What Character Is That?
An Easy-Access Dictionary of 5,000 Chinese Characters

Second Edition

BY
PING-GAM GO

SIMPLEX PUBLICATIONS

To my brother Hong

By the same author:
Understanding Chinese Characters by their Ancestral Forms
Understanding Kanji Characters by their Ancestral Forms
Read Chinese Today

Cover design by Koko Kawasaki

Simplex Publications
575 Larkspur Plaza, Suite 4
Larkspur, CA 94939
http://www.simplexpublications.com

ISBN 0-9623113-5-9

Printed in the U.S.A.

10 9 8 7 6 5 4 3 2

Please, read this Summary first !

A Chinese character consist of writing-units. *One unit tells us to which group of characters that character belongs. This unit is called the "RADICAL"* (radix = root).

THE CHARACTERS IN THIS DICTIONARY ARE GROUPED UNDER THE ENGLISH NAMES OF THEIR RADICALS; THE GROUPS ARE THEN ALPHABETICALLY ARRANGED.

The Radical is usually located on the left-hand side of the character (see p. 3). To find the name of a Radical there are the Tables WHICH RADICAL IS THAT ? (pp. 21-24) and the Tables ENGLISH NAMES OF RADICALS (pp. Eng 1-7). The latter also lists the Simplified Forms as used in China.

The Section THEIR ANCESTRAL FORMS (ETYMOL-OGY) (pp. 29-50) explains the meaning of the Radicals based on their stylus-written Ancestral Forms. It will greatly help you to remember the Radical Names.

HOW TO USE THE DICTIONARY (p. 2) and HOW TO COUNT THE NUMBER OF STROKES (pp. 12-13) will tell you how to locate a character in this Dictionary.

Many times you do not have to count the number of strokes, because most groups are small Groups allowing you to find the characters just by looking for it (A 0).

There are 11 large Groups containing over 100 characters (A 0). For these Groups you can use the RAPID-ACCESS INDEX (pp. Ra 1-Ra 46), *in which the characters are alphabetically arranged by the name of the Radical and the name* of another *writing-unit.* There is an Introduction (pp. 60-62), which you should read first.

There are a number of QUIZES to help you get familiar with the use of the Dictionary.

Before using the Dictionary, you should read the Introduction first (A0-A00).

You will find that the Dictionary also contains the PINYIN spellings and the SIMPLIFIED FORMS as used in China today (see Diagram on p. 2). The Simplified Characters are listed in the INDEX OF SIMPLIFIED CHARACTERS by the Names of their Radicals.

What Character Is That on the Front Cover?

    The Radical of a character tells us to which Group the character belongs (*radix* = root). The Radical of this character is located on top of the character. It is 士 , named SCHOLAR. (See also: *Which Radical Is That ?* (p. 21) and its Etymology – explains why it is so written (p. 44)).

    We find the Group SCHOLAR on pp. S1–S 2. Because it is a very small group of six characters only, we can easily locate the character as Character No. 6. It means **"LONGEVITY"** **("LONG LIFE")** *.

---

    * This character is very common and popular and can be seen on dinner plates, clothings, jewelry, and other items. (See colored photos W4 and 43 in *Understanding Chinese Characters by Their Ancestral Forms, 3rd Ed.,* by the same author).

Common Radicals
Simple symbols – not-so-easy to understand

*MAN	人	几	A being standing on two legs.
****** HEAD (2)	頁	頁	The head 囟 placed upon the body 儿 **.
GOLD	金	釜	Nuggets 䒑 buried (∧ cover) in **EARTH** 土 .
JADE	玉	玉	The gem • that kings 王 *** possessed.
MOUND	阜	阝	Mound 厂 with steps ≡ leading to a wood ∘∘∘.
FOOT	足	吊	Foot 止 (ankle, heel, toes) at rest ○ ****.
FOOTSTEP	彳	勿	Step ╱ taken by a person 勹 (𠆢 see **MAN** *).
PROCEED	辵	辵	The **FOOT** 止 and three footsteps 彡 .
FOOD	食	食	Pot (contents ⊙, ladle ヒ , mixing △*****).
CLOTHES	衣	衣	A robe 冖 (亼 sleeves) dragging over the floor.
SILK	糸	糸	Cocoons 8 twisted (𠆢 spindle) into thread.
WORDS	言	言	The tongue 舌 and words = produced by it.
REVELATION	示	示	Emanations 川 , signs from Heaven = .
ILLNESS	疒	疒	Ill and lying — in bed 爿 (half of **TREE** 朩).

The above 43 characters are the Radicals for 3,693 characters. This is 74% of all the characters in this 5,000 Characters Dictionary. Knowing their names will give you the "keys" to the meanings of about 3,700 characters.

---

* **MAN** or **MANKIND**, or **PERSON** (male or female).
** Two legs representing a person's body.
*** The mediator ｜ between Heaven ⏜, Earth ⏟ and Mankind —
**** Compare **PROCEED**, the **FOOT** moving (making footsteps 彡).
***** Three lines coming together.
****** **HEAD (1)** 首 is an uncommon Radical.

NOTE: The 43 Common Radicals (with their Compressed Forms and their Names), arranged by the number of their strokes , appear in the Table "**The Common Radicals**" on page 25. For purposes of reviewing them, they are arranged *alphabetically* (also with their Compressed Forms) on page 26.

How Many Do You Know ? (Quiz)

Before you do this Quiz, please, read again carefully previous pages 4 and 5. On a piece of paper, write down the names of the Radicals that you see below. You will find he *Solutions* and your *Scoring Evaluation* on the next page.

(A) The Very Easy Ones (See page 4 – top portion).

口 1	日 2	目 3	木 4	女 5	亠 6	广 7	心 8
手 9	貝 10	門 11	刀 12	竹 13	酉 14	肉 15	虫 16
犬 17	馬 18	魚 19	鳥 20				

(B) The Easy Ones (See page 4 – bottom portion).

艸 1	火 2	水 3	禾 4	石 5	土 6	大 7	巾 8
車 9							

(C) The Not-So-Easy Ones (See page 5).

人 1	頁 2	足 3	彳 4	辵 5	玉 6	金 7	糸 8
衣 9	食 10	阜 11	言 12	疒 13	示 14		

Solutions and your Scoring Evaluation are on the next page!

How Many Do You Know ?

Solutions and Evaluations

(A)
1. Mouth
2. Sun
3. Eye
4. Tree
5. Woman
6. Dwelling
7. Shelter
8. Heart
9. Hand
10. Shell
11. Door
12. Knife
13. Bamboo
14. Wine jug
15. Flesh
16. Insect
17. Dog
18. Horse
19. Fish
20. Bird

(B)
1. Grass
2. Fire
3. Water
4. Grain
5. Stone
6. Earth
7. Big
8. Cloth
9. Cart

(C)
1. Man
2. Head
3. Foot
4. Footstep
5. Proceed
6. Jade
7. Gold
8. Silk
9. Clothes
10. Food
11. Mound
12. Words
13. Illness
14. Revelation

Evaluation for (A)
18 to 20 correct – Excellent
15 to 17 correct – Good
12 to 14 correct – Satisfactory

Evaluation for (B)
8-9 correct – Excellent
6-7 correct – Good
5   correct – Satisfactory

Evaluation for (C)
13-14 correct – Excellent
11-12 correct – Good
9-10 correct – Satisfactory

If you score less than "Satisfactory", you should read again pages 4 and 5 and try again.

Compressed Common Radicals

In functioning as a Radical, many Common Characters are <u>compressed</u> in order to give maximum space to the remaining units. As a result of this, some are <u>slightly altered</u> (page 8) and some are <u>greatly altered</u> (page 9).

Original shape slightly altered :

	Original shape	Slightly altered shape
Bamboo	竹	竺
Big	大	夼
Earth	土	圡
Silk	糸	纟
*Water	水	氺
Food	食	飠
Jade	玉	王
Foot	足	𧾷
Eye	目	罒
Clothes	衣	衤
Revelation	示	礻
Man	人	亻

The **black bars** and **black squares** show the positions of the Non-Radical writing-units. <u>If they are absent, the Radical is located on the left-hand side of the character, as is usually the case.</u>

* See also the *greatly altered shape* of **WATER** on next page.

Original shape greatly altered:

	Original shape	Greatly altered shape	
Flesh	肉	月	
Grass	艸	丷	
Knife	刀	刂	
Proceed	辵	辶	辶
*Water	水	氵	氺
Heart	心	忄	忄
Fire	火	灬	
Hand	手	扌	
Mound	阜	阝	
Dog	犬	犭	

The **black bars** and **black squares** show the positions of the Non-Radical writing-units. If they are absent the Radical is located on the left-hand side of the character, as is usually the case.

* See also the *slightly altered shape* of WATER on previous page.

On the Tables **"The Common Radicals"** (pages 25 to 26), <u>all Common Radicals and their Compressed Forms (with their Names)</u> *are arranged according to the number of their strokes.*

On the Tables **"Which Radical Is That?"** (pages 20 to 24), <u>all Radicals and their Compressed Forms (with their Names)</u> *are arranged according to the number of their strokes.*

Compressed Common Radicals (Quiz)

In functioning as a Radical, many times a Common Character is <u>compressed</u> in order to give maximum space to the remaining writing units. On a piece of paper, write down the names of the Compressed Radicals shown below. Before doing this, please, study them again on pages 8 and 9.

糸 [1]	竺 [2]	士 [3]	夲 [4]	氺 [5]	趴 [6]	王 [7]	食 [8]
罒 [9]	衤 [10]	礻 [11]	亻 [12]	艹 [13]	月 [14]	灬 [15]	犭 [16]
氵 [17]	刂 [18]	辶 [19]	扌 [20]	阝 [21]	灬·忄 [22]		

To give you some help, the corresponding original forms are shown below. In addition to this, you may have to read again pages 4 and 5.

糸 [1]	竹 [2]	土 [3]	大 [4]	水 [5]	足 [6]	玉 [7]	食 [8]
目 [9]	衣 [10]	示 [11]	人 [12]	艸 [13]	肉 [14]	火 [15]	犬 [16]
水 [17]	刀 [18]	辵 [19]	手 [20]	阜 [21]	心 [22]		

You find the Solutions and your Scoring Evaluation on the next page!

Compressed Common Radicals
Solution and Evaluation

1. Silk
2. Bamboo
3. Earth
4. Big
5. Water *
6. Foot
7. Jade
8. Food
9. Eye
10. Clothes
11. Revelation
12. Man
13. Grass
14. Flesh
15. Fire
16. Dog
17. Water *
18. Knife
19. Proceed
20. Hand
21. Mound
22. Heart *

20 to 22 correct – Excellent
17 to 19 correct – Good
14 to 16 correct – Satisfactory

* Water and Heart each have two compressed forms: one form is placed at the bottom, and the other form is placed on the left-hand side of the character.

If you score less than "Satisfactory", you should read again pages 8 and 9 (and possibly also pages 4 and 5) and then do the Quiz again.

How to Count the Number of Strokes

A **"stroke"** is a **"straight line"** produced by the writing brush without lifting it from the paper. There is an exception, however, i.e. when the brush writing from left to right or from right to left, continues writing downward and produces a **"hook"**, as in B and C in the example below and as in the first stroke of **Woman** in the first diagram on the next page.

This is illustrated in the example below. The character  for **Perpetually (Always, Forever)**, is a good example of how to write a character and how to arrive at the number of strokes it contains.

The number of strokes in a character can best be found by actually writing the character, even if we do so using our finger writing in the air. There are only a few simple rules to follow. As a rule, strokes are written from top to bottom or from left to right *. And a character is either built from left to right or from top to bottom.

It looks as if this character consists of many strokes, but it actually has only *five*. This is because **B** is one stroke only, and so is **C**. In both cases the writing brush manages to make the "hook" in one continuous movement without lifting it from the paper.

Can you find the number of strokes of the following characters?

女	日	金	園	福	愛
Woman	Sun	Gold	Garden	Good luck	Love

You find the answers on the next page!

* Unless you are writing with a brush, the direction of writing is not important. When writing with a brush it is very important because the resulting "picture" could be very different. For example, to get a stroke that looks the same as D in the example of the character **Perpetually** you have to write from *right to left*.

The following diagrams should illustrate the rules given previously.

Numbers at the top-right corners are the number of strokes written so far. Asterisks (*) are placed at "hooks".

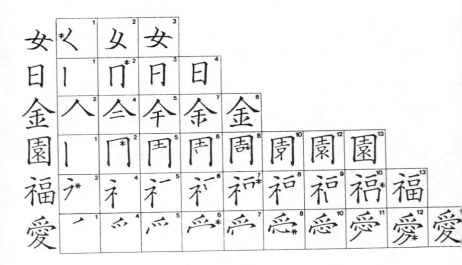

If you can not locate a character on a Table, it means that you did not get its correct number of strokes. It is then necessary for you to *look for the character under the* stroke number that is one higher or one lower. In a small Group, you can locate a character without going to the trouble of counting the number of strokes by simply looking for it, especially if it is a very simple or very complicated one.

A Walk Through Chinatown (Quiz)

Below are characters that are common in Chinatown. Can you find them in the Dictionary and write down their meanings? They all carry Common Radicals, as discussed on pages 4 and 5. (Except in **M**; these are Radicals themselves.) *Solutions are on next page!*

	Characters	*Helpful Hints*
A	大¹ 心² 日³ 金⁴ 馬⁵	These are 5 Common Radicals (4-5)*.
B	司¹ 后² 商³ 喜⁴	The Radical is part of our body (4).
C	家¹ 宮² 富³ 寶⁴	The Radical is on top and means 'house' (4).
D	餅¹ 餐² 館³ 飯⁴	The Radical is something we can eat (5).
E	洲¹ 海² 港³	The Radical (in its compressed form) is a fluid (9).
F	花¹ 華² 藥³	The Radical is on top; means some vegetation (9).
G	店¹ 廳²	The Radical shields us against the weather (4).
H	財¹ 貴²	The Radical is something formerly used as 'money' (4)
I	天¹	The Radical means 'not small' (4).
J	樓¹	The Radical is something we see in the wood (4).
K	銀¹	The Radical is a metal, which is 'not silver' (5).
L	愛¹	The Radical is **'inside'** the character. It's a vital part of the body.
M	山¹ 行² 香³ 龍⁴	Find them in **"Which Radical is That?"** after knowing their number of strokes.

* The numbers refer to pages of this book.

After you find the <u>Name of the Radical</u>, find the <u>Group that bears that name</u> in the Dictionary. Then count the number of strokes <u>of the Non-Radical writing-units</u>. The character is located within the section of the Group marked with that number. (<u>Read page 2 again for full instruction</u>.)

A Walk Through Chinatown (Solutions)

(A) **Big** (4*); **Heart** (4); **Sun** (4); **Gold** (5) **Horse** (4).

(B) **Mouth.** Manage (No.14**); Empress (No.20); Trade (No.124);
   Happy (No. 136).

(C) **Dwelling.** House (No.23); Palace (No.24); Rich (No.36); Precious (No.57).

(D) **Food.** Round cake (No.13); Food (No.19); Cultural Center (No.24);
   Cooked rice. Food (No.4).

(E) **Water.** Continent (No.58); Sea (No.72); Harbor (No. 115).

(F) **Grass.** Flower (No.12); China (No.65); Herbs (No.159).

(G) **Shelter.** Shop. Store (No.9); Hall (No.35).

(H) **Shell.** Wealth (No.5); Precious. Honorable (No.17).

(I) **Big.** Heaven (No.5).

(J) **Tree.** Multi-story house (No. 167).

(K) **Gold.** Silver (No. 37).

(L) **Heart.** Love (No.102).

(M) **Mountain** (3 strokes***); **Go** (6 strokes); **Fragrant** (9 strokes); **Dragon** (16
   strokes).

NOTE: **Names printed in bold are names of their Radicals.**

   * Numbers refer to page numbers of this book.

   ** Refers to the Character Number in the group (**Mouth**, in this case).

*** Refers to the Tables **"Which Character is That?"** . (These are Radicals themselves.)

How They Appear on Signs

(A) 大 Big. In "Big Restaurant Golden Dragon".

   心 Heart. With 中 (Center - **Rod** No.2) in 中 心 "Center" (Center
   Heart).

   日 Sun. Means also "Day (Daily)" used in "Newspaper" (Daily
   Paper).

   金 Gold. With 龍 **Dragon** (M4) in "Golden Dragon Restaurant".

   馬 Horse. With 寶 **Precious** (C4) in "Precious Horse Restaurant".

(B) 司 Manage. Seen many times with 公 (Common - **Eight** No.3) in
   公司 "Firm" or "Company" (Common. Manage(ment)).

   后 Empress. In "Empress of China Restaurant".

   商 Trade. Seen quite often, e.g. with 店 (Shop, Store - **G1**) in "Shop"
   or "Store" (Trade. Shop).

   喜 Happy. In the Chinese New Year's Wish: *Gung Hay Fat Choy !*
   (Wishing You Happiness and Expanding Wealth!). (*See* H1.)

15

(C) 家 House(hold). Appears many times with 酒 (Wine, Liquor - **Wine Jug** No. 6) in 酒家 "Restaurant serving liquor" (Wine House)

宮 Palace. In "Imperial Palace Restaurant".

富 Rich. Appears together with 貴 (Precious, Honorable - H2) to mean "Rich and Honorable". (*See* H2.)

寶 Precious. With 馬 (Horse - A5) in "Precious Horse Restaurant".

(D) 餅 Round cake. With 家 (House - C1) in "Cake House".

餐 Food. With 廳 (Hall - G2) in "Great Wall Restaurant (Food Hall)".

館 Cultural Center. With 中 (Center - Rod No.2), 華 (**China** - F2) and 會 (Association - **Speak** No.13) in "Chinese (Center. China) Association Cultural Center".

飯 Cooked rice. Meal. With 店 (Shop. Store G1) in "Szechwan Restaurant (Meal. Shop)".

(E) 洲 Continent. With 亞 ("A", short for "Asia" - **Two** No.10) in "Asia (Asia Continent) Garden Restaurant".

海 Sea. With 四 (Four - **Enclosure** No.3) in "Four Seas Restaurant".

港 Harbor. With 香 (Fragrant - M3) in 香港 "Hong Kong (Fragrant Harbor) Restaurant".

(F) 花 Flower. In "May's Flower Shop".

華 China. With 中 (Center - **Rod** No.2) in 中華 "China" (Center China, i.e. "China, the Center of the World", former belief, because formerly China had the highest civilization in the world.)

藥 Herbs With 材 (Material - **Tree** No. 21) in "China Herbs (Herbs. Material) Store".

(G) 店 Shop, Store. Seen many times as "Restaurant" (Food. Shop), "Book Store", etc.

廳 Hall. With 餐 (**Food** - D2) in "Peking Restaurant (Food. Hall)".

(H) 財 Wealth. In the Chinese New Year's Wish: *Gung Hay Fat Choy!* (Wishing You Happiness and Expanding Wealth!) (*See* B4.)

貴 Precious, Honorable. Appears together with 富 (**Rich** - C3) to mean "Rich and Honorable".

(I) 天 **Heaven**. At Chinatown Gate: "Under Heaven We All Must Work For the Common Good" (free translation).

(J) 樓 **Multi-story house.** Used by restaurants that have one or more upper-floors for dining.

(K) 銀 **Silver.** With 行 "Store" (**Go** No.1) to mean "Bank" (Silver Store), because silver was the metal used for currency. (Gold being used in jewelry and for decorative purposes.)

(L) 愛 **Love.** Appears in shop windows on jewelry items, and on clothings, e.g. child's clothing.

(M) 山 **Mountain** (a Radical). With 金 "Gold" (**Gold** No.1) to form "Gold Mountain", the Chinese name for "San Francisco".

行 **Go** (a Radical). With 銀 "Silver" (**K**) to form 銀 行 "Silver. Store" (**Go** No.1) to mean "Bank" (*see* **K**).

香 **Fragrant** (a Radical). With 港 "Harbor" (**E** 3) to form "Hong Kong" (Fragrant Harbor) (*See* E3.)

龍 **Dragon** (a Radical). With 金 "Gold" (**Gold** No.1) as in "Golden Dragon Restaurant". It also appears on the Chinese Lunar Calendar as one of the 12 animals representing the lunar cycles.

Understanding Chinese Characters by their ancestral forms, by the same author, explains 288 commonly seen characters on the basis of their ancestral forms (with 72 photos).

What's on the Menu? (Quiz)

Below are some basic items found on a Chinese Menu. They give you an idea of the rules the Chinese follow when creating their characters. For example, characters below that indicate certain 'cooking methods' all have the Radical **"Fire"**. Those for 'fishes' have **"Fish"** as Radical, etc.

The Radicals in the series **A** to **G** are **Common Radicals** and they can be located on the Tables <u>**"The Common Radicals"**</u> (pages 25 to 26). Not all Radicals in the series **H** to **I** are common and they should be located on the Tables <u>**"Which Radical Is That?"**</u> (pages 20 to 24).

Most of the time, not always, the Radical is on the left-hand side of the character. See *Helpful Hints* below.

	Characters						*Helpful Hints*
A	炒¹	炸²	烤³	烹⁴	熏⁵	燒⁶	The Radical is 'burning'
B	蛋¹	蝦²	蟹³	蠔⁴			The Radical is sometimes at the bottom.
C	鮭¹	鯉²	魷³				The Radical has 11 strokes and 'swims'.
D	鴨¹	鴿²	鷄³				The Radical is on the right-hand side.
E	菜¹	葱²	蒜³				The Radical is on top and is a 'vegetation'.
F	飯¹	餃²					The Radical has 8 strokes and is 'edible'.
G	湯¹						The Radical is in its an 'alternate' form and is a 'fluid'.
H	牛¹	肉²	米³	豆⁴	魚⁵		These are five Radicals, find them!
I	包¹	猪²	甜³	粥⁴	酸⁵	辣⁶ 麵⁷	*Helpful Hints (ctd),* see below.

Helpful Hints (cont.)

(I) [1] Radical on top (2 strokes). [2] Radical on left-side (3 strokes). [3] Radical on right-side (5 strokes). [4] Radical inside character (6 strokes). [5] Radical on left-side (7 strokes). [6] Radical on left-side (7 strokes). [7] Radical on left-side (11 strokes).

Find the <u>Radical Name</u>. Go to the Dictionary, to the <u>Group with that Name</u>. Count the <u>Number of strokes of the Non-Radical Units</u>. The Character and is inside the <u>Section of the Group marked with that Number.</u> (*Read p. 2 again, if necessary.*)

What's on the Menu? – Solution & Evaluation

(A) Fire. Stir-fry (No. 9*); Deep-fry (No.14); Bake (No.23); Boil, cook (29); Smoke (No.56); Roast (No.70).

(B) Insect. Egg (No.19); Shrimp (No.43); Crab (No.74); Oyster (No.80A).

(C) Fish. Salmon (No.11); Carp (No.13); Squid (No.4).

(D) Bird(1). Duck (No.11); Pigeon (No.17); Chicken (No.31).

(E) Grass. Vegetable (No.79); Onion (No.98); Garlic (No.113).

(F) Food. Rice (cooked) (No.4); Dumpling (No.12).

(G) Water. Soup (No.121).

(H) Radicals: **Ox** (4 strokes**); **Flesh** (4 strokes); **Rice** (6 strokes); **Bean** (7 strokes); **Fish** (11 strokes).

(I) Stuffed bun (**Wrap** No.5); Pig, pork (**Dog** No.18); Sweet (**Sweet** No.3); Porridge (**Rice** No.8); Sour (**Wine jug** No.15); Hot (**Offend** No. 4); Noodles (**Wheat** No. 5).

<u>NOTE</u>: **Names printed in bold are names of their Radicals.**

  * Number refers to the Character Number in the Group (**Fire**, in this case).
** Refers to the appropriate Table of "**Which Character is That?**" (pages 20 to 24).

> 30 to 31 correct – Excellent
> 25 to 26 correct – Good
> 20 to 21 correct – Satisfactory

If you score less than "Satisfactory", you should read again pages 4 and 5 (Common Radicals) and pages 8 and 9 (Compressed Forms of Common Radicals) and then do the Quiz again.

Which Radical Is That?

The following four Tables "**Which Radical Is That?**" (pages 21 to 24) **contain all Radicals and Compressed Radicals accompanied by their Names . They are arranged by their stroke numbers.**
All Compressed Radicals are marked by an asterisk (*) and mentioned twice:

> *(1) they are placed next to their original form (even though sometimes they do not have the same number of strokes as their original form); and*
> *(2) they are mentioned separately under their own stroke number.*

Most of the time you will be dealing with Common Radicals (pages 4-5) **and their Compressed Forms** (pages 8 and 9). **As mentioned before** (page 3), **these 43 Radicals appear in 3,693 characters, which is 74% of the 5,000 characters in this Dictionary.** They are listed separately with their Compressed Forms according to the number of their strokes in the Table "**The Common Radicals**" (page 25). *To locate a Common Radical, it is easier to use this Table. In order to review them, they are listed alphabetically* (page 26).

As a rule, Radicals are located on the <u>left-hand side</u> of the character (56% of the cases); but they can also appear on <u>top</u> (16%), at the <u>bottom</u> (12%), or on the <u>right-hand side</u> (8%) of the character. In the remaining cases (8%), we are dealing with characters where the Radical is found <u>inside</u> the character, OR where <u>the Radical alone is the character.</u>

If you can not locate a character on a Table, it means that you did not get its correct number of strokes. It is then necessary for you to look for the character under the stroke number that is one higher or one lower. *In a small Group, you can locate a character without going into the trouble of counting the number of strokes by simply looking for it, especially if it is a very simple or very complicated one, allowing you to limit your search to the very beginning or the very end of the Group.*

If after all efforts you still can not locate a character, you probably are dealing with an "odd character". These are characters that for some reason or other are really problematical. They can be found in another Section of the book: "**The Odd Ones**" (pages 51-59). *Because the Radical is not known yet, the characters here are arranged under their total number of strokes, i.e. including those of their Radicals.*

Which Radical Is That ? (1)

1	一 ONE	丨 ROD	丶 DOT	丿 LEFTSTRKE	乙 BENT	亅 DWNSTRKE				
2	二 TWO	亠 LID	人 亻 MAN	入 ENTER	八 EIGHT	冂 BORDERS	冖 COVER	冫 ICE	几 STOOL	
	凵 PIT	刀 刂 KNIFE	力 STRENGTH	勹 WRAP	匕 SPOON	匚 BASKET	十 TEN	卜 DIVNATION	卩 SEAL	厂 CLIFF
3	厶 COCOON	又 HAND (2)	阝* CITY	阝* MOUND						
	口 MOUTH	囗 ENCLSURE	土 EARTH	士 SCHOLAR	夂 PERSEVRE	夊 PURSUE	夕 EVENING	大 大 BIG	女 WOMAN	子 孓 CHILD
	宀 DWELLING	寸 INCH	小 SMALL	尢 LAME	尸 CORPSE	屮 SPROUT	山 MOUNTAN	巛 川 RIVER	工 WORK	己 SELF · 巾 CLOTH · 干 PESTLE
	幺 纟 THREAD	彡* · 廴* MOVE ON	廾 FOLD HNDS	弋 DART	弓 BOW	彐 PIG'S SNOUT	彡 LINES	彳 FOOTSTEP	犭* DOG	
	忄* HEART	辶* PROCEED	氵* WATER	艹* GRASS						

A Radical accompanied by an asterisk (*) is a Compressed Form with its number of strokes different from that of the original form.

Which Radical Is That ? (2)

4

心 HEART	戈 HALBERD	尸 DOORLEAF	手 扌* HAND (I)	支 BRANCH	攵 TAP	文 LITERATUR	斗 PECK	斤 AXE
方 SQUARE	无 旡* NOT	日 SUN	曰 SPEAK	月 MOON	木 朩* TREE	欠 BREATHE	止 STOP	歹 DISINTGRN	殳 STRIKE	毋 母* DO NOT
比 COMPARE	毛 HAIR	氏 CLAN	气 VAPOR	水 氵* 氺 WATER	火 灬 FIRE	爪 爫 CLAW	父 FATHER	爻 INTR'TWNE
爿 SPLTWD (L)	片 SPLTWD (R)	牙 TOOTH	牛 牜 OX	犬 犭 DOG	月* FLESH	王* JADE	艹* GRASS	罒 NET	耂* OLD	辶 PROCEED
礻* REVELATION

5

玄 DARK	玉 王* JADE	瓜 MELON	瓦 TILE	甘 SWEET	生 GROW	用 USE	田 FIELD	疋 ROLL.	疒 ILLNESS	癶 BOTH FEET
白 WHITE	皮 SKIN	皿 DISH	目 EYE	罒* NET	矛 LANCE	矢 ARROW	石 STONE	示 礻* REVELATION	内 TRACK	禾 GRAIN
穴 CAVE	立 STAND	衤* CLOTHES	衣 衤 CLOTHES	母* DO NOT	罒* NET	玉 JADE	氺* WATER

NOTE: A radical accompanied by an asterisk (*) is an alternate form with its number of strokes different than that of the original form.

Which Radical Is That ? (3)

6	竹 BAMBOO / 竺*	米 RICE	糸 / 糹 SILK	缶 EARTHENWR	网 / 罒* / 罓* NET	羊 SHEEP / 羋	羽 WINGS
	老 OLD / 耂*	而 BEARD	耒 PLOW	耳 EAR	聿 STYLUS	肉 / 月 FLESH	臣 MINISTER	自 NOSE (1)	至 REACH	臼 MORTAR	舌 TONGUE
	舛 OPOSITION	舟 BOAT	艮 DEFIANCE	色 COLOR	艸 / 艹* GRASS	虍* TIGER	虫 INSECT	血 BLOOD	行 GO	衣 / 衤* CLOTHES	
	西 / 襾 / 覀 STOPPER						

7	見 SEE	角 HORN	言 WORDS	谷 VALLEY	豆 BEAN	豕 PIG	豸 CAT	貝 SHELL	赤 RED	走 RUN	足 / 趴* FOOT	身 BODY
	車 CART	辛 OFFEND	辰 PERIOD	辵 / 辶* / 辶* PROCEED	邑 / 阝* CITY	酉 WINE JUG	釆 FOOTPRNT	里 VILLAGE

8	金 GOLD	長 LONG	門 DOOR	阜 / 阝* MOUND	隶 SEIZE	隹 BIRD (2)	雨 / 雨 RAIN	青 / 靑* GREEN	非 BACK-BACK

9	面 FACE	革 RAWHIDE / 韋 LEATHER	韭 LEEK	音 SOUND	頁 HEAD (2)	風 WIND	飛 FLY	食 / 飠 / 飠* FOOD	首 HEAD (1)	香 FRAGRANT

NOTE: A radical accompanied by an asterisk (*) is an alternate form with its number of strokes different than that of the original form.

Which Radical Is That ? (4)

10	馬 HORSE	骨 BONES	高 HIGH	髟 HAIRLCKS	鬥 FIGHT	鬯 WINE VESL	鬲 CALDRON	鬼 GHOST
11	魚 FISH	鳥 BIRD (1)	鹵 SALT	鹿 DEER	麥 WHEAT	麻 HEMP		
12	黃 YELLOW	黍 MILLET	黑 BLACK	黹 EMBRODRY				
13	黽 TURTLE	鼎 TRIPOD	鼓 DRUM	鼠 RAT				
14	鼻 NOSE (2)	齊 EVEN						
15	齒 TEETH							
16	龍 DRAGON	龜 TORTOISE						
17	龠 FLUTE							

The Common Radicals
(arranged by the number of their strokes)

Strokes	Radicals
2	人 亻 入 (MAN) · 刀 刂 (KNIFE) · 阝* (MOUND)
3	口 (MOUTH) · 土 圡 (EARTH) · 大 夻 (BIG) · 女 (WOMAN) · 宀 (DWELLING) · 巾 (CLOTH)
4	广 (SHELTER) · 彳 (FOOTSTEP) · 辶 (PROCEED) · 犭* (DOG) · 扌* (HAND (1)) · 忄* (HEART) · 氵* (WATER) · 艹 (GRASS) · 心 (HEART) · 礻 (HAND (1)) · 手 (HAND (1)) · 日 (SUN) · 木 (TREE) · 水 (WATER) · 火 灬 (FIRE)
5	犬 (DOG) · 月* (FLESH) · 艹* (GRASS) · 王* (JADE) · 衤* (REVLTION) · 玉 (JADE) · 疒 (ILLNESS) · 目 罒 (EYE) · 石 (STONE) · 示 (REVLTION) · 禾 (GRAIN) · 礻* (CLOTHES) · 氺* (WATER)
6	竹 ⺮ (BAMBOO) · 糸 糹 (SILK) · 肉 (FLESH) · 艸 (GRASS) · 虫 (INSECT) · 衣 (CLOTHES)
7	言 (WORDS) · 貝 (SHELL) · 足 𧾷 (FOOT) · 車 (CART) · 辵 (PROCEED) · 酉 (WINE JUG)
8	金 (GOLD) · 門 (DOOR) · 阜 (MOUND) · 食* (FOOD)
9	頁 (HEAD (2)) · 食 (FOOD)
10	馬 (HORSE)
11	魚 (FISH) · 鳥 (BIRD (1))

Those with asterisks (*) are Compressed Radicals with the number of their strokes different than that of the originals.

The Common Radicals
(alphabetically arranged)

Below is a List of the 43 Common Radicals (see again pages 4 and 5). This time they are alphabetically arranged and listed with their Compressed Forms. Sometimes you are not sure of the Name of one of them and you can use this List to verify it. But you can also use the List to review all of them.

The asterisks (*) are used to indicate their degree of importance. The numbers are the number of times they appear as Radicals of characters in the various Groups.

** BAMBOO 竹 竺	83	
* BIG 大 夳	30	
* BIRD (1) 鳥	46	
* CART 車	42	
* CLOTH 巾	33	
** CLOTHES 衣 衤	64	
* DOG 犬 犭	34	
* DOOR 門	33	
** DWELLING 宀	57	
** EARTH 土 圵	84	
** EYE 目 罒	57	
** FIRE 火 灬	89	
* FISH 魚	41	
*** FLESH 肉 月	102	
* FOOD 食 飠	47	
** FOOT 足 趴	75	
* FOOTSTEP 彳	34	
*** GOLD 金	123	
* GRAIN 禾	48	
*** GRASS 艸 艹 艹	168	
*** HAND (1) 手 扌	264	
* HEAD (2) 頁	38	

*** HEART 心 忄 小	177	
* HORSE 馬	37	
** ILLNESS 疒	72	
** INSECT 虫	87	
** JADE 玉 王	54	
** KNIFE 刀 刂	52	
*** MAN 人 亻 入	207	
* MOUND 阜 阝	47	
*** MOUTH 口	221	
** PROCEED 辵 辶 辶	84	
* REVELATION 示 礻	33	
** SHELL 貝	61	
* SHELTER 广	35	
*** SILK 糸 糹	126	
** STONE 石	52	
** SUN 日	64	
*** TREE 木	210	
*** WATER 水 氵 氺	222	
* WINE JUG 酉	32	
** WOMAN 女	85	
*** WORDS 言	143	

NR. OF RADICALS IN GROUPS

Total numbers of characters:
3, 693 (74% of 5,000).

```
*** MOST COMMON (100-264)
 ** VERY COMMON (50-99)
  * COMMON (30-49)
```

RADICALS (ENGLISH NAMES)

ARROW 矢
AXE 斤

BACK TO BACK 非
BAMBOO 竹 竺
BASKET 匸
BEAN 豆
BEARD 而
BENT 乙 乚
***BIG** 大 大
***BIRD** (1) 鳥
BIRD (2) 隹
BLACK 黑
BLOOD 血
BOAT 舟 身
BODY 身
BONES 骨
BORDERS 冂
BOTH FEET 癶
BOW 弓
BOX 匚
BRANCH 支
BREATHE 欠

CALDRON 鬲
***CART** 車
CAT 豸
CAVE 穴 空
CHILD 子 孑
CITY 邑 阝
CLAN 氏
CLAW 爪 爫
CLIFF 厂 巾
***CLOTH** 巾
****CLOTHES** 衣 衤
COCOON 厶
COLOR 色
COMPARE 比
CORPSE 尸
COVER 冖

DARK 玄
DART 弋
DEER 鹿
DEFIANCE 艮
DISH 皿
DISINTEGRATION 歹
DIVINATION 卜
***DOG** 犬 犭
DO NOT 母
***DOOR** 門
DOORLEAF 戶
DOT 丶
DOWNSTROKE 亅
DRAGON 龍
DRUM 鼓
****DWELLING** 宀

EAR 耳
****EARTH** 土 士
EARTHENWARE 缶
EIGHT 八
EMBROIDERY 黹
ENCLOSURE 囗
ENTER 入 人
EVEN 齊
EVENING 夕
****EYE** 目 罒

FACE 面
FATHER 父
FIELD 田
FIGHT 鬥
****FIRE** 火 灬
***FISH** 魚
*****FLESH** 肉 月
FLUTE 龠
FLY 飛
FOLDED HANDS 廾
***FOOD** 食 飠
****FOOT** 足 𧾷
FOOTPRINT 釆
***FOOTSTEP** 彳
FRAGRANT 香

GHOST 鬼
GO 行
*****GOLD** 金
***GRAIN** 禾
*****GRASS** 艸 艹
GREEN 青
GROW 生

HAIR 毛
HAIRLOCKS 髟
HALBERD 戈
*****HAND** (1) 手 扌
HAND (2) 又
HEAD (1) 首
***HEAD (2)** 頁
*****HEART** 心 忄 ⺗
HEMP 麻
HIGH 高
HORN 角
***HORSE** 馬

ICE 冫
****ILLNESS** 疒
INCH 寸
****INSECT** 虫
INTERTWINE 爻

****JADE** 玉 王

****KNIFE** 刀 刂

LAME 尢
LANCE 矛
LEATHER 韋
LEEK 韭
LEFTSTROKE 丿
LEGS 儿
LID 亠
LINES 彡
LITERATURE 文
LONG 長

***MAN** 人 亻 入
MELON 瓜
MILLET 黍
MINISTER 臣
MOON 月
MORTAR 臼
*MOUND** 阜 阝
MOUNTAIN 山
***MOUTH** 口
MOVE ON 夂

NET 网 罒 冈 門
NOSE (1) 自
NOSE (2) 鼻
NOT 元 无
OFFEND 辛
OLD 老 耂
ONE 一
OPPOSITION 舛
OX 牛 牜

PECK 斗
PERIOD 辰
PERSEVERE 夂
PESTLE 干
PIG 豕
PIG'S SNOUT 彑 彐 彑
PIT 凵
PLOW 耒
PROCEED 辵 辶 辶
PURSUE 夂

RAIN 雨 霝
RAT 鼠
RAWHIDE 革
REACH 至
RED 赤
*REVELATION** 示 礻
RICE 米
RIVER 川 巛
ROD 丨
ROLL 疋 正
RUN 走

SALT 鹵
SCHOLAR 士
SEAL 阝 卩
SEE 見
SEIZE 隶
SELF 己
SHEEP 羊 羋
SHELL 貝 宀
*SHELTER** 广
***SILK** 糸 糹
SKIN 皮
SMALL 小
SOUND 音
SPEAK 曰
SPLITWOOD (1) 爿
SPLITWOOD (2) 片
SPOON 匕
SPROUT 屮
SQUARE 方
STAND 立
STONE 石
STOOL 几
STOP 止
STOPPER 襾 西 西
STRENGTH 力
STRIKE 殳
STYLUS 聿
SUN 日
SWEET 甘

TAP 攴 攵
TEETH 齒
TEN 十
THREAD 幺
TIGER 虍
TILE 瓦
TONGUE 舌
TOOTH 牙
TORTOISE 龜
TRACK 禸
***TREE** 木
TRIPOD 鼎
TURTLE 黽
TWO 二

USE 用

VALLEY 谷
VAPOR 气
VILLAGE 里

***WATER** 水 氵 氺
WHEAT 麥
WHITE 白
WIND 風
*WINE JUG** 酉
WINE VESSEL 鬯
WINGS 羽
WOMAN 女
***WORDS** 言
WORK 工
WRAP 勹

YELLOW 黃

NR. CHARACTERS IN GROUPS

*** MOST COMMON (102-264)
** VERY COMMON (52-89)
* COMMON (30-48)

28

*Their Ancestral Forms (Etymology)**

Note on asterisks

*** = Most common char.
** = Very common char.
* = Common char.

ARROW 矢

Picture of an arrow .

AXE 斤

Representing an axe and c *(a chip of wood):* .

BACK TO BACK 非

Two identical objects placed opposite each other .

** BAMBOO 竹 . ⺮

Picture of bamboo trees with drooping leaves .

BASKET 匚

Picture of a basket , *turned aside* .

BEAN 豆

A simple meal of beans • on a stemmed platter: .

BEARD 而

What hangs down from the chin: .

BENT 乙 . 乚

The bent shape of a germ .

* BIG 大 .

A man with outstretched arms as if showing the size of a large object .

* BIRD (1) 鳥

Picture of a bird .

* *Understanding Chinese Characters by their Ancestral Forms*, by this Author, deals with characters seen in American Chinatowns and cities.

BIRD (2) 隹

Picture of a short-tailed bird 隹 .

BLACK 黑

Soot ⅹ *deposited by a smoky fire* 炎 *around a vent* ⊗ – 黑 .

BLOOD 血

A stemmed vessel 皿 *containing blood* – : 血 .

BOAT 舟

A hollowed tree trunk 舟 *, representing a boat.*

BODY 身

A person, shown with a conspicuous abdomen 身 .

BONES 骨

Picture of a human skeleton 骨 .

BORDERS 冂

The boundaries of some portion of space 冂 .

BOTH FEET 癶

Picture of both feet of a person or animal: 癶 .

BOW 弓

Picture of a Chinese reflex bow 弓 .

BOX 匚

Picture of a box ⊔ *turned sideways to allow other components to be written in* 匚 .

BRANCH 支

Originally 支 : *a hand* 彐 *pulling off a branch* 个 *from a tree.*

BREATHE 欠

A man 人 *breathing out air* ⫶ : 欠 .

CALDRON 鬲

Representing an ancient three-legged caldron 鬲 .

* CART 車

A cart (seen from above) 車, *showing the body* ⊕, *axle* | , *and wheels* 二 .

CAT 豸

Representing a cat-like animal 豸 .

CAVE 穴 . 空

A cave ⌒ *resulting from earth being taken away* 八 *(by the water):* 穴 .

CHILD 子

Picture of a newborn child with the legs still bound in swathes 子 .

CITY 邑 . 阝

The city ○ *and its seal* 卩 : 邑 .

CLAN 氏

Representing a floating plant that grows in abundance 屮 .

CLAW 爪 . 爫

Picture of a claw 爪 .

CLIFF 厂

Representing a steep cliff 厂.

* CLOTH 巾

Piece of cloth ∩ *for cleaning, hanging down* | *from the girdle:* 巾.

** CLOTHES 衣 . 衤

A robe and its sleeves ⊥ *and* ⋀ *its dragging over the floor:* 衣.

COCOON 厶

Picture of a cocoon ○.

COLOR 色

A man 卩 *with a red (color of a seal* 卩 *) face:* 色.

COMPARE 比

Two men 从 *standing next to each other, in order to compare their heights* 从.

CORPSE 尸

A sitting person 尸 *, representing the dead.*

COVER 冖

Picture of a cover ⌒.

DARK 玄

The thread 𢆶 *(two cocoons twisted into a thread) being dipped* 入 *into the dye, and obtaining a dark color:* 玄.

DART 弋

A dart (a small arrow), which attached to a string can be retrieved after it has been thrown to kill a small animal : 弋 .

DEER 鹿

Representing the deer 鹿 , with its head and horn ㅂ, its body へ and its feet 丬丬 .

DEFIANCE 艮

Defiance 艮 – a man 𠆢 who turns around 𠂊, to look (𠂤 eye) another person full in the face.

DISH 皿

Picture of a dish mounted on a pedestal 皿 , as used by the Chinese during banquets.

DISINTEGRATION 歹

Picture of a skeleton 𠯁 – the body after the decay of the flesh.

DIVINATION 卜

Cracks in tortoise shells 卜 , developed by heating, used as basis for fortune-telling.

* DOG 犬 . 犭

A dog, showing its two front legs and its head turned aside 犮 .

DO NOT 毋

A woman 毋 , who is being locked up — for misconduct: 毋 .

* DOOR 門

Picture of a saloon-door with swinging leaves 門 .

DOORLEAF 戶

The left-hand leaf 戶 of a swinging-door 門 .

DOT 丶

Picture of a dot • .

DOWNSTROKE 」

A crooked downstroke made by the writing-brush 」.

DRAGON 龍

A dragon 龍 *flying towards the sky (dragon* 彡*, wings* 彡 *, and the sky* ＝*).* *

DRUM 鼓

A drum 鼓 *(a hand* 彐 *holding a stick* — *beating a drum on a stand* 豆 *); a hand holding a stick (repeated):* 彐.

** DWELLING 宀

Picture of a hut - a primitive dwelling 宀.

EAR 耳

Picture of the ear 耳.

** EARTH 土 . 圡

The layer 二 *from which all things* 丨 *came out:* 土.

EARTHENWARE 缶

Picture of a vessel with a cover 缶.

EIGHT 八

A quantity consisting of two equal halves)(.

EMBROIDERY 黹

Cloth 巾 *(a radical) pierced by thread and needle* 黹 *resulting in a piece of embroidery (* 㒸 *a plant in full bloom):* 黹.

ENCLOSURE 囗

Picture of an enclosure ◯.

34

ENTER 入

Representing a plant with its roots penetrating the soil 人 *.*

EVEN 齊

A field of corn, drawn in perspective, in which the ears are of even height 𠆢坐𠆢 *.*

EVENING 夕

A wavy half-moon, just appearing above the horizon 𝒟 *.*

** EYE 目 . 罒

Picture of an eye ⟨𝐃⟩ *, set upright* ⊖ *in order to take up minimum space.*

FACE 面

The face ◯ *with the nose* ⊜ *in the center:* ⊜ *.*

FATHER 父

A hand ⇉ *holding a rod* ∣ *, to express authority:* ⇉ *.*

FIELD 田

Picture of a field with furrows ⊕ *.*

FIGHT 鬥

Two pair of hands ⋲⋺ *opposing each other:* ⟨⋲⋺⟩ *.*

** FIRE 火 . 灬

A pile of wood burning with flames 火 *.*

* FISH 魚

Picture of a fish: head 𝄽 *, scaly body* ⊜ *, and tail* 火 *:* 象

*** FLESH 肉 月

Strips of dried meat, bundled together 肉.

FLUTE 龠

Representing a bamboo 侖 tube with holes ʊʊʊ : 龠.

FLY 飛

Picture of a flying crane 飛.

FOLDED HANDS 廾

Two hands joined together and held up in a respectable greeting, the way Chinese people do 廾.

* FOOD 食 食

A pot with contents ⊙, a ladle ᠘, and the symbol △ to suggest 'mixing' (three lines coming together): 食

** FOOT 足 足

The foot 止, with the ankle, heel and toes, at rest ○: 足.

FOOTPRINT 釆

Representing the footprint of an animal 釆.

* FOOTSTEP 彳

A step J taken by the left foot 亻 (人 the two legs of a person.): 彳.

FRAGRANT 香

The sweet 曰 (a writing unit) odor of fermented (== vapors) grain 禾 (a wrriting unit): 香.

GHOST 鬼

Picture of a ghost moving through the air 鬼 (ㄙㄙ represents the swirl caused by the movement).

GO 行

Footsteps made by left and right feet: 彳亍 .

*** GOLD (METAL) 金

Four nuggets (ore) 呈 *buried (∧ cover) in the earth* 土 *(Rad):* 釜 .

* GRAIN 禾

Representing a plant (朮 *Tree) with ripening ears hanging down* ⌐
at the top: 朮

*** GRASS 艸 . 艹

Representing grass, growing in abundance 屮屮 .

GREEN 青

The color (凵 *crucible containing substance* • *colored by heat) of* 屮
young plants 屮 *emerging from the earth* 土 *(a Radical, see p. 34):* 青 .

GROW 生

A young plant 屮 *emerging from the earth* 土 *(a Radical, see p. 34):* 生 .

HAIR 毛

Picture of a bundle of hair 毛 .

HAIRLOCKS 髟

Representing long 髟 *(Rad.190) hairlocks* 彡 : 髟

HALBERD 戈

Representing a halberd – a spear ending in a battle-axe: 戈 .

*** HAND (1) 手 . 扌

Picture of the hand with the five fingers clearly shown 手 .

HAND (2) 又

The right hand seen in profile – only three fingers are seen: 彐

HEAD (1) 首

Representing the head with the hair clearly shown 甾 *.*

* HEAD (2) 頁

The head 甾 *placed upon the body* 儿 *:* 頁

*** HEART 心 . 灬 . 忄

Picture of the heart – the sac opened; the lobes and the aorta are also seen 心.

HEMP 麻

*Representing hemp (*林* plant) in storage (*广* shelter):* 麻.

HIGH 高

Picture of a tower: 高

HORN 角

Representing a striated horn 角.

* HORSE 馬

Picture of a horse with its mane blowing in the wind: 馬.

ICE 冫

Picture of ice crystals 仌.

** ILLNESS 疒

To be ill and be lying — in bed 爿 *(splitwood: half of a tree* 木*):* 疒.

INCH 寸

A hand ㄋ and a dash –, to indicate where the pulse can be felt – which is about an inch (Chin. inch < ca. .33 dm >) away from the hand: ㄋ.

** INSECT 虫

Picture of a worm or insect 㕣.

INTERTWINE 爻

To unite by twisting together 㸚.

** JADE 玉 . 王

The precious gem · that only kings 王 (the mediator | between Heaven ⼀, Earth ⼀ and Man —) could possess: 玉.

** KNIFE 刀 刂

Picture of a knife 刀; later the handle was curved upwards for compactness 刀.

LAME 尢

Picture of a person who has one leg shorter than the other, and therefore has to limp 尢.

LANCE 矛

Picture of a lance 矛.

LEATHER 韋

Two men 刀刀 stretching a piece of leather ○ to smoothen it 韋.

LEEK 韭

Picture of a leek plant 韭.

LEFTSTROKE 丿

A stroke written from right to left 丿 – general idea of action or motion.

LEGS 儿

Representing the legs of a person 儿.

LID 亠

Representing the lid of a vessel 人.

LINES 彡

Three lines – to represent rays of light, feathers, hair, etc. 彡.

LITERATURE 文

Intercrossing lines, representing waves of thoughts 文.

LONG 長

Hair 𠂤 so long that it is tied with a band—and a brooch 丫 : 𣲺.

*** MAN 人 亻

That being who is standing on two legs 𠆢.

MELON 瓜

Picture of the melon plant and its fruit 瓜.

MILLET 黍

Representing the plant 禾, the seeds of which are put 𠆢 in water 巛, to produce spirits: 黍

MINISTER 臣

Picture of a minister making a deep bow 𰀁 before the Emperor. (The character was turned upright for compactnes 臣 .)

MOON 月

Picture of a crescent moon 𝔻.

MORTAR 臼

Representing a mortar ◡ with crushed material ⌒ in it: 臼 .

* MOUND 阜. 阝

Representing a terraced embankment ⌐ with steps ☰ leading to a forest (ooo trees): 阜

MOUNTAIN 山

Picture of a mountain range ⌒⌒⌒ .

*** MOUTH 口

Picture of the mouth ▽ .

* MOVE ON 夂

Representing the long strides made by a person: 夂

NET 网. 罒. 門. ⺳

Picture of a net 网 .

NOSE (1) 自

Picture of a nose 自 .

NOSE (2) 鼻

The nose 自 on the human body (represented by 畀): 鼻

NOT 元. 兂

A man (represented by his two feet 儿) unable to stand up, beause of an obstacle 工: 兂 .

OFFEND 辛

To offend (a pestle 午 producing a grinding action) one's superior 二: 辛 .

OLD 老．耂

Hair ⼭ and beard ⼓ that have changed in color (a person ⼓ who has changed his position ⼪ – is upside down): 耂 .

ONE 一

One stroke, to represent the number 'one' : ― .

OPPOSITION 舛

Two objects placed back to back ⼡⼧ .

OX 牛．牛

Representing an ox (seen from behind): only the two hind legs and tail are seen ⼇ ; the head is shown with the horns ⼬ : 半 .

PECK 斗

Ten ⼗ ladles ⼌, which was a peck (measuring unit): ⼌⼗ .

PERIOD 辰

A woman who bends over ⼚ (cp. ⼈ person) to conceal her menses (a sitting woman with apron ⼕): 辰 .

PERSEVERE 夂

A person ⼈ who steps forward slowly despite shackles ⼂ : 夂 .

PESTLE 干

Picture of a pestle ⼲ .

PIG 豕

Picture of a pig 豕 .

PIG'S SNOUT 彑．彑．⺕

Representing a pig's snout 彑 .

PIT 凵

Representing a hole in the earth ∪ .

PLOW 耒

Representing a plow – the wooden (木 *tree) handle and a piece of wood with dents in it* 耒 : 耒 .

** PROCEED 辵 . 辶 . 辶

To proceed step by step (the foot 止 *and* 彳 *three footsteps):* 辵 .

PURSUE 夂

A man 人 *who walks despite an obstacle* ＼ : 夂 .

RAIN 雨 . 霝

Drops of water ＝＝ *falling down* ｜ *from clouds* ∧ *suspended from the sky* ￣ : 雨 .

RAT 鼠

Picture of a rat, showing its head with whiskers 臼 , *legs and tail* 比 : 鼠 .

RAWHIDE 革

A pair of hands 臼 *stretching out a sheep's skin* 羊 : 革 .

REACH 至

A bird with wings backward 至 *coming down and reaching the earth* 土 : 至 .

RED 赤

Representing an angry man 大 *– his face turning red (* 火 *fire):* 赤 .

* REVELATION 示 . 礻

Emanations 小 *from heaven* ＝ , *revealing signs from heaven:* 示 .

43

RICE 米

Four grains of rice, scattered ⅄ due to thrashing 十: 米.

RIVER 川. 巛

A big stream formed by smaller streams 巛.

ROD 丨

A vertical stroke representing a rod 丨.

ROLL 疋

The foot 止 in motion ⌒: 疋.

RUN 走

A man with his head bent downward 夭 who runs (止 foot) quickly: 夭·.

SALT 鹵

A vessel ⊗ containing grains of salt ∴ : 鹵.

SCHOLAR 士

One who has knowledge of all things (between the two units one —
and 十: 士.

SEAL 卩. 己

The right half of a broken seal 卩 given to a government official by
the Emperor (who held the left half 㔾).

SEE 見

The eye 目 of a person (a being standing on two legs 儿): 見.

SEIZE 隶

A hand ⊐ that catches a running animal by its tail 㣇 : 隶.

44

SELF 己

Representing the threads of the weft: two transversal = and one longitudinal | ; at the bottom is the shuttle ∟ : 㠯. (Etymology ?)

SHEEP 羊. 善

Picture of a sheep seen from behind: the horns Ψ, four feet and a tail 丯: 羊.

** SHELL 貝

Picture of a 'cowrie' shell, used as money in ancient China 貝.

* SHELTER 广

A hut ∧ which is half-finished that serves as a shelter: 广.

*** SILK 糸. 幺

Small threads from cocoons 8 twisted (人 spindle) into a thicker one 幺.

SKIN 皮

The skin ⌒ stripped off by a hand ⇒ holding a knife つ: 皮.

SMALL 小

An object ハ split | into two: 小.

SOUND 音

Showing the mouth ⊌, the tongue ⋎ , the sound ─ produced in the mouth and the sound waves coming out from the mouth = : 音.

SPEAK 曰

A word ∟ spoken out by the mouth ⊌ : 曰.

SPLITWOOD (LEFT) 爿

The left half of a tree 木: 爿.

SPLITWOOD (RIGHT) 片

The right half of a tree 米 : K .

SPOON 匕

Representing an ancient spoon: 大 .

SPROUT 屮

Picture of a new shoot of a plant , i.e. a sprout: Ψ .

SQUARE 方

Representing the square earth with the four regions at the corners: 丐 .

STAND 立

A man 大 *standing on the ground* — : 岙 .

** STONE 石

Showing a stone ○ *in a cliff* 厂 : 厉 .

STOOL 几

Picture of a stool 几 .

STOP 止

Representing the foot-at-rest, showing the heel ∟ , *the toe* ⌐ *and the ankle* Ϸ *of a foot:* 止 .

STOPPER 西 . 西 . 西

Picture of a stopper ⊔ *on a bottle* ⊓ : 西 .

STRENGTH 力

Picture of a muscle in its sheath: 秀 .

STRIKE 殳

The hand ⇒ *making a violent motion* 令 *in order to strike:* 殳 .

STYLUS 聿

A hand ⇒ *holding a stylus* | *writing a line* — *on a tablet* ☐ : 聿 .

** SUN 日

Picture of the sun ⊙ .

SWEET 甘

Something sweet — *being held in the mouth* � : 甘 .

TAP 攴 . 攵

A hand holding a stick : 攴 .

TEETH 齒

Representing teeth in the mouth : 齒 . *(* 止 *Serves as phonetic only.)*

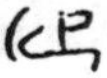

TEN 十

Symbol for a unit: 十 .

THREAD 幺

Two cocoons ○ *twisted into a thread:* 幺 .

TIGER 虎

Representing the stripes of the tiger: 虍 .

TILE 瓦

Representing a Chinese rooftile ⧄ , *turned upright in order to take up minimum writing space:* 瓦 .

TONGUE 舌

The tongue Ψ shown outside the mouth ⊟: 呂 .

TOOTH 牙

Representing a tooth: 钅 .

TORTOISE 龜

Representing a tortoise, showing its body Ψ, its shell ⊗, and its claws 彡: 𧒼 .

TRACK 内

Representing the hind legs 冗 and the tail ∂ of an animal – one that just left its track: 冘 .

*** TREE 木

Picture of a tree, showing the trunk | , with the branches ∪ and the roots ∩: 朿 .

TRIPOD 鼎

Picture of an ancient caldron with three legs, of which two only can be seen: 鼎 .

TURTLE 黽

Representing the turtle, showing its body Ψ and its gills ⊝ ▷: 黽 .

TWO 二

Two strokes, representing the number "two" : = .

USE 用

Representing an ancient bronze vessel, to be used when making offers to the ancestors: 用 . (Etymology unknown.)

VALLEY 谷

A narrow opening (⊟ mouth) which is situated between two high mountain walls 彳彳: 谷 .

VAPOR 气

Representing vapors rising from the soil 气 .

VILLAGE 里

The fields of eight families 畕 surrounding a common well • , and the soil to be cultivated (土 earth, a Radical, see p. 34): 里 .

*** WATER 水 . 氵 . 求

A stream 〳 with whirls of water 〵 : 水 .

WHEAT 麥

A plant (木 tree) with ears of grain 𠆢 , and 夂 (a man 𠂇) who advances in spite of an obstacle 乀 , indicating the relentless development of the grain): 麥 .

WHITE 白

The sun ⊙ just rising above the horizon, causing the sky to become "white": 白 .

WIND 風

Motion of air 𠂆 and an insect 虫 . (It was believed that insects were born when the wind blew.): 風 .

* WINE JUG 酉

Picture of a wine jar 酉 .

WINE VESSEL 鬯

A vessel filled with grain 米 and a ladle 匕 to remove the wine: 鬯 .

WINGS 羽

Picture of a pair of wings: 羽.

** WOMAN 女

Picture of a woman 女.

*** WORDS 言

The tongue 舌 *and words (=sound waves) being produced by it:* 言.

WORK 工

The ancient carpenter's square to symbolize 'work': 工.

WRAP 勹

A man 人 *(a being standing on his legs* 儿*) who bends his legs to envelop a large object:* 勹.

YELLOW 黃

The fiery glow 炗 *(a man* 人 *carrying a torch* 炗*) from the fields* 田 *:* 黃.

The Odd Ones – Unusual Cases

Occasionally, you will have a problem finding the Radical of a character. If "odd" is defined as "apart from what is regular, expected or planned" (Webster), then here is a List of "odd" characters; many of them are very common characters. *Because the Radical is not known, characters are arranged by the total number of their strokes.*

We can group the cases as follows:

(A) The Radical is not the one you expect.

百 The Radical is not SUN 日 , or ONE 一 , but WHITE 白 (The character means "Hundred", WHITE 2).

酒 The Radical is not WATER 氵 , as you expect, but WINE JUG 酉 . (The character means "Wine, Liquor", WINE JUG 6).

壽 The Radical is not MOUTH 口 or INCH 寸 , but SCHOLAR 士 . (The character means "Longevity", SCHOLAR 6).

(B) Unusual Radicals

房 The Radical is 戸 DOORLEAF. (The character means "House, Room", DOORLEAF 2.)

虎 The Radical is 虍 TIGER. (The character means "Tiger", TIGER 1.)

書 The Radical is 曰 SPEAK. (The character means "Book" , SPEAK 6.)

(C) The Radical is inside the character.

愛 The Radical is HEART 心 . (The character means "Love", HEART 102.)

粥 The Radical is RICE 米 . (The character means "Porridge", RICE 8.)

(D) The Radical is 'hidden', nowhere to be seen.

半 The Radical is TEN 十 ! (The character means "Half", TEN 7.)

年 The Radical is PESTLE 干 ! (The character means "Year", PESTLE 3.)

Common Characters are accompanied by their meanings.
To locate a character on this List, you have to count the total number of the strokes of the character.

It is a good idea for you to go through the pages of this Section making you aware of the problems and the solutions that could be lying ahead for you!

The Odd Ones – Unusual Cases
(arranged by the number of their strokes)

2

九 Nine
Bent 2

了 Downstroke 1

七 Seven
One 3

刁 Knife 2

3

也 Bent 5

丸 Ball. Pill
Dot 1

凡 Dot 2

才 Talent, genius
Hand (1) 2

叉 Fork
Hand (2) 2

久 Leftstroke 2

之 Leftstroke 3

丈 One 4

下 Below
One 5

三 Three
One 6

上 Above
One 7

千 Thousand
Ten 2

廿 Twenty
Ten 3

于 Two 2

4

弋 One
Dart 2

丹 Dot 3

予 Downstroke 2

公 Public. Common
Eight 3

六 Six
Eight 4

尤 Lame 2

以 Man 13

无 Not 2

不 Not, no
One 9

平 Peaceful
Pestle 2

凶 Pit 2

中 Center
Rod 2

巴 Self 4

化 Spoon 1

升 Ten 4

午 Noon
Ten 5

幻 Thread 2

云 Cloud
Two 3

互 Two 4

井 Well
Two 5

五 Five
Two 6

勿 Do not, not
Wrap 3

5

册 Borders 1

民 The people
Clan 2

弎 Two
Dart 3

卡 Divination 3

母 Mother
Do not 2

主 Master, host
Dot 4

兄 Legs 6

52

世 One i4

且 One 15

凸 Pit 3

凹 Pit 4

出 Go out / Pit 5

北 North / Spoon 2

正 Stop 2

卉 Ten 6

半 Half / Ten 7

幼 Thread 3

甩 Use 2

巨 Work 4

夷 Big 10

再 Borders 3

次 Breathe 2

式 Dart 4

死 Disintegration 2

全 Whole / Enter 4

甲 Field 2

由 Field 3

申 Field 4

寺 Inch 2

兆 Legs 7

考 Old 2

丟 One 17

年 Year / Pestle 3

州 River 2

巡 River 3

危 Seal 3

印 Seal 2

曳 Speak 2

曲 Speak 3

朱 Tree 7

百 Hundred / White 2

夾 Big 11

弟 Bow 8

局 Office, bureau / Corpse 6

良 Defiance 2

每 Each, every / Do not 3

坐 Earth 12

弄 Folded hands 4

串 Rod 3

壯 Scholar 3

卯 Seal 5

更 Speak 4

束 Tree 19

些 Two 8

求 Water 5

皂 White 4

乳 Bent 7

奉 Big 12

奇 Big 13

欣 Breathe 3

氓 Clan 3

爬 Claw 2

爭 Claw 3

居 Residence, house
Corpse 12

房 House. Room
Doorleaf 2

所 Place. Room
Doorleaf 4

事 Affair, business
Downstroke 3

兩 Two, both
Enter 5

垂 Earth 13

夜 Night, evening
Evening 5

夠 Evening 6

采 Footprint 2

承 Hand (1) 15

來 Come, arrive
Man 73

臥 Minister 2

岡 Mountain 5

者 Old 3

兩 Two, both
Enter 5

並 One 19

舞 Opposition 2

弁 Pestle 5

幸 Pestle 6

彔 Pig's snout 1

函 Pit 6

卷 Roll
Seal 6

尚 Small 4

武 Stop 6

卓 Ten 8

協 Ten 9

卑 Ten 10

卒 Ten 11

虎 Tiger
Tiger 1

果 Fruit
Tree 28

東 East
Tree 40

況 Two 9

亞 "a" (in "Asia", etc.)
Two 10

的 Adj. particle
White 5

妻 Woman 27

9

奏 Big 19

冑 Borders 4

冒 Borders 5

表 Watch
Clothes 4

屋 House. Room
Corpse 15

冠 Cover 3

毒 Do not 4

扁 Doorleaf 5

衍 Go 2

拜 Hand (1) 47

叛 Hand (2) 11

封 Inch 3

54

咫 Mouth 77

咸 **Salty, salted** Mouth 79

罕 Net 2

既 Not 3

复 Persevere 1

致 Reach 2

巷 Self 5

美 **Beautiful** Sheep 3

歪 Stop 7

要 **Want to (v)** Stopper 2

甚 Sweet 2

南 **South** Ten 12

幽 Thread 4

虐 Tiger 2

查 Tree 43

柬 Tree 55

厘 Village 2

重 **Heavy** Village 3

皇 **Emperor** White 6

皆 White 7

威 Woman 40

10

隻 Bird (2) 2

弱 Bow 13

衷 Clothes 6

衰 Clothes 10

扇 **Fan** Doorleaf 6

兼 Eight 10

眞 **Real, genuine** Eye 15

烏 Fire 26

恥 Heart 44

恭 Heart 52

將 Inch 4

乘 Leftstroke 8

朗 Moon 7

島 **Island** Mountain 12

料 Peck 2

辱 Period 2

夏 **Summer** Persevere 2

耗 Plow 2

耕 Plow 3

羔 Sheep 4

書 **Book** Speak 6

務 Strength 14

栽 Tree 82

氣 **Gas, air** Vapor 1

泰 Water 53

酒 **Wine, liquor** Wine jug 6

翅 Wings 2

11

乾 Bent 8

欲 Breathe 6

常 **Contstantly** Cloth 19

帶 **Belt, zone** Cloth 20

袋 Clothes 16

參 "Shen"("ginshen") Cocoon 3

率 Dark 3

執 Earth 28

墊 Earth 35

堂 Hall Earth 36

眾 Many, Crowd Eye 19

術 Go 3

將 Inch 7

爽 Intertwine 2

望 Moon 8

商 Trade Mouth 124

斜 Peck 3

象 Pig 3

羞 Sheep 5

匙 Spoon Spoon 3

章 Stand 3

竟 Stand 4

晝 Sun 32

甜 Sweet Sweet 3

處 Tiger 4

瓶 Bottle Tile 2

瓷 Porcelain Tile 3

野 Village 4

習 Wings 5

12

眾 Many. Crowd Blood 2

欺 Breathe 8

款 Breathe 10

為 Claw 5

裁 Clothes 22

報 Newspaper Earth 44

焦 Fire 34

街 Street Go 5

甦 Grow 4

就 Lame 3

斑 Literature 4

喬 Mouth 141

喪 Mouth 146

辜 Offend 2

粥 Porridge Rice 8

疏 Roll 2

壹 One Scholar 5

羨 Sheep 7

貳 Two Shell 22

替 Speak 9

曾 Speak 11

最 Speak 12

童 Stand 6

凱 Stool 4

勝 Strength 19

博 Ten 13

幾 How many. Few Thread 5

虛 Tiger 5

舒 Tongue 4

甯 Use 5

量 Village 5

渠 Water 119

翔 Wings 8

13

新 New Axe 6

亂 Bent 9

歇 Breathe 11

載 Cart 13

裏 Clothes 29

聖 Ear 9

愛 Love Heart 102

麼 Hemp 2

舅 Mortar 6

與 Mortar 7

農 Agriculture Period 3

幹 Pestle 7

彙 Pig's snout 3

義 Righteousness Sheep 8

會 Association Speak 13

豎 Stand 8

歲 Stop 8

募 Strength 22

肆 Four (elab.) Stylus 4

虜 Tiger 6

號 Number Tiger 7

虞 Tiger 8

禽 Track 2

業 Business Tree 141

準 Water 131

匯 Water 133

端 Beard 5

歌 Breathe 14

輝 Cart 18

幕 Cloth 27

製 Clothes 32

裏 Clothes 34

聚 Ear 10

夢 Evening 7

夥 Evening 8

鬧 Fight 2

弊 Folded hands 6

魂 Ghost 2

魁 Ghost 3

蝕 Insect 51

尵 Legs 17

興 Prosper Mortar 8

嘗 Taste (v) Mouth 170

臺 Platform Reach 3

疑 Roll 3

壺 Scholar 4

壽 Longevity Scholar 6

凳 Stool 5
暢 Sun 50
翡 Wings 9
翠 Wings 10

15

歐 Breathe 15
層 **Layer. Floor** Corpse 25
魄 Ghost 5
衝 Go 8
穀 Grain 38
髮 **Hair** Hairlocks 1
慶 Heart 128
慕 Heart 131
憂 Heart 140
黎 Millet 2
皺 Skin 4
肅 Stylus 3
舖 **Shop, store** Tongue 6

颳 Wind 2

16

艱 Defiance 3
衛 Go 10
穌 Grain 41
穎 Grain 43
靜 Green 3
舉 Mortar 9
豫 Pig 7
穀 Rice 19
賴 Shell 47
縣 Silk 81
歷 Stop 9
整 Tap 25

17

雛 Bird (2) 14
輿 Cart 33
幫 Cloth 32

褻 Clothes 53
衡 Go 11
臨 Minister 3
糞 Rice 21
隸 Seize 1
賸 Shell 52
氅 Tap 27
虧 Tiger 9
豁 Valley 2
麵 Wheat 3
膳 Words 108

18

斷 Axe 7
雞 **Chicken** Bird (2) 16
雙 **Pair, double** Bird (2) 17
雜 **Miscellaneous** Bird (2) 18
鬆 Hairlocks 7
叢 Hand (2) 15

舊 Mortar 10

羹 Sheep 13

歸 Stop 10

颭 Wind 3

翻 Wings 15

翹 Wings 16

麵 Flour. Noodles Wheat 5

飄 Wind 5

耀 Wings 17

21

屬 Corpse 26

魔 Ghost 10

25

鹽 Salt Salt 3

29

鬱 Wine vessel 1

19

歎 Breathe 16

麗 Beautiful Deer 3

鬍 Hairlocks 9

20

釉 Footprint 3

騰 Horse 27

鹹 Salted, salty Salt 2

贏 Shell 57

纂 Silk 118

響 Sound 4

競 Stand 12

22

歡 Breathe 17

襲 Clothes 63

聽 Hear, listen Ear 19

鬚 Hairlocks 11

囊 Mouth 217

23

變 Words 135

24

艷 Bean 9

艶 Color 2

衢 Go 13

59

Rapid–Access Index

The **"Rapid-Access Index"** allows you to immediately locate a character in the large Groups, i.e. in Groups of over 100 characters. It covers 1,963 characters (approx. 2,000 characters or 40% of the Dictionary) in the following Groups: **HAND** (264 chars.); **WATER** (222 chars.); **MOUTH** (221 chars.);**TREE** (210 chars); **MAN** (207 chars.); **HEART** (177 chars.); **GRASS** (168 chars); **WORDS** (143 chars); **SILK** (126 chars);**GOLD** (123 chars); **FLESH** (102 chars).

The symbol ⎡Rapid Access available⎤ is placed at the beginning of these Groups, to tell you that you should use the **"Index"** for this Group.

By naming the Radical and another writing-unit (and a third in some cases), the characters can be alphabetically arranged by the names of their writing-units.

You may encounter writing-units that are **Uncommon Writing-Units**. A List **"Uncommon Writing-Units in Rapid-Access Index"** is given on pages 61 and 62.

Take this character 葱 . What character is that? **GRASS** ⺍ is here the Radical, so we go to the Section **GRASS** in the Index. We also see another unit **HEART** 心 . Now we go down the Section until **HEART**. Here we find the character accompanied by the number 98. This means that the character is located in the Group **GRASS** in the Dictionary as Character No. 98 (**"Onion"**).

A writing-unit can consist of other smaller units. For example, in the character 愧 , we see 鬼 (GHOST), a very uncommon unit. But here we see that 田 (FIELD) is part of it. After we arrive at the Section **HEART** (忄 , a Compressed Radical), we go to **FIELD** and find the character accompanied by the number 115. This means that the character is located in the Group **HEART** in the Dictionary as Character No.115 (**"Ashamed; conscience-stricken"**).

The List **"Uncommon Writing-Units in Rapid-Access Index"** on pages 61 to 62 contains Uncommon Writing-Units that you could encounter in the "Rapid-Access Index".

Uncommon Writing-Units in Rapid-Access Index
(arranged by the number of their strokes)

1
一 ONE
丨 ROD
丶 DOT
丿 LEFTSTROKE
乙 乚 BENT
亅 DOWNSTROKE

2
二 TWO   阝 CITY
亠 LID
儿 LEGS
八 EIGHT
冂 BORDERS
冖 COVER
冫 ICE
几 STOOL
凵 PIT
力 STRENGTH
勹 WRAP
匕 SPOON
匚 BASKET
十 TEN
卜 DIVINATION
卩 㔾 SEAL
厂 CLIFF
厶 COCOON
又 HAND (2)

3
囗 ENCLOSURE
士 SCHOLAR
夂 PURSUE

夕 EVENING
子 孑 CHILD
寸 INCH
小 SMALL
尸 CORPSE
屮 SPROUT
山 MOUNTAIN
巛 RIVER
工 WORK
己 SELF
干 PESTLE
幺 THREAD
廴 MOVE ON
廾 FLDED HANDS
弋 DART
弓 BOW
彐 彑 彐 PIG'S SNOUT
彡 LINES

4
戈 HALBERD
戸 DOORLEAF
支 BRANCH
攴 攵 TAP
文 LITERATURE
斤 AXE
方 SQUARE
旡 NOT
月 MOON
欠 BREATHE
止 STOP

比 COMPARE
毛 HAIR
氏 CLAN
爪 爫 CLAW
父 FATHER
爿 SPLITWOOD (L)
片 SPLITWOOD (R)
牙 TOOTH
牛 OX

5
甘 SWEET
生 GROW
用 USE   白 WHITE
田 FIELD
疋 ROLL
癶 BOTH FEET
皮 SKIN
皿 DISH
矛 LANCE
矢 ARROW
穴 空 CAVE
立 STAND
毋 母 DO NOT

6
米 RICE
缶 EARTHNWARE
羊 善 SHEEP
羽 WINGS
而 BEARD
耳 EAR

61

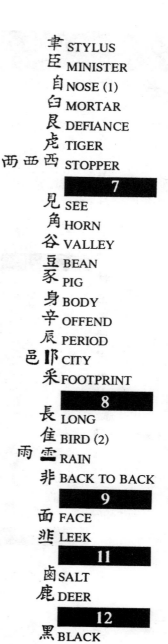

聿 STYLUS
臣 MINISTER
自 NOSE (1)
臼 MORTAR
艮 DEFIANCE
虍 TIGER
西 襾 酉 STOPPER

7

見 SEE
角 HORN
谷 VALLEY
豆 BEAN
豕 PIG
身 BODY
辛 OFFEND
辰 PERIOD
邑 阝 CITY
釆 FOOTPRINT

8

長 LONG
隹 BIRD (2)
雨 霝 RAIN
非 BACK TO BACK

9

面 FACE
韭 LEEK

11

鹵 SALT
鹿 DEER

12

黑 BLACK

13

鼠 RAT

16

龍 DRAGON

What's More on the Menu? (Quiz)

Below are 44 characters that you often see on a Chinese Menu.
To find their meanings you can use the **"Rapid-Access Index"** here.

The characters are arranged under their Radicals and the large letters are the first letters of their Names (see **"Radicals (English Names)"**, pages 27 and 28). **To locate a character you need to know the Name of its Radical and the Name of another writing-unit, which could be an Uncommon Writing-Unit.** On pages 61 and 62 you find the List **"Uncommon Writing-Units in Rapid-Access Index"**.

F	肉 1	肝 2	肚 3	腐 4	腊 5	腸 6	腿 7
臘 8	**G**	鍋 9	**G**	芋 10	芥 11	芹 12	茄 13
茶 14	荔 15	荸 16	荳 17	菇 18	菱 19	菠 20	菜 21
葱 22	蒸 23	蒙 24	蒜 25	蔔 26	蔬 27	蕃 28	薑 29
摩 30	蘑 31	蘿 32	**H**	捲 33	排 34	**S**	素 35
絲 36	**T**	李 37	核 38	桃 39	椒 40	**W**	汁 41
油 42	湯 43	滷 44				

You find the Solutions and your Scoring Evaluation on the next page!

Using the Rapid-Access Index – Solutions & Evaluation

FLESH

[1] Common Radical: <u>Flesh, Meat</u>. [2] pestle 6: <u>Liver</u>. [3] EARTH 10: <u>Stomach, Tripe</u>. [4] Shelter 54 / MAN. inch 54: **"fu"** in "tofu" (bean cake). [5] SUN. two 59: <u>Cured</u> (– meat). [6] SUN. wrap 64: <u>Sausage</u>. [7] defiance 77/ PROCEED 77: <u>Ham</u> (huôtuî). [8] river 97/ (Rat) 97: <u>Cured</u> (– meat).

GOLD

[9] MOUTH^2. borders^2 69: <u>Pot</u> in "potsticker".

GRASS

[10] downstroke 6 / two 6: <u>Taro.</u> [11] MAN. leftstroke 13: <u>Mustard green.</u> [12] axe 16: <u>Celery, Parsley, Cress.</u> [13] MOUTH. strength 28: <u>Eggplant.</u> [14] MAN. (TREE) 39: Tea. [15] strength^3 45: <u>Lichee.</u> [16] child 60 / cover 60 / ten 60: <u>Water chestnut.</u> [17] bean 61: <u>Legumes, Beans, Peas.</u> [18] MOUTH. WOMAN 67: **"gu'**, <u>Mushroom</u> (mógu). [19] EARTH 70 / pursue 70: <u>Water chestnut.</u> [20] WATER. skin 75: <u>Spinach</u> (bocài). [21] TREE. claw 79: <u>Vegetable.</u> [22] HEART 98: <u>Onion.</u> [23] FIRE (child) 104: <u>Steam (v).</u> [24] pig 109/ cover 109: **"Mêng"**, <u>Mongolian</u> (Mênggû). [25] Revelation 113 (should also have been: small 113 / two 113): <u>Garlic.</u> [26] MOUTH. Field 123: **"bo"**, <u>Turnip, Radish</u> (luóbo). [27] cocoon 124/ lid. cocoon 124 / legs 124: <u>Vegetable.</u> [28] Field. TREE 129: <u>Tomato.</u> [29] Field^2. One^2 140: <u>Ginger.</u> [30] Shelter 155 / TREE^2· HAND 155 / HAND 155: **"mo"**, <u>Mushroom</u> (mógu). [31] TREE^2· MOUTH 160 / STONE 160: **"mo"**, <u>Mushroom</u> (mógu). [32] EYE. Bird 167: **"luó"**, <u>Turnip, Radish</u> (boluó).

HAND

[33] Big. seal 105 / seal. Big 105: <u>Roll</u> in "egg roll". [34] leftstroke 113 (should also have been: back to back 113): <u>Spareribs</u> (páigû).

SILK

[35] (JADE) 21: **Vegetable** in "vegetable dish". [36] SILK
41:_Shredded_ in "shredded meat".

TREE

[37] Child 16: **Plum, Prune**. [38] lid. MAN 69 / MAN 69:
Walnut (hétaó). [39] (back to back) 80:_Peach_. [40] Hand
123 (should also have been: small 123): **Pepper(y), Hot** in
"hot food".

WATER

[41] ten 3: **Juice, Extract** (beef –). [42] Field 56: **Oil, Fat.**
[43] SUN. wrap 121: **Soup, Broth**. [44] Enclosure. divination 166 (should also have been: dot[4] 166 / divination 166):
Stew in soy sauce, **Thick gravy**.

---

36 to 44 correct – Excellent
32 to 35 correct – Good
26 to 31 correct – Satisfactory

---

*If you score less than "Satisfactory", you should
carefully study the Solutions of the ones you miss
and try again !*

FLESH

back to back 腓 53

bent 肶 9

Big 胯 37

Big 胭 43

Big 腌 62

Big 膜 80

Bird 雋 93

Bird 膌 95

borders 脯 44

Bow 胰 35

branch 肢 12

branch 臕 86

Cart 腫 66

Cave 腔 56

Child 脟 47

Child 脖 48

(clan) 脈 39

(clan) 脊 74

claw 脟 47

cliff 脈 39

cliff 脆 42

cliff 膽 91

Cloth 肺 14

(CLOTHES) 脣 49

(CLOTHES) 脹 52

(CLOTHES) 膿 88

cocoon 肬 18

cocoon 育 19

cocoon 胎 29

cocoon 能 40

cocoon 脚 46

compare 背 26

Corpse 肩 16

Corpse 臀 92

Corpse 臂 89

cover 脖 48

dart 膩 83

deer 臕 98

defiance 腿 77

Dish 臚 99

doorleaf 肩 16

dot 肘 4

dot 肩 16

dot 脯 44

dot 膊 75

dot 膳 85

DWELLING 腔 56

DWELLING 腕 61

EARTH 肚 10

EARTH 脚 46

EARTH 腔 82

eight 腆 60

Enclosure 胭 43

Enclosure 腦 68

Enclosure 膿 88

evening 腕 61

Field 胃 31

Field. Big 腌 62

Field. Dish 臚 99

Field. HEART 腮 69

Field. rod 胃 21

Field. spoon 膚 78

Field. ten 脾 57

Field. tiger 膚 78

FIRE 臕 98

FIRE 臙 100

GRASS 膜 80

GRASS 臟 101

Halberd 臟 101

Hand 肢 12

Hand 股 17

Hand 服 20

Hand 腎 58

Hand 臀 92

HEART 腮 69

HEART 臆 94

inch 肘 4

inch 腐 54

inch 腑 55

inch 膊 75

KNIFE 臍 96

leftstroke 肱 18

leftstroke 胙 30

Legs 胱 38

lid 肓 5

lid 肺 14

lid 育 19

lid 腋 63

lid 臍 96

	FLESH	
lines 膠 79	MOUTH. lines 膨 84	river 脛 45
lines 膨 84	MOUTH2. MAN3 臉 87	river 腦 68
long 脹 52	MOUTH. One 膈 73	river 臘 97
MAN. Bird 膚 95	MOUTH. pursue 胳 36	rod. leftstroke 胚 27
MAN. inch 腐 54	MOUTH. scholar 膨 84	rod. leftstroke 胙 30
MAN. inch 腑 55	MOUTH. scholar 膙 86	rod. One 肯 15
MAN. lid 腋 63	MOUTH. seal 腳 65	rod. One3 胙 30
MAN. lines 膠 79	MOUTH. Sheep 膳 85	rod. One3 脹 52
MAN3. MOUTH2 臉 87	MOUTH. ten 胡 23	rod. One6 腓 53
MAN. One4 脊 41	MOUTH3. TREE 臊 90	rod2. One 腆 60
MAN. pursue 腋 63	offend 臂 89	rod. two 肝 6
MAN. rod 骨 28	One. Bow 胰 35	rod. two 胖 24
MAN. Shelter 腐 54	One. (CLOTHES) 唇 49	roll 骨 28
MAN. Shelter 腑 55	One. cocoon 肱 18	seal. cliff 脆 42
MAN. Tap 脩 50	One3. Field 腆 66	seal. DWELLING 腕 61
MAN. Wings 膠 79	One2. leftstroke 胚 27	seal. EARTH 腳 46
minister 腎 58	One4. MAN 脊 41	seal. Hand 服 20
minister 臟 101	One. rod 肯 15	seal. rod 肥 13
MOUTH 骨 11	One3. rod 胙 30	seal. wrap 胞 25
MOUTH. borders 膈 73	One3. rod 脹 52	sheep 膳 85
MOUTH. branch 膙 86	One6. rod 腓 53	SHELL 膩 83
MOUTH. cocoon 胎 29	One. rod2 腆 60	Shelter 腐 54
MOUTH. Corpse 臂 89	One. work 脛 45	Shelter 腑 55
MOUTH2. cover 膏 72	period 唇 49	Shelter 膚 95
MOUTH. dot 脫 51	period 膿 88	Shelter 臚 98
MOUTH. EARTH 膛 82	pestle 肝 6	SILK 縢 76
MOUTH. eight 肌 22	pit 胸 34	SILK2 孿 102
MOUTH. FIRE 臊 100	PROCEED 腿 77	(small) 肖 8
MOUTH. Legs 脫 51	pursue 胳 36	splitwood 臟 101
MOUTH2. lid 膏 72	(rat) 臘 97	spoon 背 26
	Ra 2	

spoon[2] 能 40
square 脅 74
stool 肌 2
stool 股 17
stop 肯 15
Strength 肋 3
Strength[3] 脅 33
strike 股 17
strike 臀 92
SUN. GRASS 膜 80
SUN. grow 腥 70
SUN. HEART 臆 94
SUN. pursue 腹 67
SUN. spoon 脂 32
SUN. two 腊 59
SUN. wrap 腸 64
ten 肢 12
ten 脖 48
tiger 膚 78
tiger 臚 99
TREE 膝 81
TREE 膘 90
two 肝 6
two 胖 24
two 胯 37
two 脯 44
two 膩 83
WATER 膝 81
Wings 膠 79

FLESH

WOMAN 腰 71
WORDS 膽 91
WORDS 孿 102
work 肛 7
work 脛 45
work 腔 56
wrap 胞 25
wrap 胸 34

GOLD

arrow 鏃 94
axe 錾 93
back to back 銚 32
bean 鐙 97
bent 鈍 16
Big 鋏 44
Big 錡 59
Bird 錐 50
Bird 鍍 109
Bird 鑼 120
borders 銅 34
borders 鋼 53
borders 錀 117
both feet 鐙 97
Bow 銕 33
Cart 鍾 67
Cart 鏈 88
Cart 錾 93

GOLD

claw 錚 51
cliff 鏈 85
Cloth 錦 54
CLOTHES 鑲 116
cocoon 鈎 11
cocoon 銃 27
cocoon 鋑 49
Corpse 鋸 56
Corpse 鎗 83
cover 鋟 47
cover 鎊 80
defiance 銀 37
Dish 鑑 110
Dish 鑪 114
downstroke 釘 4
DWELLING 錠 61
DWELLING 鉈 20
DWELLING 鎔 84
Ear[3] 鑷 119
EARTH. EYE 鐸 107
EARTH. Field 鐘 95
EARTH[3]. lame 鏡 99
EARTH. leftstroke 銬 36
EARTH. MAN[2] 銼 48
EARTH. MOUTH 鏜 92
EARTH. Tap 鰲 90
Enclosure 錮 55
EYE. EARTH 鐸 107
EYE. eight 鎮 75

EYE. INSECT 鐲 103	Halberd 鍼 65	MOUTH. Corpse 鋸 56
EYE. minister 鑒 111	Halberd 鐵 106	MOUTH. DWELLING 鎔 84
EYE. MOUTH 鐶 102	Hand 釓 6	MOUTH. EARTH 鐺 92
(EYE). One 鉏 18	Hand 鋟 47	MOUTH. Enclosure 錮 55
EYE. SILK 鑼 120	Hand 鍍 71	MOUTH. evening 銘 31
EYE. SUN 鏝 89	Hand 鍛 72	MOUTH. EYE 鐶 102
father 釜 3	Hand 鑿 123	MOUTH. Field 鐺 105
father 鉸 30	inch 鑄 76	MOUTH[2]. GRASS 鑵 118
Field 鈿 24	INSECT. EYE 鐲 103	MOUTH. Halberd 鍼 65
Field. Dish 鑪 114	leftstroke 釗 5	MOUTH. Halberd 鐵 106
Field. EARTH 鍾 67	Legs 銃 27	MOUTH. inch 鑄 108
Field. EARTH 鐘 95	lid 銃 27	MOUTH. Legs 銳 43
Field. GRASS 錨 66	lid 鉸 30	MOUTH[2]. lid 鑲 116
Field. MOUTH 鎧 105	lid 鏘 80	MOUTH. MAN 鉿 29
Field. TREE 鍊 57	lines 鋒 39	MOUTH. MAN 鎗 83
FIRE. Grain 鍬 73	MAN[2]. Big 鋏 44	MOUTH[3]. MAN 鑰 117
FLESH 銷 42	MAN[2]. EARTH 銼 48	MOUTH. Mountain 鎧 78
FLESH 鍋 81	MAN. (JADE) 銓 35	MOUTH. One 銅 34
Footstep 銜 28	MAN. MOUTH 鉿 29	MOUTH. One 鐙 97
go 銜 28	MAN. MOUTH 鎗 83	MOUTH[2]. PROCEED 鎚 7
Grain 銹 46	MAN. MOUTH[3] 鑰 117	MOUTH. river 鑞 112
Grain 鍬 73	MAN. One 鈴 12	MOUTH. stool 鉛 26
GRASS 銑 40	MAN. One 鈴 21	MOUTH. ten 錮 55
GRASS 錨 66	minister 鑑 110	MOUTH. ten 鋸 56
GRASS 鏵 96	mortar 鍤 64	MOUTH. TREE 鍊 70
GRASS 鑊 109	Mountain 鎧 78	MOUTH[2]. WOMAN 鏤 87
GRASS 鑵 118	MOUTH 釦 7	MOUTH. wrap 鉤 17
grow 鏈 85	MOUTH[2]. Bird 鑵 118	One 鈕 14
Halberd 鉞 25	MOUTH[2]. borders[2] 鍋 69	One[4] 錘 52
Halberd[2] 錢 62	MOUTH. compare 鑱 115	One. bent 鈍 16

GOLD

One. Big 鏳 59

One. Bow 銕 33

One. downstroke 釕 4

One. (EYE) 鉏 18

One³. Field 鍾 67

One. leftstroke 鈑 23

One. use 鋪 45

period 鎄 76

pestle 釺 8

pig's snout 鍛 47

pig's snout 錚 51

pig's snout 銉 68

pig's snout 鎌 79

pig's snout 鏽 101

PROCEED 鎚 77

PROCEED 鏈 88

pursue 鋒 39

pursue 鋑 49

river 釧 5

rod. Hand 鍛 72

rod. leftstroke 釧 5

rod. pig's snout 銉 68

rod². pig's snout 鎌 79

rod. pursue 鋒 39

rod. two 釬 8

roll 錠 61

seal 鈀 15

seal 鉋 22

SHELL 鎖 82

SHELL 鑽 122

Shelter 鍍 71

Shelter 鐮 104

SILK 鑼 120

SILK² 鑾 121

small 鈔 10

splitwood² 鏽 101

(spoon) 鉈 20

square 鎊 80

square 鏊 90

square 鏇 91

square 鏃 94

stool 鍛 72

stool 鑿 123

Strength 鋤 38

strike 鍛 72

strike 鑿 123

stylus 銉 68

SUN. Cloth 錦 54

SUN. EYE 鏝 89

SUN. Legs 鏡 86

SUN. pestle 銲 41

SUN. small 鐐 98

SUN. TREE 鑠 113

SUN. two 錯 63

SUN. WATER 錫 100

SUN. wrap 錫 60

sweet 鉗 19

Tap 鏊 90

ten 針 2

ten 鏳 59

thread² 鑠 113

TREE 鐷 57

TREE 鍊 70

TREE 鍱 74

TREE 鑠 113

two 釬 8

two 鈞 13

two 銉 68

WATER 錄 58

WATER 錫 100

white 錦 54

white 鑠 113

WORDS 鑾 121

wrap 鈞 9

wrap 鈞 11

wrap 鈞 13

wrap 鈎 17

wrap 鉋 22

GRASS

arrow 蒺 115

arrow 薙 143

斤 16 axe

axe 薪 142

back to back 菲 64

basket 芒 3

basket 萁 93

bean 荳 61

Big. cover 英 37

Big. Enclosure 茵 53

Big. MAN2 荚 57

Big. One 芙 11

Big. One 莽 71

Big. One 葵 90

Bird 蕉 136

Bird 薙 143

(Bird) 薦 145

Bird 鸝 166

Bird 蘿 167

black 薰 147

both feet 葵 90

Breathe 茨 52

Cart 蕇 87

Cart 董 95

Cart 蓮 120

cat 貓 149

Child 荐 43

Child 葶 60

Cloth 蒂 94

CLOTHES 蓑 112

cocoon 芸 21

cocoon 蓋 107

cocoon 蔬 124

Corpse 蔚 127

cover 葶 60

cover 蕇 87

cover 蒂 94

cover 蒙 109

Dish 蓋 107

Dish 藍 148

Dish 蘆 161

Door 蘭 165

dot 芍 5

dot 芝 7

dot 葡 92

downstroke 芋 6

DWELLING 苧 22

DWELLING 蔻 119

DWELLING 蒨 125

EARTH 苧 49

EARTH 菱 70

EARTH 蓋 107

earthenware 菊 78

eight 萁 93

Enclosure 茵 53

Enclosure 薔 144

Enclosure 苗 41

evening 苑 38

evening 葬 96

(EYE) 苜 24

EYE 首 34

EYE. Bird 蘿 167

EYE. Halberd 蔑 121

EYE. SILK 蘿 167

EYE. SUN 薯 150

Field 苗 32

Field. borders 萬 99

Field. borders 藕 156

Field. Dish 蘆 161

Field. footprint 蕃 129

Field. Grain 蕃 129

Field. Legs 蒐 111

Field2. One3 薑 140

Field. river 畱 80

Field. thread 蓄 105

Field. TREE 蕃 129

Field. TREE 藕 156

FIRE. Bird 蕉 136

FIRE. Bird 鸝 166

FIRE. (Cart) 薰 147

FIRE. (Child) 蒸 104

FIRE. rod4 無 137

FIRE. EARTH2 藝 118

FIRE. Shelter 蔗 117

FIRE. Shelter 薦 145

FIRE. Strength 藝 118

GRASS

FIRE. Wine jug 醮 166

Fish 蘇 162

Fish 薊 139

FLESH 藤 158

FLESH 菁 81

Footstep 薇 146

ghost 蒐 111

Grain 莉 58

Grain 蒡 62

Grain 姜 84

Grain 藜 154

Grain 蘇 162

GRASS² 艸 4

GRASS 芻 8

Halberd 茂 31

Halberd 藏 151

HAND 抱 73

HAND 摩 155

Hand 芰 18

Hand 茠 77

Hand 葭 88

HEART 蔥 98

HEART 蕙 132

HEART³ 蕊 133

high 蒿 106

Ice 茨 52

ILLNESS 蕨 115

inch 蕁 49

inch 蔚 127

KNIFE. eight 芬 9

KNIFE. Fish 薊 139

KNIFE. Grain 莉 58

KNIFE. leek 韰 168

KNIFE. TREE 莉 66

KNIFE. two 荊 44

lance 茅 30

leather 葦 100

leek 韰 168

leftstroke 艾 2

leftstroke 茇 14

leftstroke 芽 19

Legs 芫 20

Legs 荒 40

Legs 葚 93

Legs 蔻 119

Legs 蔬 124

lid 芒 3

lid. Cloth 蒂 94

lid. cocoon 蔬 124

lid. leek 韰 168

lid. Legs 荒 40

MAN 芩 15

MAN². Big 英 57

MAN. cocoon 陰 128

MAN. dot 苁 26

MAN. leftstroke 芥 13

MAN. MOUTH 荅 48

MAN. MOUTH 荷 56

MAN. MOUTH 蒼 114

MAN. MOUTH 蓉 116

MAN². MOUTH 薔 144

MAN. spoon 花 12

MAN. square 菸 83

MAN. SUN 葛 89

MAN. SUN 蒨 125

MAN². ten 萃 82

MAN. (TREE) 茶 39

MAN². TREE 萊 69

MAN. WATER 藜 154

MAN. white 蒨 125

minister 藍 148

minister 藏 151

moon 菁 81

moon 藤 158

Mound 陰 128

Mountain 薇 146

MOUTH 葦 100

MOUTH². Big 蕎 130

MOUTH². borders² 蒿 101

MOUTH. cocoon 苔 36

MOUTH. Corpse 蒼 114

MOUTH. divination 苫 35

MOUTH. DWELLING 蓉 116

MOUTH. Ear 茸 97

MOUTH. Enclosure 茼 41
MOUTH. Enclosure 薔 144
MOUTH. evening 茗 47
MOUTH. Field 葍 123
MOUTH. FLESH 萌 86
MOUTH. leftstroke 若 25
MOUTH. lid 蓑 112
MOUTH. MAN 荅 48
MOUTH. MAN 荷 56
MOUTH.MAN² 薔 144
MOUTH. moon 葫 86
MOUTH. One 苛 23
MOUTH. One 若 25
MOUTH. One 蓑 112
MOUTH. stand 菩 76
MOUTH. Strength 茄 28
MOUTH. Tap 藪 157
MOUTH. ten 苦 29
MOUTH. TREE² 藺 160
MOUTH. TREE 蘭 165
MOUTH. WATER 落 91
MOUTH. WOMAN 茹 42
MOUTH. WOMAN 菇 67
MOUTH. WOMAN 藪 157
MOUTH. wrap 苟 27
MOUTH². wrap 蒿 106
offend 薪 142
One⁴ 華 65
pig 蒙 109

pig's snout 蕭 131
plow 藕 156
PROCEED 蓮 120
PROCEED 蓬 122
pursue 菱 70
Revelation² 蒜 113
Revelation 蔚 127
Rice 菊 68
river 莖 55
rod 芽 19
rod 華 65
rod 葭 88
scholar 莊 54
seal 芭 17
seal 苑 38
seal 葩 73
Shelter 蔗 117
Shelter 薦 145
Shelter 蘼 155
SILK 約 103
SILK 蘊 164
SILK 蘿 167
small 叔 77
splitwood 莊 54
splitwood² 蕭 131
splitwood 藏 151
spoon 葬 96
square 芳 10
square 菸 83

STONE 蘑 160
stool 芨 18
Strength³ 荔 45
Strength 藝 118
strike 芟 18
SUN. Big 莫 59
SUN. cat 貓 149
SUN. EARTH 著 85
SUN. EYE 蔓 126
SUN. EYE 薯 150
SUN. Enclosure 萱 63
SUN. FLESH 萌 72
SUN. MAN 葛 89
SUN. MAN 蓿 125
SUN. moon 萌 72
SUN. speak 萱 63
SUN. ten 草 50
SUN. TREE 藉 152
SUN. wrap 葛 89
Tap 蔻 119
Tap 蔽 134
Tap 薇 146
Tap 藪 157
ten 莘 60
ten² 華 65
thread 茲 51
tiger 蘆 61
tooth 芽 19

GRASS	HAND	HAND

TREE. claw 菜 79

TREE. Door 蘭 165

TREE. Field 藕 156

TREE². HAND 摩 155

TREE. KNIFE 莉 66

TREE. MAN² 萊 69

TREE². MOUTH 蘑 160

TREE. One 茉 33

TREE. One 葉 102

TREE. thread² 藥 159

TREE. white 藥 159

two 芋 6

two 荒 20

two 芸 21

two 蔻 119

valley 蓉 116

village 董 95

WATER. dot 茫 46

WATER. dot 蒲 110

WATER. Field 藩 153

WATER. FLESH 藤 158

WATER. footprint 藩 153

WATER. Grain 藩 153

WATER. Grain 藜 154

WATER. inch 薄 141

WATER. lid 茫 46

WATER. MAN 溚 108

WATER. MAN 藜 154

WATER. moon 藤 158

WATER. MOUTH 落 91

WATER. MOUTH³ 藻 163

WATER. pestle 萍 74

WATER. skin 菠 75

WATER. SUN 蕩 135

WATER. TREE 藻 163

WATER. (use) 蒲 110

Wine jug 蘸 166

WOMAN 姜 84

WOMAN 薅 138

work 莖 55

wrap 芍 5

wrap² 蒻 8

wrap 菊 68

wrap 菢 73

wrap 萄 78

wrap 葡 92

HAND

arrow 擬 237

arrow 挨 79

axe 折 13

axe 折 56

axe 掀 102

axe 掑 210

basket 拒 38

bent 扎 3

bent 托 8

bent 拖 54

bent 挖 78

Big 扶 16

Big 換 132

Big. dot 拳 67

Big. Field 掩 128

Big. MAN 挾 83

Big. rod 捧 101

Big. seal 捲 105

Big. small 捺 112

Big. two 撲 208

Bird 搗 177

Bird 推 122

Bird. basket 摳 223

Bird. Mountain 攜 158

(Bird). Mountain 搗 171

Bird. MOUTH 攤 259

Bird. rain 攉 250

Bird. Wings 擢 234

black 攩 62

boat 搬 161

bones 搰 166

borders 捕 88

borders 搆 159

both feet 揆 137

both feet 撥 207

Bow 拂 35

Bow 搦 160

Bow 撥 207

branch 技 18

Breathe 掀 102

Breathe 撖 199

Cart 揮 133

Cart 搸 246

Cave 控 107

Cave 挖 78

Cave 攛 257

(Child) 承 15

(Child) 拯 62

City 挪 86

City 擲 243

Clan 抵 53

(Clan) 扼 43

claw 抓 10

claw. Hand 授 116

claw. mortar 搯 172

claw. pig's snout 挣 98

HAND

claw. pursue 援 151

claw. TREE 採 123

cliff. Breathe 撖 199

cliff. EARTH 捱 127

cliff. seal 扼 19

cliff. tiger 攎 156

cliff. WORDS 擔 229

cloth 掃 114

(CLOTHES) 振 80

(CLOTHES) 捩 153

cocoon 拚 33

cocoon 挨 79

compare 批 24

Corpse 掘 104

Corpse 握 147

Corpse 捩 153

Corpse 擘 226

dart 拭 75

(dart) 抿 43

Dish 搵 157

do not 拇 42

Door 捫 111

Door 擱 238

Door 攔 254

doorleaf 搹 165

dragon 攏 251

DWELLING 挓 59

DWELLING 擦 235

DWELLING 擰 236

DWELLING 攟 239

DWELLING 按 73

Ear 攝 256

EARTH 挂 69

EARTH 撓 202

EARTH. Cliff 捱 127

EARTH. divination 掛 108

EARTH. inch 持 61

EARTH. leftstroke 拷 65

EARTH. MAN 挫 94

EARTH. mortar 捏 92

earthenware 搖 178

earthenware 掏 118

eight 捌 96

Enclosure 捆 85

EYE 搷 173

EYE 擇 232

EYE 擉 215

EYE 擺 247

Field. (dart) 拽 64

Field. EARTH 撞 195

Field. footprint 播 206

Field. Grain 播 206

Field. MOUTH 摺 185

Field. Rain 擂 224

Field. rod 抽 30

Field. rod 押 57

Field. SILK 摞 182

FIRE 揪 145

FIRE 撚 203

FIRE 撫 197

FIRE 撈 200

FLESH 捎 89

FLESH. cover 捐 166

FLESH. MOUTH 捐 84

FLESH. stand 攏 251

FLESH. Tap 撇 194

FLESH. Tap 撒 209

FOOT 捉 81

GRASS. Field 描 139

GRASS. MAN 搽 152

GRASS. MOUTH 搭 168

GRASS. MOUTH 擎 221

GRASS. SUN 摸 184

GRASS. SUN 摹 186

hair 撬 198

Halberd 找 11

Hand 才 2

Hand 掇 121

Hand. boat 搬 161

Hand. claw 授 116

Hand. mortar 搜 143

Hand. rod 披 50

Hand. stool 投 27

Hand. stool 撃 219

HEART 撑 236

HEART 摠 191

HEART 摁 141

HEART 擾 244

hemp 摩 183

inch 搏 188

inch 搏 162

INSECT 搔 164

(JADE) 拄 32

(JADE) 挺 91

(KNIFE) 扭 21

KNIFE 掣 99

KNIFE 扮 23

KNIFE 捌 87

KNIFE 挈 60

(lance) 抒 25

leftstroke 扔 4

leftstroke 拃 36

leftstroke 挑 77

leftstroke 排 113

lid. Bird 擁 233

lid. borders 摘 189

lid. KNIFE 擠 242

lid. MAN 披 129

lid. MOUTH 攘 253

lid. MOUTH 掠 109

lid. MOUTH 擅 227

lid. stool 抗 17

lid. ten 摔 187

MAN 拊 34

MAN 拴 76

MAN 掄 110

MAN 擒 220

mortar 掐 103

mortar 插 130

mortar 搜 143

mortar 掐 172

Mountain 拙 31

Mountain. beard 揣 131

Mountain. Bird 摧 190

Mountain. Bird 攜 255

Mountain. Corpse 掘 104

MOUTH 扣 9

MOUTH 括 70

MOUTH. basket 摳 180

MOUTH. Bird 攤 259

MOUTH. black 擋 262

MOUTH. (CLOTHES) 攘 264

MOUTH. cocoon 抬 52

MOUTH. Compare 攬 252

MOUTH. Corpse 搶 176

MOUTH. Corpse 擘 226

MOUTH. divination 扚 45

MOUTH. DWELLING 掌 97

MOUTH. Ear 揖 150

MOUTH. Field 摺 185

MOUTH. Field 擋 230

MOUTH. Field 揮 211

MOUTH. FLESH 捐 84

MOUTH. GRASS 搭 168

MOUTH. GRASS 擎 221

MOUTH. Hand 撑 192

MOUTH. HEART 撼 216

MOUTH. inch 擣 241

MOUTH. KNIFE 招 29

MOUTH . KNIFE 捌 87

MOUTH. Legs 挽 95
MOUTH. lid 掠 109
MOUTH. lid 攘 253
MOUTH. MAN 拾 74
MOUTH. MAN 揜 149
MOUTH. MAN 撿 218
MOUTH. MAN 捨 115
MOUTH. MAN 拿 71
MOUTH. Scholar 擡 240
MOUTH. SHELL 損 167
MOUTH. Shelter 搪 170
MOUTH. Shelter 掂 120
MOUTH. Strength 拐 39
MOUTH. SUN 擅 227
MOUTH. TREE 揀 136
MOUTH. TREE 操 231
MOUTH. WOMAN 拏 72
MOUTH. WOMAN 摟 181
MOUTH. WOMAN 擻 249
MOUTH. wrap 拘 37
Move on 挺 91
One 打 6
One 抵 53
One 拔 46
One 拯 62
period 振 80
pig 據 222
pig's snout 捷 125
pig's snout 掙 98
pig's snout 掃 114
PROCEED 撻 228
PROCEED 搥 155
Rain 擢 250
rat 攛 257
Rice 掬 106
rod. dot 拌 48
rod. dot 拼 63
rod. dot 掽 142
rod. two 拱 68
rod. leftstroke 拃 36
rod. two 拜 47
rod. two 捶 100
roll 擬 237
seal 把 22
seal 抑 28
seal. Big 捲 105
seal. cliff 扼 19
seal. eight 撰 196
seal. wrap 抱 49
see 攪 261
see 攬 263
SHELL 攢 260
Shelter 183 摩
Shelter 擴 245
SILK 攣 258
skin 披 50
small 抄 12
spoon 擬 237
sprout 搊 174
stand 拉 40

HAND

STONE 拓 55

stop 扯 14

Strength 抛 20

Strength 拗 58

Strength 攄 225

strike 投 27

strike 擊 219

strike 搬 161

SUN. Big 捲 193

SUN. dot 拍 51

SUN. compare 揩 135

SUN. Hand 撮 213

SUN. MAN 抻 217

SUN. old 揯 154

SUN. pestle 捍 82

SUN. pursue 搿 146

SUN. rod 措 126

SUN. (roll) 提 144

SUN. small 撩 210

SUN. spoon 指 60

SUN. spoon 揩 154

SUN. ten 掉 119

SUN. ten 撑 212

SUN. Wings 搨 169

SUN. Wings 摺 179

SUN. wrap 揭 138

SUN. wrap 揚 148

Tap. borders 撇 205

Tap. borders 撇 204

Tap. FLESH 撤 194

Tap. FLESH 撒 209

Tap. GRASS 擎 221

Tap. MOUTH 撖 249

ten 抖 26

tiger 攄 156

tiger 據 222

tiger 攄 225

tongue 括 70

TREE. Big 攀 248

TREE. claw 採 123

TREE. cover 探 117

TREE. Enclosure 捆 85

TREE. Hand 操 163

TREE. lance 揉 134

TREE. MOUTH 揀 136

TREE. Shelter 摩 183

TREE. two 抹 41

two 扭 21

two 搋 142

two 捅 93

two 拱 68

two 捕 88

use 捅 93

use 捕 88

WATER 摣 223

WATER 掌 90

white 拍 51

white 揩 135

white 摺 179

Wine jug 撙 214

Wings 摺 179

Wings 搧 165

WOMAN 拏 44

WOMAN 挐 72

WOMAN 接 124

WORDS 擔 229

WORDS 攣 258

work 扛 7

work 拭 75

work 控 107

work 搓 175

wrap. earthenware 掏 118

wrap. MOUTH 拘 37

wrap. Rice 掬 106

wrap. seal 抱 49

wrap. sprout 摵 174

HEART

axe 忟 13
axe 慚 135
basket 忙 6
basket 忘 11
beard 懦 166
Big 快 17
Big 懊 161
Big 快 42
Big 恩 54
Big 忝 21
Bird 惟 92
Bird 應 164
Bird 憔 154
blood 恤 58
Bow 悌 70
Breathe 忝 61
Breathe 愁 141
Breathe 懿 176
Cart 慚 135
cat 懇 157
Child 悖 68
Child 惇 88
Child 慈 120
claw 愛 102
Cloth 怖 34
(CLOTHES) 悵 76
cocoon 慘 136
Corpse 慰 139

HEART

Corpse 怩 26
cover 忱 19
dart 忑 7
defiance 恨 45
defiance 懇 157
defiance 慨 125
Dish 恤 58
divination 忐 8
Dog 愁 71
(do not) 悔 65
Door 悶 82
Door 憫 148
Ear 恥 44
Ear³ 懾 173
Ear 憨 144
EARTH 怯 28
EARTH 怪 30
EARTH 恃 55
eight 恭 52
Enclosure 恩 54
Enclosure 惱 101
Enclosure 悃 66
evening 怨 43
EYE. Bird 懼 174
EYE. CLOTHES 懷 169
EYE. DWELLING 憲 145
EYE. eight 慎 118
EYE. SILK 戀 168
EYE. spoon 慎 118
EYE. TREE 想 105

EYE. WATER 懷 169
face 恤 100
Field 思 37
Field. borders 愚 111
Field. legs 愧 115
Field. One 惠 79
Field. tiger 慮 129
FIRE 恢 53
FIRE 愁 71
FIRE 愁 109
FIRE 憔 154
FLESH 悄 72
FLESH 情 90
FLESH 惰 107
FLESH 態 121
FLESH 懇 119
footprint 悉 69
footstep 慫 99
footstep 懲 167
ghost 愧 115
Grain 悉 69
Grain 愁 109
GRASS. Bird 懽 175
GRASS. (Cart) 懂 162
GRASS. EYE² 憎 171
GRASS. legs 慌 113
GRASS. MOUTH 惹 96
GRASS. MOUTH 慝 134
GRASS. MOUTH² 懽 175
GRASS. SUN 慕 131

HEART

grow 性 35	lid 忘 11	MOUTH. EYE 憩 143, 127
Halberd 感 78	lines 惨 136	MOUTH². Field 憚 151
Halberd 惑 97	lines² 慧 124	MOUTH. Grain 懍 159
Halberd 感 137	literature 憫 48	MOUTH. GRASS 慝 134
Halberd 懺 172	long 悵 76	MOUTH. Halberd 惑 78
Hand 憝 123	MAN 念 18	MOUTH. Halberd 感 97
HEART 憶 163	MAN². Big 愜 98	MOUTH. Halberd 憾 156
HEART 憾 156	MAN. cocoon 惨 136	MOUTH. HEART 憾 156
HEART 惚 80	MAN. dot 念 18	MOUTH. lance 憰 146
(HEAD) 憂 140	MAN. FLESH 愈 112	MOUTH. Legs 悦 27
horn 懈 155	MAN². Halberd 懺 172	MOUTH. Legs 悦 75
Horse 憑 150	MAN. ice 恋 61	MOUTH. MAN 恰 50
ice 恋 61	MAN. KNIFE 愈 112	MOUTH. MAN 愠 110
inch 忖 10	MAN. lines 惨 136	MOUTH. (pestle) 恬 59
inch 愽 117	MAN. Mountain 懲 167	MOUTH. pursue 恪 49
inch 慰 139	MAN. MOUTH 恰 50	MOUTH. rod 忠 12
(JADE) 恙 62	MAN. small 您 67	MOUTH². rod 患 64
KNIFE 忍 4	MAN. Tap 悠 74	MOUTH. SHELL 懶 170
KNIFE 忿 14	MAN. ten 悴 91	MOUTH. Shelter 恬 86
KNIFE 惻 108	MAN. use 憊 153	MOUTH. ten 怙 23
KNIFE 懈 155	Mountain 懲 167	MOUTH. two 悟 73
KNIFE 懶 170	MOUTH. basket 惱 132	MOUTH². two 愕 103
(leek) 悲 83	MOUTH. borders 恫 60	MOUTH. WOMAN 恕 56
leek 懺 172	MOUTH. borders 恓 77	nose 息 57
leftstroke 必 2	MOUTH. Breathe 懿 176	nose 憩 143, 127
leftstroke 忧 19	MOUTH. Child 惇 88	not 慨 125
leftstroke 怎 39	MOUTH. cocoon 怡 25	One 志 8
leftstroke 怍 40	MOUTH. cocoon 息 38	One² 忸 20
Legs 恍 48	MOUTH. Dish 愠 110	One. divination 忐 9
Legs 怵 24	MOUTH. Enclosure 懍 159	One. Enclosure 恓 100

HEART

One. leftstroke 怀 15	Shelter 應 164	Tap 憨 149
One. pig's snout 恆 46	SILK 慈 120	Tap 憨 144
One³. rod 怎 39	SILK² 戀 177	Tap 懲 167
One³. rod 作 40	sound 憶 163	ten 怵 24
One⁶. rod² 慧 124	spoon 怩 26	thread 慈 122
Ox 忏 22	stool 恐 51	tiger 慮 129
Ox 懈 155	stool 憨 123	tongue 恬 59
pestle 怦 33	Strength 慟 133	tongue 憩 143, 127
pig's snout 急 29	Strength 懃 158	(TREE) 怵 24
pig's snout 慧 124	strike 憨 123	TREE 惆 66
pig's snout 恆 46	SUN 怕 32	TREE 想 105
pursue 愛 102	SUN. clan 惜 81	TREE 慄 116
pursue 憂 140	SUN. cliff 愿 114	TREE 懋 160
pursue 慶 128	SUN. dish 愠 110	two 忸 20
Rain 懦 166	SUN. dot 惶 94	two 恆 46
Revelation 慰 139	SUN. dot² 憎 152	two 惡 93
Rice 憐 147	SUN. EYE 慢 130	WATER 潍 165
river 惱 101	SUN. GRASS 慕 131	WATER. footstep 懲 99
rod² 慧 124	SUN. grow 惺 106	WATER. Shelter 慷 126
scholar 志 3	SUN. HEART 憶 163	white 怕 32
scholar 懿 176	SUN. One 怛 36	white 惶 94
seal 怨 43	SUN. One² 恒 47	white 愿 114
self 忌 5	SUN. pestle 悍 63	WOMAN 怒 31
SHELL 惻 108	SUN. pursue 復 104	WOMAN 怨 56
SHELL 慣 138	SUN. small 愿 114	WOMAN 悽 89
SHELL 憤 142	SUN. stand 意 95	WORDS 戀 177
SHELL 懶 170	SUN. ten 悼 85	work 恐 51
Shelter 恬 86	SUN. two 惜 84	wrap 忽 16, 41
Shelter 憬 126	SUN. wrap 惕 87	
Shelter 慶 128	Tap 悠 74	

MAN

(arrow) 侠 64
arrow 侯 85
arrow 候 110
arrow 俟 96
axe 儞 179
(back to back) 佻 81
basket 傻 193
beard 儒 196
bent 他 19
Big 倦 118
Big 俸 109
Big 俺 122
Big 偓 168
Big 僕 176
Bird 催 169
Bird 傕 174
borders 侖 68
borders 偏 141
Bow 佛 43
Child 仔 23
Child 俘 84
clan 低 58
claw 俘 84
claw 僞 180
cliff 仄 10
Cloth 佈 53
Cloth 佩 76
CLOTHES 依 69

MAN

cocoon 俟 96
cocoon 俊 101
compare 偕 137
Corpse 偏 141
Corpse 倔 117
Corpse 催 174
dart 代 20
Dish 儘 197
divination 仆 3
Dog 伏 28
Dog 倏 127
(do not) 侮 102
Door 們 120
doorleaf 倉 133
dot 今 7
dot 令 15
dot 以 13
DWELLING 佗 60
DWELLING 佇 42
DWELLING 傢 154
EARTH² 佳 71
EARTH³ 僥 181
EARTH. Field 俚 88
EARTH. inch 侍 78
EARTH. KNIFE 倒 131
EARTH. pestle 倖 111
EARTH. (Sheep) 倖 111
EARTH. spoon 佬 77
EARTH. square 傲 166
EARTH. Tap 傲 166

eight 供 72
eight 斳 179
Enclosure 個 114
evening[2] 侈 67
(EYE) 俱 115
EYE 值 106
father 傲 153
Field 佃 59
Field[2] 僵 184
Field[3] 偏 199
Field. Big 俺 122
Field. borders 偶 139
Field. EARTH 俚 88
(Field). leftstroke 便 93
Field. Legs 傀 156
Field. rod 伸 54
Field. ten 俾 123
FIRE 伙 31
FIRE 傒 128
FIRE 偽 180
FIRE 儘 197
FLESH 侑 83
FLESH 俏 97
folded hands 備 158
FOOT 促 100
ghost 傀 156
Grain 俐 89
GRASS 備 158
GRASS 儆 188
Halberd 伐 26

Halberd 俄 90
Halberd 儀 182
Hand 侵 98
Hand 俶 135
Hand 假 136
Head 傾 164
HEART 忈 37
HEART 億 187
HEART 優 200
horn 俑 104
inch 付 12
inch 傅 151
inch 傳 161
(JADE) 任 32
(JADE) 住 41
(JADE) 儀 182
KNIFE. disintegration 例 75
KNIFE. dot 刎 16
KNIFE. EARTH 倒 131
KNIFE. eight 份 25
KNIFE. Grain 俐 89
KNIFE. lid 儕 194
KNIFE. SHELL 側 146
leather 偉 149
leftstroke 仍 5
leftstroke. bent 仇 2
leftstroke. Cloth 佈 53
leftstroke. rod 介 6
leftstroke. rod 作 62
leftstroke. rod 併 126

leftstroke. ten 仟 22

leftstroke. pig's snout 伊 30

Legs 倪 112

lid 儕 194

lid 侅 79

lid 伉 33

lines 修 129

MAN². Big 俠 87

MAN. borders 倫 121

MAN². borders 倆 119

MAN. dot 似 55

MAN². (EYE) 俎 99

MAN. FLESH 偸 142

MAN. inch 俯 108

MAN. KNIFE 偸 142

MAN. leftstroke 价 35

MAN. lid 侅 79

MAN. MOUTH 俗 95

MAN³. MOUTH² 儉 186

MAN. One 伶 47

MAN². One 倆 119

MAN. SUN 偈 144

MAN. SUN 偺 145

MAN. SUN 儈 189

MAN⁴. ten 傘 159

MAN. TREE 來 73

mortar 倪 112

Mountain 仙 18

Mountain² 倔 117

Mountain 催 169

MOUTH² 侶 92

MOUTH³. basket 傴 170

MOUTH. Big 倚 113

MOUTH. black 儻 207

MOUTH. borders 尙 130

MOUTH². borders 僑 172

MOUTH. compare 儎 203

MOUTH. Corpse 倨 116

MOUTH. Corpse 僻 192

MOUTH. cover 停 143

MOUTH. divination 佔 40

MOUTH. doorleaf 倉 133

MOUTH. doorleaf 傖 152

MOUTH. EARTH 侗 132

MOUTH. EARTH 僅 163

MOUTH. Enclosure 個 114

MOUTH. Field 偪 140

MOUTH. FIRE 儻 207

MOUTH. GRASS 儆 188

MOUTH. inch 儔 195

MOUTH. leftstroke 佑 65

MOUTH. leftstroke 使 80

MOUTH. Legs 侃 70

MOUTH. lid 停 143

MOUTH. MAN 俗 95

MOUTH². MAN³ 儉 186

MOUTH. offend 僻 192

MOUTH. One 何 44

MOUTH. One 伺 56

MOUTH. period 儂 191

(MOUTH) pursue 傻 162

MOUTH. rod 仲 24

MOUTH. rod 偉 149

MOUTH. SHELL 償 198

MOUTH. stand 倍 124

MOUTH. Strength 伽 45

MOUTH. Tap 做 147

MOUTH. Tap 微 188

MOUTH². Tap 儆 206

MOUTH. ten 佔 46

MOUTH. ten 個 114

MOUTH. ten 居 116

MOUTH. TREE 保 91

MOUTH. wrap 儆 188

Move on 健 138

offend 覲 201

old 佬 77

One. borders 侖 68

One². deer 儷 204

One. downstroke 仃 9

One. leftstroke 仗 11

One. leftstroke 便 93

Ox 件 36

period 儂 191

pig 傢 154

pig 像 178

pig's snout 伊 30

pig's snout 侵 98

pig's snout 傭 171

pig's snout 儘 197

pursue. basket 傻 193

pursue. cocoon 俊 101

pursue. Dog 倏 127

pursue. HEART 優 200

pursue. MOUTH 傻 162

Rain 儒 196

reach 倒 131

river 俓 103

rod 他 19

rod 佛 43

rod 伴 50

rod 作 62

rod 併 126

rod 修 129

scholar 仕 17

seal 仰 39

seal 倦 118

seal 偓 168

see 覷 201

sheep 佯 82

SHELL 側 146

SHELL 偵 148

SHELL 債 160

SHELL 價 183

SHELL 償 198

SHELL 儹 205

Shelter 俯 108

Shelter 傭 171

small 余 66   SILK 係 86

small 你 48

small 係 86
small 俶 135
spoon 化 14
square 仿 27
square 倣 107
square 傍 157
square 傲 166
stand 位 63
stool 亢 33
stop 企 34
stopper 偓 168
stopper 價 183
stylus 健 138
SUN[2] 倡 105
SUN. compare 偕 137
SUN. (dot) 伯 52
SUN. dot 偕 137
SUN. dot 僧 177
SUN. EARTH 儲 202
SUN. HEART 億 187
SUN. MAN 偌 145
SUN. MAN 偈 144
SUN. MAN 儈 189
SUN. (MOUTH) 僧 177
SUN. not[2] 僭 173
SUN. One 但 57
SUN. pursue 偖 145
SUN. rod 借 134
SUN. small 僚 175
SUN. square 傲 185

SUN. Tap 傲 185
SUN. two 借 134
SUN. WOMAN 偓 150
SUN. wrap 佝 74
SUN. wrap 偈 144
SUN. wrap 傷 167
Tap 倣 107
Tap 修 129
Tap 做 147
Tap 傲 153
Tap 傲 166
Tap 儆 188
ten 什 8
ten 仟 22
thread 係 86
TREE 休 29
TREE 体 51
TREE[2] 健 190
TREE 傑 155
two 仁 4
two 伍 38
two 伴 50
two 供 72
two 併 126
use 俑 104
use 備 158
use 傭 171
valley 俗 95
village 俚 88

MAN		MOUTH	

white 伯 52

white 偕 137

white 傲 185

WOMAN 倭 49

WOMAN 倭 125

WOMAN 僂 165

WORDS 信 94

WORDS 儲 202

work 仝 21

work 佐 61

work 倥 103

MOUTH

arrow 唉 106

axe 听 57

back to back 啡 126

(back to back) 咷 90

basket 叵 12

basket 咂 72

beard 喘 134

bent 吃 25

Big 吴 54

Big. borders 唤 140

Big. Enclosure 咽 96

Big. Field 奄 122

Big. KNIFE 喫 142

Big. leftstroke 吞 50

Big. MOUTH 喬 141

Big. One 咲 89

Bird 唯 131

Bird 售 125

Bird 囉 218

black 嘿 188

borders 向 21

borders. City 嚮 210

borders. EARTH 周 58

borders. MAN 呐 48

borders. One 同 32

borders. ten 喃 148

branch 吱 34

Breathe 吹 36

Breathe 咨 93
Breathe 嗽 176
Child 吼 41
(Child) 哼 99
City 哪 105
City 嘟 184
claw 嚼 215
claw 嗳 199
cliff 唇 109
cliff 后 20
Cloth 吊 29
Cloth 咂 72
CLOTHES 哀 86
(CLOTHES) 唇 109
(CLOTHES) 喪 146
(CLOTHES) 喂 152
CLOTHES 裹 213
cocoon 台 15
cocoon. arrow 唉 106
cocoon. leftstroke 呱 73
cocoon. Legs 吭 51
cocoon. One 吆 31
cocoon. pursue 唆 111
cocoon. Wings 嗡 169
Corpse 嘱 181
Corpse 囑 219
Corpse 呎 77
Corpse 呢 68
Dog 吠 38
Dog 喉 121

Dog 嗅 158
Door 問 130
doorleaf 啓 120
doorleaf 戾 121
downstroke 吁 23
downstroke 呼 63
downstroke 呀 55
dragon 嚨 211
DWELLING 嚀 206
EARTH 吐 30
EARTH. Child 哮 98
EARTH. EARTH 哇 94
EARTH. EARTH 嚇 207
EARTH. Field 哩 103
EARTH. leftstroke 告 43
eight 只 3
eight 叭 11
eight 哄 81
Enclosure 咽 96
Enclosure 嗇 162
evening 名 28
EYE 咱 91
EYE 嗔 155
EYE 嚼 215
EYE 囉 218
EYE   219 囑
father 咬 95
Field. (CLOTHES) 喂 152
Field. GRASS 喵 144
(Field). One 哽 101

Field. rod 呻 71

Field. rod 睪 175

Field. ten 啤 115

Field. ten 嚥 208

FIRE 嘿 188

FIRE 嚥 212

FIRE 嘮 187

Fish 嚕 209

FLESH 哨 110

FLESH 啃 119

FLESH 嘲 180

Grain 和 64

GRASS 哎 76

GRASS 喵 144

GRASS 噂 185

Halberd. EARTH 哉 92

Halberd. (HAND) 哦 107

Halberd. (Head) 嘎 182

Halberd. leftstroke 咸 79

Halberd. MOUTH 喊 135

Halberd. small 喊 173

Halberd. stop 噦 204

Halberd. thread 嘰 189

Hand 吱 34

Hand 啜 117

Hand 唚 104

HAND 哲 97

Head 噸 198

HEART 噫 194

HEART 嚘 199

HEART 嚀 206

hemp 嘛 171

horn 嘴 190

Horse 嗎 159

Ice 咨 93

INSECT 噛 156

INSECT 囑 219

(JADE) 呈 35

KNIFE 召 2

KNIFE 叨 16

KNIFE. disintegration 咧 83

KNIFE. eight 吩 37

KNIFE. teeth 齰 220

KNIFE. TREE 喇 145

leftstroke 叨 17

leftstroke 史 13

leftstroke 吸 42

leftstroke. bent 吃 25

leftstroke. Big 吞 50

leftstroke. cocoon 呱 73

leftstroke. downstroke 吁 23

leftstroke. downstroke 呼 63

leftstroke. One 呔 31

leftstroke. One 唾 128

leftstroke. rod 咋 59

leftstroke. work 嗟 168

Legs 吮 51

Legs 唬 118

lid. borders 商 124

lid. Cloth 啼 151

lid. Cloth 帟 149

lid. father 咬 95

lid. leftstroke 吝 46

lid. MAN 咳 82

lid. MAN 唪 127

lid. MOUTH 哼 99

literature 吝 46

MAN 吹 36

MAN. arrow 喉 143

MAN. borders 呐 48

MAN. borders 禽 195

MAN. dot 含 40

MAN. inch 呼 61

MAN. FLESH 喻 154

MAN. KNIFE 喻 154

MAN. lid 咳 82

MAN. lid 唪 127

MAN.MAN 唪 127

MAN. MAN 嗇 162

MAN. MOUTH 哈 80

MAN. MOUTH 嗆 167

MAN. One 合 22

MAN. One 吟 56

MAN. One 命 67

MAN. pursue 咎 66

MAN. seal 命 67

melon 呱 73

Mound 阿 123

Mountain 喘 134

MOUTH 吕 47

MOUTH. basket 匝 12

MOUTH. Big 喬 141

MOUTH. Big 嘆 177

MOUTH. borders 响 78

MOUTH. borders 嗣 164

MOUTH. Cliff 嚴 214

MOUTH. (CLOTHES) 喪 146

MOUTH. (CLOTHES) 囊 217

MOUTH. Corpse 嘱 181

MOUTH. Dog 哭 102

MOUTH. Dog 器 196

MOUTH. DWELLING 嗒 157

MOUTH. Field 單 150

MOUTH. FIRE 嚥 212

MOUTH. Halberd 喊 135

MOUTH. Head 嚻 216

MOUTH. lid 哼 99

MOUTH. MAN 哈 80

MOUTH. MAN 嗆 167

MOUTH. Mound 阿 123

MOUTH. MOUTH 品 87

MOUTH. MOUTH 枭 161

MOUTH. MOUTH 嘔 174

MOUTH. MOUTH 噪 203

MOUTH. MOUTH 器 196

MOUTH. MOUTH 噩 200

MOUTH. MOUTH 嚷 213

MOUTH. MOUTH 嚻 216

MOUTH. MOUTH 囊 217

MOUTH. MOUTH 嚷 221

MOUTH. One 呵 62

MOUTH. One 哥 100

MOUTH. pig 嚎 205

MOUTH. pursue 咯 84

MOUTH. rod 噥 201

MOUTH. scholar 喜 136

MOUTH. scholar 噎 193

MOUTH. scholar 嘉 172

MOUTH. stool 咒 60

MOUTH. Strength 嘉 172

MOUTH.Tap 嚴 214

MOUTH. ten 咕 65

MOUTH. TREE 喇 145

MOUTH. TREE 嗽 176

MOUTH. TREE 噪 203

MOUTH. Wings 噲 186

nose 咱 91

nose 嗅 158

One 司 14

One. borders 同 32

One. cocoon 呟 31

One. downstroke 可 7

One. downstroke 叮 18

One. leftstroke 右 19

One. leftstroke 吏 27

One. rod 否 39

period 唇 109

period 噥 201

pig 啄 116

pig 嚎 205

pig's snout 君 45

pursue 咎 26

pursue 咎 66

pursue 唆 111

Revelation 噤 197

rod 叫 6

rod 叫 44

rod 咋 59

rod 哺 108

rod 唾 128

roll 噠 208

scholar 吉 24

seal 叩 5

seal 咆 69

seal 唧 133

seal 唧 137

self 吧 49

sheep 咩 85

sheep 善 147

SHELL 員 113

SHELL 嘖 179

SHELL 噴 202

Shelter 唐 112

Shelter 嘛 171

SILK 嗉 166

SILK 縣 192

SILK 囉 218

small 吵 33

small 呸 70

spoon 叱 4

spoon 噓 191
spoon 嘴 190
stool 唬 165
stop 嘴 190
stopper 哂 88
Strength 另 10
Strength 嘮 187
SUN. City 嘟 184
SUN. DWELLING 喧 139
SUN. DWELLING 嘗 170
SUN. Ear 嘬 183
SUN. EARTH 嗜 163
SUN. EARTH 嘟 184
SUN. Fish 嚕 209
SUN. FLESH 嘲 180
SUN. HEART 噫 194
SUN. MAN 喝 138
SUN. MOUTH 嘈 178
SUN. old 嗜 163
SUN. pursue 喀 153
SUN. SUN 唱 114
SUN. TREE 喳 132
SUN. wrap 喝 138
Tap 啓 120
ten 古 8
(ten) 喃 148
ten 嚏 208
tiger 唬 118
tiger 唬 165
tiger 噓 191

MOUTH

tooth 呀 55
TREE. Hand 嗓 160
TREE. MOUTH 梟 161
TREE. One 味 74
TREE. Revelation 噤 197
TREE. Shelter 嘛 171
TREE. SUN 喳 132
TREE.TREE 噤 197
two 啞 129
two 吾 53
use 哺 108
use 嘴 190
WATER 咏 75
Wings 嗡 169
Wings 噏 186
work 嗟 168
wrap 句 9
wrap 吻 52
wrap 咆 69

SILK

back to back 緋 54
BAMBOO 纂 118
bent 紀 5
bent 执 8
bent 純 19
Bird 維 66
borders 納 15
borders 綱 55
borders 網 65
borders 編 70
Bow 縫 100
Cart 繫 108
(Child) 紓 18
City 綁 47
clan 紙 11
claw 綏 49
claw 綵 63
claw 緩 67
claw 綰 83
claw 繇 98
Cloth 綿 61
Cloth 締 73
Cocoon 統 42
Cocoon 繒 100
Corpse 編 70
cover 索 20
cover 締 73
(dart) 線 39

SILK

Dish 縊 82
(do not) 繁 87
doorleaf 編 70
dot 执 8
dot 約 10
dot2 終 25
dot 絆 27
dot 縛 80
dot2 縊 82
DWELLING 綻 50
DWELLING 綜 64
DWELLING 縮 93
DWELLING 續 97
EARTH. EYE 繹 115
EARTH3. Legs 繞 102
EARTH. pursue 綾 57
EARTH. Shelter 纏 119
EARTH. SUN 緒 72
EARTH. Tap 緻 78
earthenware 繇 98
eight 紛 12
(EYE) 組 31
EYE 縣 81
EYE 繹 115
EYE 纂 118
EYE 續 122
EYE 纜 126
father 絞 35
Field 累 26
Field 細 30

Field3 纍 121
Field. (dart) 綍 39
Field. Grain 繙 101
Fields2. One3 繮 112
Field. rod 紬 24
Field. rod 紳 28
Field. Shelter 纊 120
Field. TREE 繰 92
FIRE2 縈 86
FLESH 絹 45
FLESH 繊 104
footprint 繙 101
Grain 綉 48
Grain 繙 101
GRASS 蘭 111
Halberd 絨 33
Halberd 緘 68
Halberd 織 99
Halberd 纖 123
Hand4 綴 53
Hand 緊 56
Hand 緞 74
Hand 繫 108
HEART 總 96
HEART 縤 107
inch 紂 4
inch 縛 80
INSECT 縄 100
INSECT 蘭 111
(JADE) 素 21

SILK

(KNIFE) 紐 7

KNIFE 紛 12

KNIFE 紹 29

KNIFE 絶 43

(lance) 紓 18

leather 緯 76

leftstroke 紈 8

leftstroke 級 14

leftstroke 紗 17

leftstroke 綁 47

Legs 統 42

lid. Cloth 締 73

lid. cocoon 統 42

lid. father 絞 35

lid. leftstroke 紋 22

lid. leftstroke 紊 23

lid. Ox 緯 89

lines 綁 47

literature 紋 22

literature 紊 23

MAN. borders 納 15

MAN. borders 繪 60

MAN. DWELLING 縮 93

MAN[2]. Footstep 縱 95

MAN[2]. leek 纖 123

MAN[2]. Halberd 纖 123

MAN. MOUTH 給 37

MAN. MOUTH 絡 58

MAN. One 紟 16

MAN. One 給 37

MAN. One 繪 60

MAN. SUN 縮 93

MAN. SUN 繪 109

minister 緊 56

minister 纜 126

mortar 綹 83

Mountain 網 55

MOUTH[2]. bent 繩 113

MOUTH. compare 纏 124

MOUTH. dot[2] 繕 105

MOUTH. Ear 緝 75

MOUTH. EARTH 綢 51

MOUTH. FLESH 絹 45

MOUTH. Halberd 緘 68

MOUTH. KNIFE 紹 29

MOUTH. MAN 給 37

MOUTH. MAN 絡 58

MOUTH. One[2] 緯 76

MOUTH[2]. PROCEED 繼 79

MOUTH. pursue 絡 38

MOUTH. scholar 結 36

MOUTH. TREE 練 69

MOUTH. WOMAN 絮 40

MOUTH[2]. WOMAN 縷 91

offend[2] 辮 117

One 系 2

One 紐 7

One 組 31

One. bent 純 19

One. Dish 縊 82

One[3]. rod 素 21

One[2]. rod 絆 27

One[6]. rod[2] 緋 54

One[3]. rod 緞 74

One[3]. rod 縫 88

One. thread[4] 繼 116

One. work 經 44

Ox 緯 89

pestle[2] 辮 117

pig 緣 77

pig 縫 114

pig's snout 綠 59

pig's snout 緣 77

pig's snout 繡 106

PROCEED 縫 79

PROCEED 縫 88

PROCEED 縫 114

pursue 終 25

pursue 絳 34

pursue 緩 67

pursue 縫 88

Revelation 綜 64

river 經 44

river 繹 92

rod 糾 3

rod 絆 27

roll 綻 50

see 纜 126

self 紀 9

SHELL 續 122

SHELL 績 94

SHELL2 纓 125

Shelter 纏 119

Shelter 纊 120

SILK 絲 41

SILK. Field 縲 90

small 紗 17

splitwood2 繡 106

spoon 紫 32

sprout2 緦 84

square 紡 13

stand2 辮 117

stop 紫 32

strike 緞 74

strike 繋 108

SUN. Big 繚 103

SUN. Cloth 綿 61

SUN. cocoon2 繒 85

SUN. EARTH 緒 72

SUN. Halberd 織 99

SUN. MAN 縮 93

SUN. MAN 繪 109

SUN. small 繚 103

SUN. Square 繳 110

SUN. Tap 繳 110

SUN. ten 綽 52

SUN. WATER 線 62

Tap 緻 78

Tap 繁 87

Tap 織 104

SILK

Tap 繳 110

ten 索 20

thread4 繼 116

TREE 細 46

TREE 綵 63

TREE 練 69

TREE 纅 92

turtle 繩 113

two 絆 27

WATER 綠 59

WATER 線 62

white 綿 61

WOMAN 絮 40

WOMAN 綏 49

WOMAN 縷 91

WOMAN 纓 125

work 紅 6

work 經 44

wrap 約 10

wrap2 緦 84

yellow 纊 120

TREE

axe 析 38

(back to back) 桃 80

back to back 桽 110

back to back 框 150

basket 柩 56

basket 框 75

basket ・ 150

basket 櫃 199

bean 橙 174

bent 札 2

Big 棒 114

Big 椅 105

Big 榛 145

Big 椿 164

Big 樊 165

Big 樸 184

Bird 梟 87

Bird 桦 157

Bird 樵 186

Bird 權 197

Bird 權 207

black 檔 209

body 榭 155

borders 束 10

borders 柵 46

borders 桐 81

borders 楠 137

borders 構 148

both feet 橙 174

Bow 梯 97

branch 枝 25

Breathe 枚 30

Breathe 橛 182

Cave 榨 144

Child 李 16

City 梆 93

City 椰 149

City 椰 142

claw 援 132

cliff 板 34

cliff 橛 182

cliff 桅 83

cliff 栀 86

Cloth 柿 37

Cloth 棉 113

cocoon 松 39

cocoon 梭 96

compare 枇 35

cover 榜 153

defiance 根 71

defiance 椰 149

defiance 概 166

Dish 檻 198

(do not) 梅 92

Door 欄 205

dot 术 5

DWELLING. leftstroke 榨 144

DWELLING. MOUTH 棺 111

DWELLING. Revelation 棕124
DWELLING. SHELL 檳200
DWELLING. spoon 柁63
DWELLING. SUN 檀133
DWELLING. valley 榕161
DWELLING. WOMAN 案78
Ear 椰142
Ear 橄177
EARTH 杜20
EARTH 桂76
EARTH 棱115
eight 松39
eight 棋106
evening 桀73
EYE 植104
EYE 楣136
EYE 楞135
EYE 櫝202
EYE 欖210
father 校72
Field 果28
Field 柚66
Field 梗89
Field 槐156
Field 榴151
FIRE 楸139
FIRE 榮160
FIRE 樵186
Fish 櫓201
FLESH 梢94

FLESH 棚116
FLESH 榆143
FLESH 槊154
ghost 槐156
Grain 梨90
Grain 榛145
Grain 檁192
GRASS 樺176
GRASS 模169
GRASS 橫175
GRASS 權207
hair 橇179
Halberd 栽82
Halberd 械85
Halberd 棧102
Halberd 機178
Hand 板34
Hand 枝25
Hand 桑79
Hand 椒123
Head 欙204
high 槁147
inch 村22
inch 榭155
inch 樹185
inch 樽187
inch 槳172
(INSECT) 櫃199
(JADE) 枉41
(JADE) 柱48

(JADE) 框 75

(JADE) 梃 100

KNIFE 梁 91

KNIFE 梨 90

KNIFE 榆 143

KNIFE 榴 151

lame 杌 23

(lame) 枕 24

(lance) 杼 26

lance 柔 52

lance 橘 183

(leek) 業 141

(leek) 樸 184

leftstroke 朵 9

leftstroke. leftstroke 18 杉

leftstroke. One 朱 7

leftstroke. rod 柞 65

leftstroke. rod 梯 97

leftstroke. rod 榨 144

leftstroke. (two) 梆 93

Legs 梳 95

Legs 椹 127

lid. Cloth 柿 107

lid. cocoon 梳 95

lid. cocoon 棄 107

lid. father 校 72

lid. MAN 核 69

lid. MAN 梓 125

lines 杉 18

MAN 枚 30

MAN 核 69

MAN 條 98

MAN 梓 125

MAN 檣 195

minister 檻 198

mortar 椿 164

MOUTH 呆 17

MOUTH 束 19

MOUTH 杏 13

MOUTH. Big 椅 105

MOUTH. black 櫄 209

MOUTH. borders 桐 81

MOUTH. Corpse 槍 159

MOUTH. Cover 棠 119

MOUTH. dot 柬 55

MOUTH. DWELLING 榕 161

MOUTH. EAR 楫 138

MOUTH. eight 枳 47

MOUTH. Enclosure 檀 193

MOUTH. Enclosure 檁 192

MOUTH. Enclosure 檣 195

MOUTH. Field 檔 194

MOUTH. FIRE 檂 209

MOUTH. Hand 極 109

MOUTH. inch 樹 185

MOUTH. lance 橘 183

MOUTH. lid 棄 107

MOUTH. MOUTH 棺 111

MOUTH. MOUTH 槁 147

MOUTH. MOUTH 樞 163

MOUTH. MOUTH 橋181

MOUTH. MOUTH 檢190

MOUTH. MOUTH 權207

MOUTH. One 柯57

MOUTH. One 栲49

MOUTH. One 桐81

MOUTH. pursue 格74

MOUTH. Strength 枷53

MOUTH. Strength 架54

MOUTH. ten 枯58

MOUTH. two 梧101

MOUTH. WOMAN 樓167

Move on 梃100

not 概166

One 末3

One 未6

One 本4

One 朽8

One. basket 某60

One. basket 柑51

One. bent 杖11

One. borders 柄61

One. downstroke 材21

One. leftstroke 朱7

One. rod 杯36

pestle 杆14

pestle 杵27

pig 橡131

pig 橡180

pig 橡203

PROCEED 槌146

pursue 梭96

pursue 椴132

Revelation 標170

rod 柞65

rod 梯97

seal 杷33

seal 柳59

seal 桅83

see 欖210

(self) 梔86

(sheep) 業141

SHELL 槙152

SHELL 檳200

SHELL 櫃199

SHELL 櫝202

SHELL 櫻206

SILK 橡203

SILK 欒208

small 杪32

splitwood 槳172

spoon 枇35

spoon 柴44

square 楞135

square 榜153

square 橄189

STONE 柘45

stop 柴44

stopper 栗77

stopper 標170

SUN 杏 42
SUN 東 40
SUN 椿 130
SUN. Big 模 169
SUN. Cloth 棉 113
SUN. compare 棍 112
SUN. compare 楷 134
SUN. divination 桌 67
SUN. dot 柏 62
SUN. dot 樂 168
SUN. dot 橄 189
SUN. DWELLING 檀 133
SUN. EARTH 楮 128
SUN. Enclosure 檀 193
SUN. Fish 櫓 201
SUN. MAN 檜 191
SUN. MOUTH 槽 171
SUN. One 查 43
SUN. One 桓 70
SUN. pestle 桿 88
SUN. ten 棹 103
SUN. ten 樟 162
SUN. TREE 楂 126
SUN. Wings 楊 158
SUN. wrap 楊 140
sweet 柑 51
sweet 某 60
Tap 枚 31
Tap 橄 177
Tap 橄 189

TREE
ten 枝 25
ten 樺 157
thread 樂 168
thread 機 178
TREE 林 29
TREE. Big 樊 165
TREE. borders 棗 122
TREE. borders 棘 108
TREE. Door 欄 205
TREE. Ear 馘 188
TREE. Field 棟 121
TREE. Field 裸 120
TREE. Hand 馘 188
TREE. One 株 68
TREE. roll 楚 129
TREE. stool 梵 84
TREE. SUN 楂 126
TREE. TREE 森 117
two 棒 114
two 棋 106
two 椹 127
use 桶 99
valley 榕 161
WATER 染 64
WATER 染 50
WATER 梁 91
WATER 樣 173
white 柏 62
white 棉 113
white 楷 134

TREE	WATER
white 樂 168	WATER
white 橄 189	bean 澄 177
Wine jug 樽 187	beard 濡 202
Wings 櫂 197	bent 汽 24
WOMAN 棲 118	bent 池 7
WOMAN 櫻 206	Big 決 19
WORDS 檐 196	Big (arrow) 湊 125
WORDS 欒 208	Big. borders 澳 194
work 杠 15	Big. claw 溪 136
wrap 杓 12	Big. dot 汰 25
	Big. Field 淹 106
	Big. HEART 添 99
	Big. leftstroke 沃 30
	Big. thread 溪 136
	Big. two 泰 53
	Big. two 涝 69
	Bird 準 131
	Bird 匯 133
	Bird 濯 200
	Bird 灘 220
	Bird 灌 218
	bones 滑 132
	borders 滴 165
	both feet 潑 185
	Bow. both feet 潑 185
	Bow. Bow 溺 140
	Bow. long 漲 149
	Bow. rod 涕 80
	Bow. rod 沸 40

WATER

Bow. WORDS 灣 222

Cart 渾 114

Cart 漸 169

Cart 連 156

Child 浮 71

Child 淳 95

Child 涵 86

Child 游 129

(clan) 泥 46

claw 淫 108

claw 淨 103

claw 滔 144

claw 溪 136

cliff 派 63

Cloth 沛 32

Cloth 滯 150

CLOTHES 滾 153

(CLOTHES) 漲 149

(CLOTHES) 濃 195

cocoon 滲 162

Corpse 泥 48

Corpse 涮 96

Corpse 漏 154

cover 沉 16

defiance 浪 75

defiance 溉 152

Dish 溢 147

Dish 濫 203

Dog 淚 89

(do not) 海 72

Door 潤 190

Door 澗 181

Door 瀾 217

doorleaf 淚 89

doorleaf 滬 170

dot 永 2

downstroke 汙 15

DWELLING. Field 演 172

DWELLING. HEART 濘 205

DWELLING. Legs 浣 74

DWELLING. MAN 淀 100

DWELLING. mortar 瀉 212

DWELLING. offend 淬 146

DWELLING. (roll) 淀 100

DWELLING. SHELL 濱 206

EARTH. cocoon 法 37

EARTH. EARTH 涯 105

EARTH. EARTH 澆 179

EARTH. Legs 洗 65

EARTH. stopper 湮 128

EARTH. thread 溼 142

eight 洪 61

Enclosure. divination 滷 166

Enclosure. Legs 泗 52

Enclosure. MAN 泅 34

Enclosure. MOUTH 涸 87

Enclosure. MOUTH 澔 196

Enclosure. pig 溷 134

evening 汐 13

EYE 渺 120

Ra 39

EYE 澤 199
EYE 濁 191
EYE 瀆 213
Field 油 56
Field 溜 137
FIRE 淡 97
FIRE 澇 184
Fish 漁 173
FLESH 消 79
FLESH 清 104
FLESH 滑 132
FLESH 潵 176
FLESH 潲 187
Grain 瀝 216
GRASS 漠 159
GRASS 濛 204
GRASS 漕 167
GRASS 灌 218
Halberd 淺 102
Halberd 減 117
Halberd 滅 138
Hand 沒 20
Hand. mortar 溲 122
Hand. pig's snout 浸 82
Hand. rod 溲 122
Hand. Shelter 渡 123
Hand. small 淑 94
Hand. stool 沒 21
Head 瀨 215
HEART 沁 28

WATER
HEART 添 99
HEART 濾 210
inch 溥 141
inch 漿 168
(JADE) 汪 29
(JADE) 注 36
(JADE) 淫 108
KNIFE. Cloth 涮 96
KNIFE. Corpse 涮 96
KNIFE. Field 溜 137
KNIFE. KNIFE 澀 186
KNIFE. MOUTH 沼 33
KNIFE. SHELL 測 124
KNIFE. SILK 潔 180
KNIFE. spoon 沏 27
leftstroke 沙 23
leftstroke 汲 18
leftstroke 泛 38
Legs 湛 112
lid 泣 44
lid. borders 漓 155
lid. cocoon 流 76
lid. KNIFE 濟 209
lid. Legs 流 76
lid. MAN 液 107
lid. MOUTH 淳 95
lid. MOUTH 涼 90
lid. MOUTH 濠 201
long 漲 149
MAN. borders 淪 92

WATER

MAN. borders 滿 157

MAN . cocoon 滲 162

MAN. Dog 狀 59

MAN. lines 滲 162

MAN. MOUTH 洽 60

MAN. square 淤 109

moon 湖 113

moon 溯 143

moon 潮 175

mortar 滔 144

MOUTH. Big 漢 151

MOUTH. Bird 灘 220

MOUTH. borders 洞 67

MOUTH. borders 淌 85

MOUTH. borders 渦 127

MOUTH. borders 滴 165

MOUTH. Child 淳 95

MOUTH. CLOTHES 滾 153

MOUTH. (CLOTHES) 濃 195

MOUTH. cocoon 治 39

MOUTH. deer 灑 219

MOUTH. divination 沾 35

MOUTH. doorleaf 滬 170

MOUTH. EARTH 浩 73

MOUTH. Enclosure 涸 87

MOUTH. Enclosure 濤 196

MOUTH. FLESH 滑 132

MOUTH. GRASS 灌 218

MOUTH. Halberd 減 117

MOUTH. inch 濤 208

MOUTH. KNIFE 沼 33

MOUTH. MAN 洽 60

MOUTH. MAN 浴 83

MOUTH. moon 湖 113

MOUTH. MOUTH 漚 160

MOUTH. MOUTH 潭 188

MOUTH. MOUTH 灑 219

MOUTH. One 河 41

MOUTH. One 灑 219

MOUTH. pestle 活 62

MOUTH. pig 濠 201

MOUTH. rod 沖 17

MOUTH. scholar 濤 208

MOUTH. small 凉 90

MOUTH. stool 沿 55

MOUTH. ten 沽 45

MOUTH. TREE 漱 163

MOUTH. TREE 澡 198

MOUTH. work 濤 208

Move on 涎 81

not 溉 152

One. bent 沌 26

One. bent 汽 24

One. borders 浦 77

One. borders 溝 135

One. downstroke 汀 6

One. dot 求 5

One. pit 泄 42

One. two 浦 77

pestle 汗 10

pig 濠 201
pig's snout 津 68
pig's snout 淨 103
pit 涵 86
PROCEED 連 156
Rain 漏 154
Rain 濡 202
Revelation 漂 161
rod 洲 58
rod 洪 61
roll 漩 164
salt 滷 166
seal 氾 4
seal 港 115
seal 滬 170
sheep 洋 70
SHELL 測 124
SHELL 漬 174
SHELL 潰 178
SHELL 濺 214
SHELL 瓚 221
Shelter 渡 123
SILK 潔 180
SILK 灣 222
skin 波 50
small 沙 23
small 涉 78
splitwood 淵 110
splitwood 漿 168
square 漩 164

WATER

stand 泣 44
stand 滴 165
stool 汎 9
stool 汎 8
stool 沉 16
stop 涉 78
stopper 洒 64
stopper 漂 161
Strength 湧 130
strike 沒 21
stylus 津 68
SUN 汨 31
SUN. Big 潦 182
SUN. cliff 源 148
SUN. compare 混 88
SUN. cover 溟 139
SUN. (dart) 洩 66
SUN. Dish 溫 126
SUN. Door 澗 190
SUN. dot 泊 51
SUN. dot 泉 54
SUN. dot 激 193
SUN. EYE 漫 158
SUN. GRASS 漠 159
SUN. GRASS 漕 167
SUN. MAN 澣 192
SUN. moon 潮 175
SUN. not 潛 183
SUN. SILK 濕 207
SUN. small 源 148

WATER

SUN. small 潦 182

SUN. Tap 激 193

SUN. ten 潭 189

SUN. ten 潄 192

SUN. TREE 渣 111

SUN. WATER 瀑 211

SUN. wrap 渴 118

SUN. wrap 湯 121

sweet 泔 43

sweet 湛 112

Tap 激 193

ten 汁 3

thread 滋 145

tongue 活 62

TREE 沐 22

TREE. basket 渠 119

TREE. Breathe 漱 163

TREE. Legs 深 93

TREE. MOUTH 漱 163

TREE. MOUTH 澡 198

TREE. One 沫 47

TREE. One 渫 116

TREE. SUN 渣 111

TREE. TREE 淋 91

TREE. WATER 漆 171

two 污 14

two 汙 15

use 涌 84

valley 浴 83

WATER 水 1

WATER 泳 57

WATER 涵 86

white 泉 54

white 泊 51

Wings 濯 200

WOMAN 汝 11

WOMAN 凄 101

WORDS 澹 197

WORDS 灣 222

work 江 12

wrap 淘 98

wrap 泡 49

WORDS

axe 訴 31

axe 誓 60

basket 詎 28

basket 誆 44

bean 證 117

bent 訖 10

bent 託 13

Big 訣 16

Big 誇 43

Bird 誰 77

Bird 譙 124

Bird2 雦 134

body 謝 107

borders 訥 18

(borders) 諷 84

borders 諞 93

borders 講 102

both feet 證 117

clan 訨 32

claw 諍 69

claw 護 87

cliff 詹 36

cliff 詭 45

cliff 諺 99

Cloth 諦 95

cocoon 訟 20

Corpse 諞 93

cover 諦 95

cover 謗 105

dart 試 49

Dish 謚 94

Dish 謚 106

divination 卦 2

Dog 誕 59

Dog 讞 142

do not 誨 55

doorleaf 諞 93

dot 訊 7

dot 評 30

dot 訴 31

dot2 誨 55

dot 謙 103

downstroke 訂 5

downstroke 諍 69

DWELLING 詫 35

DWELLING 誼 72

DWELLING 諳 85

Ear 諏 80

EARTH 詩 48

EARTH 譯 130

earthenware 謠 110

eight 訟 20

eight 詹 36

eight 謚 94

eight 謚 106

eight 譽 132

evening 謠 110

(EYE) 詛 26

EYE 詈 29

EYE 譯 130

EYE 讀 133

Field 課 74

Field 謂 97

FIRE 詼 46

FIRE2 談 78

FIRE 譙 124

FIRE 讞 136

FLESH 誚 64

FLESH 請 81

FLESH 謂 97

FLESH 諭 100

FLESH 謄 108

Grain 誘 67

Grain 諉 73

GRASS. bird 護 131

GRASS. Hand 護 131

GRASS. Legs 謊 101

GRASS. MOUTH 諾 92

GRASS. MOUTH 警 127

GRASS. One4 譁 118

GRASS. SUN 謨 114

Halberd 誠 54

Halberd 誡 58

Halberd 護 119

Halberd 識 122

Halberd 議 126

WORDS

Halberd 識 139	MAN. (JADE) 詮 52	MOUTH. eight 譽 132
HAND 誓 60	MAN2. leek 識 139	MOUTH. FIRE 讕 141
Hand 設 19	MAN. lid 該 41	MOUTH. FIRE 譏 136
Hand 諏 80	MAN. lines 診 23	MOUTH. GRASS 諾 92
Hand 諼 87	man. lines 謬 113	MOUTH. GRASS 警 12ʼ
HEART 誌 53	MAN. mortar 諛 82	MOUTH. Ice 諮 96
HEART 認 56	MAN. MOUTH 諂 96	MOUTH. KNIFE 詔 24
inch 討 12	MAN2. rod 誣 65	MOUTH. lance 譴 120
inch 詩 48	MAN. spoon 訛 17	MOUTH. leather 諱 88
inch 謝 107	MAN. SUN 謁 98	MOUTH. Legs 說 61
INSECT 諷 84	MAN. thread2 譏 119	MOUTH. lid 諄 71
(JADE) 註 27	MAN. Wings 謬 113	MOUTH. lid 諒 75
(JADE) 誆 44	mortar 諂 70	MOUTH. lid 謫 116
(JADE) 誔 59	Mountain 訕 11	MOUTH2. lid 讓 138
KNIFE 詔 24	MOUTH3. basket 謳 115	MOUTH. offend 譬 128
leather 諱 88	MOUTH. Big 誤 66	MOUTH. One 詞 33
leftstroke 詐 22	MOUTH. black 讕 141	MOUTH. One 證 117
leftstroke 誘 67	MOUTH. borders 謫 116	MOUTH. pestle 話 38
lid 該 41	MOUTH. borders 謫 120	MOUTH. rod2 諱 88
lid 諦 95	MOUTH. both feet 證 117	MOUTH. scholar 詰 42
lid 譺 99	MOUTH. Breathe 諂 96	MOUTH. small 諒 75
lid 謗 105	MOUTH. Child 諄 71	MOUTH. ten 謫 116
lines 譺 99	MOUTH2. CLOTHES 讓 138	MOUTH. tiger 讞 142
lines 謬 113	MOUTH. compare 譬 137	MOUTH. two 語 68
MAN. borders 訥 18	MOUTH. Corpse 譬 128	Move on 誕 63
MAN. borders 論 76	MOUTH. Dog 讞 142	One 訂 5
MAN. FLESH 諭 100	MOUTH. EARTH 話 57	One 託 13
MAN. Halberd 譏 119	MOUTH. EARTH 調 79	One3 詐 22
MAN2. Halberd 識 139	MOUTH. EARTH 謹 111	One2 証 25

WORDS

One2 評 30
Ox 許 15
pestle 訐 9
pestle 評 30
pig's snout 諍 69
pig's snout 謙 103
PROCEED 謎 104
pursue 諼 87
Rice 謎 104
river 訓 6
rod 詐 22
rod 評 30
rod2 謙 103
scholar 讀 133
seal 詭 45
self 記 8
Sheep 詳 50
(Sheep) 議 126
SHELL 讀 133
SHELL 讚 140
SHELL 讕 143
SILK2 變 135
sprout2 讖 109
square 訪 14
square 謗 105
stool 訊 7
stool 設 19
stop 証 25
stop 誕 63

stopper 譚 123
strike 設 19
SUN. compare 諧 86
SUN. dot 諧 86
SUN. dot 譈 125
SUN. dot2 譜 129
SUN. DWELLING 諠 85
SUN. EARTH 諸 83
SUN. EARTH 譈 125
SUN. EYE 謾 112
SUN. GRASS 謨 114
SUN. Halberd 識 122
SUN. Legs2 譜 121
SUN. MAN 謁 98
SUN. rod2 譜 129
SUN. spoon 詣 40
SUN. stand 諳 91
SUN. stopper 譚 123
SUN. ten 譚 123
SUN. wrap 詢 51
SUN. wrap 謁 98
Tap 變 135
ten 計 3
ten 評 30
thread2 譏 119
tiger 讞 142
tongue 話 38
tooth 訝 21
TREE 誅 37

TREE 誅 47
TREE 課 74
TREE 諫 89
TREE 謀 90
two 講 102
use 誦 62
WATER 詠 34
Wings 詡 39
Wings 謬 113
WOMAN 誘 73
WORDS 讟 143
work 試 49
wrap 訇 4
wrap 詢 51
wrap2 讕 109

ENGLISH NAMES OF RADICALS
(INTRODUCTION)

The following Table is an expanded version of "RADICALS (ENGLISH NAMES)" (pp. 27-28). The Radicals are listed here by the number of their strokes.

The Table includes the Simplified Forms, followed by their Traditional Forms (between parentheses). You will find them at the beginning of each List.

The Compressed Forms of the Radicals are listed separately from the Original Forms and are placed at the end of each List. They are marked with an asterisk (*).

The Traditional Forms and their Compressed Forms are listed separately, making it easier to locate each of them. It also allows for more accurate indication with reference to their occurrence.

The common forms are indicated by the letter A, as follows:

AAA for MOST COMMON

AA for VERY COMMON

A for COMMON

In "RADICALS (ENGLISH NAMES)", Radical **HEART** 心 忄 灬 is marked with three asterisks (***), as being most common. However, only the Compressed Form 忄 is the form that is used most of the time as the Radical of the character. It is marked in this Table with three A's (AAA). The Original Form 心 is marked with two A's (AA). The other Compressed Form 灬 $^{+}$ is used only three times in the Group (in HEART Nos. 21, 52, and 131) and is not marked at all with the A.

+ The black bar ▬ shows the position of the remaining units.

As a rule, to allow maximum space for the remaining units, the Compressed Form (if available) is used as the Radical of the character. This, for instance, takes place in the Group **MAN**, where the Compressed Form 亻 is the Radical used most of the time (marked AAA). The Original Form 人 (and the other Compressed Form 𠆢) are used only occasionally; they are marked with one A only.

Two previous Tables also show Radical Names:

- **"WHICH RADICAL IS THAT ?"** (pp. 21-24).
This is a compact form of four Tables, in which all Radicals acompanied by their Compressed Forms are printed close together. The Compressed Forms are also printed separately.

- **"RADICALS (ENGLISH NAMES)"** (pp. 27-28).
Radicals accompanied by their Compressed Forms are alphabetically arranged under their English Names. It is most suitable for review purposes, when you want to refresh your memory.

These two Tables may also help you to find the Name of a Radical. However, they do not contain the Simplified Forms; only the following Table **"ENGLISH NAMES OF RADICALS"** (pp. Eng 1–Eng 7) contain also the Simplified Forms.

Studying and knowing all Radicals marked A, AA and AAA, will greatly help you in finding a character in this Dictionary. The Section **"Their Ancestral Forms (Etymology)"** (pp.29-50) will help you memorizing them, by showing their ancestral forms to you.

ENGLISH NAMES OF RADICALS

1 STROKE

一	ONE
丨	ROD
丶	DOT
丿	LEFTSTROKE
乙 乚	BENT
亅	DOWNSTROKE

2 STROKES

二	TWO	
亠	LID	
人 入	MAN	A
儿	LEGS	
入 入	ENTER	
八	EIGHT	
冂	BORDERS	
冖	COVER	
冫	ICE	
几	STOOL	
凵	PIT	
刀	KNIFE	A
力	STRENGTH	

勹	WRAP	
匕	SPOON	
匚	BASKET	
匚	BOX	
十	TEN	
卜	DIVINATION	
卩 巳	SEAL	
厂	CLIFF	
厶	COCOON	
又	HAND (2)	
阝	CITY *	
阝	MOUND *	A
刂	KNIFE *	AA
𧾷	FOOT *	
亻	MAN *	AAA

3 STROKES

辶(辶)	PROCEED	AA
讠(言)	WORDS	AAA
饣(食)	FOOD	A
艹(艸)	GRASS	AAA
门(門)	DOOR	A
纟(糸)	SILK	AAA

Eng 1

爿(爿)	SPLITWOOD (L)
口	MOUTH AAA
囗	ENCLOSURE
土 圡	EARTH AA
士	SCHOLAR
夂	PURSUE
夊	PERSEVERE
夕	EVENING
大 夳	BIG A
女	WOMAN AA
子 孑	CHILD
宀	DWELLING AA
寸	INCH
小	SMALL
尢	LAME
尸	CORPSE
屮	SPROUT
山	MOUNTAIN
川 巛	RIVER
工	WORK
己	SELF
巾	CLOTH A
干	PESTLE

幺	THREAD
广	SHELTER A
廴	MOVE ON
廾	FOLDED HANDS
弋	DART
弓	BOW
彑 彐 彑	PIG'S SNOUT
彡	LINES
彳	FOOTSTEP A
犭	DOG* A
扌	HAND (1) * AAA
忄	HEART * AAA
辶	PROCEED * AA
氵	WATER * AAA

4 STROKES

见(見)	SEE
斗(鬥)	FIGHT
贝(貝)	SHELL AA
飞(飛)	FLY
车(車)	CART A
风(風)	WIND
马(馬)	HORSE A
韦(韋)	LEATHER

心	HEART	AA
戈	HALBERD	
户	DOORLEAF	
手	HAND (1)	A
支	BRANCH	
攴攵	TAP	
文	LITERATURE	
斗	PECK	
斤	AXE	
方	SQUARE	
元旡	NOT	
日	SUN	AA
曰	SPEAK	
月	MOON	
木	TREE	AAA
欠	BREATHE	
止	STOP	
歹	DISINTEGRATION	
殳	STRIKE	
毋	DO NOT	
比	COMPARE	
毛	HAIR	
氏	CLAN	
气	VAPOR	

水	WATER	
火 灬	FIRE	AA
爪 爫	CLAW	
父	FATHER	
爻	INTERTWINE	
爿	SPLITWOOD (L)	
片	SPLITWOOD (R)	
牙	TOOTH	
牛 牜	OX	
犬	DOG	
月	FLESH *	AAA
艹	GRASS *	AAA
王	JADE *	AA
罒	NET *	
耂	OLD *	
辶	PROCEED *	
礻	REVELATION *	A
灬	FIRE *	AA
忄	HEART *	

钅(金)	GOLD	AAA
龙(龍)	DRAGON	
长(長)	LONG	
发(髮)	HAIRLOCKS	

ENGLISH NAMES OF RADICALS

玄	DARK
玉	JADE
瓜	MELON
瓦	TILE
甘	SWEET
生	GROW
用	USE
田	FIELD
疋 正	ROLL
疒	ILLNESS AA
癶	BOTH FEET
白	WHITE
皮	SKIN
皿	DISH
目	EYE AA
矛	LANCE
矢	ARROW
石	STONE AA
示	REVELATION
内	TRACK
禾	GRAIN A
穴 空	CAVE
立	STAND

衤	CLOTHES * AA
罒 門	NET *
氺	WATER *
罒	EYE *

6 STROKES

齐(齊)	EVEN
鸟(鳥)	BIRD (1) A
页(頁)	HEAD (2) A
竹 ⺮	BAMBOO AA
米	RICE
糸 糹	SILK AAA
缶	EARTHENWARE
网	NET
羊 ⺶	SHEEP
羽	WINGS
老	OLD
而	BEARD
耒	PLOW
耳	EAR
聿	STYLUS
肉	FLESH
臣	MINISTER
自	NOSE (1)
至	REACH

臼	MORTAR	
舌	TONGUE	
舛	OPPOSITION	
舟	BOAT	
艮	DEFIANCE	
色	COLOR	
艸	GRASS	
虍	TIGER	
虫	INSECT	AA
血	BLOOD	
行	GO	
衣	CLOTHES	AA
西 襾 西	STOPPER	

7 STROKES

卤(鹵)	SALT	
麦(麥)	WHEAT	
龟(龜)	TORTOISE	
見	SEE	
角	HORN	
言	WORDS	AAA
谷	VALLEY	
豆	BEAN	
豕	PIG	
豸	CAT	

貝	SHELL	AA
赤	RED	
走	RUN	
足 趴	FOOT	AA
身	BODY	
車	CART	A
辛	OFFEND	
辰	PERIOD	
辵	PROCEED	
邑	CITY	
酉	WINE JUG	A
采	FOOTPRINT	
里	VILLAGE	

8 STROKES

黾(黽)	TURTLE	
齿(齒)	TEETH	
鱼(魚)	FISH	A
金	GOLD	AAA
長	LONG	
門	DOOR	A
阜	MOUND	
隶	SEIZE	
隹	BIRD (2)	
雨	RAIN	

青 GREEN

非 BACK-TO-BACK

食 FOOD *   A

鬲 CALDRON

鬼 GHOST

面 FACE

革 RAWHIDE

韋 LEATHER

韭 LEEK

音 SOUND

頁 HEAD (2)   A

風 WIND

飛 FLY

食 FOOD   A

首 HEAD (1)

香 FRAGRANT

魚 FISH   A

鳥 BIRD (1)   A

鹵 SALT

鹿 DEER

麥 WHEAT

麻 HEMP

黃 YELLOW

黍 MILLET

黑 BLACK

黹 EMBROIDERY

馬 HORSE   A

骨 BONES

高 HIGH

髟 HAIRLOCKS

鬥 FIGHT

鬯 WINE VESSEL

黽 TURTLE

鼎 TRIPOD

鼓 DRUM

鼠 RAT

ENGLISH NAMES OF RADICALS

14 STROKES

鼻 NOSE (2)

齊 EVEN

15 STROKES

齒 TEETH

16 STROKES

龍 DRAGON

龜 TORTOISE

17 STROKES

龠 FLUTE

THE INDEX OF SIMPLIFIED CHARACTERS
(INTRODUCTION)

Contrary to general belief, not all Chinese characters have been simplified in today's China . Of the 5,047 characters in this Dictionary, only 1,878 have been simplified. This leaves 3,169 characters or ca. 62% unchanged.

We can distinguish three classes of Simplified Characters. Hereunder follow some examples – the Simplified Characters are accompanied by the Traditional Characters (placed between parentheses).

CLASS A – the Radical has been simplified. (The Non-Radical portion remains unchanged):

银 (銀) Silver (GOLD, No. 37)

语 (語) Language (WORDS, No. 68)

馆 (館) Lodging (FOOD, No. 24)

CLASS B – the Non-Radical portion has been simplified. (The Radical is unchanged or simplified.)

灯 (燈) Lamp (FIRE, No. 72)

吨 (噸) Ton(nage) (MOUTH, No. 198)

汤 (湯) Soup (WATER. No. 121)

CLASS C – **(a) the Radical has been replaced by another Radical.** (The Non-Radical portion remains unchanged, or has been simplified):

体 (體) Body; trunk (BONES, No. 7)

熔 (鎔) Melt; fuse; smelt (GOLD, No. 84)

护 (護) Protect; guard (WORDS, No.131)

(b) the Radical has been removed; the Non-Radical portion becomes a Simplified Character:

面 (麵) Flour; noodles (WHEAT, No. 5)

卷 (捲) Roll (egg –) (HAND (1), No. 105)

云 (雲) Cloud (RAIN, No. 3)

(c) the character has been changed in its entirety:

厂 (廠) Factory (SHELTER, No. 28)

万 (萬) Ten thousand (GRASS, No. 99)

义 (義) Righteousness (SHEEP, No. 8)

(NOTE: page Si 000 comes after page Si 0000.)

LIST OF SIMPLIFIED RADICALS
(followed by their Traditional Forms in parentheses)

3 STROKES				5 STROKES		
辶	(辵)	PROCEED	AA	钅	(金) GOLD	AAA
讠	(言)	WORDS	AAA	龙	(龍) DRAGON	
饣	(食)	FOOD	A	长	(長) LONG	
艹	(艸)	GRASS	AAA	发	(髪) HAIRLOCKS	
门	(門)	DOOR	A	**6 STROKES**		
纟	(糸)	SILK	AAA	齐	(齊) EVEN	
扌	(爿)	SPLTWOD	(L)	鸟	(鳥) BIRD (1)	A
4 STROKES				页	(頁) HEAD (2)	A
见	(見)	SEE		**7 STROKES**		
斗	(鬥)	FIGHT		卤	(鹵) SALT	
贝	(貝)	SHELL	AA	麦	(麥) WHEAT	
飞	(飛)	FLY		龟	(龜) TORTOISE	
车	(車)	CART	A	**8 STROKES**		
风	(風)	WIND		鱼	(黽) TURTLE	
马	(馬)	HORSE	A	齿	(齒) TEETH	
韦	(韋)	LEATHER		黾	(魚) FISH	A

In **CLASS A** (30% of all Simplified Characters), only the Radical has been simplified; the Non-Radical portion has remained unchanged.

Knowing the name of the Simplified Radical (see **"List of Simplified Radicals"** on p. Si 0000) will bring you to the Group to which the Simplified Character belongs. And knowing the number of strokes of the Non-Radical portion will allow you to locate the character (see p. 2).

For this reason, you will not find Simplified Characters of CLASS A in the "INDEX OF SIMPLIFIED CHARACTERS".

In **CLASS B** (50% of all Simplified Characters), the Non-Radical portion of the character has been simplified. *For this reason it is not possible anymore to locate the character by the number of strokes of the Non-Radical portion– see p. 2).*

In **CLASS C** (20% of all Simplified Characters), the Radical has been replaced by another Radical (see CLASS C – (a)); or the Radical has been removed (see CLASS C – (b)); or the entire character has been simplified (see CLASS C – (c)).

For these reasons, it is not possible to find even the Group to which the character belongs.

The "INDEX OF SIMPLIFIED CHAR-ACTERS" does *not* contain Simplified Characters of CLASS A. The INDEX only contains Simplified Characters of CLASS B and CLASS C (i.e. 70% only of all Simplified Characters).

In many cases, a Simplified Character contains no Radical (see CLASS C – (b) and (c) on p. Si 00). In order to also include such Simplified Character in the INDEX, the definition of a Radical in the INDEX has been liberalized.

> **In the INDEX, a 'Radical' may also be a writing-unit that *only resembles a Radical*. It *does not serve the usual function* of a Radical, i.e. it *does not indicate* to which Group that character belongs.**

Examples:

The Simplified Character 义 (Righteousness) contains no Radical. It is listed under DOT, although 丶 is not the Radical of this character in the usual sense of the word.

万 (Ten thousand) is listed under ONE, and 丰 (Abundant; fine-looking) is listed under ROD, although 一 and | are not the Radicals of these characters in the usual sense of the word.

> **Characters which contain UNCOMMON RADICALS are also listed by the number of their strokes at the end of the Index.**

Examples:

卧 (Lie (down)) (MINISTER 臣 is an Uncommon Radical) is also listed under 8 STROKES (p. Si 26).

雇 (Hire, employ) (DOORLEAF 戸 is an Uncommon Radical) is also listed under 12 STROKES (p. Si 28).

肃 (Respectful; solemn) (STYLUS 肃 is an Uncommon Radical) is also listed under 8 STROKES (p. Si 26).

Remarks on the Simplified Characters

In **CLASS A**, only the Radical of the character has been simplified, leaving the Non-Radical part unchanged. Of the 214 Radicals, 28 have been simplified. *Characters of which only the Radical has been simplified, become Simplified Characters, although the Non-Radical remains unchanged.*

There are 565 characters in this Class (30% of all Simplified Characters) in this Dictionary. *They are not included in the Index, because by knowing the Name of the Simplified Character (see **List of Simplified Radicals** on p. Si 0000), we can locate the character in the usual manner (see p. 2).*

In **CLASS B**, the Non-Radical part has been simplified. The radical has been simplified, if it has a simplified form (see p. Si 0000); otherwise it has been left unchanged.

As a rule, the Non-Radical part (sometimes also called the Phonetic part) gives indication to the pronunciation of the character. *Usually the Non-Radical part has been replaced by a simple writing-unit that gives the same or closely the same pronunciation.*

灯 (燈) Teng[1] (deng) – Lamp (FIRE, No. 72).

厅 (廳) T'ing[1] (ting) – Hall (SHELTER, No. 35).

听 (聽) T'ing[1] (tìng) – Listen; hear (EAR, No. 19).

汤 (湯) T'ang[1] (tang) – Soup (WATER, No. 121).

荡 (蕩) Tang[4] (dàng) – Swing (v) (GRASS, No. 135).

烫 (燙) T'ang[4] (tàng) – Scald (v) (FIRE, No. 71).

[**Phonetic parts are: T'ing (ting)** 丁 **and T'ang (tang)** 汤].

In CLASS C (a), the Radical of the character has been replaced by another Radical. The Non-Radical part has been simplified, or has been left unchanged.

鎔 (Fuse; melt) (Rad. GOLD/METAL, No. 84) has been simplified into 熔 (Rad. FIRE). *This seems to be more appropriate, because not only Metals, but also Non-Metals (e.g. butter, ice) can 'melt'. On the other hand, in order to 'fuse', we need FIRE.*

髏 (Body, trunk) (Rad. BONES, No. 7) has been simplified into 体 (Rad. MAN/PERSON). *It seems more appropriate to use MAN/PERSON as the Radical, because when we think of 'body', we are more likely to think of 'the body of a MAN or PERSON' and are not likely to think of 'body' in connection with BONES.*

In CLASS C (b), the Radical has been removed, and the Non-Radical part by itself became a Simplified Character.

面 – Mien⁴ (miàn) is the Non-Radical (Phonetic) part of 麵 (Rad. WHEAT, No. 5). By itself this Non-Radical is used to represent 'Noodles'. *The word Mien⁴ (miàn) for 'Noodles' is a very common word, used very often, justifying the omission of the elaborate writing of the Radical (Wheat)* 麥 .

云 – Yun² (yún) is the Non-Radical (Phonetic) part of 雲 . By itself it means 'Cloud'. *This very common word justifies the omission of the additional, elaborate writing of* 雨 *(Rad. RAIN).*

In CLASS C (c), the character has been completely changed into a very simple symbol. *Many Traditional Characters are very common, but are very complex writings. Very simple symbols are now used in China, replacing them (see p. Si 00).*

INDEX SIMPLIFIED CHARACTERS
(List of characters of Class B and C – see p. Si 0)

ARROW 矢
医 W17
矫 A1

AXE 斤
斩 A2
断 A2

BAMBOO 竹 ⺮
笃 B4
笔 B2
笑 M24
笋 B3
5 笺 B4 S20
笼 B6
筝 B3
答 G15
筑 B4
筛 B4
等 G15
7 筹 B5
签 B5 B6
简 B5
箧 B4

篓 B6
箫 B5
篓 B5
10 篮 B5
篱 B6
籁 B6

BASKET 匚
区 B19
医 W17

BEAN 豆
豆 B6 G16

BENT 乚
乱 B8

BIG 大
买 S6
夸 W26
夺 B10
夹 B9
关 D9 D9
庆 H29
衾 B10

卖 S7
奋 B10
类 H21 H21
奖 B10

BIRD (1) 鸟
鸡 B12 B13
岛 M18
鸥 B12
5 鸰 B11
鸢 C6
莺 B12
鸳 B12
鸷 B12
鸾 B12
鹏 B12
鹃 B12
鹉 B12
鹦 B12

BIRD (2) 佳
难 B14
雇 M11

雏 B13
雕 B11 L4
雠 W31
耀 F8

BLOOD 血
衄 W17

BOAT 舟
舰 B15
舱 B15

BODY 身
躯 B16
躲 B16

BONES 骨
骷 B16
髅 B16

BORDERS 冂
币 C11
冈 M18
网 S14
周 P6

BOW 弓
张 B18
弥 B19
弯 B19
弹 B19
强 B18 B19

BREATHE 欠
欢 B20 H32 H35
欧 B20
钦 B20
欲 H30

CART 车
轧 C1
军 C1
轫 C2
轰 C3
转 C3
轮 C2
轻 C2
轳 C4
轿 C3
辆 C2
辔 C4
毂 C3

CAVE 穴
穷 C5
帘 B5
窃 C6
窝 C6
窍 C6
窑 C5
窜 C6
窝 C5
窦 C6
窥 C6

CHILD 子
孙 C7
学 C7
孽 C7

CITY 阝
邮 C8
邻 C8 M17
郁 W17
郑 C8

CLAN 氏
氓 C8 F2

CLIFF 厂

厂 C10 S10
厄 M15
厅 S10
历 S27 S33
厉 C10
压 E7
厌 C10
产 G22
5 严 M31
励 S28
厕 C9 S10
厘 V2 V2
厢 S10
10 厨 C9 S10
厦 S10
魇 G2

CLOTH 巾

币 C11
布 M4
帅 C11 C11
师 C11
帏 C11
帐 C11
帘 B5

帜 C11
帮 C12
带 C11
幡 S21

CLOTHES 衣

农 P2
补 C13
衬 C15
袄 C15
衿 S11
5 袓 C13 C15
袜 C15
袭 C15
裆 C15
装 C13
裤 C14
褛 C15
褒 C15
10 褴 C15
襁 C14 C15
褓 S16

COCOON 厶

么 H32 T4
乡 C8

云 R1
会 S19
县 S15
层 C18
系 M6 S17
齐 T13
参 C16
兹 G15
尝 M29

COLOR 色

艳 B7 B7 C16

COMPARE 比

毗 C16
毙 T3

CORPSE 尸

尸 C16 C17
卢 D4
尽 D4 M12
层 C18
屈 C17
届 C17
屏 C17
属 C18
屡 C17

COVER ⼍		DOG 犬 犭		DOORLEAF 户	
冗	D11	状	D5	雇	M11
写	D14	狈	D6		
冢	E5	犹	D6	**DOT** 丶	
冤	D13	狭	D6	义	S4
		狮	D7	勺	T7
DISH ⽫		独	D7	广	S10
盏	D3	7 获	D7	习	W18
盐	D4 S1	狱	D7	3 匀	W32
监	D3	猪	P3	㇒	S20
盗	D3	猎	D7	书	S19
盘	D4	猬	I10	斗	F3
盖	D4 G19	献	D7	办	O1
蓝	G21	獭	D7	为	C9
				风	W15
DISINTEGRATION 歹		**DOOR** 门		4 匆	H24
殁	D4	问	M27	对	I7
残	D5	闯	D9	业	T14
殒	D5	闲	D8	尔	I12
殓	D5	闹	F3 D8	龙	D11
殖	D4	闾	D9	头	H21
殡	D5	因	D9	兰	G22
		阆	F3	发	B17 H2
DIVINATION 卜		阐	D9	5 关	D9
卜	D5 G19	阅	F3	夹	B9 C13
处	T5			毕	F3
卧	M13				

伞	S16	丧	M28	
巩	R3	卖	S7	
庄	G16	卷	H10	
并	P2	卧	M13	
亚	T19	8 囷	D9	
当	F3	间	D9	
并	M5 M8	养	F18	
兴	M15	举	M15	
买	S6	将	I7	
协	T4	姜	G20	
尽	D4	兹	G15	
爷	F1			
寻	I7	亲	S3	
导	I7	类	H21	
夹	B9	9 爱	H28	
产	G22	羞	S4	
6 丽	D2	党	B14	
尘	E6 E7	壶	S2	
应	H31	离	B14	
寿	S2	10 着	E13 G17	
状	D5	凿	G9	
来	M5	翘	W18	
7 采	H11	辉	F6	
枣	T13	颊	H21	
单	M28	黉	Y1	
肃	S29			

DOWNSTROKE 丿

了	D10 E14
才	S17
于	S21
争	C9

DRAGON 龙

龙	D11
庞	D11
龛	D11

DWELLING 宀

宁	U1 D14
灾	F4 G17
宝	D14
宠	D14
审	D14
实	D14
帘	B5
宪	H30
宽	D14
宾	S7
寝	D14

EAR 耳

闻 E2
耻 H24
耸 E2
聂 E2
职 E2
聋 E2
联 E2
聪 E2

EARTH 土

圣 E2
尘 E6 E7
压 E7
庄 G16
考 T1
4 场 E4 E6
块 E5
坛 E7
坟 E6
坝 E7
坏 E7
坛 E6
坠 E6
坚 E4
坞 E5

5 幸 M7
垫 E6
垦 E6
垒 E7
致 S15
堕 E6
堤 M17
野 E4
10 填 C5 E5
墙 E6 S20

EARTHENWARE 缶

缶 E2
罂 E7 T5
罐 G9

ENCLOSURE 囗

回 P5
团 E10 R8
曲 W14
园 E10
卤 W10
围 E10
困 E13
囵 E10

国 E9
图 E10
圀 W8
圄 E9 E10
圆 E10

EVENING 夕

够 E11
梦 E11

EYE 目 罒

县 S15
直 E12
罗 M32 N2
罚 N2
5 真 E12
罢 N2
睁 E13
着 E13 G17
睿 H19
暖 F6
瞋 E14
瞒 E14
瞰 E14
羁 N2

FACE 面
面 F1 W14
靦 F1

FATHER 父
爷 F1

FIELD 田
电 R1
亩 F2
龟 T6
里 C13
画 F3
畅 S32
备 M10
奋 B10
单 C15 M28
毗 C16
野 E4
畴 F3
簧 Y1
翻 S16

FIRE 火 灬
灭 W9
灯 F8
灿 F8
灵 R3
灾 F4 G17
4 炖 F8
炉 F8 G9
杰 M10 T11
炮 F4 F5
5 点 B14
烁 F8
炼 F6
炽 F7
烂 F8
炸 F4 F6
炫 G2
炭 F5
6 热 F7
烧 F7
烛 F8
烟 F5 F7 G17
烦 F6
烬 F8
7 焊 G3 G5
烫 F7

焕 F6
焰 F8
10 熔 G7
熏 F8

FISH 鱼
鲈 F11
鲇 F9
稣 G12
鲟 F10
鲸 F11
鲋 F10
鲢 F10
鲨 F9
鳄 F11
鳅 F10 F10

FLESH 肉 月
肠 F14
肾 F14
肴 F19
肤 F15
肿 F15
胀 F14
肮 B16

胁 F13
5 胧 M14
胆 F16
胜 S28
胪 F16
脉 F13
胫 F13
胡 H2
6 脍 F11
脐 F16
脏 F16 B16
胶 F15
脑 F15
脓 F16
胭 F16
胳 F11 F13
衔 F16
7 脚 F13 F14
望 M14
脸 F16
8 腊 F16
腆 S3
腻 F15
腾 H35
10 静 G22

臕 F16
膻 S5
膳 F20

FOOD 饣
饥 F20
飨 F20
饯 F19
饰 F18 F19
蚀 I10
饶 F20
餍 F20
馄 F19 F19
馈 F19 F20
馋 F20
馍 F20
馕 N2

FOOT 足
趸 F24
跑 F23 S20
跃 F24 R10
践 F22
跻 F24
跷 F23 F24
踩 F21 F22

踪 F23 F23
蹄 F23 F23
蹰 F24
蹿 F24
蹶 F24

FOOTPRINT 采
释 F25

FOOTSTEP 彳
彻 F27
征 F27
径 F26 M7
徕 F26
衔 G4 M27
御 R6

GO 行
衔 G4 M27

GOLD 金 钅
针 G6
钦 B20
钩 G3 G3
钟 G6 G8
钢 G5

钥 G9
5 钱 G6
钻 G9
铁 G4 G8
铎 G8
铄 G9
鉴 G9 G9
6 铗 G5
铧 G8
铙 G8
铛 G8
铠 G7
铮 G5
铲 G7
銎 G9
锡 G8
7 铺 T6
铸 G9
链 G6 G7
锅 G6
锁 G7
锈 G8
8 錾 G8
锚 G6
锣 G9
锤 G7
螢 I10

锹 T8
9 镂 G7
镊 G9
镇 G7
13 镰 G7
镬 G9

GRAIN 禾
秆 G10 G11
种 G11
秌 G10
积 G12
称 G11
秒 G12
颖 G12
稳 G12
穑 G12
穗 S17

GRASS 艹
艺 G19
节 B4
苇 G18
芜 G20
苍 G19
芦 G22
苎 G14

苏 G22 G23
劳 S28
5 苹 G21 T18
范 B4
茎 G16
苞 G17
6 荚 G16
荤 G17
荐 G15 G21
草 G13 G15 H35
茧 S17
荞 G20
荫 G20 S10
药 G18 G21
荣 T15
荡 D4 G20
7 莲 G19
莱 G16
莅 G19
获 D7
莹 J4
莴 G18
莺 B12
萝 G22
8 萦 S15
萧 G20 B5

营	F8
10 蓟	G20
蓝	G21
蒙	E14
蔑	B14
蔷	G21
12 蕊	G20
蕴	G22
薮	G21
薇	G21
孽	C7
15 藤	B6
蘑	G21 G21
蘸	G22

HAIR 毛

毡	H1
髦	B12
氅	B12

HAIRLOCKS 髟

鬓	H2
鬟	H2

HALBERD 戈

戈	H3
戏	H4
尧	E5
咸	S1
战	H3
戚	H30

HAND (1) 手 扌

扑	H15
托	W24
扬	H12 W15
扪	H10
扫	H10
扩	H17
执	E4
扣	G3
4 扯	H14
抠	H14
抟	H14
抚	H15
扰	H17
折	H14
抡	H10
抢	H13
护	W31

报	E5
拟	H17
5 拓	H13
抵	H16
拢	H18
抻	H9
拣	H11
担	H16
拥	H17
拦	H18
拧	H17
拨	H15
择	H17
抬	H17
6 拿	H6
挣	H9
挡	H16 H18
按	H12
挛	H18
挂	H8 H10 N1
挞	H16
挟	H8
挠	H15
挥	H11
挤	H17
7 损	H13

捆 S13	摸 H14	艰 D2
捏 H9 H11	摄 H18	肾 F14
挨 H11	摈 H17	殴 S29
换 H11	摆 H17	竖 S22 B7
捞 H15	摊 H18	8 难 B14
捂 H14	携 H12 H18	爱 H28
捡 H16	摩 H14	聂 E2
捣 H13 H17	撇 H15	殷 H29
8 携 H16	12 撵 H17	毁 F8 W30
掏 H13	撺 H18	叠 F3
掩 H12	撤 H18	
捶 H12	攒 H18 M12	
捻 H15		
掷 H17		**HEAD (2)** 页
掸 H15 H15	**HAND (2)** 又	须 H2
据 H16	又 H19	顾 H22
掰 H16	双 B13	颈 H21
9 搭 H13	凤 B10	颊 H21
搁 H17	劝 S28	颠 H22
揽 H18	对 I7	颤 H22
搀 H18	发 B17 H2	颧 H22
搂 H14	圣 E2	
搅 H18	欢 B20 H32	
搜 G19	戏 H4	
10 携 H12 H18	5 坚 E4	**HEAD (1)** 首 is
摇 H14	轰 C3	an uncommon Radical, which means:"head;first; leader, chief".
	变 W31	

HEART 心 忄		
忆 H31	惫 H30	骄 H35
闷 H27	惬 H27	验 H35
志 W26	惧 H32	骚 H34
忏 H32	惊 H35	
志 W26	惮 H30	**ICE** 冫
怄 H29	惨 H30	决 W2
怀 H31	惩 H31	冲 G2 W2
忧 H30	9 惯 H30	冻 I2
怅 H26	愤 H30	净 I2
态 H29	愧 W22	凄 H27
5 怵 H23	愈 I5	凉 W6
怜 H30	10 懔 H32	准 W8
总 S16	愿 H22	凑 W8
㤉 H29	懍 H31	减 W7
恍 H23	懑 H31	凛 I2 W7
恻 H28	懒 H31	
恼 H28		**ILLNESS** 疒
恶 H27 M31	**HORN** 角	疖 I6
虑 H29	触 H33	疗 I6
恳 H31	觞 H33	疝 I5
恋 H32		疮 I5
恒 H25	**HORSE** 马	疯 I5
7 惆 H30	驱 H35	5 症 I6
悬 H31	驳 H33 H34	疱 S18
惭 H29	驴 H35	痈 I6
	驿 H35	痢 I5

痨 I6
痪 I5
痹 I4
痴 I4 I6
痱 I3
瘟 I5
10 瘪 I6
瘫 I6
瘾 I6
癞 I6
癣 I6
癫 I5

INCH 寸
对 I7
导 I7
寻 I7
寿 S2
将 I7

INSECT 虫
虫 I7 I11
虮 I11
蚀 I10
萤 S17
虾 F10 I9

蚁 I11
虽 B13
虹 I10
蚂 I10
蚕 I12
蚝 I11
5 萤 I10
蛎 I12
蛊 I12
蛮 I12
强 B19
蜈 I9
蜗 I10
8 蝈 I10
蜡 I12
蝇 I11
蝉 I11
蝶 I9
蝎 I11
蝼 I10

JADE 王 王
宝 D14
玛 J3
环 J4
现 J2

玺 J4
莹 J4
球 H1
琐 J3
琏 J4
瑶 J3
璎 J4

KNIFE 刀 刂
划 K4
则 K3
刚 K3
创 K3
5 刨 G4 K2
刮 W15
制 C14
刽 K4
剂 K4
刺 G16 K2
剐 K3
剑 K4
剃 G21
窃 C6
8 剥 K3
剧 K4
剩 S8

剿 S28

LEATHER 韦
韬 B18 L2
韫 L2

LEFTSTROKE 丿
儿 L3
么 H32 T4
升 M16 S30
归 S27
匆 H24
乔 M27
农 P2

LID 亠
丧 M28
离 B14

LINES 彡
参 C16
须 H2
彩 S14

LITERATURE 文
斋 E11

MAN 人 亻
个 B3 M7
亿 M11
² 队 M17
仓 M5
仓 M8
从 F26
仆 M11
仅 M10
什 M2 S33
³ 们 M8
仪 M11
仙 M10
丛 H19 T17
⁴ 优 M12
伛 M11
仡 M3
伤 M10
价 M11
伦 M8
伧 M10
仿 M7
伙 E11
伪 M11
传 M10
伟 M9

会 S19
众 B14
伞 M10 S16
众 E13
⁵ 两 E10 O3
体 B16
佑 R5 M5
佣 M11
余 F19
⁶ 侧 M9
倾 M9
侠 M6
侥 M11 M11
侨 M11
侩 M12
依 M12
侪 M12
舍 H10
凭 H30
⁷ 俦 M12
俭 M11
俨 M13
俩 M8
俪 M12
修 F14
⁸ 倾 M10

倏	M8 M8
倜	M8 M9
值	M7
债	M10
借	G21
耸	E2
倘	M13
健	F26
偿	M12
偻	M10
10 储	M12
傻	M10 M12

MINISTER 臣
卧	M13

MOUND 阝
队	M17
阵	M16
阳	M17
阴	M17
阶	M17
陈	M16
陆	M16
际	M17
陨	M17

险	M18
随	M18
隐	M18

MOUNTAIN 山
出	T3
击	H16
岁	S26
岂	B7
岖	M19
岛	M18
岳	M18 M19
岭	M19
岩	M18 M19
巅	M19

MOUTH 口
叶	G18
叹	B20 M29
叽	M30
只	B13 R5 R5
号	T5
占	M3
台	R4
3 回	M32 P5
同	G2 H2

吃	M27
吓	M31
吁	B6 F17
吊	B18
后	F25 M21
向	M31
问	M27
吗	M28
4 吣	M25
豆	B6 G16
吴	M23
员	M26
呕	M29
吨	M31
听	E2
呛	M29
呆	D6 T8
启	M26
谷	G12 R8 V1
乱	B8
5 咙	M31
和	F17 M23
咏	W25
咛	M31
舍	H10
周	P6

黾	T19	
6 总	S16	
虽	B13	
哕	M31	
咸	S1	
哝	M31	
胡	G2	
哗	M29	
哑	M27	
咽	M31	
哔	W30	
咱	M9	
响	S19	
咳	B20	
咨	W29	
毡	H1	
咸	S1	
战	H3	
点	B14	
胡	H2	
哄	F3	
骂	N2	
7 唤	M27	
幽	M30	
面	W14	

唠	M30	
党	B14	
竞	S22	
敌	T2	
唇	F14	
8 欲	H30	
啬	M29	
喷	M29	
营	F8	
啃	M26 T3	
啕	M25	
啮	M32	
兽	D7	
龛	D11	
9 喷	M31	
喧	W28	
喂	F19	
啼	M29	
10 嗳	M31	
辟	D9	
喷	M28	
辞	O1	
嗪	F15	
骷	B16	
12 噜	M31	
嘱	M32	
器	M32	

NET

罗	M32 N2
罚	N2
罢	N2
置	D13 N1
羁	N2

OFFEND 辛

辟	D9
辞	O1
辩	O1
辫	S17

ONE 一

与	M15
万	G18
才	S17
卫	G2 G2
乌	F5
3 气	V1
丑	W16
长	L5
升	M16 S30
写	D14
刍	G13
业	T14

兰 G22
5 异 F2
亚 T19
两 E10 O3
丽 D2
面 F1 W14
韭 G17

OX 牛
牵 O4
牺 O4
犊 O4

PERSEVERE 夂
处 T5
麦 W14
复 C14 F26 P2

PIG 豕
圂 W8
冢 E5
象 M11

PIG'S SNOUT ⇒
肃 S29
隶 S3

PIT 凵
凶 L3

PROCEED 辶
辽 P8
边 P9
3 巡 M32
迈 P9
达 P7
过 P7
迁 P8
4 连 P6
运 P7
违 P7
远 P8
进 P7
还 P9
这 P6
迟 P8
5 迩 P9
选 P8
适 P8
逊 P8
迹 F23
7 递 P8
逖 P7
逻 P9

9 遗 P8
遁 P8
逼 M9
遍 F26
遥 P8
遭 F23

RAIN 雨
霹 R2
雾 R2
霁 R2

RAWHIDE 革
鞑 R4
鞘 L2 R3

REVELATION
礼 R6 示 礻
祯 R6
祷 R6
祸 R6
禀 G11
禄 R6
禅 R6

RICE 米	**RUN** 走	觌 S3	
粘 M13	赵 R10	觎 S3	
粗 H33	赶 R10	觑 S3	
粪 R8	趋 R10		
粮 R8	趱 R10	**SHELL** 贝	
糊 F19		败 T2	
糕 F19	**SALT** 卤	贤 S7	
糜 R8	卤 S1 W10	贮 S6	
糯 G12		账 S7	
	SCHOLAR 士	购 S8	
ROD 丨	壮 S2	质 S7	
个 B3 M7	声 E2	5 贱 S7	
卜 G19	壳 S29	赃 S8	
丰 B7	壶 S2	赉 S7	
韦 L2		赎 S8	
书 S19	**SEAL** 巳	赖 S8	
升 M16 S30	厄 M15	10 罂 T5	
丑 W16	卷 H10	赘 S8	
4 归 S27		赝 S8	
业 T14	**SEE** 见	赞 S8 W31	
当 F3	观 S3		
乔 M27	规 S3	**SHELTER** 广	
曲 W14	觅 S3	庄 G16	
亚 T19	视 S3	库 S9	
7 畅 S32	览 S3	应 H31	
临 M13	觉 S3	庐 S10	
竖 B7 S22		床 S9 S20	

庞 D11	绕 S16 P8	**SPLITWOOD (1)**
庙 S10	绘 S17	妆 W19　爿
废 I5 S10	⁷绣 S13 S16	壮 S2
麻 I4	绦 S15	状 D5
廒 S10	继 S17	将 I7
廪 S10	绩 S16	
	续 S17	**SPLITWOOD (2)**
SILK 纟	绳 S17	牍 S20　片
系 S17 M6	绿 S14	
丝 S13	⁹缆 S18	**SQUARE** 方
矿 S17	缕 S16	旋 G8 S21
纤 S16 S17	缘 S17	
⁴纬 S15	缠 S17	**STAND** 立
纲 S14	缙 S15	竖 B7 S22
纵 S16	¹¹缨 S18	亲 S3
纶 S14	缰 R4	竞 S22
继 S13		
紧 S14	**SKIN** 皮	**STONE** 石
⁵线 S14 S15	皱 S18	矶 S25
练 S14		矾 S25
绎 S17	**SMALL** 小	矿 S25
织 S16	尔 I12	岩 M19
绉 S15	系 M6	码 S24
经 S13		砚 S24
累 S17		砖 S25
萦 S15		

研 S23
5 砺 S25
础 S25
确 S25
8 碍 S25
碰 H12
碌 S24
磋 S25
碱 S1
磺 S25

STOOL 几
几 S26 T4
尧 E5
壳 S29
凭 H30 H33 I2
凯 S26

STRENGTH 力
劝 S28
历 S27 S33
办 O1
为 C9
务 S28
动 S28
协 T4

5 劳 S28
劫 K2
穷 C5
劲 S28
励 S28
势 S28
勋 S28
勤 H31

STRIKE 殳
殴 S29
殷 H29
毁 F8 W30

STYLUS 聿
肃 S29

SUN 日
旧 M15
亘 T19
时 S31
旷 S33
昙 S33
5 复 C14 F26
昵 S32
显 H22

昼 S31
晕 S32
晋 S31
晒 S33
晓 S33
8 暂 S33
韵 S19
暖 F6

TAP 攵
败 T2
效 M10 T1
致 S15
敌 T2
教 T2
敢 T2
敛 T2
数 T2

TEETH 齿
龃 T3
龈 T3
龌 T3

TEN 十
卉 G13 T3
协 T4
毕 F3
华 G16
单 C15 M28

TIGER 虎
虏 T5
虚 T5
虞 T5

TILE 瓦
瓯 T5

TONGUE 舌
乱 B8
敌 T2
辞 O1

TREE 木
术 G2 T7
朱 S23
东 T9
乐 T16
权 T18

机 T16
朴 T17
朱 S23
杀 S29
朵 T7
杂 B14
³ 极 T13
杠 T7 T15
杆 T11
来 M5
条 T12
床 S9 S20
呆 D6 T8
杨 T14
⁴ 采 H11
桌 T11
松 H2
枪 G7 T15
构 H13 T15
柜 B6 T18
枢 T16
杰 M10 T11
枣 T13
⁵ 标 T16
栀 T11
栈 T12

栏 T18
柠 T18
树 T17
荣 T15
亲 S3
栋 T13
⁶ 栗 H28
桧 T17
栖 T13
档 T17 T18
桥 T17
桦 T16
桩 T16
样 T16
栾 T18
桨 T16
⁷ 麻 I4
检 T17
梦 E11
彩 S14
植 T12
楝 T18
棹 T18
榄 T18
楼 T16
楦 T14

10 剿 S28	关 D9 D9	5 浅 W7
模 T16	并 M5 M8 P2	沽 R2
槛 T18	亘 T19	泪 W6
槟 T18		泻 W13
横 T16	**VALLEY** 谷	注 W25
樱 T18	谷 G12 V1	泞 W12
樯 T17		泼 W11
12 橹 T18	**VILLAGE** 里	泽 W12
橡 T18	里 C13 V2	6 浑 W7
檐 B5	野 F4 V2	测 W8
檩 T17		浆 W10
	WATER 水 氵	洼 C5
TURTLE 黾	汉 W9	洁 W11
鼋 T19	汇 B6 P3 W8	洒 W13
	录 P3 G6	浇 W11
TWO 二	污 W2 W5	浊 W12
干 B8 P2	汤 W8	洇 W8
于 S21	4 泄 W3 W5 W7	济 W13
亏 T5	泛 W1 W1 W3	浓 W12
开 D8	沪 W10	7 涧 W11
云 R1	沥 W13	润 W12
无 F5 N3	沧 W6	涛 W13
专 B7 I7	沤 W10	涌 W6 W8
击 H16	沟 W8	涩 W11 W12
兰 G22	没 W2	浣 W5 W12
夹 B9 C13	隶 S3	涝 W11

涡 W8
涂 E5
涨 W9
涟 W10
8 渔 W11
渍 W11
渎 I2 W13
渐 W10
渊 W7
渗 W10
9 滑 W8
溃 W11
滞 W9
湿 W9 W12
溅 W13
湾 W13
10 漠 W10
满 W10
滤 W13
滥 W12
滚 W9
滨 W12
滩 W11 W13
12 澜 W13
潜 W11
濒 W13

WIND 风
飘 W15

WINE JUG 酉
酱 W17
酿 W17
酽 W17

WINGS 羽
翘 W18
翻 S16

WOMAN 女
奶 -W19 W23
妆 W19
奸 W21
妇 W21
妈 W22
妞 W19
6 娈 W23
姜 G20
娇 W23
娴 W23
娱 W21
娘 W23
宴 W31

婴 W23
婶 W23
媪 W22
10 嫔 W23
髅 B16

WORDS 言 讠
讥 W30
认 W27
让 W31
议 W31
4 讽 W28
论 W28
讴 W30
讳 W28
讲 W29
5 识 W30
证 W25
译 W31
诌 W30
诉 H29
誉 W30
挣 W27
6 誉 W31
误 W27

[8]诺	W29		
读	W31		
谎	W29		
谗	W31		
[10]谣	W30		
谟	W30		
说	W31		
谥	W29 W29		
[13]谳	W31		
谶	W31		

WRAP 勹

勺	T7
匀	W32
匆	H24

2

几	S26 T4
儿	L3
卜	G19
了	E14
厂	C10 S10

3

与	M15
亏	T5
才	S17
卫	G2
万	G18
个	B3 M7
乡	C8
习	W18
飞	F17
于	S21
勺	T7
么	H32 T4
丬	S20

4

韦	L2
专	B7
乌	F5
书	S19
厄	M15
队	M17
丑	W16
升	M16 S30
丰	B7
为	C9
开	D8
无	F5 N3
区	B19
冈	M18
匀	W32
冗	D11
仓	M8
凶	L3
币	C11

5	
龙	D11
兰	G22
外	E11
戋	H3
业	T14
专	B7 I7
卢	D4
击	H16
写	D14
卉	G13 T3
归	S27
处	T5
匆	H24
对	I7
头	H21
尔	I12
东	T9
乐	T16
刍	G13
礼	R6

6	
师	C11
亚	T19
毕	F3
朱	S23
齐	E11
当	F3
戏	H4
阵	M16
阳	M17
阴	M17
阶	M17
夹	C13
华	G16
协	T4
产	G22
网	S14
伞	S16
尧	E5
异	F2
巩	R3
考	T1
壮	S2
寻	I7
导	I7
夹	B9

乔	M27
曲	W14
岁	S26
孙	C7
妆	W19
杀	S29
观	S3
爷	F1
欢	B20 H32 H35
争	C9
农	P2

7	
卤	S1 W10
周	P6
谷	G12 V1
里	C13 V2
乱	B8
严	M31
两	E10 O3
壳	S29
邻	C8
陈	M16
陆	M16
际	M17

邮 C8
弃 T13
声 E2
寿 S2
彻 F27
系 M6
张 B18
来 M5
状 D5
医 W17
穷 C5
麦 W14

8
氓 C8 F2
庞 D11
畅 S32
单 C15 M28
赵 R10
周 P6
凭 H30 H33 I2
凯 S26
卷 H10
郑 C8
郁 W17
参 C16

幸 M7
帘 B5
征 F27
径 F26 M7
弥 B19
张 B18
学 C7
枣 T13
殁 D4
瓯 T5
觅 S3
视 S3
规 S3
败 T2
斩 A2
肴 F19
欧 B20
殴 S29
隶 S3
肃 S29
罗 M32 N2
卧 M13
虏 T5
丧 M28

9
临 M13
剃 G21
赵 R10
毗 C16
毙 T3
战 H3
咸 S1
殒 D5
险 M18
陨 M17
将 I7
类 H21
须 H2
复 C14 F26
弯 B19
姜 G20
亲 S3
残 D5
览 S3
觉 S3
牵 O4
毡 H1
钦 B20
畅 S32

罚 N2	监 D3	敛 T2
竖 B7 S22	盏 D3	教 T2
窃 C6	盐 D4 S1	敢 T2
养 F18	竟 S22	祸 R6
	皱 S18	祷 R6
10	舰 B15	断 A2
窍 C6	舱 B15	望 M14
毙 T3	羞 S4	欲 H30
圈 W8	艳 B7 B7 C16	旋 G8 S21
窎 C6	赶 R10	盗 D3
冤 D13	冢 E5	盖 D4 G19
斋 E11	难 B14	盘 D4
顾 H22		矫 A1
离 B14	**11**	莺 B12
壶 S2	衔 G4 M27	窍 C6
徕 F26	着 E13 G17	窑 C5
爱 H28	龛 D11	颈 H21
瓶 E7	彩 S14	虚 T5
牺 O4	随 M18	崒 W17
效 M10 T1	隐 M18	麸 W14
敌 T2	猪 P3	野 E4 V2
致 S15	梦 E11	躯 B16
殷 H29	够 E11	衔 G4 M27
祯 R6	弹 B19	
龛 D11	殓 D5	
罢 N2	戚 H30	

12

觞	H33
御	R6
强	B18 B19
殖	D4
觍	S3
犊	O4
掰	H16
数	T2
牍	S20
雇	M11
禅	R6
禄	R6
凿	G9
窜	C6
窝	C5
颊	H21
翘	W18
释	F25
象	M11
雳	R2
鼋	T19
辉	F6
趋	R10

13

鼓	D11
蓝	G21
触	H33
觞	H33
辟	D9
韫	L2
毂	C3
毁	F8 W30
禀	G11
置	D13
窥	C6
窦	C6
颖	G12
酱	W17
躲	B16
辞	O1
雾	R2
龃	T3
雏	B13
虞	T5
韵	S19
	F1

14

韬	B18 L2
鞑	R4
殡	D5
觐	S3
罂	E7
酿	W17
酽	W17
静	G22
霁	R2
骷	B16

15

觑	S3
飘	W15
踶	T3
鞘	L2 R3

16

氅	B12
耨	G7
颠	H22
颥	H22
辩	O1
雕	B11 L4
魇	G2

17 羴 S17 羈 N2 齷 T3		
18 雠 W31 翻 S16 髏 B16		
19 孽 C7		
20 耀 F8 鬖 H2		
21		
22		
23 顴 H22 罐 G9 鬢 H2 趲 R10		

About the Book

The idea to write an alphabetized Chinese Dictionary came when the author was working on his book *Understanding Chinese Characters by their Ancestral Forms*. He thought that it would not be difficult for anyone to remember the names of the basic Chinese characters once their ancestral forms are known.

A Chinese character consist of writing-units. One unit indicates which Group of Characters the character belongs. This unit is called the 'Radical' (*radix* = root). *Chinese characters can be alphabetically grouped under the English Names of their Radicals. By knowing the Radical Name, one can locate the Group to which the character belongs and so arrive at its meaning(s).*

In addition to an **Alphabetized Dictionary**, a **"Rapid-Access Index"** can be compiled in which the characters are alphabetically arranged by the name of the Radical and the name of another writing-unit. This has been done in this book for the large Groups of over 100 characters.

It is the author's hope that this book will give meanings to those beautiful Chinese characters that are seen more and more in our world.

A

About the Author

Ping-gam Go is a resident of San Francisco. His ancestors came from the Fukien province in China. He attended the University of Amsterdam, where he received the B.Sc. degree in Physics and Mathematics. Later in Leyden University, Holland, he received the M.Sc. degree in Geology. He did postgraduate work at the Imperial College of Science & Technology in London.

After working for the Indonesian Geological Survey, he returned to Amsterdam, where he worked for the Elsevier Publishing Company as science editor. Elsevier at that time undertook the assembling and translating of all Nobel Prize Lectures from the beginning (1901) on, which were held in different languages. For coediting the project and for his contributions to its translations, he received a letter of recognition from the Nobel Foundation in Sweden.

His other books are *Read Chinese Today* and *Understanding Chinese Characters by their Ancestral Forms.*

An Easy-Access Dictionary of 5,000 Chinese Characters

Having carefully read the previous pages and having done all the Quizes, the following 5,000 Chinese characters will no longer appear mysterious and puzzling to you.

After the Chinese invented the writing-brush, writing became easier and faster and soon the old stylus-writing system was abandoned. The brush, however, could not make the same drawings that the stylus could make. **Except for a thousand or more "pictograms"** (characters which originally consisted of pictures and symbols by which their meanings can be explained), **Chinese characters are "phonograms". They consist of two existing drawings: one gives the general idea of the meaning (the "Radical"), the other gives the pronunciation of the character.**

In this Dictionary the characters are grouped under the English Names of their Radicals. In the Groups the characters are arranged by the number of their strokes. By knowing the English Name of the Radical, the Group to which the character belongs can be found. By knowing the number of its strokes, the character with its meaning(s) can be located. **There are two situations, however, whereby you don't have to count the number of strokes:**

(1) **the Group is very small and you can find the character just by looking for it.** Especially when it is very simple or very complicated, enabling you to confine your search to the very beginning or the very end of the Group.

There are 214 Radicals and therefore 214 Groups. **Most of the Groups, namely 160, contain less than 20 characters:**
- 32 contain between 20 and 11 characters;
- 41 contain between 10 and 6 characters; and
- 87 contain 5 and less characters!

---

(2) **the Group is very large, containing more than 100 characters. For these Groups you can use the "Rapid-Access Index"** (pages 60 to 65 and Ra 1 to Ra 46). **By naming the Radical and another writing-unit, you can locate the character without having to know its stroke number.**

These 11 very large Groups, containing 1,963 characters or 39% of the Dictionary, are: **HAND** (264 characters); **WATER** (222 characters); **MOUTH** (221 characters); **TREE** (210 characters); **MAN** (207 characters); **HEART** (177 characters); **GRASS** (168 characters); **WORDS** (143 characters); **SILK** (126 characters); **GOLD** (123 characters); **FLESH** (102 characters).

A question that is frequently asked is: *"How many characters do the Chinese people really know?"* The total number of characters known are over 50,000, however only 5,000 to 8,000 are in common use and of these merely 3,000 are used for everyday purposes.*

This does not mean that the common Chinese Vocabulary consists of 8,000 words only. **All Chinese characters are pronounced with one syllable. For clarity of speech, most Chinese words are two- or three-syllables words and are therefore combinations of two or three characters. In order to understand Chinese text, you will need to consult a larger Dictionary which gives you the meanings of these character combinations. This Dictionary gives the meanings of the character and also the Pinyin notation (Mandarin pronunciation) of the character. Modern Chinese dictionaries are alphabetically arranged according to their Mandarin pronunciations (Pinyin notations).** (See also page v *(Foreword)* and page 2 *(illustration)*. An excellent modern Chinese-English Dictionary is *A Chinese-English Dictionary*, Beijing Foreign Language Institute, latest edition 1990.

Here are some important Notes on the Dictionary itself:

> Accent for the First Tone (the horizontal bar) is missing in this Dictionary, because such accent is missing on our keyboard.
> Characters for Family Names are left out if they do not have any meaning. (As a rule, Family Names have no meaning other than to serve as an 'emblem' identifying a family.)
> Meanings preceded by an asterisk (*) refer to the Simplified Form of that character only.
> A phrase between parentheses is only given as an example of use of that particular character; it is not unconditionally connected with that character.
> The notation (N) means that that particular character can serve as a "numerator" (as in "a piece of cake", where "piece" is a "numerator").

---

* "The total number of Chinese characters is estimated at more than 50,000 of which only 5,000–8,000 are in common use. Of these merely 3,000 are used for everyday purposes." (*Practical Chinese Reader*, The Commercial Press, Beijing, 1985). See also Footnote on page 3.

NOTE: It should be mentioned that 8,000 characters would include characters for Family Names (more used as 'family emblems' with no meanings) and charracters representing scientific terms.

A

ARROW 矢

Picture of an arrow .

1. 矢 **Shih³ (shî)** - Arrow; vow, swear (– to tell the truth).

2. 矣² **Yî³ (yî)** - Final particle (used in classical literature).

3. 知³ **Chih¹ (zhi)** - Know, be aware of.

4. 矩⁵ **Chü³ (jû)** - Carpenter's square; rule, law, pattern.

5. 短⁷ **Tuan³ (duân)** - Short, brief; shortcoming (**duânchu**).

6. 矬 **Ts'o² (cuó)** - Short (– woman).

7. 矮⁸ **Ai³ (aî)** - Short in stature (a – man); low in rank (– grade).

8. 矫 矯¹² **Chiao³ (jiâo)** - Correct, straighten out; strong (– and brave).

9. 矰 Tseng[1] (zeng) - Arrow for crossbow.

AXE 斤

Representing an axe ⁀ and ⊂ (a chip of wood): ⻌ .

1. 斤 Chin[1] (jin) - Axe, hatchet; catty (unit of weight: 1.33 lbs.).

2. 斥 [1] Ch'ih[4] (chì) - Scold; expel, exclude; expand (– trade).

3. 斧 [4] Fu[3] (fǔ) - Axe, hatchet.

斩 4. 斬 [7] Chan[3] (zhân) - Chop, cut in two; decapitate, behead.

5. 斯 [8] Szu[1] (si) - This, that.

6. 新 [9] Hsin[1] (xin) - New, fresh, recent.

断 7. 斷 [14] Tuan[4] (duàn) - Break, cut off; decide, judge; absolutely.

B

BACK TO BACK 非

Two identical objects placed opposite each other 非 .

1. 非 **Fei[1] (fei)** - Not; wrong; short for Africa.

2. 靠 **K'ao[4] (kào)** - Lean against (– a tree); depend on, rely on.

3. 靡 **Mi[2] (mî)** - Extravagant. **Mi[3] (mî)** - windblown; no, not.

BAMBOO 竹 竺

Picture of bamboo trees with drooping leaves 竹 .

1. 竹 **Chu[2] (zhú)** - Bamboo.

2. 竿 **Kan[1] (gan)** - Pole, rod, cane.

3. 竽 **Yü[2] (yú)** - Ancient reed organ.

4. 笊 [4] **Chao⁴ (zhào)** - Bamboo ladle or strainer; bamboo wicker.

5. 笆 **Pa¹ (ba)** - Basketry; bamboo fence.

6. 笑 **Hsiao⁴ (xiào)** - Laugh, smile; laugh at, ridicule.

7. 笋 **Sun³ (sûn)** - Bamboo shoots; bamboo sprouts.

8. 笞 [5] **Ch'ih¹ (chi)** - Beat (w. bamboo stick, cane, etc.), flog.

9. 笥 **Szu⁴ (sì)** - Bamboo-plaited basket or suitcase.

10. 符 **Fu² (fú)** - Tally; tally/coincide with; amulet, talisman.

11. 笨 **Pen⁴ (bèn)** - Stupid, foolish; awkward, clumsy.

12. 筥 **P'o³ (pô)** - Shallow basket.

13. 笙 **Sheng¹ (sheng)** - Chinese reed pipe.

14. 第 **Ti⁴ (dì)** - Series, sequence; rank, order; residence, mansion.

15. 笠 **Li⁴ (lì)** - Large bamboo or straw sunhat w. broad rim.

16. 笤 **T'iao² (tiáo)** - Small broom w. handle (clothes brush).

17. 笛 **Ti² (dí)** - Bamboo flute; whistle (steam −).

18. 笄 **Chi¹ (ji)** - Hairpin; marriageable.

19. 筋 [6] **Chin¹ (jin)** - Muscle, sinew, tendon.

20. 筏 **Fa² (fã)** - Bamboo raft; pontoon.

21. 筐 **K'uang¹ (kuang)** - Basket.

22. 筆 筆 **Pi³ (bî)** - Pen, pencil; write, compose.

笋 23. 筍 **Sun³ (sûn)** - Bamboo shoot, bamboo sprout.

24. 答 **Ta² (dá)** - Reply, answer; reciprocate, return (– a visit).

25. 等 **Teng³ (dêng)** - Class, grade; equal; await; et cetera (etc.).

26. 筒 **T'ung³ (tông)** - Pipe, tube; tube-shaped object.

27. 策 **Ts'e⁴ (cè)** - Plan, scheme, strategy; whip (– a horse).

28. 箸 ⁷ **Chu⁴ (zhù)** - Chopsticks.

29. 筠 **Yün² (yún)** - Bamboo skin; bamboo splint.

30. 筷 **K'uai⁴ (kuài)** - Chopsticks.

31. 筲 **Shao¹ (shao)** - Bamboo pail; bucket.

32. 筮 **Shih⁴ (shì)** - Divine (tell fortune) using bamboo slips.

33. 算 **Suan⁴ (suàn)** - Calculate, compute; plan.

34. 筵 **Yen² (yán)** - Bamboo mat; banquet, feast (wedding –).

筝 35. 筝 ⁸ **Cheng¹ (zheng)** - Stringed instrument, like a cither; kite.

36. 箕 **Chi¹ (ji)** - Winnowing basket; dustpan.

个 37. 箇 **Ke⁴ (gè)** - Numerator (N), same as 個 ; individual.

38. 箍 **Ku¹ (gu)** - Belt, band; bind around (– package w. string).

39. 管 **Kuan³ (guân)** - Tube, pipe; manage, run (– a business).

40. 箔 **Po⁴ (bò)** - Bamboo screen; foil (gold –).

笺 42. 41. 算 **Suan⁴ (suàn)** - Calculate, compute; plan (– a trip).

42. 箋 **Chien¹ (jian)** - Writing paper; letter; notes, annotations.

43. 箴 **Chen¹ (zhen)** - Needle; admonish, give advice.

44. 箸 ⁹ **Chu⁴ (zhù)** - Chopsticks.

45. 篆 **Chuan⁴ (zhuàn)** - Ancestral form of a character.

范 46. 範 **Fan⁴ (fàn)** - Pattern, model, standard.

节 47. 節 **Chieh² (jíe)** - Joint; section; festival; economize.

箧 48. 篋 **Ch'ieh⁴ (qiè)** - Trunk (– travelling), small suitcase.

49. 箬 **Jo⁴ (ruò)** - Broad leaf bamboo; bamboo sheath.

50. 篇 **P'ien¹ (pian)** - Sheet (– of paper); piece of writing.

51. 箱 **Hsiang¹ (xiang)** - Box, chest, trunk.

52. 箭 **Chien⁴ (jiàn)** - Arrow.

筑 53. 築 ¹⁰ **Chu⁴ (zhù)** - Build (– a dike); construct (– a road).

54. 篡 **Ts'uan⁴ (cuàn)** - Usurp, seize (– power); rebel.

55. 篙 **Kao¹ (gao)** - Bamboo pole; punt pole.

56. 篦 **Pi⁴ (bì)** - Double-edged fine-toothed comb; comb (v).

筛 57. 篩 **Shai¹ (shai)** - Sieve, sift (– rice), screen (–ashes from coal).

笃 58. 篤 **Tu³ (dû)** - Sincere, true, genuine; serious (– illness).

59. 邃 Ti² (dí) - Flute, fife; whistle (steam –).

篓 60. 簍 ¹¹ Lou³ (lôu) -Basket, hamper.

61. 簏 Lu⁴ (lù) - Basket.

62. 篾 Mieh⁴ (miè) - Bamboo strips.

63. 簇 Ts'u⁴ (cù) - Cluster, crowd (v); bunch (– of grapes).

64. 篷 P'eng² (péng) - Covering (on car, boat); awning; sail.

65. 簧 ¹² Huang² (huáng) - Reed (– organ); spring (of a clock).

简 66. 簡 Chien³ (jiān) - Bamboo slip; letter, note; simple, brief.

萧 67. 簫 Hsiao¹ (xiao) - Vertical bamboo flute.

68. 簪 Tsan¹ (zan) - Flat hairpin, clasp; wear in one's hair.

帘 69. 簾 ¹³ Lien² (lián) - Blinds (bamboo –); curtain, screen.

70. 簸 Po³ (bô) - Winnowing fan; winnow (– grain).

71. 簿 Pu⁴ (bù) - Account book, note book; register.

签 72. 簽 Ch'ien¹ (qian) - Bamboo slip; label, sticker; sign(v).

檐 73. 簷 Yen² (yán) - Eaves of a house; ledge; brim (of a hat).

筹 74. 籌 ¹⁴ Ch'ou² (chóu) - Calculate; prepare, plan; chip, counter, token.

篮 75. 籃 Lan² (lán) - Basket (–ball game).

76. 籍 Chi² (jí) - Record, register; birthplace; membership.

藤 77. 籐 [15] **T'eng²** (téng) - Rattan, cane; vine, creeping plant.

笼 78. 籠 [16] **Lung²** (lóng) - Bamboo steamer. **Lung³** (lông) - Cover (v).

籁 79. 籟 **Lai⁴** (lài) - Reed instrument; creaking, moaning sound.

签 80. 籤 [17] **Ch'ien¹** (qian) - Same as 72.

篱 81. 籬 [19] **Li²** (lí) - Bamboo fence; hedge.

箩 82. 籮 **Lo²** (luó) - Square-bottomed bamboo basket.

吁 83. 籲 [26] **Yü⁴** (yù) - Invoke, implore; appeal, plead.

BASKET 匚

Picture of a basket ⋃ , turned aside 匚 .

1. 匡 [4] **K'uang¹** (kuang) - Correct, reform; assist, help

2. 匠 **Chiang⁴** (jiàng) - Craftsman, artisan; mechanic.

3. 匣 [5] **Hsia²** (xía) - Small box, case; casket.

4. 匪 [8] **Fei³** (fèi) - Bandit, robber; not (– far off).

汇 5. 匯 [11] **Hui⁴** (huì) - Converge; collect(ion); remit (– money).

柜 6. 匱 [12] **Kuei⁴** (guì) - Cupboard, cabinet, wardrobe.

BEAN 豆

A simple meal of beans • on a stemmed platter: 🖔 *.*

1. 豆 **Tou⁴** (dòu) - Beans, peas; ancient stemmed vessel.

岂 2. 豈 [3] Ch'i[3] (qǐ) - How?; Isn't it?; etc.

3. 豉 [4] Chih[1] (zhī) - Salted and dried oysters, beans, olives, etc.

4. 豊 [6] Li[3] (lǐ) - Sacrificial vessel.

5. 登 Teng[1] (dēng) - Ascend, climb; enter (– in diary); publish.

竖 6. 竪 [8] Shu[4] (shù) - Vertical, perpendicular; upright; set upright.

7. 豌 Wan[1] (wān) - Garden pea.

丰 8. 豐 [11] Feng[1] (fēng) - Abundant; graceful; fine-looking.

艳 9. 艷 [17] Yen[4] (yàn) - Gorgeous, colorful; gaudy; amorous.

艳 10. 豓 [21] Yen[4] (yàn) - Beautiful, fascinating; seductive.

BEARD 而

What hangs down from the chin: 帀.

1. 而 Erh[2] (ér) - Beard; conjunctive (and, but, yet, etc.).

2. 耐 Nai[4] (nài) - Bear, endure.

3. 耍 Shua[3] (shuâ) - Play; play (tricks); flourish (– a sword).

专 4. 耑 Chuan[1] (zhuān) - Special (– program); monopolize.

5. 端 Tuan[1] (duān) - End (this –); item; cause; proper; carry.

BENT 乙 . ㄴ

The bent shape of a germ ㇄ .

1. 乙 Yi[3] (yǐ) - Second (2nd) (– grade).

2. 九^{1} **Chiu^3 (jîu)** - Nine; many (bridge w. – turns).

3. 乜 **Mieh^1 (mie)** - Squint; half-closed (– eyes).

4. 乞^{2} **Ch'i^3 (qî)** - Beg, ask for.

5. 也 **Yeh^3 (yê)** - Also, too, as well as; either.

6. 乩^{5} **Chi^1 (ji)** - To divine using a willow stick or a planchette.

7. 乳^{7} **Ju^3 (rû)** - Breasts; milk; newborn, suckling (– pig); squab, fledgling pigeon (**rûge**).

干 8. 乾^{10} **Kan^1 (gan)** - Dry, dried (– food); empty; exhausted. * Interfere; oppose. **Kan^4 (gàn)** - Trunk; do, work; able.

乱 9. 亂^{12} **Luan^4 (luàn)** - Confusion, disorder; confused; rebellion.

BIG 大. 

A man with outstretched arms as if showing the size of a large object .

1. 大 **Ta^4 (dà)** - Big, great; heavy (– rain); main (– course).

2. 夫^{1} **Fu^1 (fu)** - Husband; man (– and wife); laborer, coolie.

3. 夬 **Chüeh^2 (jué)** - Fork (v); past; settled; differing.

4. 太 **T'ai^4 (tài)** - Too (– much); very, extremely (- happy).

5. 天 **T'ien^1 (tian)** - Heaven, sky; day; weather; season.

6. 夭 **Yao^1 (yao)** - Die yong; tender, young (– and beautiful).

7. 夯^{2} **Hang^1 (hang)** - Pile driver, earth pounder.

8. 失 Shih[1] (shi) - Lose, miss (– the train); mistake.

9. 央 Yang[1] (yang) - Center; beg, entreat; finish, conclude.

10. 夷[3] Yi[2] (yí) - Barbarians; level (to the ground), exterminate.

夹 11. 夾[4] Chia[1] (jia) - Squeeze; clip; mingle. Chia[2] (jiá) - Lined.

12. 奉[5] Feng[4] (fèng) - Offer w. respect; receive; serve (– master).

13. 奇 Ch'i[2] (qí) - Strange, rare; surprise (– visit); extraordinary.

14. 奈 Nai[4] (nài) - How (– to handle it); do sth. to a person.

15. 奄 Yen[3] (yân) - Cover; suddenly.

16. 契[6] Ch'i[4] (qì) - Contract, deed, bond, agreement.

17. 奎 K'uei[2] (kúi) - Used as phonetic (e.g. kuíníng: 'quinine').

18. 奔 Pen[1] (ben) - Run away; hurry, rush; flee (– for freedom).

19. 奏 Tsou[4] (zòu) - Play (music); perform (at concert); achieve.

20. 奕 Yi[4] (yì) - In full spirit; great and lasting (– dynasty).

21. 奘[7] Chuang[3] (zhuâng) - Big and thick, stout.

22. 奚 Hsi[1] (xi) - How? why? what? where?

23. 套 T'ao[4] (tào) - Cover(ing), case; harness (– a horse).

24. 奢[9] She[1] (she) - Luxurious, lavish; excessive (– drinking).

25. 奠 Tien[4] (diàn) - Establish, settle; make offerings to the dead.

2ს. 奥 Ao[4] (aò) - Profound (- meaning); difficult to understand.

夺 27. 奪[11] To² (duó) - Take by force, seize; force one's way.

奖 28. 奬 Chiang³ (jiâng) - Encourage; praise, reward; prize, award.

奁 29. 奩 Lien² (lián) - Trousseau, a woman's dressing case.

奋 30. 奮[13] Fen⁴ (fèn) - Act vigorously, rouse, excite; raise, lift.

BIRD (1) (long-tail) 鳥

Picture of a bird 鳥.

鸟 1. 鳥 Niao³ (niâo) - Bird.

鸠 2. 鳩[2] Chiu¹ (jiu) - Turtledove, pigeon.

凤 3. 鳳[3] Feng⁴ (fèng) - Phoenix (fènghuáng).

鸣 4. 鳴 Ming² (míng) - Cry of birds, insects, etc.; sound (v).

鸢 5. 鳶 Yüan¹ (yuan) - Kite, hawk; kite (paper –).

鸩 6. 鴆[4] Chen⁴ (zhèn) - Bird w. poisonous feathers; poison (v).

鸦 7. 鴉 Ya¹ (ya) - Crow (wuya) (lâogua[18]).

鸱 8. 鴟[5] Ch'ih¹ (chi) - Owl (chixiu).

鸮 9. 鴞 Hsiao¹ (xiao) - Owl (xiaoyôu).

鸰 10. 鴒 Ling² (líng) - Wagtail (jílíng).

鸭 11. 鴨 Ya¹ (ya) - Duck.

鸯 12. 鴦 Yang¹ (yang) - Mandarin duck (yuan[14]yang).

鸪 13. 鴣 **Ku¹ (gū)** - Partridge (**zhè³⁵gu**).

鸳 14. 鴛 **Yüan¹ (yuan)** - Mandarin duck (**yuanyang¹²**); couple.

鸿 15. 鴻⁶ **Hung² (hóng)** - Swan goose (**hóngyàn**); great, grand.

16. 雋 **Jen⁴ (rèn). Chen¹ (zhen)** - Feather; headdress.

鸽 17. 鴿 **Ke¹ (ge)** - Dove, pigeon (**bóge**).

鸹 18. 鴰 **Kua¹ (gua)** - Crow (**lâogua**) (**wuya⁷**).

鹅 19. 鵝⁷ **O² (é)** - Goose.

鹈 20. 鵜 **T'i² (tí)** - Pelican (**tíhú²⁸**).

鹄 21. 鵠 **Hu² (hú)** - Swan. **Ku³ (gû)** - Target (in archery, shooting).

鹉 22. 鵡 **Wu³ (wû)** - Parrot (**ying⁴³wû**) (**yingge**).

鹌 23. 鵪⁸ **An¹ (an)** - Quail (**anchún²⁵**).

鹏 24. 鵬 **P'eng² (péng)** - Roc (monstrous legendary bird).

鹑 25. 鶉 **Ch'un² (chún)** - Quail (**an²³chún**).

雕 26. 鵰 **Tiao¹ (diao)** - Vulture; carve, engrave.

鹊 27. 鵲 **Ch'üeh⁴ (què)** - Magpie.

鹕 28. 鶘⁹ **Hu² (hú)** - Pelican (**tí²⁰hú**).

鹤 29. 鶴¹⁰ **Ho⁴ (hè)** - Crane; longevity.

鸰 30. 鶵 **Ch'u² (chú)** - Nestling, fledgling, young (– bird).

鸡 31. 鷄 Chi[1] (jī) - Chicken.

鷀 32. 鷀 Tz'u[2] (cí) - Cormorant (lúcí).

33. 鷻 Shun[3] (shûn) - Kestrel (small falcon).

莺 34. 鶯 Ying[1] (yīng) - Warbler, oriole, yellow bird.

鷓 35. 鷓 [11] Che[4] (zhè) - Partridge (zhègu[13]).

鸷 36. 鷙 Chih[4] (zhì) - Hawk; bird of prey; ferocious, violent.

鸥 37. 鷗 Ou[1] (ou) - Gull (sea–).

氅 38. 氅 Ch'ang[3] (chǎng) - Down of crane, etc.; cloak.

鹇 39. 鷼 Hsien[2] (xián) - Silver pheasant (báixián).

鸶 40. 鷥 [12] Szu[1] (si) - Egret, snowy heron (lú[42]si).

鹰 41. 鷹 [13] Ying[1] (yīng) - Hawk, eagle, falcon.

鹭 42. 鷺 Lu[4] (lù) - Egret, snowy heron, paddy bird (lùsi[40]).

鹦 43. 鸚 [17] Ying[1] (yīng) - Parrot, cockatoo (yingge) (yingwu[22]).

鹳 44. 鸛 [18] Kuan[4] (guàn) - Stork, heron, crane.

鹂 45. 鸝 [19] Li[2] (lí) - Oriole, mango bird, yellow bird (huánglí).

鸾 46. 鸞 Luan[2] (luán) - Mythical bird, similar to phoenix.

BIRD (2) (short-tail) 隹

Picture of a short-tailed bird 隺 .

1. 隹 **Chui¹ (zhui)** - Short-tailed bird; single, one only; (N).

只 2. 隻² **Chih¹ (zhi)** - Single, one only; (N).

3. 隼 **Sun³ (sûn)** - Kestrel, falcon.

4. 雀³ **Ch'üeh⁴ (què)** - Sparrow.

5. 雄⁴ **Hsiung² (xióng)** - Male (of birds, etc.); powerful; grand.

6. 雇 **Ku⁴ (gù)** - Hire, employ (labor), rent (car, boat).

7. 集 **Chi² (jí)** - Gather, collect; fair, market; volume, part.

8. 雅 **Ya³ (yâ)** - Correct; refined; section.

9. 雁 **Yen⁴ (yàn)** - Wild goose.

10. 雉⁵ **Chih⁴ (zhì)** - Pheasant.

11. 雌 **Tz'u² (cí)** - Female (of animals or plants).

12. 雍 **Yung¹ (yong)** - Wagtail; harmony.

13. 雕⁸ **Tiao¹ (diao)** - Vulture; carve, engrave.

虽 14. 雖⁹ **Sui¹ (sui)** - Although, though; even if.

雏 15. 雛¹⁰ **Ch'u² (chú)** - Young (bird), squab (fledgling pigeon)

鸡 16. 雞 **Chi¹ (ji)** - Chicken.

双 17. 雙 **Shuang¹ (shuang)** - Pair, double; twin; even (number).

杂 18. 雜 Tsa² (zá) - Mixed, assorted, miscellaneous.; mix, mingle.

离 19. 離[11] Li² (lí) - Leave; be away from; be without (– food).

难 20. 難 Nan²(nán) - Difficult; bad. **Nan⁴ (nàn)** - Disaster.

BLACK 黑

Soot ⋋ deposited by a smoky fire 炎 around a vent ⊕ – 熏 .

1. 黑 **Hei¹ (hei)** - Black; dark; sinister; secret (– society).

2. 黔[4] **Ch'ien² (qián)** - Black; Kweichou (Guizhou) province.

3. 默 **Mo⁴ (mò)** - Silent; write from memory.

4. 黜[5] **Ch'u⁴ (chù)** - Dismiss, remove, expel (– from school).

5. 黛 **Tai⁴ (dài)** - Umber (dark pigment for painting eyebrows).

点 6. 點 **Tien³ (diān)** - Speck, spot, point (boiling –); o'clock.

7. 黧[8] **Li² (lí)** - Dark (– complexion).

党 8. 黨 **Tang³ (dǎng)** - Party (political –), clique, gang; kinsfolk.

BLOOD 血

A stemmed vessel 皿 containing blood – : 血 .

1. 血 **Hsüeh⁴ (xuè)** - Blood.

众 2. 衆[6] **Chung⁴ (zhòng)** - A crowd, multitude; many, numerous.

蔑 3. 衊[15] **Mieh⁴(miè)** - Disdain; smear; none.

BOAT 舟

A hollowed tree trunk 舟, representing a boat.

1. 舟 **Chou[1] (zhou)** - Boat, vessel.

2. 舡 [3] **Ch'uan[2] (chuán)** - Same as 5.

3. 航 [4] **Hang[2] (háng)** - Navigation, navigate (boat or plane).

4. 般 **Pan[1] (ban)** - Manner, way; kind, sort, class.

5. 船 [5] **Ch'uan[2] (chuán)** - Boat, ship, vessel.

6. 舶 **Po[2] (bó)** - Seaworthy ship.

7. 舵 **To[4] (duò)** - Helm, rudder.

8. 艇 [7] **T'ing[3] (tîng)** - Light boat, barge, canoe, punt.

9. 艑 **Pien[1] (pian)** - Small boat, skiff.

10. 艘 [10] **Sou[1] (sou)** - (N) for ships.

舱 11. 艙 **Ts'ang[1] (cang)** - Cabin, hold (of ship/plane); module.

舰 12. 艦 [14] **Chien[4] (jiàn)** - Naval vessel, warship, battleship.

BODY 身

A person, shown with a conspicuous abdomen 身 .

1. 身 **Shen[1] (shen)** - Body, person; trunk; life (–'s experience).

2. 躬 [3] **Kung[1] (gong)** - Personally (be there –); bend, bow.

3. 眈 ⁴ **Tan¹ (dan)** - Delay; indulge in.

躲 4. 躱 ⁶ **To³ (duô)** - Hide, conceal; dodge, avoid, shun.

5. 躺 ⁸ **T'ang³ (tâng)** - Lie down, recline.

躯 6. 軀 ¹¹ **Ch'ü¹ (qu)** - The human body.

BONES 骨

Picture of a human skeleton 🦴 .

1. 骨 **Ku³ (gû)** - Bone; skeleton; rib, frame (of umbrella).

肮 2. 骯 ⁴ **Ang¹ (ang)** - Filthy, dirty.

3. 骰 **T'ou² (tóu)** - Dice.

4. 骸 ⁶ **Hai² (hái)** - Bones; skeleton.

髅 5. 髏 ¹¹ **Lou² (lóu)** - Human skull (death's head) **(dúlóu) (kulóu)**; human skeleton **(kulóu)** (see 8).

6. 髓 ¹³ **Sui³ (suî)** - Marrow (bone –), pith (– of a stem).

体 7. 體 **T'i³ (tî)** - Body; substance; style; system (political –). **T'i¹ (ti)** - Intimate; private savings **(tiji)**.

骷 8. 髑 **K'u¹ (ku)** - Human skeleton; human skull (death's head) **(kulóu)** (see 5).

脏 9. 髒 **Tsang¹ (zang)** - Dirty, filthy. **Tsang⁴ (zàng)** - Viscera.

BORDERS 冂

The boundaries of some portion of space 冂.

1. 册 Ts'e[4] (cè) - Book, register; volume, copy (one – missing).

2. 冉 Jan[3] (rân) - Slowly, gradually.

3. 再 Tsai[4] (zài) - Again; second (– edition); come back again.

4. 冑 Chou[4] (zhòu) - Helmet; offspring, descendants, posterity.

5. 冒 Mao[4] (mào) - Risk, brave (– the rain); falsify (– records).

6. 冓 Kou[4] (gòu) - Inner chamber; ten billion.

7. 冕 Mien[3] (miân) - Crown, coronet.

BOTH FEET 癶

Picture of both feet of a person or animal: 癶.

1. 癸 Kuei[3] (guǐ) - The Tenth Heavenly Stem (used in divination).

2. 登 Teng[1] (deng) - Ascend, go up; record, publish; step on.

发 3. 發 Fa[1] (fa) - Send out, issue; express; discharge; expand.

BOW 弓

Picture of a Chinese reflex bow 弓.

1. 弓 Kung[1] (gong) - Bow; arch; bend.

吊 2. 弔[1] Tiao[4] (diaò) - Hang; condole; mourn; withdraw; revoke.

3. 引 Yin[3] (yîn) - Lead, guide; stretch; attract; cause (– laughter).

4. 弗[2] Fu[2] (fú) - Not, neither, no.

5. 弘 Hung[2] (hóng) - Great, grand, magnificent; expand, enlarge.

6. 弛 Chih[2] (chí) - Release the arrow; relax; annul, abolish.

7. 弛[4] Pa[4] (bà) - Part of a bow grasped.

8. 弟 Ti[4] (dì) - Younger brother.

9. 弦[5] Hsien[2] (xián) - String (of bow/violin); spring (of watch).

10. 弩 Nu[3] (nû) - Crossbow.

韜 11. 弢 T'ao[1] (tao) - Sheath, case; hide; strategy (in war).

12. 弭[6] Mi[3] (mî) - Remove; check, stop, put down (– rebellion).

13. 弱[7] Jo[4] (ruò) - Weak, feeble; inferior; young (– and old).

14. 弰 Shao[4] (shao) - Release the arrow.

张 15. 張[8] Chang[1] (zhang) - Open (up); stretch; exaggerate; (N).

强 16. 強 Ch'iang[2] (qiáng) - Strong; violent. Ch'iang[3] (qîang) - make an effort. Chiang[4] (jiàng) - Stubborn; unyielding.

17. 弸 Peng[1] (beng) - A stiff bow; complete.

18. 強[9] Ch'iang[2] (qiáng) - Same as 16.

19. 彀[10] Kou[4] (gòu) - Bow drawn in full; full, sufficient, enough.

弹 20. 彈 [12] **T'an²(tán)** - Shoot; flick. **Tan⁴ (dàn)** - Pellet; bullet.

强 21. 彊 [13] **Ch'iang² (qiáng)** - Same as 16.

弥 22. 彌 [14] **Mi² (mí)** - Full, whole; fill (– a hole), make up (– for loss).

23. 疆 [16] **Chiang¹ (jiang)** - Boundary, border.

弯 24. 彎 [19] **Wan¹ (wan)** - Draw a bow; curved, arched, crooked, bent.

BOX ⊏

Picture of a box ⊔ turned sideways to allow other components to be written in ⊏ .

1. 匹 [2] **P'i³ (pî)** - Be a match for; be equal to; (N).

2. 匾 [9] **Pien³ (biân)** - Signboard; silk banner with inscriptions.

3. 匿 **Ni⁴ (nì)** - Hide, conceal; anonymous (– letter).

区 4. 區 **Ch'ü¹ (qu)** - Area, district, region; distinguish, classify.

BRANCH 支

Originally 支 : a hand ∋ pulling off a branch 个 from a tree.

1. 支 **Chih¹ (zhi)** - Branch (– office); erect (– a tent); (N).

2. 攲 [8] **Ch'i¹ (qi)** - Inclined, leaning, tilted.

BREATHE 欠

A man 人 breathing out air 彡 : 无 .

1. 欠 **Ch'ien⁴ (qiàn)** - Owe (– money); lacking, wanting.

2. 次 ² **Tz'u⁴ (cì)** - Order, sequence; second (– son); next (– day).

3. 欣 ⁴ **Hsin¹(xin)** - Glad, happy, joyful.

咳 4. 欬 ⁶ **K'e² (ké)** - Cough.*Hai¹ (hai) - Exclamation of regret, etc.

5. 軟 ⁷ **Shu⁴ (shù)** - Suck in, absorb (– moisture).

6. 欲 **Yü⁴ (yù)** - Longing (– for food); wish; about to (– rain).

7. 欻 ⁸ **Ch'ua¹ (chua)** - Sound imitation. **Hsü¹ (xu)** - Suddenly.

8. 欺 **Ch'i¹ (qi)** - Deceive, swindle, take advantage of; bully.

钦 9. 欽 **Ch'in¹ (qin)** - Admire, respect; imperial (by – decree).

10. 款 **K'uan³ (kuân)** - Sincere; entertain; funds; paragraph.

11. 歇 ⁹ **Hsieh¹ (xie)** - Stop (– for a rest); close (– one's business).

12. 歆 **Hsin¹ (xin)** - Taste; extol, praise highly; excite.

13. 歉 ¹⁰ **Ch'ien⁴ (qiàn)** - Apology (offer –); bad harvest.

14. 歌 **Ke¹ (ge)** - Song (– book); ballad; sing.

欧 15. 歐 ¹¹ **Ou¹ (ou)** - Short for Europe.

叹 16. 歎 ¹⁵ **T'an⁴ (tàn)** - Sigh; exclaim in admiration, praise.

欢 17. 歡 ¹⁸ **Huan¹ (huan)** - Cheerful, merry; vigorously.

C

CALDRON 鬲

Representing an ancient three-legged caldron.

1. 鬲 **Li[4] (lì)** - Ancient three-legged caldron.

2. 鬻 **Yü[4] (yù)** - Sell; rear. **Chou[1] (zhou)** - Rice porridge.

CART 車

A cart (seen from above), showing the body ⊕, axle | , and wheels 二 .

车 1. 車 **Ch'e[1] (che)** - Vehicle (motor –), carriage; lathe; machine.

轧 2. 軋[1] **Ya[4] (yà). Cha[2] (zhá)** - Roll, roling (steel –); run over, oust.

军 3. 軍[2] **Chün[2] (jun)** - Armed forces, army, troops; military.

轨 4. 軌 **Kuei³ (guî)** - Rail (–road); track, path, course.

轩 5. 軒³ **Hsüan¹ (xuan)** - Veranda, porch; ancient carriage; lofty.

轫 6. 軔 **Jen⁴ (rèn)** - Wooden brake; brake, block a wheel.

软 7. 軟⁴ **Juan³ (ruân)** - Soft, pliable; mild, gentle; weak, feeble.

轭 8. 軛 **E⁴ (è)** - Yoke; restraint.

轴 9. 軸⁵ **Chou² (zhóu)** - Axle, axis (earth's –), shaft; reel; (N).

轲 10. 軻 **K'e¹ (ke)** - Wheels with axle.

辈 11. 輩 **Pei⁴ (bèi)** - Generation; lifetime.

较 12. 較⁶ **Chiao⁴ (jiào)** - Compare, comparatively, rather (– easy).

载 13. 載 **Tsai³ (zâi)** - Year; record. **Tsai⁴ (zài)** - Carry (– people).

辄 14. 輒⁷ **Che² (zhé)** - Always, often; then, consequently.

辅 15. 輔 **Fu³ (fû)** - Assist, help; supplementary (– courses).

轻 16. 輕 **Ch'ing¹ (qing)** - Light (not heavy); minor (– injury).

挽 17. 輓 **Wan³ (wân)** - Pull, draw (– a carriage); lament sb's death.

辉 18. 輝 **Hui¹ (hui)** - Brightness, splendor; shine, illuminate.

辊 19. 輥⁸ **Kun³ (gûn)** - Roller (steam –).

辆 20. 輛 **Liang⁴ (liàng)** - (N) for vehicles.

辇 21. 輦 **Nien³ (niân)** - Imperial man-drawn carriage.

轮 22. 輪 **Lun² (lún)** - Wheel; disc; by turns; steamer (river –); (N).

辈 23. 輩 **Pei⁴ (bèi)** - People of certain kind; generation; lifetime.

辎 24. 輜 **Tzû¹ (zi)** - Ancient covered wagon; baggage wagon.

辐 25. 輻 ⁹ **Fu² (fú)** - Spokes of a wheel.

26. 輵 **Ke⁴,² (gè, gé)** - Turmoil; confusion.

辏 27. 輳 **Tsou⁴ (zòu)** - Hub; focus.

输 28. 輸 **Shu¹ (shu)** - Transport; donate (– blood); be defeated.

辑 29. 輯 **Chi⁴ (jì)** - Compile, put together.

辗 30. 輾 ¹⁰ **Chan³ (zhân)** - Through many hands/places; toss about.

辖 31. 轄 **Hsia² (xía)** - Linchpin of a wheel; govern, administer.

毂 32. 轂 **Ku³ (gû)** -Hub.

與 33. 輿 **Yü² (yú)** - Carriage, chariot; territory; public (– opinion).

辕 34. 轅 **Yüan² (yuán)** - Shaft; outer gate of an ancient govt. office.

转 35. 轉 ¹¹ **Chuan³ (zhuân)** - Turn. **Chuan⁴ (zhuàn)** - Revolve.

36. 轇 **Chiao⁴ (jiào)** - Confused, mixed, complicated.

辙 37. 轍 **Che² (zhé)** - Rut, track of a wheel; rhyme.

轿 38. 轎 **Chiao⁴ (jiào)** - Sedan chair.

39. 轕 ¹³ **Ke⁴,² (gè, gé)** - Hubbub, confusion.

轰 40. 轟 ¹⁴ **Hung¹ (hong)** - Bombard; bang, roll (– of thunder).

彎 41. 轡 [15]   P'ei⁴ (pèi) - Reins, bridle.

轳 42. 轤 [16]   Lu² (lú) - Pulley, windlass (lùlu); roller (steam –).

CAT 豸

Representing a cat-like animal 豸.

1. 豸   Chai⁴ (zhài) - Cat-like animal.

2. 豺 [3]   Ch'ai² (chái) - Jackal; wicked, cruel.

3. 豹   Pao⁴ (bào) - Leopard, panther.

4. 貂 [5]   Tiao¹ (diao) - Sable, marten.

5. 狸 [7]   Li² (lí) - Wild cat; racoon.

6. 貌   Mao⁴ (mào) - Looks (good –), appearance, face; view.

7. 貓 [9]   Mao¹ (mao) - Cat.

CAVE 穴 . 空

A cave ∩ *resulting from earth being taken away* 八 *(by the water):* 穴 .

1. 穴   Hsüeh² (xué) - Cave, hole, den; grave; acupuncture point.

2. 究 [2]   Chiu¹ (jiu) - Investigate; go to the bottom of the matter.

3. 穹 [3]   Ch'iung² (qióng) - Vault, dome; the sky.

4. 空 K'ung[1] (kong) - Empty; hollow; fruitless; the sky.

5. 穿[4] Ch'uan[1] (chuan) - Bore through; wear, put on (– shoes).

6. 突 T'u[1] (tu) - Rush out; suddenly; sticking out; chimney.

7. 窄[5] Chai[3] (zhâi) - Narrow; narrow-minded; badly off.

8. 窊 Wa[1] (wa) - Depression; low.

9. 窈 Yao[3] (yâo) - Gentle and graceful (of a woman); secluded.

10. 窒[6] Chih[4] (zhì) - Obstruct, block; stop up (– a hole).

11. 窕 T'iao[4] (tiâo) - Refined, elegant.

12. 窗[7] Ch'uang[1] (chuang) - Window.

13. 窖 Chiao[4] (jiào) - Cellar, pit (for storing); store (in pit, cellar).

14. 窘 Chiung[3] (jiông) - Awkward (– situation); embarrass; poor.

15. 窠[8] K'e[1] (ke) - Nest, burrow; pit (arm–).

16. 窟 K'u[1] (ku) - Cave; hole (in the ground); den (robber's –).

17. 窩 窝[9] Wo[1] (wo) - Nest; harbor (–refugees); hold in (– anger).

18. 窨 Yin[4] (yìn) - Basement, cellar.

19. 注 窪 Wa[1] (wa) - Hollow; depression, low-lying (– ground).

20. 穷 窮[10] Ch'iung[2] (qióng) - Poor; limit, end (–less); thoroughly.

21. 窑 窯 Yao[2] (yáo) - Kiln (pottery –), pit (coal –); cave dwelling.

22. 填 窴 T'ien[2] (tián) - Fill in (– form), stuff (– pillow).

窥 23. 窺 [11] **K'uei¹ (kui)** - Peep, spy.

窎 24. 窵 **Tiao⁴ (diào)** - Deep; distant; secluded (– corner).

25. 窿 [12] **Lung² (lóng)** - Hole (rat –), cavity.

窍 26. 竅 [13] **Ch'iao⁴ (qiào)** - Aperture, hole; key to a problem.

窜 27. 竄 **Ts'uan⁴ (cuàn)** - Flee; expel; change (– wording).

窦 28. 竇 [15] **Tou⁴ (dòu)** - Hole, burrow; sinus (nasal –).

窃 29. 竊 [17] **Ch'ieh⁴ (qiè)** - Steal, pilfer, usurp (– the throne); secretly.

CHILD 子 . 孑

Picture of a newborn child with the legs still bound in swathes 孑 .

1. 子 **Tzu³ (zǐ)** - Child, son; person; seed, egg; young, tender.

2. 孔 **K'ung³ (kông)** - Hole, opening, aperture.

3. 孕 [2] **Yün⁴ (yùn)** - Pregnant.

4. 存 [3] **Ts'un² (cún)** - Live, exist; deposit (– money); accumulate.

5. 字 **Tzu⁴ (zì)** - Chinese character.

6. 孚 [4] **Fu² (fú)** - Inspire confidence; confidence, trust(worthy).

7. 孝 **Hsiao⁴ (xiào)** - Filial piety (respect to parents); mourning.

8. 孛 **Po⁴ (bò)** - Plants shooting up. **Pei⁴ (bèi)** - Comet.

9. 孜 **Tzu¹ (zi)** - Diligent, untiring.

10. 季 [5] **Chi⁴ (jì)** - Season (the four -s); youngest among brothers.

11. 孤 **Ku¹ (gu)** - Orphan(ed); alone, single.

12. 孟 **Meng⁴ (mèng)** - First in appearance; eldest (- brother).

13. 孥 **Nu² (nú)** - Child, children (wife and -).

14. 孩 [6] **Hai² (hái)** - Child(ren).

孙 15. 孫 [7] **Sun¹ (sun)** - Grandson; great grandson.

16. 孰 [8] **Shu² (shú)** - Who? Which? What?

17. 孳 [10] **Tzu¹ (zi)** - Multiply, propagate; breed, produce; diligent.

学 18. 學 [13] **Hsüeh² (xué)** - Learn(ing), study; school (elementary -).

19. 孺 **Ju² (rú)** - Child (women and -ren); baby, suckling.

孽 20. 孽 [17] **Nieh⁴ (niè)** - Evil (- deeds), sin; misfortune.

CITY 邑 . 阝

The city ○ and its seal 冖: ㊗ .

1. 邑 **Yi⁴ (yì)** - City, town; county.

2. 邕 [3] **Yung¹ (yong)** - Harmony, harmonious.

3. 那 [4] **Na⁴ (nà)** - That; there (over -); which?; then, in that case.

4. 邦 **Pang¹ (bang)** - Nation, state, country.

5. 邪 **Hsieh² (xié)** - Evil, wicked; disease-causing environment.

6. 邱 [5] **Ch'iu¹ (qiu)** - Mound, hillock; grave; (N).

7. 邸 **T'i³ (dǐ)** - Residence of a high official.

8. 郊 [6] **Chiao¹ (jiao)** - Suburbs, outskirts; countryside.

9. 郡 [7] **Chün⁴ (jùn)** - Prefecture, administrative district.

10. 郎 **Lang² (láng)** - Ancient official title.

11. 郭 [8] **Kuo¹ (guo)** - Outer wall of a city.

12. 部 **Pu⁴ (bù)** - Department; board, ministry; headquarters; (N).

邮 13. 郵 **Yu² (yóu)** - Post (office), postal (– service); mail (–box).

14. 都 [9] **Tu¹ (du)** - Capital, metropolis. **Tou¹ (dou)** - All; already.

乡 15. 鄉 [10] **Hsiang¹ (xiang)** - Country(side); village; home town.

16. 鄙 [11] **Pi³ (bǐ)** - Low, vulgar; humble (my – opinion); remote.

郑 17. 鄭 [12] **Cheng⁴ (zhèng)** - Serious (zhèngzhòng).

邻 18. 鄰 **Lin² (lín)** - Neighbor(ing); near, next (– room), close by.

CLAN 氏

Representing a floating plant that grows in abundance 屮 .

1. 氏 **Shih⁴ (shì)** - Surname; *née* (Mrs. Wang, *née* Li); Celsius.

2. 民 [1] **Min² (mín)** - The people; folk (– song); civil (– law).

3. 氓 [4] **Meng² (méng)** - The common people. **Mang² (máng)** - Vagabond (**líumáng**).

CLAW 爪 . 爫

Picture of a claw 爪.

1. 爪　Chao³ (zhâo). Chua³ (zhuâ) - Claw, talon.

2. 爬⁴　P'a² (pá) - Claw; creep, climb, clamber, scramble.

爭 3. 爭　Cheng¹ (zheng) - Contend, fight for; argue; wanting.

4. 爰⁵　Yüan² (yúan) - Whence, from where; hence, therefore.

为 5. 爲⁸　Wei² (wéi) - Do; become; be. Wei⁴ (wèi) - For (benefit of).

6. 爵¹⁴　Chüeh² (jué) - Peerage, nobility.

CLIFF 厂

Representing a steep cliff 厂.

1. 厄²　E⁴ (è) - Be stranded / in distress; misfortune; disaster.

2. 厚⁷　Hou⁴ (hòu) - Thick (- clothing); generous; rich (in flavor).

3. 原⁸　Yüan² (yuán) - Primary (- color); original; excuse.

4. 厝　Ts'o⁴ (cuò) - Place, put; carve, engrave; bury.

厕 5. 厠⁹　Ts'e⁴ (cè) - Toilet (cèsuô). Szu⁴ (sì) - Latrine (máosi).

6. 厥¹⁰　Chüeh² (jué) - Faint; his, her, its, their.

厨 7. 厨　Ch'u² (chú) - Kitchen.

8. 厦　Sha⁴ (shà) - High-rise building; mansion.

厂 9. 厰 [12] **Ch'ang³ (châng)** - Factory, plant, yard (ship-); depot.

10. 厮 **Szu¹ (sī)** - Male servant; fellow (nice –); together (play –).

厌 11. 厭 **Yen⁴ (yàn)** - Fed up with; disgusted with; detest **(yànwù)**.

厉 12. 厲 [13] **Li⁴ (lì)** - Whetstone; grind, sharpen; strict, stern, severe.

CLOTH 巾

Piece of cloth ∏ *for cleaning, hanging down* | *from the girdle:* 巾.

1. 巾 **Chin¹ (jīn)** - Towel, scarf, handkerchief, napkin.

2. 市 [2] **Shih⁴ (shì)** - Market (cattle –); city, municipality.

3. 布 **Pu⁴ (bù)** - Cloth; announce; publish; spread (– disease).

4. 帆 [3] **Fan¹ (fān)** - Sail, canvas.

5. 希 [4] **Hsi¹ (xī)** - Rare, scarce; hope.

6. 帚 [5] **Chou³ (zhôu)** - Broom.

7. 帙 **Chih⁴ (zhì)** - Cloth slip-case for books.

8. 帘 **Lien² (lián)** - Flag (as shop sign), curtain, screen (door –).

9. 帕 **P'a⁴ (pà)** - Handkerchief, veil.

10. 帛 **Po² (bó)** - Silk, plain white silk.

11. 帑 **T'ang³ (tâng)** - State treasury.

12. 帖 **T'ieh³ (tiê)** - Invitation; card; note; dose (– of medicine).

帅 13. 帥 [6] **Shuai⁴ (shuài)** - Commander-in-chief; beautiful, graceful.

14. 帝 **Ti⁴ (dì)** - The Supreme Being; emperor; imperialism.

师 15. 師 [7] **Shih¹ (shi)** - Teacher, master; model; division; army.

16. 席 **Hsi² (xí)** - Mat; seat, place; feast, banquet.

帐 17. 帳 [8] **Chang⁴ (zhàng)** - Curtain, net (mosquito –); account; debt.

18. 帡 **P'ing² (píng)** - Screen, awning.

19. 常 **Ch'ang² (cháng)** - Constantly; common; frequently.

带 20. 帶 **Tai⁴ (dài)** - Belt, girdle; zone, region; lead (– troops).

21. 帷 **Wei² (wéi)** - Curtain, tent.

22. 幅 [9] **Fu² (fú)** - Width of cloth; size (large – print); (N).

23. 帽 **Mao⁴ (mào)** - Headgear, hat, cap, cap-like cover.

帏 24. 幃 **Wei² (wéi)** - Tent; curtain.

25. 幌 [10] **Huang³ (huâng)** - Signboard; smoke screen, pretence.

26. 幔 [11] **Man⁴ (màn)** - Curtain, screen.

27. 幕 **Mu⁴ (mù)** - Curtain (stage), screen (movie); act (Act II).

28. 幙 **Mu⁴ (mù)** - Same as 27.

币 29. 幣 [12] **Pi⁴ (bì)** - Money, currency (foreign –), coin.

帜 30. 幟 **Chih⁴ (zhì)** - Flag, banner.

31. 幡 **Fan¹ (fan)** - Banner, streamer (hung before shrine).

帮 32. 幫 ¹⁴ **Pang¹ (bang)** - Help, assist; gang, band; outer leaf.

33. 懞 **Meng² (méng)** - Covering, screen, awning.

CLOTHES 衣 衤

A robe and its sleeves 亠 and ∩ its dragging over the floor: 衣.

1. 衣 **Yi¹ (yi)** - Clothes, garment; covering, coating (sugar –).

2. 卒 ² **Tsu² (zú)** - Soldier; servant; finish, end; die (– of cancer).

3. 衩 ³ **Ch'a⁴ (chà)** - Slit in the sides of a garment.

4. 表 **Piao³ (biâo)** - Exterior, surface; show; model; watch; list.

5. 衫 **Shan¹ (shan)** - Unlined upper garments (shirts, etc.).

6. 衷 ⁴ **Chung¹ (zhong)** - Inner clothing; heart, mind, feelings.

7. 衿 **Chin¹ (jin)** - Lapel of a coat.

8. 衾 **Ch'in¹ (qin)** - Large quilt.

9. 衲 **Na⁴ (nà)** - Patch, mend; patched robe of Buddhist monk.

10. 衰 **Shuai¹ (shuai)** - Decay; wane, decline, fade.

11. 袂 **Mei⁴ (mèi)** - Sleeve (of a robe).

12. 袁 **Yüan² (yuán)** - Long robe.

13. 袍 ⁵ **P'ao² (páo)** - Robe, gown.

14. 被 Pei[4] (bèi) - Quilt, bedspread; wear; by (killed – bandits).

15. 袖 Hsiu[4] (xiù) - Sleeve; put inside the sleeve; pocket (– radio).

16. 袋 Tai[4] (dài) - Bag, sack; pocket, pouch.

17. 袒 T'an[3] (tân) - Lay bare part of upper body; shield, shelter.

18. 袱[6] Fu[2] (fú) - Cloth for wrapping clothes.

19. 裉 K'en[4] (kèn) - Insert in a garment for reinforcement.

20. 袷 Chia[2] (jiá) - Lined garment.

21. 裂 Lieh[4] (liè) - Split, crack, rend, tear, rip open.

22. 裁 Ts'ai[2] (cái) - Cut (– cloth); reduce; judge, decide; dismiss.

23. 裝 Chuang[1] (zhuang) - Dress up as; pretend; load; install.
    装

24. 裔 Yi[4] (yì) - Descendants; descent (of Chinese –); frontier.

25. 裌 Chia[2] (jiá) - Double layered, lined (– jacket).
    夹

26. 裘 Ch'iu[2] (qíu) - Fur coat.

27. 裙 Ch'ün[4] (qún) - Skirt.

28. 裡 Li[3] (lǐ) - Same as 29.

29. 裏 Li[3] (lǐ) - Lining; inside, inner; hometown; unit of length.
    里

30. 補 Pu[3] (bû) - Repair; make up for; nourish.
    补

31. 裕 Yü[4] (yù) - Abundant, generous, rich; enrich.

制 32. 製 [8] **Chih⁴ (zhì)** - Make, made (**zhìzào**) (– in China); system.

33. 褂 **Kua⁴ (guà)** - Chinese style unlined garment; gown.

34. 裹 **Kuo³ (guô)** - Bind, wrap (– parcel).

35. 裸 **Lo³ (luô)** - Bare (–foot), naked, exposed (– wire).

36. 裴 **P'ei² (péi)** - Long robe.

37. 裨 **Pei⁴ (bèi)** - Assist, aid; advantage; inferior, small (– tribe).

38. 裱 **Piao³ (biâo)** - Paste, mount (– photos).

39. 裳 **Ch'ang² (cháng)** - Skirts (worn in ancient China).

复 40. 複 [9] **Fu⁴ (fù)** - Duplicate. * Turn round; again; answer.

41. 褒 **Pao¹ (bao)** - Praise, honor, commend.

42. 褓 **Pao³ (bâo)** - Swaddling clothes.

43. 褙 **Pei⁴ (bèi)** - Paste together two pieces of cloth or paper.

44. 褥 [10] **Ju⁴ (rù)** - Mattress (cotton-padded); cushion.

裤 45. 褲 **K'u⁴ (kù)** - Trousers, pants.

46. 褦 **Nai⁴ (nài)** - Stupid, ignorant.

47. 褡 **Ta¹ (da)** - Long broad girdle; loin cloth.

48. 褪 **T'un⁴ (tùn)** - Slip out. **T'ui⁴ (tui)** - Disrobe, cast (– skin).

49. 褯 **Chieh⁴ (jiè)** - Baby napkin, diaper.

褒 50. 襃[11] Pao[1] (bao) - Same as 41.

裢 51. 褳 Lien[2] (lián) - Pouch; purse.

52. 襄 Hsiang[1] (xiang) - Help, assist; assistant (– manager).

亵 53. 褻 Hsieh[4] (xiè) - Disrespectful; obscene; indecent.

单 54. 禪[12] Tan[1] (dan) - Unlined clothing. * Single; odd; simple.

55. 襁 Ch'iang[3] (qiâng) - Swaddling clothes.

56. 襟[13] Chin[1] (jin) - Lapel (of a coat).

袄 57. 襖 Ao[3] (âo) - Short coat or jacket (Chinese style).

袒 58. 襢 T'an[3] (tân) - Same as 17.

裆 59. 襠 Tang[1] (dang) - Crotch of trousers; crotch.

褴 60. 襤[14] Lan[2] (lán) - Ragged, shabby.

袜 61. 襪[15] Wa[4] (wà) - Stockings, socks, hose.

衬 62. 襯[16] Ch'en[4] (chèn) - Lining; serve as background.

袭 63. 襲 Hsi[2] (xí) - Make surprise attack; carry on (– old tradition).

64. 襻[19] P'an[4] (pàn) - Loop; fasten w. rope or string; tie, strap.

COCOON 厶

Picture of a cocoon ◌.

1. 去 Ch'ü[4] (qù) - Go, leave; remove; last year's (– winter).

2. 叁 San¹ (san) - Elaborate form of 三 (three) to prevent fraud.

参 3. 参 Shen¹ (shen) - In 'ginseng'. Ts'an¹ (can) - Join; consult.

COLOR 色

A man 卩 with a red (color of a seal 㔾) face: 㿟.

1. 色 Se⁴ (sè) - Color; looks (good –); kind (of all –s); scenery.

艳 2. 艷 Yen⁴ (yàn) - Colorful; gorgeous; romantic; admire, envy.

COMPARE 比

Two men 人 standing next to each other, in order to compare their heights 从.

1. 比 Pi³ (bǐ) - Compare; compete; gesture; ratio; than (taller –).

2. 毗 P'i² (pí) - Adjoining to, contiguous (- fields).

毗 3. 毘 P'i² (pí) - Same as 2.

CORPSE 尸

A sitting person 尸, representing the dead.

1. 尸 Shih¹ (shi) - Corpse, carcass; remains.

2. 尺 Ch'ih³ (chǐ) - Chin. unit of length; ruler, rule (slide –).

3. 尹 Yin³ (yǐn) - Govern, rule, direct; director; sincere, honest.

4. 尼 ² **Ni² (ní)** - Buddhist nun; phonetic in nylon, nicotine.

5. 尻 **K'ao¹ (kao)** - Buttocks, bottom.

6. 局 ⁴ **Chü² (jú)** - Office, bureau, shop; party, banquet; situation.

7. 尿 **Niao⁴ (niâo)** - Urine, urinate.

8. 屁 **P'i⁴ (pì)** - Wind from the bowels.

9. 尾 **Wei³ (wêi)** - Tail; end (- of the line); remnant; (N).

10. 屆 居 ⁵ **Chieh⁴ (jiè)** - Same as 11.

11. 届 **Chieh⁴ (jiè)** - Become due; session (a joint -); (N).

12. 居 **Chü¹ (ju)** - Residence, house; occupy (- a position); claim.

13. 屈 **Ch'ü¹ (qu)** - Bend, bow; subdue; to be wronged, injustice.

14. 尸 屍 ⁶ **Shih¹ (shi)** - Corpse, esp. of a murdered person.

15. 屋 **Wu¹ (wu)** - House; room (inner -).

16. 屎 **Shih³ (shî)** - Excrement (faeces, etc.); secretion, discharge.

17. 展 ⁷ **Chan³ (zhân)** - Open up, spread out; prolong; exhibition.

18. 屑 **Hsieh⁴ (xiè)** - Scraps (- of paper), crumbs; trivial.

19. 屏 屏 **P'ing² (píng)** - Screen. **Ping³ (bîng)** - Reject, hold (v).

20. 屜 屜 **T'i⁴ (ti)** - Bamboo food steamer w. trays; tray, drawer.

21. 屠 ⁹ **T'u² (tú)** - Slaughter, massacre (inhabitants of a city).

22. 屢 屢 ¹¹ **Lü³ (lü)** - Repeatedly, frequently, time and again.

23. 屣 **Hsi³ (xǐ)** - Straw sandals, slippers, shoe.

24. 履 [12] **Lü³ (lü)** - Shoe; walk on; tread (caterpillar –); carry out.

层 25. 層 **Ts'eng² (céng)** - Layer, stratum, story, floor (second –).

属 26. 屬 [18] **Shu³ (shû)** - Category, class; belong to, dependent.

COVER 冖

Picture of a cover ⌒.

1. 冗 [2] **Jung³ (rông)** - Superfluous; full of small details.

2. 尢 **Yin² (yín)** - Move on.

3. 冠 [7] **Kuan¹ (guan)** - Hat, cap. **Kuan⁴ (guàn)** - Cap (v); the best.

4. 冢 [8] **Chung³ (zhōng)** - Mound, knoll; tomb, grave.

5. 冥 **Ming² (míng)** - Dark, obscure; stupid; underworld.

6. 冤 **Yüan¹ (yuan)** - Injustice, be wronged; hatred, enmity.

D

DARK 玄

The thread 𢆶 *(two cocoons twisted into a thread) being dipped* 入
into the dye, and obtaining a dark color: 𢆥.

1. 玄 **Hsüan² (xúan)** - Dark, black; mysterious; profound.

2. 兹 **Tzu¹ (zi)** - This; now, recently (– received).

3. 率 **Shuai⁴ (shuai)** - Lead, command; rash; straight(forward).

DART 弋

A dart (a small arrow), which attached to a string can be retrieved
after it has been thrown to kill a small animal : 𰀲 .

1. 弋 **Yi⁴ (yì)** - Dart (a small arrow – *see above*).

2 弍 **Yi¹ (yì)** - Elaborate form of "one", used on checks, etc.

3. 弍 **Erh⁴ (èr)** - Elaborate form of "two", used on checks, etc.

4. 式 **Shih⁴ (shì)** - Style, format; ceremony; formula.

5. 弑 **Shih⁴ (shì)** - Kill a sovereign, superior, father.

DEER 鹿

Representing the deer 鹿 *, with its head and horn* 屮 *, its body* ⼍ *and its feet* 比 *.*

1. 鹿 **Lu⁴ (lù)** - Deer.

2 麒 **Ch'i² (qí)** - Unicorn.

丽 3. 麗 **Li⁴ (lì)** - Beautiful.

4. 麝 **She⁴ (shè)** - Musk deer.

5. 麟 **Lin² (lín)** - Unicorn (female).

DEFIANCE 艮

Defiance 艮 *– a man* 人 *who turns around* ⼍ *, to look (* 目 *eye) another person full in the face.*

1. 艮 **Ken³ (gên)** – Defiance; tough (meat), hard; straightforward.

2 良 **Liang² (liáng)** – Good (– soldier), virtuous; very (– much).

艰 3. 艱 **Chien¹ (jian)** – Difficult (task), hard (work).

DISH 皿

Picture of a dish mounted on a pedestal 皿 , as used by the Chinese during banquets.

1. 皿 **Min³ (mîn)** - Household utensil.

2. 盂 ³ **Yü² (yú)** - Broad-mouthed recptacle (e.g. spittoon); basin.

3. 盅 ⁴ **Chung¹ (zhong)** - Cup (handleless, e.g. teacup).

4. 盆 **P'en² (pén)** - Basin (wash–); pot (flower–); tub (bath–).

5. 盃 **Pei¹ (bei)** - Cup (tea–); cup (trophy, e.g. silver cup).

6. 盈 **Ying² (yíng)** - Have a surplus of; be filled with (– tears).

7. 盍 ⁵ **Ho² (hé)** - Why not ?

8. 益 **Yi⁴ (yì)** - Benefit, advantage; increase, prolong (life).

9. 盒 ⁶ **Ho² (hé)** - Box (– of matches), case, carton.

10. 盔 **K'uei¹ (kui)** - Helmet.

11. 盜 **Tao⁴ (dào)** - Steal, rob; thief, robber.

12. 盛 **Sheng⁴ (shèng)** - Flourishing; grand (opening); widespread.

13. 盜 ⁷ **Tao⁴ (dào)** - Same as 11.

14. 盞 ⁸ **Chan³ (zhân)** - Small cup (e.g. winecup); (N) for cups.

15. 盟 **Meng² (méng)** - Alliance, league (– of nations); oath.

16. 監 ⁹ **Chien¹ (jian)** - Supervise. **Chien⁴ (jiàn)** - Imperial office.

尽 17. 盡 **Chin⁴ (jìn)** - Exhausted. **Chin³ (jǐn)** - To the utmost.

盖 18. 蓋 **Kai⁴ (gài)** - Cover; shell (of crab, etc.); seal.

盘 19. 盤 ¹⁰ **P'an² (pán)** - Plate, dish, tray; wind (-ing path).

20. 盥 ¹¹ **Kuan⁴ (guàn)** - To wash (hands or face); wash (–room).

卢 21. 盧 **Lu² (lú)** - As *lú* in *lúbî* (rupee), etc.

荡 22. 盪 ¹² **Tang⁴ (dàng)** - Move, agitate; bathtub.

盐 23. 鹽 ¹⁹ **Yen² (yán)** - Salt (table –).

DISINTEGRATION 歹 歺

Picture of a skeleton 歺 *– the body after the decay of the flesh.*

1. 歹 **Tai³ (dâi)** - Bad, evil, wicked, vicious.

2 死 ² **Szu³ (sî)** - Die, dead, death.

殁 3. 殁 ⁴ **Mo⁴ (mò)** - Die, perish.

4. 殆 ⁵ **Tai⁴ (dài)** - Danger; almost, nearly.

5. 殄 **T'ien³ (tiân)** - Exterminate, root out.

6. 殃 **Yang¹ (yang)** - Misfortune, disaster; bring disaster to.

7. 殊 ⁶ **Shu¹ (shu)** - Different, special (treatment); extremely.

8. 殉 **Hsün⁴ (xùn)** - Bury; die for (one's country).

殖 9. 殖 ⁸ **Chih² (zhí)** - Breed, reproduce.

殘 10. 殘 Ts'an[2] (cán) - Incomplete (set); remnants; disabled.

殞 11. 殞[10] Yün[3] (yûn) - Perish, die.

殮 12. 殮[13] Lien[4] (liàn) - Encoffin, put a body into a coffin.

殯 13. 殯[14] Pin[4] (bìn) - Put coffin in memorial hall; carry to burial.

DIVINATION 卜

Cracks in tortoise shells 卜 *, developed by heating, used as basis for fortune-telling.*

1. 卜 Pu[3] (bû) - Divination, fortune-telling; foretell, forecast.

2. 占 Chan[1] (zhan) - Divine, foretell.

3. 卡 Ch'ia[3] (qîa) - Clipper (nail-); get stuck (fishbone in throat).

4. 卦 Kua[4] (guà) - Diagram used in divination; divination.

DOG 犬．犭

A dog, showing its two front legs and its head turned aside 犬 *.*

1. 犬 Ch'üan[3] (quân) - Dog.

2. 犯 Fan[4] (fàn) - Offend (the law), violate (treaty); attack.

3. 狀 Chuang[4] (zhuàng) - Form, shape, condition (excellent –).

4. 狂 K'uang[2] (kuáng) - Mad, crazy, violent, wild.

5. 狎 Hsiá[2] (xiá) - Be improperly familiar with a person.

6. 狐 Hu[2] (hú) - Fox.

7. 狗 Kou[3] (gôu) - Dog.

8. 狠[6] **Hen³ (hên)** - Ruthless, cruel(-hearted); firm, resolute.

9. 狡 **Chiao³ (jiâo)** - Crafty (politician), cunning (animal); sly.

狭 10. 狹[7] **Hsia² (xiá)** - Narrow.

11. 狼 **Lang² (láng)** - Wolf.

狈 12. 狽 **Pei⁴ (bèi)** - Jerboa, legendary wolf w. short foreleg.

13. 狸 **Li² (lí)** - Raccoon; wild cat.

14. 猛[8] **Meng³ (mêng)** - Violent (storm), fierce (animal).

15. 猖 **Ch'ang¹ (chang)** - Mad.

16. 猜 **Ts'ai¹ (cai)** - Guess, suspect.

17. 猝 **Ts'u⁴ (cù)** - Abrupt, suddenly, unexpected.

18. 猪[9] **Chu¹ (zhu)** - Pig; pork (–chop).

19. 猴 **Hou² (hóu)** - Monkey

20. 猫 **Mao¹ (mao)** - Cat.

21. 猬 **Wei⁴ (wèi)** - Porcupine, hedgehog.

犹 22. 猶 **Yu² (yóu)** - Like (it looks – gold); still (– valid).

23. 猷 **Yu² (yóu)** - Scheme, plan.

24. 猾[10] **Hua² (huá)** - Cunning, treacherous, sly.

呆 25. 獃 **Tai¹ (dai)** - Slow-witted, dull; stay (– at home).

獅 26. 獅 Shih[1] (shī) - Lion.

狱 27. 獄 [11] Yü[4] (yù) - Lawsuit, litigation; prison.

独 28. 獨 [13] Tu[2] (dú) - Single, alone (live –), solitary (life).

获 29. 獲 [14] Huò[4] (huò) - Capture; obtain; reap (– profits).

猎 30. 獵 [15] Lieh[4] (liè) - Hunt wild animals.

兽 31. 獸 Shou[4] (shòu) - Wild animal; beast(ly), brutal.

献 32. 獻 [16] Hsien[4] (xiàn) - Offer, present (gift); show (off one's wealth)..

獭 33. 獺 T'a[3] (tâ) - Otter.

34. 獾 [18] Huan[1] (huan) - Badger.

DO NOT 毋

A woman 㐅 , who is being locked up — for misconduct: 㐅 .

1. 毋 Wu[2] (wú) - Do not; no, not.

2. 母 Mu[3] (mû) - Mother.

3. 每 Mei[3] (mêi) - Each, every; always, constantly.

4. 毒 Tu[2] (dú) - Poison (n/v), poisonous; cruel, malicious.

DOOR 門

Picture of a saloon-door with swinging leaves 門 .

门 1. 門 **Men² (mén)** - Door; gate.

闩 2. 閂 **Shuan¹ (shuan)** - Bolt, bolt (the door).

闪 3. 閃² **Shan³ (shân)** - Dodge, evade; flash (of light).

闭 4. 閉³ **Pi⁴ (bì)** - Close, shut; obstruct.

闲 5. 閑⁴ **Hsien² (xián)** - Unoccupied, vacant (lot).

闲 6. 閒 **Hsien² (xián)** - Leisure (– hour); vacant (– land).

闰 7. 閏 **Jun⁴ (rùn)** - Intercalary, leap (year).

开 8. 開 **K'ai¹ (kai)** - Open (the door); start, operate (a business).

间 9. 間 **Chien¹ (jian)** - Between, among. **Chien⁴(jiàn)** -Separate.

闵 10. 閔 **Min³ (mîn)** - Grieve, mourn; misfortune; encourage.

闸 11. 閘⁵ **Cha² (zhá)** - Sluice gate.

闹 12. 鬧 **Nao⁴ (nào)** - Noisy; make noise/trouble.(See **FIGHT** No. 2).

阀 13. 閥⁶ **Fa² (fá)** - Magnate; warlord.

阁 14. 閣 **Ke² (gé)** - Pavilion; chamber; cabinet.

阁 15. 閤 **Ke² (gé)** - Same as 14.

闺 16. 閨 **Kuei¹ (gui)** - Boudoir, private room.

阃 17. 閫 **K'un³ (kûn)** - Women's apartments; threshold.

闾	閭 [7]	**Lû² (lǘ)** - Lane, alley.
阅	閱	**Yüeh⁴ (yuè)** - Read; review (troops).
阊	閶	**Ch'ang¹ (chang)** - The gate of heaven.
阍	閽 [8]	**Hun¹ (hun)** - Entrance of a gate; gatekeeper.
阉	閹	**Yen¹ (yan)** - Castrate (males); spay (females).
阎	閻	**Yen² (yán)** - Gate to a lane.
阔	闊 [9]	**K'uo⁴ (kuò)** - Broad, wide; rich; long (time).
阑	闌	**Lan² (lán)** - Late (in time); railing.
闯	闖 [10]	**Ch'uang³ (chuâng)** - Rush in, dash ahead.
阖	闔	**Ho² (hé)** - Whole (family), entire (world); close (door).
阙	闕	**Ch'üeh⁴ (què)** - Watchtower; imperial palace.
关	關	**Kuan¹ (guan)** - Same as 30.
关	關 [11]	**Kuan² (guan)** - Close, shut (door), shut off (the radio).
阐	闡 [12]	**Ch'an³ (chân)** - Explain, disclose.
辟	闢 [13]	**P'i⁴ (pì)** - Open up (land); refute (rumours).
闼	闥	**T'a⁴ (tà)** - Door to inner room (e.g. to the women's room).

DOORLEAF 戶

The left-hand leaf 戶 of a swinging-door 門.

1. 戶 **Hu⁴ (hù)** - Door; family, household.

2. 房 **Fang² (fáng)** - House, room, dwelling.

3. 戾 **Li⁴ (lì)** - Rebellious, perverse; crime, sin.

4. 所 **So³ (suô)** - Place, room, building.

5. 扁 **Pien³ (biân)** - Flat, thin.

6. 扇 **Shan⁴ (shàn)** - Fan (paper –); scallops **(shànbèi)**.

7. 扉 **Fei¹ (fei)** - Door (with one leaf); cottage.

DOT ヽ

Picture of a dot •.

1. 丸 **Wan² (wán)** - Ball (meat-), pellet; pill.

2. 凡 **Fan² (fán)** - All, every, any; commonplace, ordinary.

3. 丹 **Tan¹ (dan)** - Red; medicinal pill or powder.

4. 主 **Chu³ (zhû)** - Master; owner; host.

DOWNSTROKE ↓

A crooked downstroke made by the writing-brush).

1. 了 **Liao³ (liâo)** - Understand; finish, end; final particle.

2. 予 ³ **Yü³ (yü)** - Bestow, grant, confer, give.

3. 事 ⁷ **Shih⁴ (shì)** - Affair (world –s); business; occupation; job.

DRAGON 龍

A dragon 🐉 *flying towards the sky (dragon* 🐉*, wings* 〻*, and the sky* 二*).*

龙 1. 龍 **Lung² (lóng)** - Dragon.

庞 2. 龐 **P'ang² (páng)** - Huge, great; disordered.

龛 3. 龕 **K'an¹ (kan)** - Niche, shrine.

* It was believed that dragons would fly towards the sky and thereby caused rain, after sitting in the well during the dry season.

DRUM 鼓

A drum 鼓 *(a hand* 彐 *holding a stick* — *beating a drum on a stand* 豆 *); a hand holding a stick (repeated):* 支 *.*

1. 鼓 **Ku³ (gǔ)** - Drum; beat (the drum); rouse, excite.

2. 鼕 **T'ung¹ (tong)** - Rattle of drums.

DWELLING 宀

PIcture of a hut - a primitive dwelling ⌂ *.*

1. 它 **T'a¹ (ta)** - It.

冗 2. 宂 **Jung³ (róng)** - Superfluous.

3. 安 **An¹ (an)** - Safe, secure, peaceful, quiet, calm.

4. 守 **Shou³ (shǒu)** - Guard, defend; abide by, obey (the law).

5. 宅 **Chai² (zhái)** - House, residence.

6. 宇 **Yü³ (yǔ)** - Eaves (of a roof); house; space.

7. 宏 **Hung² (hóng)** - Vast, spacious; grand, great.

8. 宋 **Sung⁴ (sòng)** - Sung Dynasty.

9. 完 **Wan² (wán)** - Whole; complete, finish.

10. 宙 ⁵ **Chou² (zhòu)** - All times (past, present and future).

11. 宜 **Yi² (yí)** - Suitable, proper; should.

12. 官 **Kuan¹ (guan)** - Official, officer; governmental.

13. 宕 **Tang⁴ (dàng)** - Delay, procrastinate.

14. 定 **Ting⁴ (dìng)** - Stable, fixed; decide; certainly.

15. 宗 **Tsung¹ (zong)** - Ancestor; clan; sect, faction.

16. 宛 **Wan³ (wân)** - Winding; as if; similar to.

17. 宦 ⁶ **Huan⁴ (huàn)** - Eunuch; official (during ancient times).

18. 客 **K'e⁴ (kè)** - Guest, visitor; passenger, traveller; customer.

19. 室 **Shih⁴ (shì)** - Room (waiting-); house (tea-).

20. 宣 **Hsüan¹ (xuan)** - Proclaim, announce, declare.

21. 宥 **Yu⁴ (yòu)** - Pardon, forgive.

22. 害 ⁷ **Hai⁴ (hài)** - Harm, injure; harmful.

23. 家 **Chia¹ (jia)** - Household, family; home, house; specialist.

24. 宫 **Kung¹ (gong)** - Palace, temple.

25. 宵 **Hsiao¹ (xiao)** - Night (all - long).

26. 宰 Tsai³ (zâi) - Slaughter, butcher.

27. 宴 Yen⁴ (yàn) - Banquet; entertain (at a banquet).

28. 容 Jung² (róng) - Hold, contain; tolerate, permit; appearance.

29. 寄 ⁸ Chi⁴ (jì) - Send, mail; entrust.

30. 寇 K'ou⁴ (kòu) - Bandit; enemy; invader.

31. 密 Mi⁴ (mì) - Close, dense; intimate; secret.

32. 宿 Su³ (sù) - Lodge. Xiu³ (xîu) - Night .

33. 寂 Chi⁴ (jì) - Quiet, still; solitary, lonely.

34. 寅 Yin² (yín) -Third (in ranking).

冤 35. 冤 Yüan¹ (yuan) -Wrong, injustice; hatred, enmity.

36. 富 ⁹ Fu⁴ (fù) - Rich; abundant.

37. 寒 Han² (hán) - Cold; poor, needy.

38. 寐 Mei⁴ (mèi) - Sleep.

实 39. 定 Shih² (shí) - Same as 48.

40. 寓 Yü⁴ (yù) - Live, reside; residence.

置 41. 寘 ¹⁰ Chih⁴ (zhì) - Place, put; establish, install; buy.

42. 察 ¹¹ Ch'a² (chá) - Examine, look into, scrutinize.

43. 寨 Chai⁴ (zhài) - Stockade; camp.

44. 寡 Kua³ (guâ) - Few; single; widow (guâfù).

45. 寥 Liao² (liáo) - Few, scanty; deserted; vacant.

46. 寞 Mo⁴ (mò) - Still, silent; alone; deserted.

宁 47. 寧 Ning² (níng) - Peaceful. Ning⁴ (nìng) - Would rather.

实 48. 實 Shih² (shí) - True, real, honest; solid; fruit, seed.

寝 49. 寢 Ch'in¹ (qîn) - Sleep; rest; stop.

50. 寤 ₁₂ Wu⁴ (wù) - Awake.

宽 51. 寬 K'uan¹ (kuan) - Broad, spacious; relax.

52. 寮 Liao² (liáo) - Hut, small house.

审 53. 審 Shen³ (shên) - Careful; examine, try (in court).

写 54. 寫 ₁₃ Hsieh³ (xiê) - Write; draw, sketch.

55. 寰 ₁₆ Huan² (huán) - Domain (Emperor's).

宠 56. 寵 ₁₇ Ch'ung³ (chông) - Grant favors, pamper.

宝 57. 寶 Pao³ (bâo) - Precious; jewel, gem.

E

EAR 耳

Picture of the ear ⊖.

1. 耳 **Erh³ (êr)** - Ear; only (it's – one mile from here).

2. 聋 ³ **Ta¹ (da)** - Big-eared.

3. 耶 **Yeh¹ (ye)** - Used for its pronunciation (e.g. *Yesu* < Jesus >).

4. 耿 ⁴ **Keng³ (gêng)** - Bright, honest; straightforward.

5. 聊 ⁵ **Liao² (liáo)** - Merely, just (– to thank you); chat.

6. 聆 **Ling² (líng)** - Hear, listen; pay attention.

7. 聒 ⁶ **Kuo¹ (guo)** -Nosiy; clamor (of an angry crowd).

8. 聘 ⁷ **P'in⁴ (pìn)** - Betroth, promise to marry; employ (a psn.).

圣 9. 聖 **Sheng⁴ (shèng)** - Holy, sacred; sage.

10. 聚 [8] **Chü² (jù)** - Gather, assemble.

闻 11. 聞 **Wen² (wén)** - Hear; news; fame, famous.

联 12. 聯 [11] **Lien² (lián)** - Unite, join.

声 13. 聲 **Sheng¹ (sheng)** - Sound; voice.

耸 14. 聳 **Sung³ (sŏng)** - High, towering; shock, excite.

聪 15. 聰 **Ts'ung¹ (cong)** - Acute hearing; clever **(congming)**.

职 16. 職 [12] **Chih² (zhí)** - Duty, position, job.

聂 17. 聶 **Nieh⁴ (niè)** - Whisper.

聋 18. 聾 **Lung² (lóng)** - Deaf; hard of hearing.

听 19. 聽 **T'ing¹ (ting)** - Hear, listen; obey.

EARTH 土. 圡

The layer 二 from which all things | came out: 土.

1. 土 **T'u³ (tû)** - Earth, soil, land, ground.

2. 圭 [3] **Kuei¹ (gui)** - Ancient jade scepter; sundial.

3. 地 **Ti⁴ (dì)** - Earth, land ground, field.

4. 在 **Tsai⁴ (zài)** - Be present at.

5. 址 [4] **Chih³ (zhî)** - Location, place.

6. 坊 Fang¹ (fang) - Lane, alley.

7. 坎 K'an³ (kân) - Pit, hole.

8. 坑 K'eng¹ (keng) - Pit, hole.

9. 均 Chūn¹ (jun) - Equal, even.

10. 坍 T'an¹ (tan) - Collapse.

11. 坯 P'i¹ (pi) - Unburnt brick; semi-finished product.

12. 坐 Tso⁴ (zuò) - Sit; go (by car, boat, train, plane).

13. 垂⁵ Ch'ui² (chuí) - Hang down, droop; drop; condescend.

14. 坤 K'un¹ (kun) - Female (– artist), feminine; the earth.

15. 坭 Ni² (ní) - Mud.

16. 坏 P'i¹ (pi) - Same as 11.

17. 坡 P'o¹ (po) - Slope (hill –).

18. 坼 Ch'e⁴ (chè) - Crack, split.

19. 坦 T'an³ (tân) - Level, smooth; composed, calm.

20. 型⁶ Hsing² (xíng) - Mould, type, model; group (blood –).

21. 垛 To³ (duô) - Battlements, buttress.

22. 垢 Kou⁴ (goù) - Dirt, filth; dirty, filthy; disgrace.

23. 垤 Tieh² (dié) - Hillock.

24. 垣 Yüan[2] (yuán) - Wall (city –).

25. 埋 Mai[2] (mái) - Cover up, bury, conceal.

26. 城 Ch'eng[2] (chéng) - City wall, wall (The Great Wall).

27. 埃 Ai[1] (ai) - Dust; angstrom (A 0.00000001 cm).

执 28. 執 Chih[2] (zhí) - Hold, grasp; manage; stick to (– promise).

29. 基 Chi[1] (ji) - Foundation, base; as phonetic (Jidu <Jesus>).

30. 埽 Sao[3] (sâo) - Sweep, clean up.

坚 31. 堅 Chien[1] (jian) - Hard, solid, strong; resolute(ly).

32. 堇 Chin[3] (jîn) - Loess.

33. 培 P'ei[2] (péi) - Bank up with earth; strengthen; cultivate.

34. 埠 Pu[4] (bù) - Port; market ('China market' = Chinatown).

35. 埶 Yi[4] (yì) - Skill, craft.

36. 堂 T'ang[2] (táng) - Hall, court (Court of Justice).

37. 堆 Tui[1] (dui) - Heap, pile, stack (hay –).

野 38. 埜 Yeh[3] (yê) - Wild (cat), savage; uncultivated (land).

39. 埳 K'an[3] (kân) - Pit.

40. 域 Yü[4] (yù) - Land, region.

场 41. 場 Ch'ang[3] (châng) - Meeting place; stage.
Ch'ang[2] (cháng) - Level open space.

E 4

42. 堪 K'an[1] (kan) - Bear, endure; capable of.

43. 堡 Pao[3] (bâo) - Earthwork, rampart.

报 44. 報 Pao[4] (baò) - Report, announce; newspaper, periodical.

45. 堤 Ti[1] (di) - Dike, embankment.

46. 堞 Tieh[2] (dié) - Battlements.

47. 堵 Tu[3] (dû) - Block up, stop; suffocate.

尧 48. 堯 Yao[2] (yáo) - Lofty; eminent; legendary Emperor Yao.

49. 堭 Huang[2] (huáng) - City moat.

块 50. 塊[10] K'uai[4] (kuài) - Clod, lump (of clay), piece (of cake).

冢 51. 塚 Chung[3] (zhông) - Tomb, grace.

52. 塞 Se[4] (sè) - Stop, block.

53. 塑 Su[4] (sù) - Mould, model (in clay).

54. 塌 T'a[1] (ta) - Collapse, cave in.

55. 塔 T'a[3] (tâ) - Pagoda, tower (water -).

56. 塘 T'ang[2] (táng) - Dike, embankment; pond (fish -).

填 57. 塡 T'ien[2] (tían) - Fill up (a glass), fill in (a form).

涂 58. 塗 T'u[2] (tú) - Smear, apply (lipstick); erase.

坞 59. 塢 Wu[4] (wù) - Wall around village; shipyard, dock.

尘 60. 塵[11] Ch'en² (chén) - Dust, dirt.

场 61. 塲 Ch'ang³ (cháng) - Same as 41.

62. 境 Ching⁴ (jìng) - Boundary; place, area; situation.

63. 墓 Mu⁴ (mù) - Grave, tomb.

64. 墅 Shu⁴ (shù) - Cottage, villa.

65. 塾 Shu² (shú) - Private school.

垫 66. 墊 Tien⁴ (diàn) - Pad, cushion; advance money.

坠 67. 墜[12] Chui⁴ (zhuì) - Fall down, sink; weigh down.

坟 68. 墳 Fen² (fén) - Grave, tomb.

69. 墨 Mo⁴ (mò) - China (black) ink; pitch-dark.

70. 墩 Tun¹ (dun) - Mound; large block of stone or wood.

堕 71. 隳 To⁴ (duò) - Fall down, sink.

72. 增 Tseng¹ (zeng) - Add, increase.

垦 73. 墾[13] K'en³ (kěn) - Break new soil, plow; reclaim land.

74. 壁 Pi² (bì) - Wall, partition; cliff.

坛 75. 壇 T'an² (tán) - Altar; platform. * Jug (wine –).

墙 76. 牆 Ch'iang² (qiáng) - Wall.

77. 壅 Yung¹ (yong) - Heap soil around roots; dam (a river).

78. 壕 ¹⁴ Hao² (háo) - Moat, trench.

79. 壑 Ho⁴ (hè) - Gully, valley; pool, puddle.

压 80. 壓 Ya¹ (ya) - Press (down), hold; keep under control.

垒 81. 壘 ¹⁵ Lei³ (lêi) - Rampart; pile up bricks, stones, etc.

坏 82. 壞 ¹⁶ Huai⁴ (huài) - Bad; spoil; ruin.

83. 壤 ¹⁷ Jang³ (râng) - Soil, earth; place, region.

坝 84. 壩 ²¹ Pa⁴ (bà) - Dam; dike; embankment.

EARTHENWARE 缶

Picture of a vessel with a cover ⊕.

1. 缶 Fou³ (fôu) - Earthenware, wine jar.

2. 缸 ³ Kang¹ (gang) - Jar, crock, vat.

3. 缺 ⁴ Ch'üeh¹ (que) - Deficient, lack of; imperfect; vacancy.

瓶 4. 缾 ⁶ P'ing² (píng) - Bottle; pitcher; jar.

5. 罄 ¹¹ Ch'ing⁴ (qìng) - Exhausted; empty.

坛 6. 罈 ¹² T'an² (tán) - Earthenware jar, jug.

7. 甕 Weng⁴ (wèng) - Earthenware jar, pot, urn.

罂 8. 罌 ¹⁴ Ying¹ (ying) - Jar with small mouth and ears; vase.

9. 罐 ¹⁸ Kuan⁴ (guàn) - Pot, jar, can, tin (of sardines).

EIGHT 八

A quantity consisting of two equal halves)(.

1. 八   **Pa¹ (ba)** - Eight.

2. 兮   **Hsi¹ (xi)** - Interjection of inquiry, doubt, admiration.

3. 公   **Kung¹ (gong)** - Public; common; male (animal).

4. 六   **Liu⁴ (liù)** - Six.

5. 共   **Kung⁴ (gòng)** - Share; common; altogether.

6. 兵   **Ping¹ (bing)** - Weapons; soldier; army; military.

7. 其   **Ch'i² (qí)** - He, she, it, etc.; his, her, its, etc.; this, that, etc.

8. 具   **Chü⁴ (jù)** - Utensil; prepare (document); possess (power).

9. 典   **Tien³ (diân)** - Canon, law; ceremony; records (ancient).

10. 兼   **Chien¹ (jian)** - Both, together; unite; simultaneously.

11. 冀   **Chi⁴ (jì)** - Hope, look forward to.

EMBROIDERY 黹

Cloth 巾 (a radical) pierced by thread and needle 㡒 resulting in a piece of embroidery (丵 a plant in full bloom): 黹.

1. 黹   **Chih³ (zhî)** - Embroidery, needlework.

ENCLOSURE 口

Picture of an enclosure ○.

1. 口　Wei² (wéi) - Enclosure.

2. 囚 ²　Ch'iu² (qíu) - Prisoner; imprison; prison (– camp).

3. 四　Szu⁴ (sì) - Four.

4. 回 ³　Hui² (huí) - Return, go back; answer, reply; chapter.

5. 因　Yin¹ (yin) - Cause, reason; because.

6. 囫 ⁴　Hu² (hú) - Whole (the snake swallows the mouse –), entire.

7. 困　K'un⁴ (kùn) - Tired, weary; sleepy; surround; poor, needy.

8. 囤　Tun⁴ (dùn) - Bin to hold grain.

9. 囮　Yu² (yóu) - Decoy, inveigle.

10. 固 ⁵　Ku⁴ (gù) - Firm, strong, resolute; originally, inherently.

11. 囹 ⁶　Ling² (líng) - Prison, jail.

12. 囿 ⁷　Yu⁴ (yòu) - Enclosure, animal farm; restrained, limited.

13. 圃　P'u³ (pû) - Vegetable garden; nursery.

14. 圄 ⁸　Yü³ (yû) - Prison; imprison.

15. 圈　Chüan¹ (juan) - Lock up. **Chüan⁴(juàn)** - Pen, sty (pig's).

国 16. 國　Kuo² (guó) - Country, state, nation; national.

囵 17. 圇 **Lun² (lún)** - Whole **(húlún)** (swallow sth. –).

圄 18. 圉 ⁹ **Yü⁴ (yù)** - Stable; prison; the frontier.

囲 19. 圍 **Wei² (wéi)** - Surround; around (– us are mountains).

圆 20. 圓 ¹⁰ **Yüan² (yúan)** - Round, circular; dollar; ball (meat –).

园 21. 園 **Yüan¹ (yuán)** - Garden; park.

图 22. 圖 ¹¹ **T'u² (tú)** - Picture, drawing; chart, map; plan.

团 23. 團 **T'uan² (tuán)** - Round; round mass; group; society.

ENTER 入 · 人

Representing a plant with its roots penetrating the soil 人 .

1. 入 **Ju⁴ (rù)** - Enter, go into; join, become member of.

2. 内 **Nei⁴ (nèi)** - Within, inside; inner.

3. 仝 **Ch'üan² (quán)** - Same as 4 .

4. 全 **Ch'üan² (quán)** - Whole, complete, entire.

两 5. 兩 **Liang³ (liâng)** - Two, both (–sides); a few; tael (weight).

6. 俞 **Yü² (yú)** - Assent, agree to willingly.

EVEN 齊

A field of corn, drawn in perspective, in which the ears are of even height 徐 .

齐 1. 齊 **Ch'i⁴ (qì)** - Even, uniform; together (sing –).

斋 2. 齋³ **Chai¹ (zhāi)** - Abstain, fast; studio, shop; pure, dignified.

EVENING 夕

A wavy half-moon, just appearing above the horizon ⊅ .

1. 夕 **Hsi¹ (xī)** - Evening; sunset.

2. 外² **Wai⁴ (wài)** - Outside; foreign.

3. 夙³ **Su⁴ (Sù)** - Dawn; old, long-standing.

4. 多 **To¹ (duō)** - Many, much; too many/much, excessive.

5. 夜⁵ **Yeh⁴ (yè)** - Night, evening (– classes).

够 6. 夠 **Kou⁴ (gòu)** - Enough, sufficient; reach (– the standard).

梦 7. 夢¹¹ **Meng⁴ (mèng)** - Dream.

伙 8. 夥 **Huo³ (huô)** - Group; band; partner(ship).

EYE 目 . 罒

Picture of an eye ⵊⵏ , set upright ⊖ in order to take up minimum space.

* In a few cases, the horizontal position is maintained ⵊⵏ . (See Nos. 19, 28, 38).

1. 目 **Mu⁴ (mù)** - Eye; look at; item; cataloque.

首 2. 直³ **Chih² (zhí)** - Straight(forward); vertical; erect.

3. 盲 **Mang² (máng)** - Blind.

4. 盼⁴ **P'an⁴ (pàn)** - Long for, hope for; look (– around).

5. 看 **K'an⁴ (kàn)** - Look at, watch; read (– a newspaper, book).

6. 眉 **Mei² (méi)** - Eyebrow.

7. 眇 **Miao³ (miâo)** - Blind on one eye; minute, small.

8. 盻 **Hsi⁴ (xì)** - Look at angrily.

9. 省 **Sheng³ (shêng)** - Save; omit (– a sentence); province.

10. 相 **Hsiang¹ (xiang)** - Mutual, reciprocal; inspect, examine.

11. 眈 **Tan¹ (dan)** - Delay; indulge in (– gambling and drinking).

12. 盾 **Tun⁴ (dùn)** - Shield.

13. 眪 **Tun³ (dûn)** - Doze (– off).

14. 眨⁵ **Cha³ (zhâ)** - Blink, wink (– at a person).

眞 15. 眞 **Chen¹ (zhen)** - Real , genuine, true.

16. 眠 **Mien² (mián)** - Sleep (not enough –)

17. 眩 Hsüan⁴ (xuàn) - Dizzy; confused, bewildered.

18. 眵 ⁶ Ch'ih¹ (chi) - Eye secretion; eyes blurred and sore.

众 19. 眾 Chung⁴ (zhòng) - Many, numerous; the people, a crowd.

20. 眷 Chüan⁴ (juàn) - Family, relatives; care for.

21. 眶 K'uang⁴ (kuàng) - Eye socket.

22. 眸 Mou² (móu) - Eye pupil; eye.

23. 眯 Mi¹ (mi) - Narrowing one's eyes; take a nap.

24. 眼 Yen³ (yǎn) - Eye; aperture, small hole; main point.

困 25. 睏 ⁷ K'un⁴ (kùn) - Be hard pressed; surround; tired; sleepy.

26. 着 Chao¹ (zhao) - Move (in chess); trick. Chao² (zháo) - Touch (down); catch (cold). Cho² (zhuó) - Wear (clothes); touch (down). Chê (zhe) -
眤 27. 睁 ⁸ Cheng¹ (zheng) - Open (– your eyes).   Auxliary word.

28. 睘 Ch'iung² (qióng) - Alone, solitary; dejected; desolate.

29. 睖 Leng⁴ (lèng) - Stare (– blankly).

30. 睦 Mu⁴ (mù) - Harmonious, peaceful; friendly.

31. 睥 Pi⁴ (bì) - Look with suspicion or disapproval.

32. 睡 Shui⁴ (shuì) - Sleep; sleeping (– dress).

33. 督 Tu¹ (du) - Superintend, supervise.

34. 睧 Hun¹ (hun) - Dusk, dim, gloomy; confused.

35. 睬 Ts'ai³ (cǎi) - Pay attention to (– a person).

36. 睫 Chieh² (jié) - Eyelash.

37. 睛 Ching¹ (jing) - Eyeball.

瞷 42. 38. 翠 Yi⁴ (yì) - Keep a watchful eye (– on a person); spy .

39. 睿 Jui⁴(ruì) - Farsighted.

40. 睹⁹ Tu³ (dû) - See, look at, observe.

41. 瞅 Ch'ou³(chôu) - Take a look; glance at.

瞷 42. 瞋¹⁰ Ch'en¹ (chen) - Stare angrily at (– somebody).

43. 瞎 Hsia¹ (xia) - Blind; aimlessly (talk –); foolishly (spend –).

44. 瞌 K'e¹(ke) - Sleepy (feel –), drowsy.

45. 瞑 Ming²(míng) - Close the eyes (– to die).

瞒 46. 瞒¹¹ Man² (mán) - Conceal the truth from someone.

47. 瞟 P'iao³ (piâo) - Cast a glance at.

了 48. 瞭¹² Liao³ (liâo). Lê (le) - Understand; finish. **Liao⁴ (liào)** - Look from afar.

49. 瞬 Shun⁴ (shùn) - Blink, wink (disappear in a –); twinkling.

50. 瞶 K'uei⁴ (kuì) - Dim-sighted; blurred vision.

瞰 51. 瞰 K'an⁴ (kàn) - Look down from a height.

52. 瞳 T'ung² (tóng) - Pupil of the eye.

53. 瞧 Ch'iao² (qiáo) - Look, see.

54. 瞻¹³ Chan¹ (zhan) - Look up; look ahead (– to the future).

55. 瞽 Ku³(gû) - Blind.

56. 瞿 Ch'ü² (qú) - Look at wildly; nervous; frightened.

蒙 57. 矇¹⁴ Meng¹ (meng) - Cheat; make a wild guess; unconscious.

F

FACE 面

The face ◯ with the nose ◉ in the center: 面 .

1. 面 **Mien⁴ (miàn)** - Face, face (v) (the house is –ing the sea).

2. 靦 **T'ien³ (tiân)** - Ashamed, shy; blush.

FATHER 父

A hand ⇒ holding a rod |, to express authority: 父 .

1. 父 **Fu⁴ (fù)** - Father; male relative of older generation.

2. 爸 **Pa⁴ (bà)** - Dad, pa, father.

3. 爹 **Tieh¹ (die)** - Father, dad, daddy.

4. 爺 **Yeh² (yé)** - Yeh² (yé) - Father; grandfather; uncle.

FIELD 田

Picture of a field with furrows ⊕.

1. 田 **T'ien² (tián)** - Field, farmland.

2. 甲¹ **Chia³ (jiǎ)** - First (– class); shell (tortoise –); nail.

3. 由 **Yu² (yóu)** - Cause; because of; by (– land); from (– here).

4. 申 **Shen¹ (shen)** - State, explain; express (– thanks).

5. 男² **Nan² (nán)** - Man, male; son.

6. 甸 **Tien⁴ (diàn)** - Imperial domain; pasture.

7. 甿 ³ **Mang² (máng)** -Fugitives, gypsies. 眠

8. 界⁴ **Chieh⁴ (jiè)** - Boundary, frontier; field (– of vision).

9. 畏 **Wei⁴ (wèi)** - Fear, be afraid of; respect (treat with –).

10. 畜⁵ **Ch'u⁴ (chù)** - Livestock, domestic animals.

11. 留 **Liu² (líu)** - Ask; ask to stay (– for dinner), detain.

12. 畝 **Mu³ (mǔ)** - Chinese acre (0.0667 hectare); 亩

13. 畚 **Pen³ (běn)** - Receptacle w. long handle; scoop up.

14. 畔 **P'an⁴ (pàn)** - Side (river–); bank (river –).

15. 畦⁶ **Ch'i² (qí)** - Field 50 mu (see 12) large; bed (vegetable –).

16. 異 **Yi⁴ (yì)** - Different; strange; separate; another (–day). 异

17. 略 **Lüeh⁴ (lüè)** - Brief (– account); summary, resumé.

毕 18. 畢 **Pi⁴ (bì)** - Finish; conclude, complete; totally.

19. 番⁷ **Fan¹ (fan)** - Barbarians, savages; time (several –s).

画 20. 畫 **Hua⁴ (huà)** - Draw(ing), paint(ing), picture.

当 21. 當⁸ **Tang¹ (dang)** - Equal to; should. **Tang⁴ (dàng)** - Proper; regard as.

22. 疃⁹ **T'uan³ (tuân)** - Village; alley.

23. 畿¹⁰ **Chi¹ (ji)** - Imperial domain; limit; threshold.

24. 畾 **Lei³ (lêi)** - Fields separated by dikes.

畴 25. 疇¹⁴ **Ch'ou² (chóu)** - Farmland; division, class, category.

26. 疆 **Chiang² (jiang)** - Boundary, border, frontier.

叠 27. 疊¹⁷ **Tieh² (dié)** - Pile up; repeat; fold (–letter).

FIGHT 鬥

Two pair of hands 𝄁𝄂 opposing each other: 𝄁𝄂 .

斗 1. 鬥 **Tou⁴ (dòu)** - Fight, contest with.

闹 2. 鬧 **Nao⁴ (nào)** - Noisy; cause trouble; suffer from (– pains).

哄 3. 鬨 **Hung⁴ (hòng)** - Noise of battle; clamor, uproar.

阋 4. 鬩 **Hsi⁴ (xì)** - Quarrel, dispute.

阄 5. 鬮 **Chiu¹ (jiu)** - Lot (draw –s), ballot ticket.

FIRE 火 . 灬

A pile of wood burning with flames 炎 .

1. 火 **Huo³ (huô)** - Fire, flame; anger; ammunitions.

2. 灰 ² **Hui¹ (hui)** - Ashes; dust; grey; disheartened.

3. 灼 ³ **Cho² (zhuó)** - Burn; scorch; bright; luminous; clear, distinct.

4. 灯 **Hung¹ (hong)** - Same as 22.

5. 灸 **Chiu³ (jîu)** - Moxibustion.

灾 6. 災 **Tsai¹ (zai)** - Disaster, calamity, adversity.

7. 灾 **Tsai¹ (zai)** - Same as 6.

8. 灶 **Tsao⁴ (zào)** - Kitchen range, stove; mess, canteen.

9. 炒 ⁴ **Ch'ao³ (châo)** - Sitr-fry; *sauté*.

10. 炙 **Chih⁴ (zhì)** - Broil, roast; dry or toast before a fire.

11. 炊 **Ch'ui¹ (chui)** - Cook food (steam, boil, bake, etc.).

12. 炕 **K'ang⁴ (kàng)** - Brick bed warmed by fire.

13. 炎 **Yen² (yán)** - Hot; burning, blazing; inflammation.

14. 炸 ⁵ **Cha² (zhá)** - Deep fry. **Cha⁴ (zhà)** - Explode, blow up.

15. 炷 **Chu⁴ (zhù)** - Wick (of lamp or candle); incense stick.

16. 炫 **Hsüan⁴ (xuàn)** - Dazzle; show off, brag.

炮 17. 炰 **P'ao¹ (pao)** - Same as 18.

18. 炮 **P'ao[1] (pao)** - Quick-fry, *sauté* ; roast (in ashes); cannon.

19. 炳 **Ping[3] (bǐng)** - Bright; splendid, brilliant, luminous.

炭 20. 炭 **T'an[4] (tàn)** - Charcoal.

21. 烝 [6] **Cheng[1] (zheng)** - Evaporate; steam (food).

22. 烘 **Hung[1] (hong)** - Dry or warm by the fire, bake; set off.

23. 烤 **K'ao[3] (kâo)** - Bake, roast, grill, toast.

24. 烈 **Lieh[4] (liè)** - Strong, energetic, fierce; high-principled.

25. 烙 **Lao[4] (lào)** - Brand (–ing iron); iron (– clothes).

乌 26. 烏 **Wu[1] (wu)** - Crow; black; alas, how.

27. 烟 **Yen[1] (yan)** - Smoke, mist; tobacco, cigarette, opium.

28. 烽 [7] **Feng[1] (feng)** - Beacon.

29. 烹 **P'eng[1] (peng)** - Boil, cook (**pengtiáo**), brew, quick-fry.

30. 焉 **Yen[1] (yan)** - Here, herein; how, why.

31. 焚 [8] **Fen[2] (fén)** - Burn (– incense); set on fire.

32. 然 **Jan[2] (rán)** - Right, correct; so, like that; but, however. *
* Also, a suffix converting word or phrase into adjective or adverb.

33. 焙 **Pei[4] (bèi)** - Bake or dry over a fire.

34. 焦 **Chiao[1] (jiao)** - Burnt, scorched; anxious; harassed.

无 35. 無 **Wu[2] (wú)** - Not, no; nothing, none, nil; without.

36. 焰 **Yen⁴ (yàn)** - Flame, blaze, flare. (Same as 76.)

37. 尉 **Yün⁴ (yùn)** - Iron, press (–suit).

38. 照 ⁹ **Chao⁴ (zhào)** - Shine; photograph; license; according to.

炸 39. 煠 **Cha² (zhá)** - Deep fry.

40. 煅 **Tuan⁴ (duàn)** - Forge (– metal), temper.

41. 煮 **Chu³ (zhû)** - Boil (– eggs), cook (– rice).

烦 42. 煩 **Fan² (fán)** - Annoyed; trouble (may I – you for a match?).

43. 熙 **Hsi¹ (xi)** - Bright, prosperous; gay, merry.

44. 煳 **Hu² (hú)** - Burnt (of food).

焕 45. 煥 **Huan⁴ (huàn)** - Bright, brilliant, shining, glowing.

辉 46. 輝 **Hui¹ (hui)** - Bright, luminous, shine.

47. 煌 **Huang² (huáng)** - Bright, luminous, glittering.

暖 48. 煖 **Nuan³ (nuân)** - Warm, genial; warm up.

炼 49. 煉 **Lien⁴ (liàn)** - Smelt (– metal), temper; refine (– sugar).

50. 煤 **Mei² (méi)** - Coal.

51. 煞 **Sha⁴ (shà)** - Evil spirit, demon, goblin; very.

52 煨 **Chiao⁴ (qiāo)** - Sorrowful, melancholic; stern.

53. 煎 **Chien¹ (jian)** - Fry (– fish, eggs); decoct (– herbs).

53A. 煲 **Pao¹ (bao)** - Boil; heat (v); claypot (– style cooking).

54. 煨 **Wei¹ (wei)** - Stew, simmer; roast in the ashes (– chestnuts).

烟 55. 煙 **Yen¹ (yan)** - Same as 27.

56. 熏 [10] **Hsün¹ (xun)** - Smoke (–d fish); fumigate.

57. 熊 **Hsiung² (xióng)** - Bear.

58. 煽 **Shan¹ (shan)** - Fan a fire; incite, instigate, stir up.

59. 熄 **Hsi¹ (xi)** - Extinguish, put out (– a candle).

60. 熨 **Yün⁴ (yùn)** - Smooth out, iron.

热 61. 熱 [11] **Je⁴ (rè)** - Heat (up), hot; fever; warmhearted, popular.

62. 熬 **Ao¹ (ao)** - Boil, stew. **Ao² (aó)** - Boil, decoct; endure.

63. 熰 **Ou³ (ôu)** - Heat and drought.

64. 熟 **Shu² (shú)** - Ripe; cooked (– meat); familiar with.

65. 熨 **Yün⁴ (yùn)** - Same as 37.

炽 66. 熾 [12] **Ch'ih⁴ (chì)** - Ablaze; burning fiercely (**chìliè**).

67. 燔 **Fan² (fán)** - Burn, roast meat.

68. 燃 **Jan² (rán)** - Burn; ignite, light, set on fire.

69. 燎 **Liao² (liáo)** - Burn, set fire; illuminate.

烧 70. 燒 **Shao¹ (shao)** - Burn; cook; heat (v); roast; braise; fever.

烫 71. 燙 **T'ang⁴ (tàng)** - Burn, scald; press (– suit); perm (– hair).

灯 72. 燈 **Teng¹ (deng)** - Lamp, lantern, light; valve (radio –).

炖 73. 燉 **Tun⁴ (dùn)** - Stew; boil (– tea); warm up (– wine).

74. 燋 **Chiao¹ (jiao)** - Scorch, char, cauterize; torch.

75. 燕 **Yen⁴ (yàn)** - Swallow.

焰 76. 燄 **Yen⁴ (yàn)** - Flame, blaze, flare. (Same as 36.)

烛 77. 燭¹³ **Chu² (zhú)** - Candle; illuminate; watt (a 50– lightbulb).

毁 78. 燬 **Hui³ (huî)** - Destroy by fire; blazing fire; bright, splendid.

79. 燥 **Tsao⁴ (zào)** - Dry, arid, scorched; dry by the fire.

灿 80. 燦 **Ts'an⁴ (càn)** - Magnificent, glorious, bright **(cànlàn)**.

营 81. 營 **Ying² (yíng)** - Camp, seek (– profits); operate (– factory).

耀 82. 燿¹⁴ **Yao⁴ (yào)** - Shine, dazzle; boast, show off.

熏 83. 燻 **Hsün¹ (xun)** - Smoke, treat with smoke (–d fish).

烬 84. 燼 **Chin⁴ (jìn)** - Cinder, ashes, embers; remains, remnant.

85. 爆¹⁵ **Pao⁴ (bào)** - Explode, burst; quick-fry (–ied tripe).

烁 86. 爍 **Shuo⁴ (shuò)** - Bright, shining; glitter, sparkle **(shuòshuò)**.

炉 87. 爐¹⁶ **Lu² (lú)** - Stove, furnace, oven, fireplace.

烂 88. 爛 **Lan⁴ (làn)** - Rotten; worn out; cooked very soft (– meat).

89. 爨²⁵ **Ts'uan⁴ (cuàn)** - Earthen cooking stove; cook (– rice).

FISH 魚

Picture of a fish: head 勺, scaly body ⊘, and tail 火 : 枭

鱼 1. 魚   Yü[2] (yú) - Fish.

鲁 2. 魯[4]   Lu[3] (lŭ) - Stupid; vulgar, rude.

鲨 3. 鮅   Sha[1] (sha) - Shark.

鱿 4. 魷   Yu[2] (yóu) - Squid, cuttlefish.

鲅 5. 鮁[5]   Pa[4] (bà) - Bonito fish; Spanish mackerel.

鲊 6. 鮓   Cha[3] (zhǎ) - Salted or pickled fish.

鲋 7. 鮒   Fu[4] (fù) - Carp; perch.

鲍 8. 鮑   Pao[4] (bào) - Abalone; pickled or salted fish.

鲜 9. 鮮[6]   Hsien[1] (xian) - Fresh, new. Hsien[3] (xîan) - Rare, seldom.

鲛 10. 鮫   Chiao[1] (jiao) - Shark.

鲑 11. 鮭   Kuei[1] (gui) - Salmon.

鲨 12. 鯊[7]   Sha[1] (sha) - Shark.

鲤 13. 鯉   Li[3] (lî) - Carp.

鲫 14. 鯽   Chi[4] (jì) - Silver carp.

鲸 15. 鯨[8]   Ching[1] (jing) - Whale.

鲞 16. 鯗   Hsiang[3] (xiâng) - Dried fish.

鲇 17. 鯰   Nien[2] (nían) - Catfish.

鯖 18. 鯖 **Ch'ing¹ (qing)** - Mackerel.

鰉 19. 鰉 [9] **Huang² (huáng)** - Sturgeon.

鰍 20. 鰍 **Ch'iu¹ (qiu)** - Loach (carp-like fish) (níqiu).

虾 21. 鰕 **Hsia¹ (xia). Ha² (há)** - Shrimp, prawn.

鰍 22. 鰌 **Ch'iu¹ (qiu)** - Same as 20.

鰂 23. 鰂 **Tsei² (zéi)** - Cuttlefish, squid.

鰒 24. 鰒 **Fu⁴ (fù)** - Abalone.

鰥 25. 鰥 [10] **Kuan¹ (guan)** - Bachelor; widower; alone.

鰣 26. 鰣 **Shih² (shí)** - Shad (herring-type fish).

鰱 27. 鰱 **Lien² (lián)** - Silver carp.

鰨 28. 鰨 **T'a³ (tâ)** - Sole.

鳕 29. 鳕 [11] **Hsüeh³ (xûe)** - Cod.

鳞 30. 鳞 [12] **Lin² (lín)** - Fish scales; scaly; overlapping.

鳖 31. 鳖 **Pieh¹ (bie)** - Turtle.

鳗 32. 鳗 **Man² (mán)** - Eel.

鳝 33. 鳝 **Shan⁴ (shàn)** - Eel; finless eel.

鱔 34. 鱔 **Shan⁴ (shàn)** - Same as 33.

鲟 35. 鱘 **Hsün² (xún)** - Sturgeon.

鱖 36 鱖[13] **Kuei[4] (guì)** - Mandarin fish.

脍 37. 鱠 **K'uai[4] (kuài)** Minced meat (fish, etc.); mince.

鲚 38. 鱭 **Chi[3] (jî)** - Anchovy.

鳢 39. 鱧 **Li[3] (lî)** - Black fish.

鲈 40. 鱸[16] **Lu[2] (lú)** - Perch.

鳄 41. 鱷 **E[4] (è)** - Crocodile, alligator; rapacious (living on prey).

FLESH 肉 · 月 ┌─────────────┐ │ **Rapid Access** │ │ *available* │ └─────────────┘

Strips of dried meat, bundled together 肉.

1. 肉 **J ou[4] (ròu)** - Flesh, meat.

2. 肌[2] **Chi[1] (ji)** - Muscle, flesh.

3. 肋 **Lei[4] (lèi)** - Ribs.

4. 肘[3] **Chou[3] (zhôu)** - Elbow.

5. 肓 **Huang[1] (huang)** - Vitals.

6. 肝 **Kan[1] (gan)** - Liver.

7. 肛 **Kang[1] (gang)** - Anus, rectum.

8. 肖 **Hsiao[4] (xiào)** - Resemble, be like.

胳 9. 肐 **Ke[1] (ge)** - Same as 36.

10. 肚 **Tu[4] (dù)** - Belly, abdomen, stomach. **Tu[3] (dû)** - Tripe.

11. 肙   **Yüan[1] (yuan)** - Worm; surround; twist.

12. 肢 [4]   **Chih[1] (zhi)** - Limb.

13. 肥   **Fei[2] (féi)** - Fat; fertilizer.

14. 肺   **Fei[4] (fèi)** - Lungs.

15. 肯   **K'en[3] (kên)** - Agree, be willing to; permit.

16. 肩   **Chien[1] (jian)** - Shoulder.

17. 股   **Ku[3] (gû)** - Thigh; section, division.

18. 肱   **Hung[2] (hóng)** - Humerus, bone in the upper arm.

19. 育   **Yü[4] (yù)** - Give birth; raise (– children).

20. 服   **Fu[4] (fù)** - Dose (of medicine).

21. 胄 [5]   **Chou[4] (zhòu)** - Descendents, posterity; helmet.

22. 胑   **Chih[4] (zhì)** - Upper arm.

23. 胡   **Hu[2] (hú)** - Reckless, careless; how, why.

24. 胖   **P'ang[4] (pàng)** - Fat, plump.

25. 胞   **Pao[1] (bao)** - Placenta, afterbirth.

26. 背   **Pei[4] (bèi)** - Back of the body, of an object; learn by heart.

27. 胚   **P'ei[1] (pei)** - Embryo.

28. 胥   **Hsü[1] (xu)** - Clerk, petty official; all, each and every.

29. 胎   **T'ai[1] (tai)** - Embryo, fetus.

30. 胙 Tso⁴ (zuò) - Sacrificial meal (in ancient times).

31. 胃 Wei⁴ (wèi) - Stomach.

32. 脂⁶ Chih¹ (zhi) - Fat, grease; cosmetics (rouge, powder, etc.).

胁 33. 脅 Hsieh² (xié) - The sides; flanks; ribs; coerce; force.

34. 胸 Hsiung¹ (xiong) - Chest, breast; feelings, mind.

35. 胰 Yi² (yí) - Pancreas.

36. 胳 K'e¹ (ge) - Arm.

37. 胯 K'ua¹ (kua) - Hip. K'ua⁴ (kuà) - Thigh.

38. 胱 Kuang¹ (guang) - Bladder.

脉 39. 脈 Mai⁴ (mài) - Blood vessels; vein (ore –); pulse.

40. 能 Neng² (néng) - Ability, skill; energy (atomic –).

41. 脊 Chi² (jí) - Spine, back(bone); ridge (mountain –).

42. 脆 Ts'ui⁴ (cuì) - Brittle, crisp; loud and clear (voice).

43. 胭 Yen¹ (yan) - Rouge, cosmetics (rouge, powder, etc.).

44. 脯⁷ Fu³ (fǔ) - Dried meat; preserved fruit.

胫 45. 脛 Ching⁴ (jìng) - Shin.

46. 脚 Chiao³ (jiâo) - Foot; base, bottom.

47. 脬 P'ao¹ (pao) - Bladder.

48. 脖 **Po² (bó)** - Neck.

唇 49. 唇 **Ch'un² (chún)** - Lips.

修 50. 脩 **Hsiu¹ (xiu)** - Dried meat; teacher's salary.

51. 脱 **T'o¹ (tuo)** - Undress, take off (– shoes); shed (skin).

胀 52. 脹⁸ **Chang⁴ (zhàng)** - Expand; swell (up).

53. 腓 **Fei² (féi)** - Calf (of the leg).

54. 腐 **Fu³ (fǔ)** - Rotten, decayed, corrupt.

55. 腑 **Fu³ (fǔ)** - Bowels, viscera.

56. 腔 **Ch'iang¹ (qiang)** - Cavity (nasal –); accent (Hunan –).

57. 脾 **P'i² (pí)** - Spleen.

肾 58. 腎 **Shen⁴ (shèn)** - Kidney.

59. 腊 **La⁴ (là)** - Cured (– fish, meat, etc.).

60. 腆 **T'ien³ (tiân)** - Sumptious; rich (– food).

61. 腕 **Wan⁴ (wàn)** - Wrist.

62. 腌 **Yen¹ (yan)** - Salted (– fish); pickled (– vegetables); cured.

63. 腋 **Yeh⁴ (yè)** - Armpit.

肠 64. 腸⁹ **Ch'ang² (cháng)** - Intestines; sausage (**chángr**).

脚 65. 腳 **Chiao³ (jiâo)** - Same as 46.

肿 66. 腫 Chung³ (zhŏng) - Swollen; swelling.

67. 腹 Fu⁴ (fù) - Abdomen, belly, stomach.

脑 68. 腦 Nao³ (nâo) - Brain.

69. 腮 Sai¹ (sai) - Cheek.

70. 腥 Hsing¹ (xing) - Raw fish (or meat); having a fishy smell.

71. 腰 Yao¹ (yao) - Waist; kidney (**yaozi**) ; cashew (**yaoguô**).

72. 膏 ¹⁰ Kao¹ (gao) - Fat, grease; paste (tooth–); ointment.

73. 膈 Ke² (gé) - Diaphragm, midriff.

74. 膂 Lü³ (lü̂) - Backbone.

75. 膊 Po² (bó) - Arm.

嗉 76. 膆 Su⁴ (sù) - Crop of a bird.

77. 腿 T'ui³ (tûi) - Leg, thigh; ham (**huôtuî**).

肤 78. 膚 ¹¹ Fu¹ (fu) - Skin; shallow, superficial (**fufàn**).

胶 79. 膠 Chiao¹ (jiao) - Glue(stick); sticky; rubber (– shoes).

80. 膜 Mo² (mó) - Membrane, film (thin coating).

81. 膝 Hsi¹ (xi) - Knee.

82. 膛 T'ang³ (tang) - Breast, thorax, chest.

腻 83. 膩 ¹² Ni⁴ (nì) - Greasy; sick and tired of.

84. 膨 P'eng² (péng) - Fat, swollen, bloated.

85. 膳 Shan⁴ (shàn) - Food, meals, board (room and –).

86. 臌 [13] Ku³ (gǔ) - Swollen, bloated, puffy.

脸 87. 臉 Lien³ (liân) - Face; front (– of a building).

脓 88. 膿 Nung² (nóng) - Pus.

89. 臂 Pi⁴ (bì) - Arm; upper arm.

90. 臊 Sao⁴ (sao) - Foul smell; rancid.

胆 91. 膽 Tan³ (dân) - Gallbladder; courage, guts.

92. 臀 T'un² (tún) - Buttocks.

93. 膾 Ts'uan¹ (cuan) - Stew (v).

94. 臆 Yi⁴ (yì) - Chest, breast; subjective (– opinion).

95. 膺 Ying¹ (ying) - Breast; receive (– a decoration).

脐 96. 臍 [14] Ch'i² (qí) - Navel.

腊 97. 臘 [15] La⁴ (là) - Cured (fish, meat); sausage (làcháng); the 12th lunar month.

膘 98. 臕 Piao¹ (biao) - Fat (a – cow).

胪 99. 臚 [16] Lu² (lú) - Spread out, display, exhibit.

胭 100. 臙 Yen¹ (yan) - Rouge (yanzhi).

脏 101. 臟 [18] Tsang⁴ (zàng) - Viscera (internal organs of the body).

脔 102. 臠 [19] Lüan² (luán) - Meat in small slices.

FLUTE 龠

Representing a bamboo 㡀 *tube with holes* ∪∪∪ : 龠 .

1. 龠 **Yüeh⁴ (yuè)** - Flute; ancient measure.

2. 龡 **Ch'ui¹ (chui)** - Blow (– out the lamp).

和 3. 龢 **Ho² (hé)** - Harmonious, amiable, gentle.

吁 4. 籲 **You⁴ (yù)** - Appeal; plead. **Hsü¹ (xu)** - Sigh.

FLY 飛

Picture of a flying crane 飛 .

飞 1. 飛 **Fei¹ (fei)** - Fly; swiftly, speedy.

FOLDED HANDS 廾

Two hands joined together and held up in a respectable greeting, the way Chinese people do 廾 .

1. 廾 **Kung³ (gông)** - Hands folded.

2. 廿 **Nien⁴ (niân)** - Twenty.

3. 弁 **Pien⁴ (biàn)** - Man's cap (Chou dynasty).

4. 弄 **Nung⁴ (nòng)** - Play with; do. **Lung⁴ (lòng)** - Alley.

5. 弈 **I⁴ (yì)** - Chinese chess; play chess.

6. 弊 **Pi⁴ (bì)** - Abuses, fraud, malpractice; disadvantage.

FOOD 食 食

A pot with contents ⊙, a ladle ヒ, and the symbol △ to suggest 'mixing'
(three lines coming together): 食

1. 食   Shih² (shí) - Food; eat, edible; eclipse (lunar –).

饥   2. 飢 ² Chi¹ (jī) - Hunger, famine, crop failure; hungry, starving.

饬   3. 飭 ⁴ Ch'ih⁴ (chì) - Put in order; order (strict –s); well-behaved.

饭   4. 飯   Fan⁴ (fàn) - Cooked rice; meal, food.

饪   5. 飪   Jen⁴ (rèn) - Cook food with care.

饨   6. 飩   T'un² (tún) – Used in 'húntun' ('wonton').

饮   7. 飲   Yin³ (yǐn) - Drink (– wine); drink, beverage.

饱   8. 飽 ⁵ Pao³ (bǎo) - Satiated, have eaten enough.

饰   9. 飾   Shih⁴ (shì) - Decorations; impersonate.

饲   10. 飼   Szu⁴ (sì) - Raise, rear; feed, fodder.

饷   11. 餉 ⁶ Hsiang³ (xiǎng) - Entertain (with meals); pay (soldier's –).

饺   12. 餃   Chiao³ (jiǎo) - Meat dumplings (stuffed with meat).

饼   13. 餅   Ping³ (bǐng) - Round flat cake (e.g., mooncake), pancake.

14. 餂   T'ien³ (tiǎn) - Lick, taste.

养   15. 養   Yang³ (yǎng) - Support (– family); raise (– ducks); cultivate.

饿   16. 餓 ⁷ O⁴ (è) - Hungry, starving.

饽 17. 餑 Po¹ (bo) - Cakes, biscuits.

饰 18. 餙 Shih⁴ (shì) - Same as 9.

19. 餐 Ts'an¹ (can) - Food, meal; eat.

余 20. 餘 Yü² (yú) - Surplus, spare (– time); beyond, after (– work).

肴 21. 餚 ⁸ Yao² (yáo) - Food, dishes, delicacies; feast.

馅 22. 餡 Hsien⁴ (xiàn) - Stuffing for pastry, etc.

馄 23. 餛 Hun² (hún) - Used in 'húntun' ('wonton').

馆 24. 館 Kuan³ (guân) - Lodging; service center (restaurant, etc.); cultural center.

饯 25. 餞 Chien⁴ (jiàn) - Give a farewell dinner.

喂 26. 餧 Wei⁴ (wèi) - Hello! Hey! Feed (– a child).

糊 27. 餬 ⁹ Hu² (hú) - Gruel, porridge; seek a living.

28. 餪 Nuan³ (nuân) - Present of food; house-warming.

29. 餮 T'ieh³ (tiê) - Gluttonous, very greedy for food.

馄 30. 餫 Hun² (hún) - Same as 23.

糕 31. 餻 ¹⁰ Kao¹ (gao) - Cakes, pastry, pudding.

馈 32. 餽 K'uei⁴ (kuì) - Present sth. as a gift or as an offering.

馏 33. 餾 Liu⁴ (liù) - Heat up food (in a steamer).

馊 34. 餿 Sou¹ (sou) - Sour; spoiled (– food).

饉 35. 饉[11] **Chin³ (jîn)** - Dearth, famine, crop failure.

馒 36. 饅 **Man² (mán)** - Cakes, steamed bread.

馐 37. 饈 **Hsiu¹ (xiu)** - Savory food, delicacies.

馔 38. 饌[12] **Chuan⁴ (zhuàn)** - Food, banquet (a sumptious –).

饶 39. 饒 **Jao³ (ráo)** - Abundant, plentiful; spare (– one's life).

膳 40. 饍 **Shan⁴ (shàn)** - Food, meals, board (room and –).

饥 41. 饑 **Chi⁴ (ji)** - Be hungry, starve; famine, crop failure.

馈 42. 饋 **K'uei⁴ (kuì)** - Same as 32.

飨 43. 饗[13] **Hsiang³ (xiāng)** - Sacrifice; make offering (to the gods).

44. 饕 **T'ao¹ (tao)** - Gluttonous (greedy for food); fierce, cruel.

餍 45. 饜[14] **Yen⁴ (yàn)** - Satiated, fully satisfied.

馍 46. 饝[16] **Mo² (mó)** - Steamed bread, steamed bun.

馋 47. 饞[17] **Ch'an² (chán)** - Gluttonous, to love to eat; greedy.

FOOT 足 . 𧾷

The foot 止 , with the ankle, heel and toes, at rest ○ : 足.

1. 足 **Tsu² (zú)** - Foot, leg; enough, ample (– food).

2. 趴[2] **P'a¹ (pa)** - Lie prone; bend over.

3. 趷[3] **Ke¹ (ge)** - Thumping, jolting.

4. 趵 Pao⁴ (bào) - Leap.

5. 趾⁴ Chih³ (zhǐ) - Toe, foot.

6. 跶 T'a¹ (ta) - Tread down.

7. 距⁵ Chü⁴ (jù) - Be at a distance from; bird's spur.

8. 跑 P'ao³ (pâo) - Run (away), escape.

9. 跛 Po³ (bô) - Lame, crippled.

10. 跋 Pa² (bá) - Travel, walk; postscript.

11. 跌 Tieh¹ (die) - Fall, stumble, slip; drop (prices –).

12. 跎 T'o² (tuó) - Slip, miss; misstep.

13. 踮 Tien³ (diân) - Stand on tiptoe.

14. 跙 Ch'ieh² (qiè) - Slanting, inclined.

15. 踩 Ts'ai³ (câi) - Step on, trample, stamp (w. the foot).

踩 16. 踏⁶ Ts'ai³ (câi) - Same as 15.

17. 跤 Chiao¹ (jiao) - Wrestle; slip down.

18. 踹 Chuai³ (zhuâi) - Waddle, limp.

19. 跟 Ken¹ (gen) - Heel; follow; to, from, with.

20. 跨 K'ua⁴ (kuà) - Straddle, span; extend; cut across.

21. 跪 Kuei⁴ (gùi) - Kneel, go down on one's knees.

22. 路 Lu⁴ (lù) - Road, path, route; region; class, grade.

23. 跳 T'iao⁴ (tiào) - Jump, leap; palpitate, beat (heart–).

24. 跺 To⁴ (duò) - Stamp (one's foot).

25. 跡 Chi⁴ (jì) - Footprints, traces, clues.

26. 踉 ⁷ Lang¹ (lang) - Stagger, totter.

27. 踊 Yung³ (yŏng) - Jump up, leap up.

28. 踩 Ts'ai³ (câi) - Same as 15.

29. 踝 ⁸ Huai² (huái) - Ankle.

30. 踦 Yi³ (yî) - Crippled, lame.

31. 踞 Chü⁴ (jù) - Squat, sit; crouch; occupy.

32. 踡 Ch'üan² (juán) - Curled up, the legs drawn up.

33. 踏 T'a⁴ (ta) - Tread, trample (– on plants), walk (– on grass).

34. 踢 T'i¹ (ti) - Kick (– the ball); play football.

35. 蹦 Peng⁴ (bèng) - Jump, bounce, hop.

践 36. 踐 Chien⁴ (jiàn) - Trample, tread; carry out (– promise).

37. 踪 Tsung¹ (zong) - Trace (leaves not a –), footprint, track.

38. 踜 Leng² (léng) - A slip, pitch of body.

39. 踒 Wo¹ (wo) - Sprain (ankle or wrist); strain.

40. 踏 [9] Ch'a³ (châ) - Trudge (in mud, snow, etc.).

41. 踹 Ch'uai⁴ (chuài) - Stamp, kick (– the door open), trample.

42. 踵 Chung³ (zhōng) - Heel; follow close behind.

43. 蹂 Jou² (róu) - Tread (on); trample beneath one's feet.

44. 蹄 T'i² (tí) - Hoof (of a horse, ox, etc.).

45. 蹻 Yü² (yú) - Transgress, exceed.

46. 蹇 [10] Chien³ (jiǎn) - Lame; weak; dangerous, distressed.

47. 蹋 T'a⁴ (tà) - Tread heavily, stamp.

48. 蹈 Tao³ (dǎo) - Step, trip, skip, tread (on).

蹄 49. 蹏 T'i² (tí) - Same as 44.

50. 蹉 Ts'o¹ (cuo) - Slip; miss, err.

跄 51. 蹌 Ch'iang⁴ (qiàng) - Stagger (qiàngliàng).

踪 52. 蹝 [11] Hsi³ (xǐ) - Straw sandals, slippers.

Tsung¹ (zōng) - Footprint; track; trace.

遭 53. 蹧 Tsao¹ (zao) - Meet with (– disaster); suffer (– setbacks).

迹 54. 蹟 Chi⁴ (jì) - Same as 25.

55. 蹙 Ts'u⁴ (cù) - Press upon; urgent; wrinkled.

踪 56. 蹤 Tsung¹ (zōng) - Same as 37.

跷 57. 蹻 [12] Ch'iao¹ (qiao) - Lift up (– leg); hold up (– finger); on tip-toe (walk –).

跷 58. 蹺 **Ch'iao[1] (qiao)** - Same as 57.

59. 蹶 **Chüeh[2] (jué)** - Fall, suffer a setback.

60. 蹬 **Teng[1] (deng)** - Step upon; pedal (– a bike), wear (– shoes).

61. 蹭 **Ts'eng[4] (cèng)** - Rub; smeared with; dawdle, loiter.

62. 蹴 **Ts'u[4] (cù)** - Tread on, kick.

63. 蹲 **Tun[1] (dun)** - Squat (on heels), crouch.

64. 躇[13] **Ch'u[2] (chú)** - Irresolute, wavering, undecided.

趸 65. 蠆 **Tun[3] (dûn)** - Wholesale; buy wholesale.

66. 蹋 **T'a[1] (tà)** - To slip.

67. 躁 **Tsao[4] (zào)** - Rash, hasty, impetuous, quick-tempered.

跻 68. 躋[14] **Chi[1] (ji)** - Ascend, mount.

跃 69. 躍 **Yüeh[4] (yuè)** - Leap, jump, skip.

70. 躔[15] **Ch'an[2] (chán)** - Orbit (of celestial body).

蹰 71. 躕 **Ch'u[2] (chú)** - Hesitate, waver, undecided.

72. 躐 **Lieh[4] (liè)** - Overstep, go beyond (– what is proper).

73. 躘[16] **Lung[2] (lóng)** - Walk unsteadily.

蹿 74. 躥[18] **Ts'uan[1] (cuan)** - Jump upwards, leap up, prance.

躜 75. 躦[19] **Tsuan[1] (zuan)** - Jump up, dash forward.

FOOTPRINT 釆

Representing the footprint of an animal 米.

1. 釆 **Pien⁴ (biàn)** - Discriminate, sort out.

2. 采 **Ts'ai³ (cǎi)** - Pluck, gather.

3. 釉 **Yu⁴ (yòu)** - Glaze (–d porcelain); glossy.

释 4. 釋 **Shih⁴ (shì)** - Explain, clear up; release (– prisoner).

FOOTSTEP 彳

A step 丿 *taken by the left foot* 彳 (彳 *the two legs of a person.*): 少 .

1. 彳 **Ch'ih⁴ (chì)** - Walk slowly.

2. 彷⁴ **Fang³ (fǎng)** - Copy, imitate; resemble, be like.

3. 役 **Yi⁴ (yì)** - Service (military –), servant; battle, campaign.

4. 彿⁵ **Fu² (fú)** - Like, resembling; as if.

5. 征 **Cheng¹ (zheng)** - Take a journey; ask for; levy (– taxes).

6. 彼 **Pi³ (bǐ)** - That, those; the other party, he, she.

7. 往 **Wang³ (wǎng)** - Go (coming and –ing); previous (– year).

8. 徂 **Ts'u² (cú)** - Same as 7.

9. 很⁶ **Hen³ (hěn)** - Very (– good), quite (– correct).

后 10. 後 **Hou⁴ (hòu)** - Behind, rear; after(wards). * Empress, queen.

* Additional meanings referring only to the Simplified Form.

11. 徊 **Hui² (húi)** - Pace to and fro; wander about.

12. 律 **Lü⁴ (lù)** - Law, rule, statute; restrain, discipline.

13. 待 **Tai⁴ (dài)** - Wait for; treat (– others right); about to (– go).

14. 徇 **Hsün⁴ (xùn)** - Everywhere; follow after; quick; give in.

径 15. 徑⁷ **Ching⁴ (jìng)** - Path, way; directly (deal –); diameter.

16. 徐 **Hsü² (xú)** - Slowly, gradually, gently.

17. 徒 **T'u² (tú)** - On foot; follower, apprentice; merely; in vain.

18. 徘⁸ **P'ai² (pái)** - Pace up and down; hesitate, waver.

徕 19. 徠 **Lai² (lái)** - Solicit (– business, customers) (zhaolái).

20. 徙 **Hsi³ (xǐ)** - Move one's residence; shift; remove.

21. 得 **Te² (dé)** - Get, obtain, gain; suitable; complacent.

从 22. 從 **Ts'ung² (cóng)** - From; follow, obey.

23. 徜 **Ch'ang² (cháng)** - Wander about to and fro, irresolute.

24. 御 **Yü⁴ (yù)** - Drive (a carriage); withstand, resist.

复 25. 復⁹ **Fu⁴ (fù)** - Turn round; again; answer. *Duplicate.

健 26. 健 **Chien⁴ (jiàn)** - Healthy, strong; strengthen, invigorate.

遍 27. 徧 **Pien⁴ (biàn)** - Everywhere, all over; (N).

28. 徨 **Huáng² (huáng)** - Hesitating, doubtful, irresolute.

29. 循 **Hsün² (xún)** - Follow, according to, abide by (– the rules).

30. 微¹⁰ **Wei¹ (wei)** - Minute, small; declining; micro (– film).

彻 31. 徹[12] Ch'e[4] (chè) - Thorough; penetrating.

征 32. 徵 Cheng[1] (zheng) - Same as 5.

33. 德 Te[2] (dé) - Virtue, morality, ethics; kindness.

34. 徽[14] Hui[1] (hui) - Emblem, badge, insigna.

FRAGRANT 香

The sweet 日 *(a Radical) odor of fermented (= = vapors) grain* 禾
(a Radical): 香 .

1. 香 Hsiang[1] (xiang) - Fragrant, scented; popular; incense.

2. 馨 Hsin[1] (xin) - Strong pervasive fragrance; good reputation.

G

GHOST 鬼

Picture of a ghost moving through the air 鬼 *(*⁄⁄ *represents the swirl caused by the movement).*

1. 鬼 **Kuei³ (guî)** - Ghost, spirit, demon, devil; dirty trick.

2. 魂 ⁴ **Hun² (hún)** - Soul, spirit; mind, wits, faculties.

3. 魁 **K'uei² (kúi)** - Chief, head (department –); the best.

4. 魅 ⁵ **Mei⁴ (mèi)** - Evil spirit, demon.

5. 魄 **P'o⁴ (pò)** - Soul, spirit; form, shape.

6. 魉 ⁸ **Liang³ (liâng)** - Supernatural being (nymph, fairy, etc.)

7. 魍 **Wang³ (wâng)** - Same as 6.

8. 魏 **Wei⁴ (wèi)** - One of the Three Kingdoms (220-265).

9. 魑 [11] **Ch'ih¹ (chi)** - Evil spirit, demon, monster.

10. 魔 **Mo² (mó)** - Evil spirit, demon, monster; mystic (– power).

魇 11. 魘 [14] **Yen³ (yân)** - Bad dreams, nightmare.

GO 行

Footsteps made by left and right feet: 彳亍 .

1. 行 **Hsing² (xíng)** - Go, travel; circulate; store; perform.

2. 衍 [3] **Yen³ (yân)** - Spread out; amplify; abundant, superfluous.

术 3. 術 [5] **Shu⁴ (shù)** - Art; skill, technique, tactics.

炫 4. 衒 **Hsüan⁴ (xuàn)** - Dazzle (–ing beauty); brag, show off.

5. 街 [6] **Chieh¹ (jie)** - Street, road; market, country fair.

同 6. 衕 **T'ung⁴ (tòng)** - Lane, alley.

7. 衙 [7] **Ya² (yá)** - Public office; court, tribunal.

冲 8. 衝 [9] **Ch'ung⁴ (chòng)** - Vigorously.* **Ch'ung¹ (chong)** - Rinse; rush.

胡 9. 衚 **Hu² (hú)** - Cross street; side street.

卫 10. 衛 [10] **Wei⁴ (wèi)** - Guard, protect.

11. 衡 **Heng² (héng)** - Scale; weigh, measure, judge.

卫 12. 衞 **Wei⁴ (wèi)** - Same as 10.

13. 衢 [18] **Ch'ü² (qú)** - Thoroughfare, highway.

GOLD (METAL) 金

Four nuggets (ore) 金 buried (𠆢 cover) in the earth 土 (Rad): 釜 *.*

1. 金 **Chin¹ (jīn)** - Gold; metal.

针 2. 針² **Chen¹ (zhēn)** - Needle; injection; acupuncture.

3. 釜 **Fu³ (fǔ)** - Ancient cauldron; pan.

钉 4. 釘 **Ting¹ (dīng)** - Nail; follow closely, press, urge.

钏 5. 釧³ **Ch'uan³ (chuàn)** - Bracelet.

钗 6. 釵 **Ch'ai¹ (chāi)** - Hairpin.

扣 7. 釦 **K'ou⁴ (kòu)** - Button, buckle; button up; discount; arrest.

焊 8. 釬 **Han⁴ (hàn)** - Weld, solder.

钓 9. 釣 **Tiao⁴ (diào)** - Fish w. hook and line; fishhook.

钞 10. 鈔⁴ **Ch'ao¹ (chāo)** - Bank notes, paper money.

钩 11. 鈎 **Kou¹ (gōu)** - Hook (fishing –); check mark.

钤 12. 鈐 **Ch'ien² (qián)** - Seal; affix a seal.

钧 13. 鈞 **Chün¹ (jūn)** - Ancient unit of weight (30 catties).

钮 14. 鈕 **Niu³ (nîu)** - Handle, knob, button; bond (– of friendship).

钯 15. 鈀 **Pa⁴ (bà)** - Harrow, rake; harrow (v).

钝 16. 鈍 **Tun⁴ (dùn)** - Blunt, dull; stupid, dull-witted.

钩 17. 鈎⁵ **Kou¹ (gōu)** - Same as 11.

钼 18. **鉏** Ch'u² (chú) - Hoe (tool); hoe (v), weed.

钳 19. **鉗** Ch'ien² (qián) - Pincers, pliers, forceps; grip; restrain.

铊 20. **鉈** T'o² (tuó) - Stone roller; sliding weight on a steelyard.

铃 21. **鈴** Ling² (líng) - Bell (door-).

刨 22. **鉋** Pao⁴ (bào) - Plane (n)(v). * P'ao² (páo) - Dig, excavate.

钹 23. **鈸** Po² (bó) - Cymbals.

钿 24. **鈿** Tien⁴ (diàn) - Filigree (ornament of gold and silver wire).

钺 25. **鉞** Yüeh⁴ (yuè) - Ancient battle axe.

铅 26. **鉛** Ch'ien¹ (qian) - Lead.

铳 27. **銃**⁶ Ch'ung⁴ (chòng) - Blunderbuss, gun.

衔 28. **銜** Hsien² (xián) - Hold in the mouth; rank, title.

铪 29. **鉿** Ke⁴ (gè) - Creaking sound.

铰 30. **鉸** Chiao³ (jiâo) - Hinge; scissors; cut with scissors.

铭 31. **銘** Ming² (míng) - Engrave; memorize (engrave on mind).

铫 32. **銚** Tiao⁴ (diào) - Sauce pan.

铁 33. **銕** T'ieh³ (tiê) - Iron; arms; unalterable, determined.

铜 34. **銅** T'ung² (tóng) - Copper, bronze, brass.

铨 35. **銓** Ch'üan² (quán) - Measure, weigh; estimate; select, choose.

铐 36. 銬 **K'ao⁴ (kào)** - Handcuffs.

银 37. 銀 **Yin² (yín)** - Silver.

锄 38. 鋤⁷ **Ch'u² (chú)** - Hoe; hoe (v), weed; eliminate.

锋 39. 鋒 **Feng¹ (feng)** - Sharp edge or point of sword; front(al).

铓 40. 鋩 **Mang² (máng)** - Edge, sharp point.

焊 41. 銲 **Han⁴ (hàn)** - Same as 8.

销 42. 銷 **Hsiao¹ (xiao)** - Melt (– metal); cancel; sell; spend.

锐 43. 鋭 **Jui⁴ (ruì)** - Sharp, acute; vigor, fighting spirit.

铗 44. 鋏 **Chia² (jiâ)** - Pincers, tongs.

铺 45. 鋪 **P'u⁴ (pù)** - Shop. **P'u¹ (pu)** - Spread; extend, unfold.

锈 46. 銹 **Hsiu⁴ (xìu)** - Rust; become rusty.

锓 47. 鋟 **Ch'in¹ (qîn)** - Engrave, carve.

锉 48. 銼 **Ts'o⁴ (cùo)** - File (tool); file(v).

49. 鋑 **Chien¹ (jian)** - Engrave, carve.

锥 50. 錐⁸ **Chui¹ (zhui)** - Awl, gimlet; drill, bore.

铮 51. 錚 **Cheng¹ (zheng)** - Clang of metal.

锤 52 錘 **Ch'ui² (chuí)** - Hammer; hammer (v); weight on steelyard.

钢 53. 鋼 **Kang¹ (gang)** - Steel.

锦 54. 錦 **Chin³ (jīn)** - Brocade, tapestry; ornamented, flowered.

锢 55. 錮 **Ku⁴ (gù)** - Held in custody, imprison.

锯 56. 鋸 **Chü⁴ (jù)** - Saw; saw (v).

锞 57. 錁 **K'o⁴ (kè)** - Bullion; ingot (of gold or silver).

录 58. 錄 **Lu⁴ (lù)** - Record, copy; employ, hire.

锛 59. 錛 **Pen¹ (ben)** - Adze (cutting tool w. arched blade).

锡 60. 錫 **Hsi¹ (xi)** - Tin; pewter.

锭 61. 錠 **Ting⁴ (dìng)** - Ingot; ingot-shaped tablet (of Chin. ink, etc.)

钱 62. 錢 **Ch'ien² (qián)** - Money; cash; fund (public –s).

错 63. 錯 **Ts'o⁴ (cuò)** - Grindstone; wrong, mistaken.

锸 64. 鍤 ⁹ **Ch'a¹ (cha)** - Spade.

针 65. 鍼 **Chen¹ (zhen)** - Same as 2.

锚 66. 錨 **Mao² (máo)** - Anchor.

钟 67. 鍾 **Chung¹ (zhong)** - Bell; clock; o'clock; handleless cup.

键 68. 鍵 **Chien⁴ (jiàn)** - Key (of piano, typewriter); bolt.

锅 69. 鍋 **Kuo¹ (guo)** - Caldron; pot (–sticker), pan (sauce –).

链 70. 鍊 **Lien⁴ (liàn)** - Smelt, temper (metal); chain (iron –).

镀 71. 鍍 **Tu⁴ (dù)** - Gilding; plating (electro–).

锻 72. 鍛 **Tuan⁴ (duàn)** - Forge, temper (metal).

锹 73. 鍬 **Ch'iao¹ (qiao)** - Shovel, spade.

74. 鍱 **Yeh⁴ (yè)** - Thin iron plate.

镇 75. 鎮¹⁰ **Chen⁴ (zhèn)** - Suppress; ease (– pain); calm; cool in ice.

耨 76. 鎒 **Nou⁴ (nòu)** - Hoe, weed.

锤 77. 鎚 **Ch'ui² (chúi)** - Hammer, hammer (– into shape); weight.

铠 78. 鎧 **K'ai³ (kâi)** - Suit of armor.

镰 79. 鎌 **Lien² (lián)** - Sickle, scythe.

镑 80. 鎊 **Pang⁴ (bàng)** - Pound sterling. **P'ang³ (pâng)** - Hoe (v).

81. 鎙 **So⁴ (suò)** - Large spear.

锁 82. 鎖 **So³ (suô)** - Lock, lock up.

枪 83. 鎗 **Ch'iang¹ (qiang)** - Gun, rifle; spear, lance.

熔 84. 鎔 **Jung² (róng)** - Melt, smelt; fuse.

铲 85. 鏟¹¹ **Ch'an³ (chân)** - Shovel, spade; spade (v), shovel (v).

镜 86. 鏡 **Ching⁴ (jìng)** - Mirror, lens (optical –).

镂 87. 鏤 **Lou⁴ (lòu)** - Carve, engrave.

链 88. 鏈 **Lien⁴ (liàn)** - Chain. **Lien² (lián)** - Lead or tin ore.

镘 89. 鏝 **Man⁴ (màn)** - Trowel, spread mortar.

90. 鏊 **Ao⁴ (aò)** - Iron griddle.

旋 91. 鏇 **Hsüan⁴ (xuàn)** - Whirl (adj). * **Hsüan² (xuán)** - Revolve; return; soon.

镗 92. 鏜 **T'ang¹ (tang)** - Sound of gong. **T'ang² (táng)** - Boring.

鏨 93. 鏨 **Tsan⁴ (zàn)** - Chisel, engrave (on gold or silver).

镞 94. 鏃 **Tsu² (zú)** - Arrowhead; head of javelin.

钟 95. 鐘¹² **Chung¹ (zhong)** - Bell; clock; o'clock; handleless cup.

铧 96. 鏵 **Hua² (húa)** - Plowshare.

镫 97. 鐙 **Teng⁴ (dèng)** - Stirrup.

镣 98. 鐐 **Liao⁴ (liào)** - Fetters, shackles.

铙 99. 鐃 **Nao² (náo)** - Big (hand) cymbals.

锡 100. 鐋 **T'ang⁴ (tàng)** - Plane (carpenter's tool); smooth (v).

锈 101. 鏽 **Hsiu⁴ (xìu)** - Rust (of metal); rusty.

镮 102. 鐶¹³ **Huan² (huán)** - Metal ring, bracelet.

镯 103. 鐲 **Cho² (zhuó)** - Bracelet.

镰 104. 鐮 **Lien³ (lián)** - Sickle, scythe, reaping hook.

铛 105. 鐺 **Tang¹ (dang)** - *Clang!* **Ch'eng¹ (cheng)** - Shallow flat pan.

铁 106. 鐵 **T'ieh³ (tiē)** - Iron; arms; unalterable; determined.

铎 107. 鐸 **To² (duó)** - Large bell, formerly used in times of war.

铸 108. 鑄[14] **Chu⁴ (zhù)** - Cast, found metal.

镬 109. 鑊 **Huo⁴ (huò)** - Pot, caldron.

鉴 110. 鑑 **Chien⁴ (jiàn)** - Bronze mirror; reflect; inspect, examine.

鉴 111. 鑒 **Chien⁴ (jiàn)** - Same as 110.

镴 112. 鑞[15] **La⁴ (là)** - Tin; solder.

铄 113. 鑠 **Shuo⁴ (shuò)** - Melt (a metal); weaken; destroy.

炉 114. 鑪[16] **Lu² (lú)** - Stove, furnace, fireplace.

镵 115. 鑱[17] **Ch'an² (chán)** - Cut into, carve, chisel.

镶 116. 鑲 **Hsiang¹ (xiang)** - Inlay; mount; rim, border.

钥 117. 鑰 **Yao⁴ (yào)** - Key (yàoshi). **Yüeh⁴ (yùe)** - Key.

罐 118. 鑵[18] **Kuan⁴ (guàn)** - Can, jar, pot, tin (– of condensed milk).

镊 119. 鑷 **Nieh⁴ (niè)** - Forceps, tweezers; pick up w. tweezers.

锣 120. 鑼[19] **Lo² (luó)** - Gong.

銮 121. 鑾 **Luan² (luán)** - Small tinkling bell.

钻 122. 鑽 **Tsuan¹ (zuan)** - Drill (v). **Tsuan⁴ (zuàn)** - Drill (n); diamond.

凿 123. 鑿[20] **Tsao² (záo)** - Chisel; punch (– a hole), dig.

GRAIN 禾

Representing a plant (木 Tree) with ripening ears hanging down
at the top: 禾

1. 禾   Ho² (hé) - Grain in the field (esp. rice), paddy.

2. 秀 ²   Hsiu⁴ (xiù) - Beautiful, elegant; excellent.

3. 私   Szu¹ (si) - Private, personal; secret, illegal.

4. 禿   T'u¹ (tu) - Bald, barren; blunt; unsatisfactory.

5. 秆 ³   Kan³ (gân) - Stalk, stem (of paddy, etc.).

6. 秉   Ping³ (bîng) - Grasp, hold; control, preside over.

7. 籼   Hsien¹ (xian) - Long-grained nonglutinous rice.

8. 科 ⁴   K'o¹ (ke) - Branch of study; department; sentence (v).

9. 秒   Miao³ (miâo) - Second (1/60 of a minute).

10. 秕   Pi³ (bî) - Withered grain; blighted.

11. 秋   Chiu¹ (qiu) - Autumn; harvest time; time (troubled –s).

12. 秩 ⁵   Chih⁴ (zhì) - Order (observe –), decade.

13. 秤   Ch'eng⁴ (chèng) - Scales; balance; steelyard.

14. 秘   Mi⁴ (mì) - Secret, mysterious; keep sth. secret.

秫 15. 秫   Shu² (shú) - Sorghum.

16. 秦   Ch'in² (qín) - Ch'in Dynasty (221-207 B.C.).

17. 租 **Tzu[1] (zu)** - Rent, lease; hire (- car), charter (- bus).

18. 秧 **Yang[1] (yang)** - Rice seedlings; young (- pigs).

19. 移[6] **Yi[2] (yí)** - Move, remove, shift; change, alter.

20. 秸 **Chieh[1] (jie)** - Stalks left after thrashing, straw.

21. 稀[7] **Hsi[1] (xi)** - Rare, scarce, sparse; dilute, thin (- gruel).

22. 程 **Ch'eng[2] (chéng)** - Regulation; journey; procedure.

秆 23. 稈 **Kan[3] (gân)** - Same as 5.

24. 粳 **Ching[1] (jing)** - Round-grained nonglutinous rice.

25. 稍 **Shao[1] (shao)** - A little, somewhat, slightly (- better).

26. 税 **Shui[4] (shuì)** - Tax, duty, toll.

27. 稠[8] **Ch'ou[2] (chóu)** - Crowded, dense, thick (- porridge).

28. 稚 **Chih[4] (zhì)** - Young, immature, childish.

29. 稔 **Jen[3] (rên)** - Ripe grain; harvest; be familiar with sb.

30. 稜 **Leng[2] (léng)** - Edge, corner; ridge (-s of a washboard).

禀 31. 稟 **Ping[3] (bîng)** - Stipend, rations; report to superior.

32. 稗 **Pai[4] (bài)** - Barnyard grass, weeds; insignificant.

称 33. 稱[9] **Ch'eng[1] (cheng)** - Call, name (v). **Ch'en[4] (chèn)** - Fit (v).

种 34. 種 **Chung[3] (zhông)** - Species; seed. **Chung[4] (zhòng)** - Grow.

35. 稿 Kao³ (gâo) - Stalk, straw; sketch, manuscript. [10]

36. 稽 Chi¹ (ji) - Investigate, examine; delay, procrastinate.

37. 稼 Chia⁴ (jià) - Farming (sow and reap grain); cereals, grain.

谷 38. 穀 Ku³ (gû) - Cereal; grain. * Valley; gorge.
*Refers to the simplified only, when it is also a traditional.

39. 稻 Tao⁴ (dào) - Rice (while growing in the field), paddy.

40. 穆 Mu⁴ (mù) - Solemn, reverent. [11]

穌 41. 穌 Su¹ (su) - Revive.

积 42. 積 Chi¹ (ji) - Accumulate; long-pending (- case); indigestion.

颖 43. 穎 Ying³ (yîng) - Grain husk; tip (- of a brush); clever.

44. 穗 Sui⁴ (suì) - Ear or spike of grain; tassel, fringe. [12]

穑 45. 穡 Se⁴ (sè) - Ripe grain; farming (sow and reap). [13]

秽 46. 穢 Hui⁴ (huì) - Weeds among grain; filthy, dirty, abominable.

糯 47. 穤 No⁴ (nuò) - Glutinous (- rice), sticky. [14]

稳 48. 穩 Wen³ (wên) - Firm, steady, stable; sure (are you -?).

GRASS 艸 · 丷 艹 Rapid Access available

Representing grass, growing in abundance 丱 .

草 1. 艸 **Ts'ao³ (cǎo)** - Grass, straw; hasty (– writing), rough; draft.

艾 2. 艾² **Ai⁴ (ài)** - Chinese mugwort *(Artemisia argyi)* ; end, stop.

芒 3. 芒³ **Mang² (máng)** - Mango; awn or beard of grains.

卉 4. 芔 **Hui⁴ (huì)** - Grass (various kinds), plants, herbs.

芍 5. 芍 **Shao² (sháo)** - Peony.

芋 6. 芋 **Yü⁴ (yù)** - Taro, any edible tuber.

芝 7. 芝⁴ **Chih¹ (zhi)** - Medical fungus.

刍 8. 芻 **Ch'u² (chú)** - Hay; fodder; cut grass (v).

芬 9. 芬 **Fen¹ (fen)** - Fragrance.

芳 10. 芳 **Fang¹ (fang)** - Fragrant, good (of – reputation), virtuous.

芙 11. 芙 **Fu² (fú)** - Hibiscus.

花 12. 花 **Hua¹ (hua)** - Flower; variegated; fireworks; blurred; spend.

芥 13. 芥 **Chieh⁴ (jiè)** - Mustard greens.

芨 14. 芨 **Chi¹ (ji)** - Orchid.

芩 15. 芩 **Ch'in² (qín)** - Salt-marsh plant.

芹 16. 芹 **Chin² (qín)** - Celery, parsley, cress.

芭 17. 芭 **Pa¹ (ba)** - Banana (**bajiao**); ballet (**balêiwû**).

芟 18. 芟 **Shan¹ (shan)** - Cut grass or herbs; weed out, eliminate.

芽 19. 芽 **Ya² (yá)** - Shoot, sprout, bud.

芫 20. 芫 **Yüan² (yuán)** - Lilac daphne, coriander.

芸 21. 芸 **Yün² (yún)** - Rue, strong-scented herb; deep yellow.

苧 22. 苧 ⁵ **Chu⁴ (zhù)** - Hemp, ramie (Asiatic hemp) (**zhùmá**).

苛 23. 苛 **K'o¹ (ke)** - Cruel, harsh; severe, exacting.

24. 苢 **Yi³ (yǐ)** - Same as 26.

若 25. 若 **Je⁴ (rè)** - If (– so), as if, as (– it were); follow.

苡 26. 苡 **Yi³ (yǐ)** - Job's tears (pearly seeds of Asiatic grass).

苟 27. 苟 **Kou³ (gôu)** - Careless; if (– you study, you'll pass).

茄 28. 茄 **Ch'ieh² (qié)** - Eggplant, aubergine (fruit of eggplant).

苦 29. 苦 **K'u³ (kû)** - Bitter; pains, suffering; painstaking.

茅 30. 茅 **Mao² (máo)** - Cogon grass (Philip. grass used for roof).

茂 31. 茂 **Mao⁴ (maò)** - Exuberant, flourishing; abundant.

苗 32. 苗 **Miao² (miáo)** - Seedling , sprouts; vaccine.

茉 33. 茉 **Mo⁴ (mò)** - White jasmine.

苜 34. 苜 **Mu⁴ (mù)** - Alfalfa, lucerne.

苫 35. 苫 **Shan⁴ (shàn)** - Cover with straw, cloth, etc.

苔 36. 苔 **T'ai² (tái)** - Moss, lichen.

英 37. 英 **Ying¹ (ying)** - Flower; superior, outstanding; English.

苑 38. 苑 **Yüan⁴ (yuàn)** - Garden (Imperial –s); centre of sci. & arts.

茶 39. 茶⁶ **Ch'a² (chá)** - Tea.

荒 40. 荒 **Huang¹ (huang)** - Wasteland; famine; shortage.

茴 41. 茴 **Hui² (húi)** - Fennel, anise-seed.

茹 42. 茹 **Ju² (rú)** - Eat.

荐 43. 荐 **Chien⁴ (jiàn)** - Grass, straw, strawmat; recommend.

荆 44. 荆 **Ching¹ (jing)** - Bramble (prickly shrub); thorn.

荔 45. 荔 **Li⁴ (lì)** - Lichee.

茫 46. 茫 **Mang² (máng)** - Boundless, vast, vague; ignorant.

茗 47. 茗 **Ming² (míng)** - Tender leaves or leaf buds of tea.

答 48. 荅 **Ta¹ (da)** - Undertake.

等 49. 荨 **Teng³ (dêng)** - Wait; grade; equal; and so on; plural sign.

草 50. 草 **Ts'ao³ (câo)** - Same as 1.

兹 51. 兹 **Tzu¹ (zi)** - This, here; now, recently (– seen); year (this –).

茨 52. 茨 **Tz'u² (cí)** - Thatch (roof); caltrop (plant w. spined flowers).

茵 53. 茵 **Yin¹ (yin)** - Mattress; cushion; mat.

庄 54. 莊⁷ **Chuang¹ (zhuang)** - Village; thoroughfare; store; serious.

茎 55. 莖 **Ching¹ (jing)** - Stem or salk of plant.

荷 56. 荷 **Ho² (hé)** - Lotus, water lily.

荚 57. 莢 **Chia² (jiá)** - Pod (long seed-vessel); seed.

莉 58. 莉 **Li⁴ (lì)** - White jasmine.

莫 59. 莫 **Mo⁴ (mò)** - Not, do not; no one; nothing, none.

荸 60. 荸 **Pi² (bí)** - Water chestnut **(bíqi)**.

豆 61. 荳 **Tou⁴ (dòu)** - Legumes, beans, peas; sacrificial vessel.

莠 62. 莠 **Yu³ (yôu)** - Green bristlegrass; bad people.

菖 63. 菖⁸ **Ch'ang¹ (chang)** - Calamus, sweet flag (marsh herb).

菲 64. 菲 **Fei³ (fêi)** - Red turnip; poor, humble, simple (– meal).

华 65. 華 **Hua² (huá)** - China, Chinese; prosperous; magnificent.

刺 66. 莿 **Tz'u⁴ (cì)** - Thorn; sarcastic.

菇 67. 菇 **Ku¹ (gu)** - Mushroom **(mógu)** (see No. 155), fungus.

菊 68. 菊 **Chü² (jú)** - Chrysanthemum.

莱 69. 萊 **Lai² (lái)** - Goosefoot (herb).

菱 70. 菱 **Ling² (líng)** - Water chestnut.

莽 71. 莽 **Mang³ (mâng)** - Clusters of grass; rough, rash (– person).

萌 72. 萌 **Meng² (méng)** - Sprout, shoot, bud, germinate.

苞 73. 苞 **Pao¹ (bao)** - Bud; luxuriant, profuse, thick.

萍 74. 萍 **P'ing² (píng)** - Duckweed.

菠 75. 菠 **Po¹ (bo)** - Spinach (**bocài**); pineapple (**boluó**).

菩 76. 菩 **P'u² (pú)** - Bodhi tree.

菽 77. 菽 **Shu¹ (shu)** - Edible seeds (e.g. peas, beans).

萄 78. 萄 **T'ao² (táo)** - Grape (– wine).

菜 79. 菜 **Ts'ai⁴ (cài)** - Vegetable; dish, course; cuisine.

灾 80. 菑 **Tsai¹ (zai)** - Calamity, disaster, adversity.

菁 81. 菁 **Ching¹ (jing)** - Lush, luxuriant; essence.

萃 82. 萃 **Ts'ui⁴ (cùi)** - Assemble; gathering, collection (stamp –).

烟 83. 菸 **Yen¹ (yan)** - Smoke, mist; tobacco, cigarette; opium.

萎 84. 萎 **Wei¹ (wei)** - Decline, wither, dying; rotten.

著
* 着 85. 著⁹ **Chu⁴ (zhù)** - Outstanding; write (– book); writings, book.
* **Cho² (zhuó)** - Wear (clothes); touch (down); apply (color).

葫 86. 葫 **Hu² (hú)** - Calabash, gourd.

荤 87. 葷 **Hun¹ (hun)** - Meat or fish dish; onion, garlic, leek.

葭 88. 葭 **Chia¹ (jia)** - Rush (marsh plant), reed.

韭 88A. 韭 **Chiu³ (jîu)** - (Chinese) chives; leeks.

葛 89. 葛 **Ke² (gé)** - Kudzu vine (Asiatic creeping vine).

葵 90. 葵 **K'uei² (kuí)** - Mallow (plant w. large flowers), sunflower.

落 91. 落 **Lao⁴ (lào)** - Fall, drop, go down, set (the sun has –).

葡 92. 葡 **P'u² (pú)** - Grapes.

葚 93. 葚 **Jen⁴ (rèn)** - Mulberry.

蒂 94. 蒂 **Ti⁴ (dì)** - Base of a fruit or flower.

董 95. 董 **Tung³ (dǒng)** - Direct, superintend; director, trustee.

葬 96. 葬 **Tsang⁴ (zàng)** - Bury, inter.

葺 97. 葺 **Ch'i⁴ (qì)** - Thatch (cover roof w. straw); repair a house.

葱 98. 葱 **Ts'ung¹ (cong)** - Onion; green onion; scallion.

万 99. 萬 **Wan⁴ (wàn)** - Ten thousand, myriad (very large number).

苇 100. 葦 **Wei³ (wěi)** - Reed.

莴 101. 萵 **Wo¹ (wo)** - Lettuce (woju).

叶 102. 葉 **Yeh⁴ (yè)** - Leaf, foliage; period (– of the Ch'ing Dynasty).

药 103. 藥 **Yao⁴ (yào)** - Medicinal (– herbs), medicine; cure, remedy.

蒸 104. 蒸¹⁰ **Cheng¹ (zheng)** - Steam (– food); evaporate.

蓄 105. 蓄 **Hsü⁴ (xù)** - Save up, store up; harbor (– resentment).

蒿 106. 蒿 **Hao¹ (hao)** - Wormwood (*Artemisia*, used in medicine).

盖 107. 蓋 **Kai⁴ (gài)** - Lid; seal (n/v); shell (tortoise –); build.

莅 108. 莅 **Li⁴ (lì)** - Arrive at; be present at, attend (– a meeting).

蒙 109. 蒙 **Meng¹ (meng)** - Cheat; guess wildly; unconscious. **Meng²** **(méng)** - Cover (v); ignorant. **Meng³ (mêng)** - Mongolian.

蒲 110. 蒲 **P'u² (pú)** - Cattail (tall marsh reed w. flat leaves).

搜 111. 蒐 **Sou¹ (sou)** - Hunt, search, drill.

蓑 112. 蓑 **So¹ (suo)** - Straw or palm-leaf rain cape.

蒜 113. 蒜 **Suan⁴ (suàn)** - Garlic.

苍 114. 蒼 **Ts'ang¹ (cang)** - Azure, deep-green; sky blue; grey.

蕀 115. 蕀 **Chi² (jí)** - Gorse, furze (yellow-flowered evergreen).

蓉 116. 蓉 **Jung² (róng)** - Cottonrose hibiscus.

蔗 117. 蔗[11] **Che⁴ (zhè)** - Sugar-cane.

艺 118. 蓺 **Yi⁴ (yì)** - Art, skill (**yìshù**).

蔻 119. 蔻 **K'ou⁴ (kòu)** - Cardamon (herb of ginger family).

莲 120. 蓮 **Lien² (lián)** - Lotus.

蔑 121. 蔑 **Mieh⁴ (miè)** - Slight, disdain, slander; nothing, none.

蓬 122. 蓬 **P'eng² (péng)** - Fleabane (*Erigeron*); disheveled.

卜 123. 蔔 **Po (bo)** - Turnip, radish (**luóbo**). * **Pu³ (bû)** - Divination.

蔬 124. 蔬 **Shu¹ (shu)** - Vegetables (**shucài**).

苜 125. 蓿 Hsü⁴ (xù) - Clover, lucerne, alfalfa.

蔓 126. 蔓 Wan⁴ (wàn) - Tendrilled vine. Man⁴ (màn) - Graceful.

蔚 127. 蔚 Yü⁴ (yù) - Azure, sky blue; luxuriant; colorful.

荫 128. 蔭 Yin⁴ (yìn) - Shady. Yin¹ (yin) - Shade.

蕃 129. 蕃 ¹² Fan¹ (fan) - Foreigners; tomato (fanqié). Fan² (fán) - Luxuriant; multiply.

荞 130. 蕎 Ch'iao² (qiáo) - Buckwheat.

萧 131. 蕭 Hsiao¹ (xiao) - Desolate, dreary; lonely.

蕙 132. 蕙 Hui⁴ (huì) - Fragrant marshy orchid.

蕊 133. 蕊 Jui³ (ruî) - Stamen, pistil (of a flower).

蔽 134. 蔽 Pi⁴ (bì) - Cover, hide; shelter.

荡 135. 蕩 Tang⁴ (dàng) - Swing; rinse; sweep off; pond, marsh.

蕉 136. 蕉 Chiao¹ (jiao) - Banana (xiangjiao), plantain (banana-like tree).

芜 137. 蕪 Wu² (wú) - Overgrown w. weeds; uncultivated; disorderly.

薅 138. 薅 ¹³ Hao¹ (hao) - Pull out (weeds).

蓟 139. 薊 Chi⁴ (jì) - Thistle.

姜 140. 薑 Chiang¹ (jiang) - Ginger.

薄 141. 薄 Pao² (báo) -Thin, weak, light (– wine).

薪 142. 薪 Hsin¹ (xin) - Firewood, fuel; salary, wage.

剃 143. 薙 T'i⁴ (ti) - Shave.

薔 144. 薔 Ch'iang² (qiáng) - Rose (qiángwei). (See 146.)

荐 145. 薦 Chien⁴ (jiàn) - Recommend; grass; strawmat. (Same as 43).

薇 146. 薇 Wei¹ (wei) - Herbs; fern; rose (qiángwei). (See 144.)

薰 147. 薰¹⁴ Hsün³ (xun) - Sweet grass; fragrance, perfume, odor.

蓝 148. 藍 Lan² (lán) - Blue; indigo plant.

藐 149. 藐 Miao³ (miâo) - Petty, small, insignificant; slight, despise.

薯 150. 薯 Shu³ (shû) - Potato (sweet –); yam, cassava.

藏 151. 藏 Ts'ang² (cáng) - Conceal, hide; store (– grain).

借 152. 藉 Chieh⁴ (jiè) - Make use of; use as pretext. * Borrow; lend.

¹⁵ *Refers to the simplified form only.

藩 153. 藩 Fan¹ (fan) - Fence, hedge; frontier.

藜 154. 藜 Li² (lí) - Pigweed; lamb's quarters (herb).

蘑 155. 摩 Mo² (mó) - Mushroom.

藕 156. 藕 Ou³ (ôu) - Lotus root, arrowroot.

薮 157. 藪 Sou³ (sôu) - Marshy preserve for game and fish.

藤 158. 藤 T'eng² (téng) - Cane, rattan; creepers, climbers; vine.

药 159. 藥 Yao⁴ (yào) - Herbs, medicine, drugs; cure (w. medicine).

蘑 160. 蘑¹⁶ Mo² (mó) - Mushroom.

苹 160A 蘋 P'ing² (píng) - Apple (píngguô). P'in² (pín) - Duckweeds.

芦 161. 蘆 Lu² (lú) - Reeds, rushes; asparagus (lúsûn).

苏 162. 蘇 Su¹ (su) - Revive, come to; Soviet (Chinese – area).

藻 163. 藻 Tsao³ (zâo) - Algae, aquatic grasses.

蕴 164. 蘊 Yün⁴ (yùn) - Accumulate; hold in store; contain.

兰 165. 蘭¹⁷ Lan² (lán) - Orchid.

蘸 166. 蘸¹⁹ Chan⁴ (zhàn) - Dip (– in ink, sauce); soak (– in water).

萝 167. 蘿 Lo² (luó) - Creeping plants; turnip, radish (luóbo).

168. 虀²¹ Chi¹ (ji) - Mix, blend; some kind of leek.

GREEN 青

*The color (円 crucible containing substance • colored by heat) of 岩
young plants ψ emerging from the earth 土 (a Radical, see p. 34): 岩 .*

1. 青 Ch'ing¹ (qing) - Blue, green, black; young (– people).

2. 靛 Tien⁴ (diàn) - Indigo blue.

静 3. 靜 Ching⁴ (jìng) - Calm, quiet, peaceful; still (– life painting).

GROW 生

A young plant ψ emerging from the earth 土 (a Radical, see p. 34): 屮

1. 生 Sheng¹ (sheng) - Grow, live; life; raw (– meat), unripe.

产 2. 產 Ch'an³ (chân) - Give birth to; produce, product; property.

3. 甥 Sheng[1] (sheng) - Nephew (sister's son).

苏 4. 甦 Su[1] (su) - Revive, resuscitate, rise from apparent death.

H

HAIR 毛

Picture of a bundle of hair 𝒫 .

1. 毛　**Mao² (máo)** - Hair, wool; gross (– profit); dime (10 cent).

2. 毫 [7]　**Hao² (háo)** - Fine long hair; writing brush; milli- (–metre).

球 3. 毬　**Ch'iu² (qiú)** - Ball, sphere, globe, the earth.

4. 毯 [8]　**T'an³ (tân)** - Rug, carpet, blanket.

5. 毻 [9]　**T'o⁴ (tuò)** - Molt, shed.

6. 毽　**Chien⁴ (jiàn)** - Shuttlecock.

毡 7. 氈 [13]　**Chan¹ (zhan)** - Felt (– hat), rugs, carpet, blanket.

HAIRLOCKS 髟

Representing very long 髟 (Rad.) hairlocks 彡 : 彡.

发 1. 髮 [5]   Fa⁴ (fà) - Hair.

2. 髯   Jan² (rán) - Beard, whiskers.

3. 髫   T'iao² (tiáo) - Child's hair tuft.

4. 髭   Tzu¹ (zi) - Moustache.

5. 髻 [6]   Chi⁴ (jì) - Woman's hair worn in a bun or coil.

6. 髽 [7]   Chua¹ (zhua) - Ancient woman's hairdress.

松 7. 鬆 [8]   Sung¹ (song) - Loose(n); dried minced meat. * Pine tree.
     * Additional meaning for the Simplified Form.

8. 鬃   Tsung¹ (zong) - Mane (horse's –); bristles (pig's –).

胡 9. 鬍 [9]   Hu² (hú) - Moustache, beard. * Recklessly; outrageously.
     * Additional meanings for the Simplified Form.

10. 鬒 [10]   Chen³ (zhên) - Bushy hair.

须 11. 鬚 [12]   Hsü¹ (xu) - Beard, mustache.

鬟 12. 鬟 [13]   Huan² (huán) - Hair bun.

鬓 13. 鬢 [14]   Pin⁴ (bìn) - Hair on the temples; temples.

14. 鬣 [15]   Lieh⁴ (liè) - Mane, bristles.

HALBERD 戈

Representing a halberd – a spear ending in a battle-axe: 戋 .

1. 戈   **Ke[1] (ge)** - Halberd; spear, lance.

2. 戊[1]   **Wu[4] (wù)** - Fifth of the Ten Celestial Stems; flourishing.

3. 戉   **Yüeh[4] (yuè)** - Halberd w. crescent blade.

4. 戎[2]   **Jung[2] (róng)** - Military, army.

5. 戒[3]   **Chieh[4] (jiè)** - Guard against; admonish, warn.

6. 成   **Ch'eng[2] (chéng)** - Accomplish, succeed.

7. 我   **Wo[3] (wô)** - I, my; self (–sacrifice).

8. 或[4]   **Huo[4] (huò)** - Or, perhaps, probably.

9. 戕   **Ch'iang[1] (qiang)** - Kill; injure **(qiangzéi)**.

戈 10. 戋   **Chien[1] (jian)** - Wound (v); hurt; small; narrow; cramped.

11. 戚[7]   **Ch'i[1] (qi)** - Relative; sad, sorrow.

12. 戟[8]   **Chi[3] (jî)** - Halberd, very long lance.

13. 戥   **Teng[3] (dêng)** - Small steelyard (e.g. for weighing gold).

14. 戠   **Chih[1] (zhi)** - Sword.

15. 截[10]   **Chieh[2] (jié)** - Cut off, sever, intercept; stop (– traffic).

16. 戮[11]   **Lu[4] (lù)** - Kill, execute; unite, join (– hands).

战 17. 戰[12]   **Chan[4] (zhàn)** - War, battle, fight; tremble, shiver.

戏 18. 戲[13] **Hsi⁴ (xì)** - Play (v)(n); make fun; show (theatrical); drama.

19. 戳 **Ch'o¹ (chuo)** - Poke, stab, pierce; stamp, seal.

20. 戴 **Tai⁴ (dài)** - Wear (– glasses), put on (– hat); respect, honor.

HAND (1) 手 扌 | Rapid Access available |

Picture of the hand with the five fingers clearly shown 𠂇 .

1. 手 **Shou³ (shôu)** - Hand; hold; personal (– letter).

2. 才[1] **Ts'ai² (cái)** - Talent, ability; capable person, genius.

3. 扎 **Cha¹ (zha)** - Stick (a needle, etc.) into, plunge into.

4. 扔[2] **Jeng¹ (reng)** - Throw away, cast aside.

5. 扒 **Pa¹ (ba)** - Hold on to; tear down; strip off, skin (– rabbit).

6. 打 **Ta³ (dâ)** - Beat; fight; build (– a dam); from; a dozen.

7. 扛[3] **K'ang² (káng)** - Carry on the shoulder; shoulder (– a gun).

8. 托 **T'o¹ (tuo)** - Support with the hand; serve as a contrast.

9. 扣 **K'ou⁴ (kòu)** - Button up (– a coat); arrest; discount (v).

10. 抓[4] **Chua¹ (zhua)** - Catch, arrest, seize; scratch.

11. 找 **Chao³ (zhâo)** - Look for; give change.

12. 抄 **Ch'ao¹ (chao)** - Copy, plagiarize; search and confiscate.

13. 折 **Che² (zhé)** - Break, bend; convert into; turn back; discount.

14. 扯 **Ch'e³ (chê)** - Pull; tear; buy (– cloth, thread); chat.

15. 承 Ch'eng² (chéng) - Carry (– load); undertake (– job).

16. 扶 Fu² (fú) - Support oneself using the hand; assist, aid.

17. 抗 K'ang⁴ (kàng) - Resist; refuse (– paying tax).

18. 技 Chi⁴ (jì) - Skill, talent, ability; trick. **Chih¹ (zhi)** - Branch, twig.

19. 扼 O⁴ (è) - Seize, clutch, hold (– key position).

20. 抛 P'ao¹ (pao) - Cast, fling; leave behind (– other runners).

21. 扭 Niu³ (niû) - Turn around, twist; sprain (– a muscle).

22. 把 Pa³ (bâ) - Hold, grasp; handle (– of knife); guard (– gate).

23. 扮 Pan⁴ (bàn) - Dress up as; disguise oneself as.

24. 批 P'i¹ (pi) - Criticize; slap (– sb's face); wholesale (buy –).

25. 抒 Shu¹ (shu) - Convey, express (– one's feelings).

26. 抖 Tou³ (dôu) - Tremble, shake, shiver; rouse, stir up.

27. 投 T'ou² (tóu) - Throw, fling; deliver (– letter); join (– army).

28. 抑 Yï⁴ (yì) - Restrain, repress, curb.

29. 招⁵ Chao¹ (zhao) - Beckon; enrol; invite (– disaster); trick.

30. 抽 Ch'ou¹ (chou) - Draw (– blood); take out (– application).

31. 拙 Cho¹ (zhuo) - Clumsy, awkward; dull; my (– writing).

32. 拄 Chu³ (zhû) - Lean on (– a stick).

33. 拚 **P'in¹ (pin)** - Clap hands. **Fan¹ (fan)** - Sweep; reject; soar.

34. 拊 **Fu³ (fŭ)** - Clap (– hands), beat, tap.

35. 拂 **Fu² (fú)** - Wipe away, shake off; go against sb's wishes.

36. 拃 **Cha³ (zhâ)** - (Hand)span; measure by handspans.

37. 拘 **Chü¹ (ju)** - Arrest; restrict; inflexible.

38. 拒 **Chü⁴ (jù)** - Refuse, reject; resist, oppose.

39. 拐 **Kuai³ (guâi)** - Turn (– to the left); swindle; limp (– along).

40. 拉 **La¹ (la)** - Pull, drag; play (– the violin); help.

41. 抹 **Mo³ (mô)** - Apply, put on; wipe (– face); erase.

42. 拇 **Mu³ (mû)** - Thumb, big toe.

43. 抿 **Min³ (mîn)** - Smooth hair w. brush; close tightly, tuck .

拿 44. 拏 **Na² (ná)** - Hold, carry (– a gun), take, seize, arrest.

45. 拈 **Nien¹ (nian)** - Pick up w. thumb and fingers.

46. 拔 **Pa² (bá)** - Pull out (– tooth); select (– candidate).

47. 拜 **Pai⁴ (bài)** - Pay respect, show submission to; make visit.

48. 拌 **Pan⁴ (bàn)** - Mix.

49. 抱 **Pao⁴ (bào)** - Hold in the arms, hug; cherish.

50. 披 **P'i¹ (pi)** - Wrap around one's shoulder; open (– a book).

51. 拍 **P'ai¹ (pai)** - Clap (– one's hands); racket; take (pictures).

52. 抬 **T'ai¹ (tái)** - Raise, lift up; carry (– a stretcher).

53. 抵 **Ti³ (dǐ)** - Resist; mortgage (– a house); arrive at.

54. 拖 **T'o¹ (tuo)** - Drag, pull, haul; delay, procrastinate.

55. 拓 **T'o⁴ (tuò)** - Reclaim, develop (– wasteland).

56. 拆 **Ch'ai¹ (chai)** - Tear down, dismantle; take apart.

57. 押 **Ya¹ (ya)** - Mortgage (– a house), pledge; detain; signature.

58. 拗 **Niu⁴ (niù)** - Obstinate, stubborn, difficult (– person).

59. 挓 ⁶ **Cha¹ (zha)** - Open, expand.

60. 指 **Chih³ (zhǐ)** - Finger; point out, direct, indicate.

61. 持 **Ch'ih² (chí)** - Hold, support; manage; maintain.

62. 拯 **Cheng³ (zhêng)** - Save, rescue, help.

63. 拼 **P'in¹ (pin)** - Put together, assemble.

64. 拽 **Chuai⁴ (zhuài)** - Fling, throw, hurl.

65. 拷 **K'ao³ (kâo)** - Beat, flog, torture.

66. 挈 **Ch'ieh⁴ (qiè)** - Lift, raise; lead, take along (– one's family).

67. 拳 **Ch'üan² (quán)** - Fist; boxing.

68. 拱 **Kung³ (gông)** - Salute with folded hands; arched (– bridge).

69. 挂 **Kua⁴ (guà)** - Hang (– painting); register (– at hospital).

70. 括 **K'uo⁴ (kuò)** - Contract (– a muscle); include.

71. 拿 **Na² (ná)** - Take (– it away); hold, seize, capture.

72. 拏 **Na² (ná)** - Same as 71.

73. 按 **An⁴ (àn)** - Press (– button); control; note (editor's –).

74. 拾 **Shih² (shí)** - Pick up; ten (elaborate form on checks, etc.)

75. 拭 **Shih⁴ (shì)** - Wipe away (– her tears), rub.

76. 拴 **Shuan¹ (shuan)** - Fasten, tie (– horse to a tree).

77. 挑 **T'iao¹ (tiao)** - Carry on a shoulder-pole; choose, select.

78. 挖 **Wa¹ (wa)** - Dig, excavate.

79. 挨⁷ **Ai¹ (ai)** - Near, next to (– each other); by turns, in sequence.

80. 振 **Chen⁴ (zhèn)** - Shake, flap (– wings); excite, stimulate.

81. 捉 **Cho¹ (zhuo)** - Catch, capture, arrest; clutch, hold.

82. 捍 **Han⁴ (hàn)** - Defend, (safe)guard.

挟 83. 挟 **Hsieh² (xié)** - Hold under the arm; coerce; harbor (v).

84. 捐 **Chüan¹ (juan)** - Contribute, donate; taxation (– on houses).

85. 捆 **K'un³ (kûn)** - Tie up, bind; bundle (– of newspapers).

86. 挪 **No² (nuó)** - Move, shift, remove.

87. 捌 **Pa¹ (ba)** - Eight (elaborate form used on checks, etc.).

88. 捕 **Pu³ (bû)** - Catch (– fish), seize, arrest.

89. 捎 **Shao¹ (shao)** - Send (– letter), bring (– cookies home).

90. 挲 **So¹ (suo)** - Stroke, caress.

91. 挺 **T'ing³ (tîng)** - Straight, erect (stand –); quite (– cold).

捏 92. 捏 **Nieh¹ (nie)** - Pinch; knead (– flour); fabricate. Same as 140.

93. 捅 **T'ung³ (tông)** - Poke, stab; disclose, give away (– secret).

94. 挫 **Ts'o⁴ (cuò)** - Oppress, repress; deflate (– his arrogance).

95. 挽 **Wan³ (wân)** - Pull, draw (– a bow); roll up (– one's sleeve).

抻 96. 抻⁸ **Ch'en¹ (chen)** - Stretch (out) (–ed noodles), pull out.

97. 掌 **Chang³ (zhâng)** - Palm (of hand); slap; wield (– power).

挣 98. 掙 **Cheng⁴ (zhèng). Cheng¹ (zheng)** - Struggle to get free; earn (- a living).

99. 挈 **Ch'e⁴ (chè)** - Pull, tug; draw (– lots).

100. 捶 **Ch'ui² (chúi)** - Beat w. stick or fist, cudgel, pound.

101. 捧 **P'eng³ (pêng)** - Hold or carry in both hands; flatter.

102. 掀 **Hsien¹ (xian)** - Lift (– cover of pot).

103. 掐 **Ch'ia¹ (qia)** - Pinch (w. fingers), nip off (– flowers); cut.

104. 掘 **Chüeh² (júe)** - Dig (– a well), excavate, hollow out.

卷 105. 捲 **Chüan³ (juân)** - Roll up; roll. * **Chüan⁴ (juàn)** - Book; volume.

106. 掬 **Chü¹ (ju)** - Hold or grasp w. both hands.

107. 控 **K'ung⁴ (kòng)** - Accuse, charge; control, dominate.

挂 108. 掛 **Kua⁴ (guà)** - Same as 69.

109. 掠 **Lüeh⁴ (lüe)** - Plunder, rob; sweep (plane –s across sky).

抡 110. 掄 **Lun² (lún)** - Select, choose. * **Lun¹ (lun)** - Swing (v).

扪 111. 捫 **Men² (mén)** - Lay hand on, touch, stroke.

112. 捺 **Na⁴ (nà)** - Press down; restrain, control (– temper).

113. 排 **P'ai² (pái)** - Arrange; row; drain; spareribs (**páigû**).

扫 114. 掃 **Sao³ (sâo)** - Sweep; clear away (– snow).

舍 115. 捨 **She³ (shê)** - Give up, abandon. * **She⁴ (shè)** - House, shed.

116. 授 **Shou⁴ (shòu)** - Instruct, teach; confer, grant.

117. 探 **T'an⁴ (tàn)** - Find out, explore; lean out (– of window).

118. 掏 **T'ao¹ (tao)** - Pull out (– coins from pocket); dig (– hole).

119. 掉 **Tiao⁴ (diào)** - Fall, drop; lose; (ex)change; turn back.

120. 掂 **Tien¹ (dian)** - Weigh in the hand.

121. 掇 **To¹ (duo)** - Pick up, collect.

122. 推 **T'ui¹ (tui)** - Push (forward); infer, deduce; shirk, evade.

* Additional pronunciation and meaning(s) referring only to the Simplified Form.

采 123. 採 **Ts'ai³ (câi)** - Pick, pluck (– flowers); mine (– coal); select.

124. 接 **Chieh¹ (jie)** - Connect, join; receive; take over (– job).

125. 捷 **Chieh² (jié)** - Victory, triumph; quick, prompt.

126. 措 **Ts'o⁴ (cuò)** - Arrange, manage.

挨 127. 捱 **Ai² (ái)** - Suffer, endure; drag out, procrastinate.

128. 掩 **Yen³ (yân)** - Cover, shut; hide, conceal; attack by surprise.

129. 掖 **Yeh⁴ (yè)** - Support, help, promote.

130. 插⁹ **Ch'a² (cha)** - Insert, pierce; interfere, meddle with.

131. 揣 **Ch'uai³ (chuâi)** - Estimate, guess; surmise, conjecture.

换 132. 換 **Huan⁴ (huàn)** - Change; exchange, barter, trade.

挥 133. 揮 **Hui¹ (hui)** - Wave, wield (– sword); wipe (– tears); scatter.

134. 揉 **Jou² (róu)** - Knead (– dough); make flexible; rub (– eyes).

135. 揩 **K'ai¹ (kai)** - Wipe (– the table), rub, clean.

拣 136. 揀 **Chien³ (jiân)** - Select, choose, pick up (– from floor).

137. 揆 **K'uei² (kúi)** - Calculate, estimate; consider (– condition).

138. 揭 **Chieh¹ (jie)** - Take off (– from the wall); uncover, expose.

139. 描 **Miao² (miáo)** - Trace, copy; sketch, paint (– portrait).

捏 140. 揑 **Nieh¹ (nie)** - Same as 92.

141. 摋 **Sai¹ (sai)** - Move; shake; choose.

碰 142. 挳 **P'eng⁴ (pèng)** - Touch (don't – it), meet unexpectedly.

143. 搜 **Sou¹ (sou)** - Search; examine.

144. 提 **T'i² (tí)** - Carry; raise; propose; draw. **Ti¹ (di)** - Guard.

145. 揪 **Chiu¹ (jiu)** - Hold tight, seize, grasp; pull, drag.

146. 攅 **Tsan³ (zân)** - Accumulate, hoard up, save.
Ts'uan² (cuán) - Assemble. Same as 260 & MAN 205.

147. 握 **Wo⁴ (wò)** - Grasp, hold, take by the hand.

扬 148. 揚 **Yang² (yáng)** - Raise (– one's hand); make known.

掩 149. 揜 **Yen³ (yân)** - Same as 128.

150. 揖 **Yi¹ (yi)** - Make a bow w. hands clasped.

151. 援 **Yüan² (yuán)** - Hold fast; quote, cite; help, aid.

152. 搽¹⁰ **Ch'a² (chá)** - Apply, put on (– powder on the face).

153. 搌 **Chan³ (zhân)** - Sop up liquid, blot (– ink).

154. 搘 **Chih¹ (zhi)** - Prop up (– a window).

捶 155. 搥 **Ch'ui² (chúi)** - Same as 100.

156. 搋 **Ch'uai¹ (chuai)** - Rub; knead (– dough).

按 157. 搇 **An⁴ (àn)** - Same as 73.

携 158. 攜 **Hsieh² (xié)** - Carry; bring along (– one's children).

构 159. 搆 **Kou⁴ (gòu)** - Drag; incur; reach.

160. 搦 **Ni⁴ (nì)** - Lay the hand on, grasp, seize.

161. 搬 **Pan¹ (ban)** - Move (change residence); remove (– tables).

162. 搏 **Po² (bó)** - Fight, combat, struggle; beat (heart –).

163. 搡 **Sang³ (sâng)** - Push violently.

164. 搔 **Sao¹ (sao)** - Scratch (– one's head).

165. 搧 **Shan¹ (shan)** - Fan (– away chaff); strike, slap the face.

166. 搰 **Ku⁴ (gù)** - Mix, stir, twist.

损 167. 損 **Sun³ (sûn)** - Harm, damage, destroy; decrease; loss.

搭 168. 搭 **Ta¹ (da)** - Build (– bridge); hang; travel by (– plane).

拓 169. 搨 **T'a⁴ (tà)** - Make rubbings from inscriptions. * **T'o⁴ (tuò)** - Open up, develop (– land).

170. 搪 **T'ang² (táng)** - Keep out (– the wind); evade (– creditors).

捣 171. 搗 **Tao³ (dâo)** - Pound w. pestle, beat, attack; harass, disturb.

掏 172. 搯 **T'ao¹ (tao)** - Pull out (– cash from pocket); dig (– hole).

173. 搷 **Tien¹ (dian)** - Beat, jolt, knock.

174. 搊 **Ch'ou¹ (chou)** - Grasp, crumple up.

175. 搓 **Ts'o¹ (cuo)** - Rub or roll between hands or fingers; twist.

抢 176. 搶 **Ch'iang³ (qiâng)** - Rob, snatch; scramble for; scrape; rush.

捂 177. 搗 **Wu³ (wû)** - Cover up tightly, muffle; seal.

摇 178. 搖 **Yao² (yáo)** - Shake, wave (– a fan); turn (– windlass).

折 179. 摺¹¹ **Che² (zhé)** - Break; bend; discount; turn back.

抠 180. 摳 **K'ou¹ (kou)** - Dig, delve into; carve.

搂 181. 摟 **Lou¹ (lou)** - Rake together; extort. **Lou³ (lôu)** - Hug, embrace.

182. 摞 **Lo⁴ (luò)** - Pile up, stack up; pile, stack.

摩 183. 摩 **Mo² (mó)** - Rub, scrape; touch; mull over, ponder.

摸 184. 摸 **Mo¹ (mo)** - Feel, touch; feel for, grope for.

185. 撂 **Liao⁴ (liào)** - Put down, leave behind; shoot down.

186. 摹 **Mo² (mó)** - Imitate, follow a pattern, copy, trace.

187. 摔 **Shuai¹ (shuai)** - Fall, tumble, plunge; break (– a glass).

抟 188. 摶 **T'uan² (tuán)** - Roll sth. into a ball.

189. 摘 **Chai¹ (zhai)** - Pick (– cotton), take off (– glasses); select.

190. 摧 **Ts'ui¹ (cui)** - Break, destroy, devastate.

191. 摠 **Tsung³ (zông)** - Sum up; general (– crisis), chief.

192. 撑¹² **Ch'eng¹ (cheng)** - Pole (– a boat); prop up, support; open.

扯 193. 撦 **Ch'e³ (chê)** - Same as 14.

194. 撤 **Ch'e⁴ (chè)** - Withdraw (– troops), remove (– from office).

H 14

抚 195. 撞 **Chuang⁴ (zhuàng)** - Strike; collide; meet by chance.

196. 撰 **Chuan⁴ (zhuàn)** - Compose, write (– books).

抚 197. 撫 **Fu³ (fǔ)** - Comfort, console; stroke, caress; nurture, foster.

198. 撬 **Ch'iao⁴ (qiào)** - Pry, force open (– a box).

199. 撅 **Chüeh¹ (jüe)** - Stick up, pout (– one's lip); break, snap off.

捞 200. 撈 **Lao¹ (lao)** - Dredge; gain through improper means.

201. 撩 **Liao¹ (liao)** - Raise. **Liao² (liáo)** - Stir up; tease, provoke.

挠 202. 撓 **Nao² (náo)** - Scratch; hinder, disturb.

捻 203. 撚 **Nien³ (niân)** - Twist sth. w. the fingers; pinch.

204. 撇 **P'ieh¹ (pie)** - Skim off (– grease), cast aside, abandon.

撇 205. 擎 **P'ieh³ (pîe)** - Same as 204.

206. 播 **Po¹ (bo)** - Sow, spread, disseminate; broadcast.

拨 207. 撥 **Po¹ (bo)** - Stir, poke; allot or appropriate (– funds).

扑 208. 撲 **P'u¹ (pu)** - Throw oneself on; rush at; attack; flutter.

209. 撒 **Sa¹ (sa)** - Cast (– net), let go. **Sa³ (sâ)** - Scatter, disperse.

210. 撕 **Szu¹ (si)** - Tear (apart), break into pieces, rip (open).

掸 211. 撣 **T'an² (tán)** - Pluck. **Tan³ (dân)** - Brush away, whisk.

掸 212. 撣 **Tan³ (dân)** - Same as 211.

213. 撮 Ts'o¹ (cuo) - Bring together. Tso³ (zuô) - Pinch (– of salt).

214. 撙 Tsun³ (zûn) - Save, hoard up; economize; regulate, adjust.

215. 擉¹³ Ch'o¹ (chuo) - Spear (v); pinch.

216. 撼 Han⁴ (hàn) - Shake, move; excite, stir up.

217. 擀 Kan³ (gân) - Roll (– dough); polish.

捡 218. 撿 Chien³ (jiân) - Pick up, collect, gather.

击 219. 擊 Chi¹ (ji) - Strike, hit; attack; bump into.

220. 擒 Ch'in² (qín) - Seize, capture, catch.

221. 擎 Ch'ing² (qíng) - Elevate, lift up; prop up, hold up.

据 222. 據 Chü⁴ (jù) - Occupy; according to, base on; certificate.

扪 223. 擓 K'uai³ (kuâi) - Scratch; carry on the arm.

224. 擂 Lei² (léi) - Pound, grind; pestle.

掳 225. 擄 Lu³ (lû) - Capture; plunder, loot (lûlüè).

掰 226. 擘 Pai¹ (bai) - Break off w. fingers and thumb, split.

227. 擅 Shan⁴ (shàn) - Act without permission; be good at.

挞 228. 撻 Ta⁴ (tà) - Whip, flog.

担 229. 擔 Tan¹ (dan) - Carry on pole; undertake. Tan⁴ (dàn) - Load; burden; *dan* (50 kg).

挡 230. 擋 Tang³ (dâng) - Keep off (– wind). Tang⁴ (dàng) - Put in order (bìngdàng).

择 232. 操 Ts'ao¹ (cao) - Hold, grasp; drill, exercise; control, manage.

择 232. 擇 Tse² (zé). Chai² (zhái) - Select, choose; prefer.

拥 233. 擁 Yung¹ (yong) - Embrace, hug; crowd (v), press; possess.

234. 擢¹⁴ Cho² (zhuó) - Promote, raise (in rank); extract, pull out.

235. 擦 Ts'a¹ (ca) - Rub, wipe; brush (– past sb.); apply, put on.

拧 236. 擰 Ning² (níng) - Twist, pinch. Ning³ (nîng) - Screw (v).

拟 237. 擬 Ni³ (nî) - Intend, plan to; draw up, draft; imitate, mimic.

搁 238. 擱 Ke¹ (ge) - Put (– this there); put aside, postpone.

摈 239. 擯 Pin⁴ (bìn) - Discard, get rid of, reject.

抬 240. 擡 T'ai² (tái) - Lift up; carry on a pole betw. two people.

捣 241. 擣 Tao³ (dâo) - Pound w. a pestle, beat; harass, disturb.

挤 242. 擠 Chi³ (jî) - Squeeze, crowd (v), press, push against.

掷 243. 擲¹⁵ Chih¹,⁴ (zhi, zhì) - Throw, cast.

扰 244. 擾 Jao³ (râo) - Trouble, harass, annoy; trespass on hospitality.

扩 245. 擴 K'uo⁴ (kuò) - Expand, stretch; enlarge, extend.

撵 246. 攆 Nien³ (niân) - Drive out, oust, expel; catch up (– w. a psn.).

摆 247. 擺 Pai³ (bâi) - Put, place; arrange; state clearly; wave (v), sway; pendulum.

248. 攀 P'an¹ (pan) - Climb, clamber; implicate, involve.

撒 249. 撒 Sou³ (sôu) - Enliven, rouse.

250. 攉[16] Huo¹ (huo) - Shovel coal; knead, mix up.

拢 251. 攏 Lung³ (lông) - Assemble, gather; grasp; reach (- shore).

搀 252. 攙[17] Ch'an¹ (chan) - Support sb. w. one's hand; mix.

253. 攘 Jang³ (râng) - Resist (- aggression); push up one's sleeves.

拦 254. 攔 Lan² (lán) - Stop, bar, block, hold back.

携 255. 攜[18] Hsieh² (xié) - Same as 158.

摄 256. 攝 She⁴ (shè) - Absorb, assimilate; take photograph; act for.

挥 257. 攛 Ts'uan¹ (cuan) - Fling; do in a hurry; fly into a rage.

挛 258. 攣[19] Lüan² (luán) - Tie, bind; bend; crooked.

摊 259. 攤 T'an¹ (tan) - Spread out; take share in; stand, stall (book-).

攒 260. 攢 Tsan³ (zân) - Accumulate, hoard up, save.

搅 261. 攢[20] Ts'uan² (cuán) - Assemble. Same as 146 & MAN 205.
Chiao³ (jiâo) - Stir, mix, disturb, annoy, trouble.

挡 262. 攩 Tang³ (dâng) - Same as 230.

揽 263. 攬[21] Lan³ (lân) - Take into one's arm; grasp, monopolize.

264. 攮[22] Nang³ (nâng) - Stab; fend off, push from.

HAND (2) 又

The right hand seen in profile – only three fingers are seen: ⺕

1. 又 **Yu⁴ (yòu)** - Again, moreover, also, and; but.

2. 叉 **Ch'a¹ (cha)** - Fork, fork (v) (– hay); cross (v), intersect. ¹

3. 反 **Fan³ (fǎn)** - Turn over; on the contrary; rebel against. ²

4. 及 **Chi² (jí)** - Reach; while (eat – it's hot); up to; as well as.

5. 收 **Shou¹ (shou)** - Receive, accept; collect (– taxes); harvest.

6. 友 **Yu³ (yôu)** - Friend, friendly (– nation).

7. 圣 **Sheng⁴ (shèng)** - Sage, saint; sacred, holy. ³

8. 受 **Shou⁴ (shòu)** - Receive; bear, endure; pleasant (– to hear). ⁶

9. 叔 **Shu¹ (shu)** - Father's younger brother; uncle.

10. 取 **Ch'ü³ (qǔ)** - Lay hold on, take, get; receive; choose, select.

11. 叛 **P'an⁴ (pàn)** - Rebel against; betray. ⁷

12. 叙 **Hsü⁴ (xù)** - Talk, chat; narrate, describe.

13. 叟 **Sou³ (sôu)** - An old man. ⁸

睿 14. 叡 **Jui⁴ (ruì)** - Far-sighted, profound, shrewd. ¹⁴

丛 15. 叢 **Ts'ung² (cóng)** - Crowd together; grove; collection. ¹⁶

HEAD (1) 首

Representing the head with the hair clearly shown 首 .

1. 首   **Shou³ (shôu)** - Head; first; leader, chief.

HEAD (2) 頁

The head 首 *placed upon the body* 儿 : 頁

页 1. 頁   **Yeh⁴ (yè)** - Head; page, leaf (loose –), sheet (– of paper).

顷 2. 頃 ²   **Ch'ing³ (qîng)** - Unit of area (6.6667 ha); an instant.

顶 3. 頂   **Ting³ (dîng)** - Top (mountain–); oppose, go against.

预 4. 預 ³   **Han¹ (han)** - Thick (– thread).

项 5. 項   **Hsiang⁴ (xiàng)** - Nape (of the neck); item (– by –).

顺 6. 順   **Shun⁴ (shùn)** - Compliant, obedient; favorable.

须 7. 須   **Hsü¹ (xu)** - Beard, moustache; must, necessary; wait.

颁 8. 頒 ⁴   **Pan¹ (ban)** - Proclaim, make known; confer; issue.

颂 9. 頌   **Sung⁴ (sòng)** - Praise, commend; ode, eulogy.

顿 10. 頓   **Tun⁴ (dùn)** - Pause; suddenly, immediately; arrange.

顽 11. 頑   **Wan² (wán)** - Stupid; stubborn, obstinate; naughty.

预 12. 預   **Yü⁴ (yù)** - In advance, beforehand.

领 13. 領 ⁵   **Ling³ (lîng)** - Neck; collar; receive (– prize); main point.

颇 14. 頗 P'o^1 (po) - Oblique; quite (– good); rather (– easy).

颏 15. 頦 ^{6} K'o^1 (ke) - Chin.

颐 16. 頤 Yi^2 (yí) - Cheek; chin; jaw; keep fit; recuperate.

颔 17. 頷 ^{7} Han^4 (hàn) - Chin; jaw; nod (– gently).

颊 18. 頰 Chia^2 (jiá) - Cheek.

颈 19. 頸 Ching^3 (jǐng) - Neck.

赖 20. 賴 Lai^4 (laì) - Rely, depend; deny; blame sb. wrongly.

频 21. 頻 P'in^2 (pín) - Frequently, repeatedly; hurried.

头 22. 頭 T'ou^2 (tóu) - Head; chief, first (– class); top (hill–).

颓 23. 頹 T'ui^2 (túi) - Decadent; faded; ruined.

颖 24. 穎 Ying^3 (yǐng) - Tip (– of writing brush); clever.

颗 25. 顆 ^{8} K'o^1 (ke) - Anything small and round (pearl, etc.); grain.

类 26. 類 ^{9} Lei^4 (leì) - Class, category; similar to.

额 27. 額 O^2 (é) - Forehead; a specified number or amount.

题 28. 題 T'i^2 (tí) - Subject, topic, theme; inscribe.

颜 29. 顏 Yen^2 (yán) - Color; face, countenance; prestige.

类 30. 類 ^{10} Lei^4 (lèi) - Same as 26.

颡 31. 顙 Sang^3 (sǎng) - Forehead.

顛 32. 顚 **Tien¹ (dian)** - Crown (of the head), top; jolt, upset.

愿 33. 願 **Yüan⁴ (yuàn)** - Hope, wish, desire; be willing; vow.

颟 34. 顢 ^11 **Man¹ (man)** - Foolish, inept.

顾 35. 顧 ^12 **Ku⁴ (gù)** - Turn around and look; look at; attend to.

颤 36. 顫 ^13 **Chan⁴ (zhàn)** - Tremble. **Ch'an⁴ (chàn)** - Quiver, vibrate.

显 37. 顯 ^14 **Hsien³ (xiân)** - Apparent, show; display (v); illustrious.

颧 38. 顴 ^18 **Ch'üan² (quán)** - Cheekbones.

| Rapid Access |
| available |

HEART 心 忄 忄

Picture of the heart – the sac opened; the lobes and the aorta are also seen 心.

1. 心 **Hsin¹ (xin)** - Heart; feeling, emotion; centre, core.

2. 必 ^1 **Pi⁴ (bì)** - Certainly, surely; necessarily, must.

3. 志 ^3 **Chih⁴ (zhì)** - The will, determination; annals, records.

4. 忍 **Jen³ (rên)** - Endure, bear, tolerate; patience.

5. 忌 **Chi⁴ (jì)** - Abstain from (– wine), avoid; fear; jealous of.

6. 忙 **Mang² (máng)** - Busy, fully occupied; make haste, hurried.

7. 忒 **T'e⁴ (tè)** - Err, error, mistake; too (– young).

8. 忐 **T'an³ (tân)** - Nervous, timorous; mentally disturbed.

9. 忑 **T'e⁴ (tè)** - Downhearted.

10. 忖 Ts'un³ (cûn) - Ponder, speculate, consider.

11. 忘 Wang⁴ (wàng) - Forget, neglect.

12. 忠 ⁴ Chung¹ (zhong) - Loyal, sincere, devoted.

13. 忻 Hsin¹ (xin) - Delight, joy; cheerful.

14. 忿 Fen⁴ (fèn) - Anger, indignation, resentment.

15. 怀 Huai² (huái) - Bosom; breast; cherish; think of.

16. 忽 Hu¹ (hu) - Neglect (v); overlook; suddenly.

17. 快 K'uai⁴ (kuài) - Quick, fast; sharp (- knife); happy.

18. 念 Nien⁴ (niàn) - Think about, thought; study, read aloud.

19. 忱 Ch'en² (chén) - Sincere, honest, trustworthy.

20. 忸 Niu⁴ (niù) - Stubborn.

21. 忝 T'ien³ (tiân) - Disgrace; unworthy of the honor.

22. 忤 Wu³ (wû) - Obstinate, disobedient.

23. 怙 ⁵ Hu⁴ (hù) - Rely on.

怵 24. 怵 Ch'u⁴ (chù) - Fear (- apprehensive).

25. 怡 Yi² (yí) - Happy, joyful; pleased.

26. 怩 Ni² (ní) - Blush(ing), look ashamed.

恍 27. 怳 Huang³ (huâng) - As if (- in a dream); suddenly; confused.

28. 怯 Ch'ieh[4] (qiè) - Timid; cowardly; nervous.

29. 急 Chi[2] (jí) - Impatient, anxious, urgent; rapid, swift.

30. 怪 Kuai[4] (guài) - Strange; quite (– heavy); blame.

31. 怒 Nu[4] (nù) - Angry, furious; resentment.

32. 怕 P'a[4] (pà) - Fear, dread, be afraid of; perhaps, I suppose.

33. 怦 P'eng[1] (peng) - Eager; impulsive.

34. 怖 Pu[4] (bù) - Be afraid of, alarmed.

35. 性 Hsing[4] (xìng) - Nature, character, temper; sex (– organ).

36. 怛 Ta[2] (dá) - Distressed, grieved, alarmed.

37. 思 Szu[1] (si) - Think of (– one's parents), thought; consider.

38. 怠 Tai[4] (dài) - Idle; remiss; negligent.

39. 怎 Tsen[3] (zên) - Why, how.

40. 怍 Tso[4] (zuò) - Ashamed (feel –).

匆 41. 忽 Ts'ung[1] (cong) - Hastily; hurriedly.

42. 怏 Yang[4] (yàng) - Disgruntled, dissatisfied, unhappy.

43. 怨 Yüan[4] (yuàn) - Resentment; blame, complain, grumble.

耻 44. 恥 [6] Ch'ih[3] (chî) - Disgrace, shame, humiliation.

45. 恨 Hen[4] (hèn) - Hate, resentment; regret, sorry.

恒 46. 恆 **Heng² (héng)** - Permanent, constant; perseverance.

47. 恒 **Heng² (héng)** - Same as 46.

48. 恍 **Huang³ (huâng)** - As if (– in a dream); suddenly.

49. 恪 **K'o⁴ (kè)** - Respectful, faithful.

50. 恰 **Ch'ia⁴ (qìa)** - Exactly (– what I want); appropriate.

51. 恐 **K'ung³ (kông)** - Fear(ful); intimidate.

52. 恭 **Kung¹ (gong)** - Respect(ful), reverent.

53. 恢 **Hui¹ (hui)** - Great, magnanimous; enlarge; extensive.

54. 恩 **En¹ (en)** - Kindness, benevolence; show favor.

55. 恃 **Shih⁴ (shì)** - Depend upon, rely on.

56. 恕 **Shu⁴ (shù)** - Pardon, forgive, excuse.

57. 息 **Hsi¹ (xi)** - Breath; news; stop (v); interest (annual –).

58. 恤 **Hsü⁴ (xuè)** - Sympathize with, pity; compassionate.

59. 恬 **T'ien² (tián)** - Quiet, calm, tranquil, unperturbed.

60. 恫 **T'ung² (tóng)** - Moaning (from pain), sighing.

61. 恣 **Tzu⁴ (zì)** - Licentious, without restraint.

62. 恙 **Yang⁴ (yàng)** - Sickness, illness, ailment.

63. 悍 ⁷ **Han⁴ (hàn)** - Overbearing, fierce, brave, bold.

64. 患 Huan⁴ (huàn) - Disaster, affliction, misery; suffer from.

65. 悔 Hui³ (huǐ) - Regret, repent.

66. 悃 K'un⁴ (kùn) - Sincere; single-minded.

67. 您 Nin² (nín) - Thou (respectful form of "you").

68. 悖 Pei⁴ (bèi) - Contrary to (– reason); perverse.

69. 悉 Hsi¹ (xi) - Know (– all our names); all, completely.

70. 悌 T'i⁴ (tì) - Love and resepct for one's elder brother.

71. 愓 T'i⁴ (tì) - Cautious, vigilant, watchful.

72. 悄 Ch'iao³ (qiâo) - Quiet; silent; sad.

73. 悟 Wu⁴ (wù) - Awaken, become aware, realize.

74. 悠 Yu¹ (you) - Far, far-reaching; long-drawn-out; leisurely.

75. 悦 Yüeh⁴ (yuè) - Please (– sb.); pleased, delighted, happy.

怅 76. 怅 ⁸ Ch'ang⁴ (chàng) - Disappointed, sorry.

77. 惝 Ch'ang³ (châng) - Alarmed, nervous, apprehensive.

78. 惑 Huo⁴ (huò) - Puzzled; doubt, suspicion; mislead.

79. 惠 Hui⁴ (huì) - Favor (receive –); be kind to, benevolent.

80. 惚 Hu¹ (hu) - Doubt, hesitation; obscure, indistinct.

81. 惛 Hun¹ (hun) - Confused; stupid, dull.

闷 82. 悶 **Men⁴ (mèn)** - Bored, depressed; air-tight, sealed.

83. 悲 **Pei¹ (bei)** - Sad, grieved; sorrow, melancholy.

84. 惜 **Hsi¹ (xi)** - Cherish, value highly; pity.

85. 悼 **Tao⁴ (dào)** - Mourning; grieved, sad.

86. 惦 **Tien³ (diàn)** -Think constantly of (– his family).

87. 惕 **T'i⁴ (tì)** - Same as 71.

88. 惇 **Tun¹ (dun)** - Sincere, honest.

凄 89. 悽 **Ch'i¹ (qi)** - Grieved; suffering.

90. 情 **Ch'ing² (qíng)** - Feelings; love, passion; favor; condition.

91. 悴 **Ts'ui⁴ (cùi)** - Distressed, sad, downhearted.

92. 惟 **Wei² (wéi)** - Only; but; think about.

恶 93. 惡 **E³·E⁴ (ê.è)** - Evil; mean; fierce. **Wu⁴ (wù)** - Hate, detest.

94. 惶 **Huang² (huáng)** - Frightened; fear, anxiety.

95. 意 **Yi⁴ (yì)** - Meaning, idea, opinion, wish, intention.

96. 惹 **Je³ (rê)** - Ask for; provoke, tease; cause (– us to laugh).

97. 感 **Kan³ (gân)** - Feel; move, touch; affected; feeling, emotion.

惬 98. 愜 **Ch'ieh⁴ (qiè)** - Be satisfied, pleased.

99. 愆 **Ch'ien¹ (qian)** - Fault, error, transgression.

100. 恓 **Mien³ (miân)** - Reflect, consider; shy, modest.

恼 101. 惱 **Nao³ (nâo)** - Angry, displeased, annoyed; worried.

爱 102. 愛 **Ai⁴ (ài)** - Love, be fond of; affection.

103. 愕 **O⁴ (è)** - Stunned, startled, amazed.

104. 愎 **Pi⁴ (bì)** - Stubborn, self-willed; wilful (– child).

105. 想 **Hsiang³ (xiâng)** - Think, suppose; long for, want.

106. 惺 **Hsing¹ (xing)** - Intelligent, clear-headed, wise.

107. 惰 **To⁴ (duò)** - Lazy, indolent, sluggish.

恻 108. 惻 **Ts'e⁴ (cè)** - Sympathize, grieve for, pity; sorrowful, sad.

109. 愁 **Ch'ou² (chóu)** - Mournful, sad; worry.

110. 愠 **Yün⁴ (yùn)** - Angry, irritated.

111. 愚 **Yü² (yú)** - Foolish, stupid; make a fool of.

112. 愈 **Yü⁴ (yù)** - Recover; more and more; the more...the more...

113. 慌 ¹⁰ **Huang¹ (huang)** - Flurried, become agitated and confused.

114. 愿 **Yüan⁴ (yuàn)** - Hope, wish, desire; be willing; vow.

115. 愧 **K'uei⁴ (kùi)** - Ashamed, bashful; conscience-stricken.

栗 116. 慄 **Li⁴ (lì)** - Terrified, afraid.

117. 愽 **Po² (bó)** - Rich, abundant, ample; win, gain; gamble.

118. 慎 Shen[4] (shèn) - Careful, cautious, prudent.

诉 119. 愬 Su[4] (sù) - Tell; complain; appeal to (– higher court).

120. 愻 Hsün[4] (xùn) - Abdicate, give up; modest; inferior.

态 121. 態 T'ai[4] (tài) - Form, appearance; attitude; state (liquid –).

122. 慈 Tzu[2] (cí) - Kind, loving, compassionate; mother (my –).

殷 123. 慇 Yin[1] (yin) - Abundant, rich; eager.

124. 慧 [11] Hui[4] (huì) - Bright, intelligent; wisdom.

125. 慨 K'ai[3] (kâi) - Generous, noble; indignant, angry.

126. 慷 K'ang[1] (kang) - Generous, noble, warm-hearted.

127. 憩 Ch'i[4] (qì) - Rest.

庆 128. 慶 Ch'ing[4] (qìng) - Congratulate, celebrate.

虑 129. 慮 Lü[4] (lù) - Consider, think over it; anxious, concerned.

130. 慢 Man[4] (màn) - Slow, sluggish; rude; postpone.

131. 慕 Mu[4] (mù) - Admire; yearn for.

怄 132. 慪 Ou[4] (où) - Irritate, annoy.

恸 133. 慟 T'ung[4] (tòng) - Grief; moved, excited.

134. 慝 T'e[4] (tè) - Dissolute, loose in morals, lewd.

惭 135. 慚 Ts'an[2] (cán) - Ashamed.

惨 136. 惨 Ts'an³ (cân) - Miserable; cruel, inhuman; seriously.

戚 137. 感 Ch'i¹ (qi) - Sorrow, woe; relative.

惯 138. 慣 Kuan⁴ (guàn) - Accustomed to; pamper (– a child), spoil.

139. 慰 Wei⁴ (wèi) - Console, comfort; be relieved, pleased.

忧 140. 憂 Yu¹ (you) - Worry, concern; sorrow.

欲 141. 慾 Yü⁴ (yù) - Desire, lust; wish; about to.

愤 142. 憤 Fen⁴ (fèn) - Anger, resentment.

143. 憩 Ch'i⁴ (qì) - Rest (a short –).

144. 憨 Han¹ (han) - Silly, foolish; simple, naive; straightforward.

宪 145. 憲 Hsien⁴ (xìan) - Statute, constitution, law.

146. 憰 Chüeh² (júe) - Cheat, swindle.

怜 147. 憐 Lien² (lián) - Sympathize, pity.

悯 148. 憫 Min³ (mîn) - Condole, sympathize, pity; sorrow.

149. 憋 Pieh¹ (bie) - Suppress, hold back; suffocate, choke.

凭 150. 憑 P'ing² (píng) - Lean against, depend on; evidence, proof.

惮 151. 憚 Tan⁴ (dàn) - Dread, fear.

152. 憎 Ts'eng¹ (zeng) - Abhore, detest, hate.

惫 153. 憊 Pei⁴ (bèi) - Exhausted, worn out, fatigued.

154. 憔 Ch'iao² (qiáo) - Grievious, depressed, pining.

155. 懈 ¹³ Hsieh⁴ (xiè) - Lazy, idle.

156. 憾 Han⁴ (hàn) - Hatred; regret(ful).

恳 157. 懇 K'en³ (kên) - Sincere(ly); beg, request.

勤 158. 懃 Ch'in² (qín) - Zealous, eager; earnest.

懔 159. 懍 Lin³ (lîn) - Fear, be afraid of.

160. 懋 Mou⁴ (mòu) - To be great or energetic; rejoice.

161. 懊 Ao⁴ (aò) - Regretful, annoyed, irritated.

162. 懂 Tung³ (dông) - Understand, know.

忆 163. 憶 Yi⁴ (yì) - Recall; recollect.

应 164. 應 Ying¹ (yìng) - Should. Ying⁴ (yìng) - Answer; deal with.

懑 165. 懑 ¹⁴ Men⁴ (mèn) - Same as 82.

166. 懦 No⁴ (nùo) - Cowardly; weak.

惩 167. 懲 ¹⁵ Ch'eng² (chéng) - Punish, penalize, chastise.

悬 168. 懸 ¹⁶ Hsüan² (xuán) - Hang (up), suspend; pending.

怀 169. 懷 Huai² (huái) - Same as 15.

懒 170. 懶 Lan³ (lân) - Lazy, sluggish.

171. 懵 Meng³ (mêng) - Ignorant, stupid.

忏 172. 懺 [17] **Ch'an⁴ (chàn)** - Repent, regret.

慑 173. 懾 [18] **She⁴ (shè). Che⁴** - Fear (v); be afraid of; frightened.

惧 174. 懼 **Chü⁴ (jù)** - Fear, dread.

欢 175. 懽 **Huan¹ (huan)** - Merry, cheerful; vigorously.

176. 懿 **Yi⁴ (yì)** - Virtuous; admirable.

恋 177. 戀 [19] **Lien⁴ (liàn)** - Love (n); long for; feel attached to.

HEMP 麻

Representing hemp (𣏟 plant) in storage (广 shelter): 麻.

1. 麻 **Ma² (má)** - Hemp; rough; pockmarked; anesthesia.

么 2. 麼 **Me (me)** - Interrogative particle.

3. 麾 **Hui¹ (hui)** - Signal flag; commander's banner; command.

HIGH 高

Picture of a tower: 高

1. 高 **Kao¹ (gao)** - High, tall; loud (– voice); high-priced.

HORN 角

Representing a striated horn 角.

1. 角 **Chiao³ (jiâo)** - Horn; corner; angle. **Chüeh² (jué)** -Role (in drama or movie); compete.

粗 2. 觕 [4] **Ts'u¹ (cu)** - Thick (– rope); rough, coarse; rude, vulgar.

3. 觚 [5] **Ku¹ (gu)** - Wine vessel, beaker, goblet; writing tablet.

4. 解 [6] **Chieh³ (jiê)** - Loosen, untie; explain; understand.

5. 觫 [7] **Su⁴ (sù)** - Tremble with fear.

6. 觭 [8] **Ch'i² (qí)** - Single; not matched.

觞 7. 觴 [11] **Shang¹ (shang)** - Wine cup, goblet.

触 8. 觸 [13] **Ch'u⁴ (chù)** - Touch, strike; offend.

HORSE 馬

Picture of a horse with its mane blowing in the wind: 馬.

马 1. 馬 **Ma³ (mâ)** - Horse.

凭 2. 馮 [2] **P'ing² (píng)** - Rely on.

驭 3. 馭 **Yü⁴ (yù)** - Drive (a carriage); imperial; resist, keep out.

驰 4. 馳 [3] **Ch'ih² (chí)** - Speed, gallop; spread (– reputation).

驯 5. 馴 **Hsün² (xún)** - Tame, docile; domesticate, tame (v).

驮 6. 馱 **T'o² (túo)** - Carry on the back.; load, burden.

驳 7. 駁 [4] **Po² (bó)** - Refute, contradict; barge (ship).

駐 8. 駐 [5] Chu⁴ (zhù) - Lodge, stay (temporary); be stationed.

驾 9. 駕 Chia⁴ (jià) - Drive (– car); fly (– plane); sail (– boat).

驹 10. 駒 Chü¹ (ju) - Colt or foal (young horse, donkey, mule).

驽 11. 駑 Nu² (nú) - Inferior horse; old horse.

驶 12. 駛 Shih³ (shî) - Speed (of a car); drive, sail.

驷 13. 駟 Szu⁴ (si) - Team of four horses.

驼 14. 駝 T'o² (tuó) - Camel; hunchbacked.

驵 15. 駔 Tsang³ (zâng) - Fine horse; steed.

骇 16. 駭 [6] Hai⁴ (hài) - Astonished, startled, shocked.

骆 17. 駱 Lo⁴ (luò) - Legendary white horse w. black mane.

驳 18. 駮 Po² (bó) - Same as 7.

骈 19. 駢 P'ien² (pián) - Pair of horses; joined together; parallel.

骏 20. 駿 [7] Chün⁴ (jùn) - Fine horse; steed.

骑 21. 騎 [8] Ch'i² (qí) - Ride (– horse, bicylcle); cavalry.

骒 22. 騍 K'e⁴ (kè) - Mare (female horse or donkey).

骗 23. 騙 [9] P'ien⁴ (piàn) - Deceive, cheat, swindle.

骘 24. 騭 [10] Chih¹ (zhi) - Stallion (male horse); promote; determine.

骚 25. 騷 Sao¹ (sao) - Disturb, upset.

骗 26. 騸 Shan[4] (shàn) - Castrate, spay.

腾 27. 騰 T'eng[2] (téng) - Jump, soar (prices –); vacate.

草 28. 騲 Ts'ao[3] (cáo) - Female (of animals); * Grass; careless; draft.

驱 29. 驅 [11] Ch'ü[1] (qu) - Drive (– a car); expel; disperse.

骡 30. 騾 Lo[2] (luó) - Mule.

骄 31. 驕 [12] Chiao[1] (jiao) - Proud, arrogant, conceited.

惊 32. 驚 [13] Ching[1] (jing) - Frighten, terrify, alarm; surprise.

验 33. 驗 Yen[4] (yàn) - Examine, test; effective.

驿 34. 驛 Yi[4] (yì) - Post, station, stop (bus –).

骤 35. 驟 [14] Chou[4] (zhòu) - Suddenly; trot (rather fast horse steps).

驴 36. 驢 [16] Lü[2] (lú) - Donkey, ass.

欢 37. 驩 [18] Huan[1] (huan) - Merry, jubilant; vigorously, in full swing.

I

ICE 冫

Picture of ice crystals 仌 .

1. 冬 ³ **Tung¹ (dong)** - Winter.

2. 冲 ⁴ **Ch'ung¹ (chong)** - Pour boiling water on (– tea); rush.

3. 决 **Chüeh² (jué)** - Determine; certainly; execute (– prisoner).

4. 冰 **Ping¹ (bing)** - Ice; icy (– wind); put on ice (– beer).

5. 冷 ⁵ **Leng³ (lêng)** - Cold; cool (– it off first); cold-hearted.

6. 冶 **Yeh³ (yê)** - Smelt, fuse; seductively dressed or made up.

7. 准 ⁸ **Chun³ (zhûn)** - Allow, permit; exact(ly), certain(ly).

8. 凉 **Liang² (liáng)** - Cool; cold. **Liang⁴ (liàng)** - Cool off.

9. 凌 **Ling² (líng)** - Ice; insult; approach; rise, soar.

10. 凋 **Tiao¹ (diao)** - Wither; fade.

净 11. 淨 **Ching⁴ (jìng)** - Clean (– water); completely; net (– weight).

12. 凄 **Ch'i¹ (qi)** - Cold, chilly; bleak, sad, miserable.

冻 13. 凍 **Tung⁴ (dòng)** - Freeze, frozen (– meat); frostbitten.

凭 14. 馮 ⁹ **P'ing² (píng)** - Lean against; rely on; proof, evidence.

15. 減 **Chien³ (jiân)** - Subtract, reduce, decrease.

16. 湊 **Ts'ou⁴ (còu)** - Collect together; happen by chance.

17. 濅 ¹³ **Chin⁴ (jìn)** - Cold, chilled.

凛 18. 凜 **Lin³ (lîn)** - Cold, strict, severe; awe-inspiring.

19. 凝 ¹⁴ **Ning² (níng)** - Congeal, solidify; concentrate.

渎 20. 瀆 ¹⁵ **Tu² (dú)** - Treat contemptuously.

ILLNESS 疒

To be ill and be lying ___ in bed 爿 (splitwood: half of a tree 朩): 疒 .

1. 疔 ² **Ting¹ (ding)** - Malignant boil.

2. 疙 ³ **Ke¹ (ge)** - Pimple; knot.

3. 疚 **Chiu⁴ (jìu)** - Chronic disease; remorse, regret.

4. 疝 **Shan⁴ (shàn)** - Hernia, rupture.

5. 疥 ⁴ **Chieh⁴ (jiè)** - Scabies.

6. 疤   **Pa[1] (ba)** - Scar.

7. 疫   **Yi[4] (yì)** - Plague, pestilence; epidemic disease.

8. 疣   **Yu[2] (yóu)** - Wart.

9. 痄 [5]   **Cha[4] (zhà)** - Mumps.

10. 疹   **Chen[3] (zhên)** - Rash, measles.

11. 症   **Cheng[4] (zhèng)** - Disease, sickness, illness.

痱 12. 痹   **Fei[4] (fēi)** - Prickly heat.

13. 疴   **K'e[1] (ke)** - Illness.

14. 疳   **Kan[1] (gan)** - Children's malnutrition disease.

15. 疲   **P'i[2] (pí)** - Tired, weary, exhausted.

16. 病   **Ping[4] (bíng)** - Ill, sick; disease.

17. 疼   **T'eng[2] (téng)** - Pain, ache; love dearly.

18. 疱   **P'ao[4] (pào)** - Blister.

19. 疾   **Chi[2] (jí)** - Sickness, hate; quick.

20. 疵   **Tz'u[1] (ci)** - Flaw, defect, blemish, fault.

21. 痔 [6]   **Chih[4] (zhì)** - Hemorrhoids, piles.

22. 痕   **Hen[2] (hén)** - Mark, scar, stain.

23. 痍   **Yi[2] (yí)** - Wound, trauma.

24. 痊 **Chüan² (quán)** - Convalescent, recover from illness.

25. 痒 **Yang³ (yâng)** - Itch(y), itching.

26. 痣 [7] **Chih⁴ (zhì)** - Mole (spot on the body).

27. 痢 **Li⁴ (lì)** - Dysentery, diarrhea.

28. 痧 **Sha¹ (sha)** - Acute disease (cholera, sunstroke, etc.).

29. 痠 **Suan¹ (suan)** - Muscular pains.

30. 痘 **Tou⁴ (dòu)** - Smallpox.

31. 痞 **P'i³ (pî)** - Swelling in the abdomen; constipation; rascal.

32. 痛 **T'ung⁴ (tòng)** - Pain, ache (head–); sorrow; bitterly (cry –).

33. 痴 [8] **Ch'ih¹ (chi)** - Silly, foolish, stupid; insane, mad.

麻 34. 痳 **Ma² (má)** - Paralysis (infantile –).

35. 痲 **Peng¹ (beng)** - Menorrhagia.

痹 36. 痺 **Pi⁴ (bì)** - Rheumatism; numbness.

37. 痰 **T'an² (tán)** - Phlegm; sputum.

38. 瘁 **Ts'ui⁴ (cùi)** - Overworked, tired, worn-out.

39. 痿 **Wei³ (wêi)** - Paralysis; weakness.

40. 瘀 **Yü¹ (yu)** - Stasis (of blood); have a blood clot.

41. 瘌 [9] **La¹ (la)** - Bald (from skin disease).

疯 42. 瘋 **Feng[1] (feng)** - Insane, mad, crazy.

43. 瘊 **Hou[2] (hóu)** - Wart.

愈 44. 瘉 **Yü[4] (yù)** - Recover. * More and more; the more...the more...

痪 45. 瘓 **Huan[4] (huàn)** - Paralysis, palsy.

疮 46. 瘡 [10] **Ch'uang[1] (chuang)** - Sore spot on body; wound (sword –).

47. 瘤 **Liu[2] (líu)** - Tumor.

48. 瘠 **Chi[2] (jí)** - Lean, thin; poor (– soil), barren (– land).

疟 49. 瘧 **Yao[4] (yaò). Nüeh[4] (nüè)** - Malaria.

50. 瘩 **Ta[2] (dá)** - Swelling on the skin; pimple.

51. 瘢 **Pan[1] (ban)** - Scar on the skin, mark.

52. 瘦 **Shou[4] (shòu)** - Thin (– in the face), lean (– meat); barren.

癲 53. 瘨 **Tien[1] (dian)** - Mentally deranged; insane.

瘟 54. 瘟 **Wen[1] (wen)** - Acute communicable disease.

55. 瘴 [11] **Chang[4] (zhàng)** - Miasma.

56. 瘸 **Ch'üeh[2] (qué)** - Lame, limp.

57. 瘰 **Lo[3] (luô)** - Scrofula, scrofulous swelling.

痫 58. 癇 [12] **Hsien[2] (xián)** - Epilepsy.

废 59. 癈 **Fei[4] (fèi)** - Cast aside, waste, cancel.

疗 60. 療 **Liao² (liáo)** - Cure, heal; treat (– a patient).

痨 61. 癆 **Lao² (láo)** - Consumption, tuberculosis.

62. 癖 [13] **P'i³ (pî)** - Addiction, craving for; indigestion.

痴 63. 癡 **Ch'ih¹ (chi)** - Same as 33.

瘪 64. 癟 [14] **Pieh³ (biê)** - Shrivelled, shrunken; flat (– tire).

症 65. 癥 [15] **Cheng¹·⁴ (zheng. zhèng)** - Disease; illness.

疖 66. 癤 **Chieh¹ (jie)** - Furuncle, boil (n); knot (in wood).

癞 67. 癩 [16] **Lai⁴ (lài)** - Leprosy; favus (skin disease) of the scalp.

癣 68. 癬 [17] **Hsüan³ (xuân)** - Ringworm; fungus disease of the skin.

瘾 69. 癮 **Yin³ (yîn)** - Addiction; strong interest (in sports, etc.).

痈 70. 癰 [18] **Yung¹ (yong)** - Carbuncle; abscess.

瘫 71. 癱 [19] **T'an¹ (tan)** - Palsy; paralysis, paralysed.

72. 癲 **Tien¹ (dian)** - Same as 53.

INCH 寸

A hand ⇛ and a dash –, to indicate where the pulse can be felt – which is about an inch (Chin. inch < ca. .33 dm >) away from the hand : ⇛

1. 寸 **Ts'un⁴ (cùn)** - Inch; small, very little (– progress).

2. 寺 [3] **Szu⁴ (si)** - Temple, monastry.

3. 封 [6] **Feng¹ (feng)** - Seal (– letter); blockade; confer; envelope.

4. 将 ⁷ **Chiang¹ (jiang)** - Same as 7.

5. 射 **She⁴ (shè)** - Shoot (out); inject; radiate (– light, heat).

专 6. 專 ⁸ **Chuan¹ (zhuan)** - Special; expert, specialist **(zhuanjia)**; monopolize.

将 7. 將 **Chiang¹ (jiang)** - About to. **Chiang⁴ (jiàng)** - General; commander in chief.

8. 尉 **Yü⁴ (yù). Wei⁴ (wèi)** - Pacify, quiet, soothe.

寻 9. 尋 ⁹ **Hsün² (xún)** - Search, seek, look for.

10. 尊 **Tsun¹ (zun)** - Senior; honor, respect; your (– wife).

对 11. 對 ¹¹ **Tui⁴ (dùi)** - Answer; opposite; correct.

导 12. 導 ¹³ **Tao³ (dâo)** - Lead, guide, conduct (– electricity, heat).

INSECT 虫

Picture of a worm or insect ⌇ .

1. 虫 **Ch'ung² (chóng)** - Insect, worm.

2. 虱 ² **Shih¹ (shi)** - Louse.

3. 虹 ³ **Hung² (hóng)** - Rainbow.

4. 虺 **Hui³ (hûi)** - Poisonous serpent w. big head and small neck.

5. 虼 **Ke⁴ (gè)** - Flea.

6. 蚩 ⁴ **Ch'ih¹ (chi)** - Ignorant, stupid.

7. 蚣 **Kung¹ (gong)** - Centipede.

8. 蚌 **Pang⁴ (bàng)** - Freshwater mussel, clam.

9. 蚪 Tou³ (dôu) - Tadpole.

10. 蚊 Wen² (wén) - Mosquito.

11. 蚤 Tsao³ (zâo) - Flea.

12. 蛰 ⁵ Cha² (zhá) - Small cicada.

13. 蚱 Cha³ (zhâ) - Some kind of locust.

14. 蛄 Ku¹ (gu) - Some kind of cicada; mole cricket.

15. 蛀 Chu⁴ (zhù) - Moth that eats books, etc.; moth-eaten.

16. 蚖 Ku¹ (gu) - Same as 14.

17. 蛇 She² (shé) - Snake, serpent.

18. 蚯 Ch'iu¹ (qiu) - Earthworm.

19. 蛋 Tan⁴ (dàn) - Egg; egg-shaped.

20. 蛆 Ch'ü¹ (qu) - Maggots.

21. 蛉 Ling² (líng) - Sand fly.

22. 蛛 ⁶ Chu¹ (zhu) - Spider (**zhuzhu**).

23. 蛔 Hui² (húi) - Roundworm.

24. 蛟 Chiao¹ (jiao) - Flood dragon (mythical dragon of floods).

25. 蛤 Ha² (há) - Frog (**háma**). Ke² (gé) - Clam.

26. 蛐 Ch'ü¹ (qu) - Cricket.

27. 蛙 **Wa¹ (wa)** - Frog.

28. 蜇⁷ **Che² (zhé)** - Jellyfish.

28 A. 蚬 **Hsien³ (xiân)** - Clam; mussel.

29. 蜂 **Feng¹ (feng)** - Bee, wasp.

30. 蜋 **Lang² (láng)** - Mantis.

31. 蜊 **Li² (lí)** - Clam.

32. 蛾 **O² (é)** - Moth.

33. 蜀 **Shu³ (shû)** - Silkworm; Szechuan province.

34. 蜓 **T'ing² (tíng)** - Dragonfly (**qingtíng**).

蜈 35. 蜈 **Wu² (wú)** - Centipede (**wúgong**).

36. 蜘⁸ **Chih¹ (zhi)** - Spider (**zhizhu**).

37. 蜢 **Meng³ (mêng)** - Grasshopper.

38. 蜜 **Mi⁴ (mì)** - Honey; sweet (– talk).

蝶 39. 蝶 **Tieh² (dié)** - Butterfly.

40. 蜻 **Ch'ing¹ (qing)** - Dragonfly (**qingtíng**).

41. 蝠⁹ **Fu² (fú)** - Bat.

42. 蝮 **Fu⁴ (fù)** - Viper.

虾 43. 蝦 **Hsia¹ (xia)** - Shrimp.

44. 蝴 **Hu² (hú)** - Butterfly.

45. 蝗 Huang^2 (huáng) - Locust.

46. 蝌 K'e^1 (ke) - Tadpole.

蜗 47. 蜗 Wo^1 (wo) - Snail (woniú).

虻 48. 虻 Meng^2 (méng) - Horsefly, gadfly.

49. 蝻 Nan^3 (nân) - Nymph of a locust.

50. 蝙 Pien^1 (bian) - Bat (bianbú).

蚀 51. 蚀 Shih^2 (shí) - Lose (– money); corrode; eclipse.

52. 蝶 Tieh^2 (dié) - Butterfly.

猬 53. 猬 Wei^4 (wèi) - Porcupine, hedgehog.

54. 蝘 Yen^3 (yân) - Lizard.

55. 蝣 Yu^2 (yóu) - Mayfly (fúyóu).

56. 螂 Lang^2 (láng) - Mantis (tángláng). [10]

蚂 57. 螞 Ma^4 (mà) - Locust (màzha). Ma^3 (mâ) - Ant (mâyî).

58. 螃 P'ang^2 (páng) - Crab (pángxiè) (see No. 74).

59. 融 Jung^2 (róng) - Melt, thaw; blend harmoniously.

萤 60. 螢 Ying^2 (yíng) - Glowworm, firefly.

蝈 61. 蟈 Kuo^1 (guo) - Long-horned grasshopper. [11]

蝼 62. 螻 Lou^2 (lóu) - Mole cricket (lóugu).

63. 螺 **Lo² (lúo)** - Conch; spiral univalve shell; screwlike.

64. 蟆 **Ma (ma)** - Frog, toad.

65. 蟄 **Che¹ (zhe)** - Sting; poison; poisonous.

66. 蟀 **Shuai⁴ (shuài)** - Cricket (**xishuài**).

67. 螳 **T'ang² (táng)** - Mantis.

虫 68. 蟲 ¹² **Ch'ung² (chóng)** - Insect; worm.

虮 69. 蟣 **Chi³ (jî)** - Nit (egg of a louse).

70. 蟒 **Mang³ (mâng)** - Python, boa (**mângshé**).

71. 蟠 **P'an² (pán)** - Curl, coil.

蝉 72. 蟬 **Ch'an² (chán)** - Cicada.

73. 蟮 **Shan⁴ (shàn)** - Earthworm (**qushan**).

74. 蟹 ¹³ **Hsieh⁴ (xiè)** - Crab (**pángxiè**) (see No. 58).

蝎 75. 蠍 **Hsieh¹ (xie)** - Scorpion.

蚁 76. 蟻 **Yi³ (yî)** - Ant (**mâyî**).

77. 蟺 **Shan⁴ (shàn)** - Same as 73.

78. 蟾 **Ch'an² (chán)** - Toad (**chánchú**).

蝇 79. 蠅 **Ying² (yíng)** - Fly.

80. 蠓 ¹⁴ **Meng³ (mêng)** - Midge (small two-winged fly).

蚝 80A. 蠔 **Hao² (háo)** - Oyster.

81. 蠢 [15] **Ch'un³ (chūn)** - Foolish, stupid; wriggle (like a worm).

蜡 82. 蠟 **La⁴ (là)** - Wax; candle; polish (floor –).

83. 蠡 **Li³ (lǐ)** - Wood-boring insect.

蛎 84. 蠣 **Li⁴ (lì)** - Oyster.

蛊 85. 蠱 [17] **Ku³ (gǔ)** - Legendary poisonous insect.

蚕 86. 蠶 [18] **Ts'an² (cán)** - Silkworm.

蛮 87. 蠻 [19] **Man² (mán)** - Savage, barbarous; southern barbarians.

INTERTWINE 爻

To unite by twisting together 爻 .

1. 爻 **Yao² (yáo)** - Intertwine; mix, blend; crosswise.

2. 爽 **Shuang³ (shuǎng)** - Cheerful; bright, clear; comfortable.

尔 3. 爾 **Erh³ (ěr)** - You; that (– morning); like that.

J

JADE 玉 . 王

The precious gem · that only kings 王 *(the mediator* | *between Heaven* ￣ *, Earth* ＿ *and Man* — *) could possess:* 玉 .

1. 玉 **Yū⁴ (yù)** - Jade; beautiful (– woman).

2. 王 **Wang² (wáng)** - King, ruler.

3. 玎 **Ting¹ (ding)** - Ding-dong, jingling noise.

4. 玖 **Chiu³ (jĭu)** - Nine (elaborate form used on checks, etc.).

5. 珏 **Chüeh² (júe)** - Two pieces of jade bound together.

6. 玫 **Mei² (méi)** - *Rugosa rose* ; rose (red –).

7. 玫 **Mei² (méi)** - Same as 6.

8. 玩 **Wan² (wán)** - Play, have fun; treat things lightly.

9. 珍 [5] **Chen[1] (zhen)** - Treasure; precious; delicious (– taste).

10. 玻 **Po[1] (bo)** - Glass (boli).

11. 珀 **P'o[4] (pò)** - Amber (hûpò).

12. 珊 **Shan[1] (shan)** - Coral (w. 33: shanhú).

13. 玷 **Tien[4] (diàn)** - Flaw, blemish, defect; disgrace.

14. 玳 **Tai[4] (dài)** - Turtle (dàimaò).

15. 珠 [6] **Chu[1] (zhu)** - Pearl; bead.

16. 珥 **Erh[3] (êr)** - Earring made of jade or pearl.

17. 珞 **Lo[4] (luò)** - Celluloid (sàilùlùo).

18. 珪 **Kuei[1] (gui)** - Jade sceptre, symbol of authority of rulers.

19. 班 **Pan[1] (ban)** - Class (– A); team; shift (night –).

现 20. 現 [7] **Hsien[4] (xiàn)** - Present (– condition); appear; cash (money).

21. 球 **Ch'iu[2] (qíu)** - Sphere (hemi–), ball; the earth.

22. 琅 **Lang[2] (láng)** - White jade-like stone.

23. 理 **Li[3] (lî)** - Texture (in wood, etc.); reason; manage.

24. 琉 **Liu[2] (líu)** - Colored glaze (líuli).

25. 琢 [8] **Cho[2] (zhuó)** - Work on a gem: chisel, carve, cut.

26. 琥 **Hu[3] (hû)** - Amber (hûpò).

27. 琴 Ch'in² (qín) - String instrument; Chinese zither.

28. 琨 K'un¹ (kun) - Some kind of jade.

29. 琳 Lin² (lín) - Fine jade; gem.

30. 琶 P'a² (pá) - *Arpeggio* (muscial term) (páyin).

31. 琵 P'i² (pí) - *Pipa,* plucked string instrument.

32. 瑕 Hsia² (xía) - Flaw (blemish or crack) in jade. [9]

33. 瑚 Hu² (hú) - Coral (w. 12: shanhú).

34. 瑁 Mao⁴ (mào) - Hawksbill turtle (dàimào).

35. 瑙 Nao³ (nâo) - Agate (mânâo).

36. 瑟 Se⁴ (sè) - Instrument w. 25 strings, similar to zither.

37. 瑞 Jui⁴ (rùi) - Auspicious; good omen; lucky.

38. 瑛 Ying¹ (ying) - Luster of gems.

39. 瑜 Yü² (yú) - Fine jade; luster of gems; virtues.

40. 瑰 Kuei¹ (gui) - Kind of jasper; precious, rare; marvellous. [10]

41. 瑯 Lang² (láng) - Same as 22.

玛 42. 瑪 Ma³ (mâ) - Agate (w. 35: mânâo).

琐 43. 瑣 So³ (suô) - Trivial, petty, minute.

瑶 44. 瑤 Yao² (yáo) - Beautiful jade or stone; green jasper.

莹 45. 瑩 Ying[2] (yíng) - Jade-like stone; lustrous and transparent.

46. 璋 [11] Chang[1] (zhang) - Ancient jade or stone sceptre.

47. 瑾 Chin[3] (jǐn) - Fine jade, beautiful gem; lustrous, brilliant.

48. 璃 Li[2] (lí) - Glass (w. 10: **boli**); colored glaze (w. 24: **líuli**).

琏 49. 璉 Lien[3] (lián) - Sacrificial vessel.

环 50. 環 [13] Huan[2] (huán) - Ring, bracelet; surround, encircle.

51. 璧 Pi[4] (bì) - Round flat piece of jade w. hole (for ceremonies).

玺 52. 璽 [14] Hsi[3] (xǐ) - Imperial seal.

53. 璺 Wen[4] (wèn) - Crack in crockery or glassware; flaw.

瓔 54. 瓔 [17] Ying[1] (ying) - Fine pebble; jewel; necklace.

K

KNIFE 刀 刂

Picture of a knife 刀; later the handle was curved upwards for compactness 刀.

1. 刀   **Tao¹ (dao)** - Knife, sword.

2. 刁   **Tiao¹ (diao)** - Cunning, sly, tricky.

3. 刃   **Jen⁴ (rèn)** - Edge or blade of knife, sword; kill w. sword.

4. 分   **Fen¹ (fen)** - Divide, separate, distinguish; branch (firm –).

5. 刈   **Yi⁴ (yì)** - Mow; cut (– grass); cut down and reap.

6. 切   **Ch'ieh¹ (qie)** - Cut. **Ch'ieh⁴ (qiè)** - Correspond; anxious.

7. 刊   **K'an¹ (kan)** - Print; publish, publication, periodical.

8. 召   **Chao⁴ (zhào)** - Call (together) (– meeting), summon.

9. 刑 [4] **Hsing² (xíng)** - Punishment (on convicts), torture.

10. 划 **Hua² (huá)** - Paddle (– boat); pay (it doesn't –); scratch.

11. 列 **Lieh⁴ (liè)** - Arrange, line up; row, line.

12. 初 [5] **Ch'u¹ (chu)** - At the beginning of; first (– train); original.

劫 13. 刼 **Chieh² (jié)** - Rob, plunder; coerce; misfortune.

14. 利 **Li⁴ (lì)** - Sharp (– knife); profit, interest (on money).

15. 判 **P'an⁴ (pàn)** - Distinguish, discriminate; judge, decide.

16. 刨 **P'ao² (páo)** - Dig, excavate; minus. **Pao⁴ (bào)** - Level off; plane sth. down; plane (n).

17. 别 **Pieh² (bié)** - Leave, depart; other; distinguish; do not.

18. 删 **Shan¹ (shan)** - Delete, erase, cancel.

19. 刹 [6] **Ch'a⁴ (chà)** - Buddhist temple.

20. 制 **Chih⁴ (zhì)** - Make, manufacture (**zhìzào**); system (**zhìdù**).

21. 刻 **K'e⁴ (kè)** - Carve, engrave; quarter of an hour.

22. 券 **Ch'üan⁴ (quàn)** - Ticket (admission –), certificate; bond.

23. 刮 **Kua¹ (gua)** - Scrape; extort; blow (the wind –s).

24. 刺 **Tz'u⁴ (cì)** - Thorn; prick, stab; assassinate; visiting card.

25. 刷 **Shua¹ (shua)** - Brush (tooth–); scrub, cleanse.

26. 到 **Tao⁴ (dào)** - Reach, arrive; go to; up to, until.

27. 剁 **To[4] (duò)** - Chop, mince, cut fine.

28. 尅 [7] **K'e[4] (kè)** - Subdue, destroy.

29. 剌 **La[4] (là)** - Perverse, disagreeable.

30. 削 **Hsiao[1] (xiao). Hsüeh[1] (xue)** - Pare (peel) w. a knife; cut.

31. 剃 **T'i[4] (tì)** - Shave (– one's head).

32. 则 則 **Tse[2] (zé)** - Standard, model; rule; follow (– example).

33. 前 **Ch'ien[2] (qián)** - Front (– door); before; first (– three rows).

34. 刚 剛 [8] **Kang[1] (gang)** - Firm, unyielding; just (– right); just now.

35. 剖 **P'ou[1] (pou)** - Cut open; analyze, dissect.

36. 剥 剝 **Pao[1] (bao). Po[1] (bo)** - Peel (– orange); skin (– rabbit).

37. 剔 **T'i[1] (ti)** - Scrape off; pick (– one's teeth); pick out and reject.

38. 剜 **Wan[1] (wan)** - Cut out, scoop out.

39. 副 [9] **Fu[4] (fù)** - Assistant, vice- (– president); supplementary.

40. 剐 剮 **Kua[3] (guâ)** - Cut a criminal to pieces; cut, hack.

41. 剩 **Sheng[4] (shèng)** - Surplus, remnant.

42. 剪 **Chien[3] (jiân)** - Scissors; cut w. scissors; exterminate.

43. 创 創 [10] **Ch'uang[1] (chuang)** - Wound. **Ch'uang[4] (chuàng)** - Start.

44. 割 **Ke[1] (ge)** - Cut (– grass, meat).

劃

45. 剿 [11] Chiao³ (jiâo) - Put down (– bandits), wipe out (– enemy).

划 46. 劃 [12] Hua⁴ (huà) - Plan (v); mark (v). * Hua² (huá) - Row (v); scratch.

剑 47. 劍 [13] Chien⁴ (jiàn) - Sword, dagger, sabre.

剧 48. 劇 Chü⁴ (jù) - Theatrical performance, play; severe (– pain).

刽 49. 劊 Kuei⁴ (guì) - Cut off, chop off.

50. 劈 P'i¹ (pi) - Split, chop; wedge. P'i³ (pî) - Split, strip (off).

51. 劐 [14] Huo¹ (huo) - Slit or cut w. a knife; hoe (v).

剂 52. 劑 Chi⁴ (jì) - Dose; prescription; pharmaceutical preparation.

L

LAME 尢

Picture of a person who has one leg shorter than the other, and therefore has to limp .

1. 尢 **Wang^{1} (wang)** - Lame; crooked.
2. 尤 **Yu^{2} (yóu)** - Especially, in particular; blame.
3. 就 **Chiu^{4} (jiù)** - Come near (– the fire); only, merely; at once.

LANCE 矛

Picture of a lance .

1. 矛 **Mao^{2} (máo)** - Spear, lance.
2. 矜 **Ching^{1} (jing)** - Pity, boast, attend to.

LEATHER 韋

Two men 刀刀 *stretching a piece of leather* ○ *to smoothen it* 幸 .

韋 1. 韋　**Wei² (wéi)** - Leather, hide.

鞘 2. 鞘　**Ch'iao⁴ (qiào)** - Sheath (for a knife, sword, etc.).

韜 3. 韜　**T'ao¹ (tao)** - Sheath, bow case; hide, conceal; art of war.

韫 4. 韞　**Yün⁴ (yùn)** - Orange (color); bow case; store (v); conceal.

LEEK 韭

Picture of a leek plant 韭 .

1. 韭　**Chiu³ (jiû)** - Leek, scallions, Chinese chives.

2. 韱　**Ch'ien¹ (qian)** - Wild garlic, wild onion.

LEFTSTROKE ノ

A stroke written from right to left ノ *– general idea of action or motion.*

1. 乃　**Nai³ (nâi)** - Be; your (– father).

2. 久　**Chiu³ (jiû)** - For a long time, long, lasting.

3. 之　**Chih¹ (zhi)** - Of (sound – drums); this; go (where to – ?).

4. 乍　**Cha⁴ (zhà)** - First (at – glance); suddenly.

5. 乏　**Fa² (fá)** - Short of (– teachers); tired, exhausted.

6. 乎　**Hu¹ (hu)** - Word at end of sentence expressing doubt, etc.

7. 乖　**Kuai¹ (guai)** - Well-behaved (– child); shrewd, perverse.

8. 乘　**Ch'eng² (chéng)** - Ride (– a bus). **Sheng⁴(shèng)** - Chariot.

L 2

LEGS 儿

Representing the legs of a person 儿.

1. 儿 **Jen² (rén)** - Man, human being, person, people.

2. 兀 ¹ **Wu⁴ (wù)** - Rising to a height, towering; bald.

3. 元 ² **Yüan² (yuán)** - First (– day); chief; dollar.

4. 允 **Yün³ (yûn)** - Permit, allow; fair (– treatment), just .

5. 充 ³ **Ch'ung¹ (chong)** - Fill, charge (– battery); act as; ample.

6. 兄 **Hsiung¹ (xiong)** - Elder brother.

7. 兆 ⁴ **Chao⁴ (zhào)** - Sign, omen; million, mega- (megahertz).

凶 8. 兇 **Hsiung¹ (xiong)** - Ominous; fierce; act of violence.

9. 光 **Kuang¹ (guang)** - Light; honor; scenery; smooth.

10. 先 **Hsien¹ (xian)** - Earlier, first; late (my – husband).

11. 克 ⁵ **K'e⁴ (kè)** - Can, able to; overcome, subdue; gram (weight).

12. 免 **Mien³ (miân)** - Avoid; exempt; remove (– from office).

13. 兔 **T'u⁴ (tù)** - Rabbit, hare.

14. 兑 **Tui⁴ (duì)** - Exchange, barter; add (– water in wine).

儿 15. 兒 ⁶ **Erh² (ér)** - Child, son; male (– horse).

16. 兜 ¹⁰ **Tou¹ (dou)** - Pocket, bag, helmet; wrap up sth. in cloth, etc.

17. 兢 ¹² **Ching¹ (jing)** - Cautious; anxious; watchful.

LID 亠

Representing the lid of a vessel 人 .

1. 亡 [1] Wang[2] **(wáng)** - Flee, escape; lose; perish, die; subdue.

2. 亢 [2] K'ang[4] **(kàng)** - Haughty, proud; severe (– drought).

3. 亥 [4] Hai[4] **(hài)** - Time period from 9 to 11 in the evening.

4. 交 Chiao[1] **(jiao)** - Hand over, deliver; intersect; intercourse.

5. 亦 Yi[4] **(yì)** - Also, too.

6. 亨 [5] Heng[1] **(heng)** - Go smoothly; succesful, prosperous.

7. 享 [6] Hsiang[3] **(xiâng)** - Enjoy.

8. 京 Ching[1] **(jing)** - Capital city; short for Beijing; 10, 000, 000.

9. 亮 [7] Liang[4] **(liàng)** - Bright; loud and clear.

10. 亭 T'ing[2] **(tíng)** - Pavillion, kiosk.

LINES 彡

Three lines – to represent rays of light, feathers, hair, etc. 彡 .

1. 形 [4] Hsing[2] **(xíng)** - Form, shape; appear(ance); compare.

2. 彦 [6] Yen[4] **(yàn)** - A man of virtue and ability.

雕 3. 彤 [8] Tiao[1] **(diao)** - Carve, engrave, cut.

4. 彪 Piao[1] **(biao)** - Young tiger; stripes (– of a tiger).

5. 彩 Ts'ai[3] **(câi)** - Colors (bright –); applause; prize.

6. 彬 **Pin[1] (bin)** - Refined (– manner).

7. 彭 [9] **P'eng[2] (péng)** - Surname (sound of the drum).

8. 彰 [11] **Chang[1] (zhang)** - Clear (– to see), obvious; conspicuous.

9. 影 [12] **Ying[3] (yîng)** - Shadow; image; photo; movie (– theatre).

LITERATURE 文

Intercrossing lines, representing waves of thoughts 交.

1. 文 **Wen[2] (wén)** - Literature, writing; language (Chinese –).

2. 斐 **Fei[3] (fêi)** - Veins, streaks; elegant, graceful, polished.

3. 斌 **Pin[1] (bin)** - Refined (manner), elegant.

4. 斑 **Pan[1] (ban)** - Spot or stripe (in a gem); variegated.

LONG 長

Hair 〈 so long that it is tied with a band—and a brooch 丫: 芥.

长 1. 長 **Ch'ang[2] (cháng)** - Long - **Chang[3] (zhâng)** - Grow.

M

MAN 人 . 亻 . 人 Rapid Access available

That being who is standing on two legs 𠆢 .

1. 人 **Jen² (rén)** - Man, human being, person, people.

2. 仇² **Ch'ou² (chóu)** - Enemy; hatred, enmity.

3. 仆 **P'u¹ (pu)** - Fall prostrate, fall to the ground.

4. 仁 **Jen² (rén)** - Benevolence; humanity; kernel; meat
(shrimp –).

5. 仍 **Jeng² (réng)** - Yet, still (– effective), as before.

6. 介 **Chieh⁴ (jiè)** - Interpose, lie between; armor; shell.

7. 今 **Chin¹ (jin)** - Modern; now; this (– year).

8. 什 Shih² (shí) - Assorted, miscellaneous.

9. 仃 Ting¹(ding) - Left alone without help or lonely (língdíng).

10. 仄 Chai³ (zhâi) - Narrow; inclined, slanting.

11. 仗³ Chang⁴ (zhàng) - Battle, war; rely on.

12. 付 Fu⁴ (fù) - Hand over; pay (– back).

13. 以 Yi³ (yǐ) - Use; according to; because of; in order to.

14. 化 Hua⁴ (huà) - Change, transform, melt; chemistry.

15. 令 Ling⁴ (lìng) - Command, order; your (– son).

16. 仞 Jen⁴ (rèn) - Ancient measure (7 or 8 *chi* < feet >).

17. 仕 Shih⁴ (shì) - Become an official.

18. 仙 Hsien¹ (xian) - Immortal being, fairy, genie.

19. 他 T'a¹ (ta) - He; other, another (– country).

20. 代 Tai⁴ (dài) - Generation; dynasty; era (geological –).

21. 仝 T'ung² (tóng) - Together; same, similar.

22. 仟 Ch'ien¹ (qian) - Elaborate form of 1, 000.

23. 仔 Tzu³ (zǐ) - Young (– pig); careful, prudent.

24. 仲⁴ Chung⁴ (zhòng) - Second (– eldest brother); middle.

25. 份 Fen⁴ (fèn) - Part, portion, share.

26. 伐 Fa² (fá) - Cut down. strike; attack.

27. 仿 Fang³ (fǎng) - Imitate, copy; resemble, be similar.

28. 伏 Fu² (fú) - Bend over; lie prostrate; hide.

29. 休 Hsiu¹ (xiu) - Stop, cease; rest; cast off one's wife.

30. 伊 Yi¹ (yi) - He, she.

31. 伙 Huo³ (huǒ) - Board, meals; partner; group.

32. 任 Jen⁴ (rèn) - Appoint; official position; allow, let.

33. 伉 K'ang⁴ (kàng) - Married couple (kànglì).

34. 企 Ch'i³ (qǐ) - Stand on tiptoe; look forward to.

35. 价 Chia⁴ (jià) - Same as (simplified form of): 價

36. 件 Chien⁴ (jiàn) - Item, article, piece (– of work); case (law –).

37. 伈 Hsin³ (xǐn) - Nervous, timid.

38. 伍 Wu³ (wǔ) - Elaborate form of 5 (five); army.

39. 仰 Yang³ (yǎng) - Look up toward a psn., admire; rely on.

占 40. 佔 ⁵ Chan⁴ (zhàn) - Occupy, seize; constitute (– the majority).

41. 住 Chu⁴ (zhù) - Live, reside, stay; stop, cease.

仁 42. 伫 Chu⁴ (zhù) - Stand for a long time.

43. 佛 Fo² (fó) - Buddha, Buddhism.

44. 何 **Ho² (hé)** - Who, what, which, why, how.

45. 伽 **Ka¹ (ga)** - Used phonetically: 'ga', as in 'gamma' (–rays).

46. 估 **Ku¹ (gu)** - Estimate, guess, appraise.

47. 伶 **Ling² (líng)** - Actor, actress.

48. 你 **Ni³ (nî)** - You.

49. 佞 **Ning⁴ (nìng)** - Given to flattery; flattery, artful speech.

50. 伴 **Pan⁴ (bàn)** - Companion, partner; accompany.

51. 体 **T'i³ (tî)** - Body; substance; style (literary –); system.

52. 伯 **Po² (bó)** - Uncle (father's elder brother) **(bóbo)**.

布 53. 佈 **Pu⁴ (bù)** - Cloth; announce, publish; spread (– disease); arrange, deploy.

54. 伸 **Shen¹ (shen)** - Extend, stretch (– out one's hand).

55. 似 **Szu⁴ (sì)** - Like, similar; seem, appear.

56. 伺 **Tz'u⁴ (cì)** - Wait upon, serve **(cìhou)**.

57. 但 **Tan⁴ (dàn)** - But, yet; nevertheless; only, merely.

58. 低 **Ti¹ (di)** - Low; lower, hang down (– one's hand).

59. 佃 **Tien⁴ (diàn)** - Till the soil; lease land from landlord; hunt.

60. 佗 **T'o² (tuó)** - He, she, it, that, etc.

61. 佐 **Tso³ (zuô)** - Assist, aid, help; assistant.

62. 作 **Tso⁴ (zuò)** - Make, do (– homework); write, compose.

63. 位 **Wei⁴ (wèi)** - Place, seat, position; throne.

64. 佚 **Yî⁴ (yì)** - Ease, leisure; idle (– walk); escape.

65. 佑 **Yu⁴ (yòu)** - Help; protect; bless.

66. 余 **Yü² (yú)** - I, me, myself.

67. 侈 ⁶ **Ch'ih³ (chî)** - Wasteful, extravagant; exaggerate.

仑 68. 侖 **Lun² (lún)** - Logical sequence; coherence.

69. 依 **Yi¹ (yi)** - Depend on; comply with; according to.

70. 侃 **K'an³ (kân)** - Upright; plainspoken; calmly and assuredly.

71. 佳 **Chia¹ (jia)** - Good, fine, beautiful.

72. 供 **Kung¹ (gong)** - Supply. **Kung⁴ (gòng)** - Offerings.

来 73. 來 **Lai² (lái)** - Come, arrive; future, next (– year).

74. 徇 **Hsün⁴ (xùn)** - Be buried w. the dead; die for (– a cause).

75. 例 **Li⁴ (lì)** - Example; precedent; rule, regulation.

76. 佩 **P'ei⁴ (pèi)** - Wear at the waist; pendant; respect, remember.

77. 佬 **Lao³ (lâo)** - Less respectful term for a man: fellow, guy.

78. 侍 **Shih⁴ (shì)** - Wait upon, serve; look after.

79. 侅 **Kai¹ (gai)** - Complete, full.

并 79A. 併 **Ping⁴ (bìng)** - Combine; unite. * Equal (– attention).

80. 使 **Shih³ (shǐ)** - Send (– sb. out); envoy; use; if, supposing.

81. 佻 **T'iao¹ (tiao)** - Frivolous (qingtiao).

82. 佯 **Yang² (yáng)** - Feign, pretend.

83. 侑 **Yu⁴ (yòu)** - Urge sb. to eat or drink; urge.

84. 俘 ⁷ **Fu² (fú)** - Capture (– enemy soldiers); prisoner of war.

85. 侯 **Hou² (hóu)** - Marquis; nobleman.

系 86. 係 **Hsi⁴ (xì). Chi⁴ (jì)** -Fasten, bind. * **Hsi⁴ (xì)** - Department; faculty; system.

侠 87. 俠 **Hsia² (xía)** - Strong and chivalrous man (**xiákè**).

88. 俚 **Li³ (lǐ)** - Vulgar, rude (– speech); rustic (– songs).

89. 俐 **Li⁴ (lì)** - Clever or quick-witted (**línglì**).

90. 俄 **O² (é)** - Instantly; presently; suddenly.

91. 保 **Pao³ (bâo)** - Protect; defend; guarantee.

92. 侶 **Lü³ (lû)** - Companion, associate.

93. 便 **Pien⁴ (biàn)** - Convenient, handy; ordinary, plain (– clothes).

94. 信 **Hsin⁴ (xìn)** - Faith; sincerity; believe, trust; letter.

95. 俗 **Su² (sú)** - Custom; convention; popular, common; vulgar.

96. 俟 **Szu⁴ (sì)** - Await, wait (– for an opportunity).

97. 俏 **Ch'iao⁴ (qiào)** - Handsome; in great demand, popular.

98. 侵 Ch'in[1] (qīn) - Invade, infringe on; approaching (– dawn).

99. 俎 Tsu[3] (zǔ) - Ancient three-legged sacrificial vessel.

100. 促 Ts'u[4] (cù) - Hurried, urgent; promote, urge; near, close to.

101. 俊 Chün[4] (jùn) - Handsome, pretty.

102. 侮 Wu[3] (wǔ) - Bully, insult.

径 103. 俓 Ching[4] (jìng) - Footpath; directly (go – to); diameter.

104. 俑 Yung[3] (yǒng) - Wooden image, puppet.

105. 倡 [8] Ch'ang[4] (chàng) - Initiate, introduce (– a principle).

值 106. 值 Chih[2] (zhí) - Value, cost; be on duty.

仿 107. 倣 Fang[3] (fǎng) - Imitate, copy; resemble, be alike.

108. 俯 Fu[3] (fǔ) - Bow (one's head); condescend.

109. 俸 Feng[4] (fèng) - Salary, pay.

110. 候 Hou[4] (hòu) - Wait, await; time, season.

幸 111. 倖 Hsing[4] (xìng) - Good fortune; fortunate, lucky; hope.

112. 倪 Yi[2] (yí) - Beginning; young, delicate; limit.

113. 倚 Yi[3] (yǐ) - Lean on, rely on; biased, partial (–partial).

个 114. 個 Ke[4] (gè) - Numerator of widest use; individual.

115. 俱 Chü[4] (jù) - All, complete.

116. 倨 **Chü⁴ (jù)** - Haughty, proud, arrogant.

117. 倔 **Chüeh² (jué)** - Stubborn (**juéjiàng**). **Chüeh⁴ (juè)** - Surly.

118. 倦 **Chüan⁴ (jüàn)** - Tired, exhausted.

倆 119. 倆 **Lia³ (liǎ)** - Two, some, several.

们 120. 們 **Men (men)** - Sign of plural: we (**wômen**), etc.

伦 121. 倫 **Lun² (lún)** - Human relations; logic; ethics (**lúnlǐ**).

122. 俺 **An³ (ân)** - I, we.

123. 俾 **Pi³ (bǐ)** - In order to; so that; cause, enable.

124. 倍 **Pei⁴ (bèi)** - Times (three –), –fold (ten–); double.

125. 倭 **Wo¹ (Wo)** - Japan (old name).

并 126. 併 **Ping⁴ (bìng)** - Combine, unite. * Equal (pay – attention).

127. 倏 **Shu¹ (shu)** - Suddenly, quickly.

倏 128. 焂 **Shu¹ (shu)** - Same as 127.

129. 修 **Hsiu¹ (xiu)** - Decorate; repair; study; construct; trim.

130. 倘 **T'ang³ (tâng)** - If, supposing; in case (– of accident).

131. 倒 **Tao³ (dâo)** - Collapse, bankrupt. **Tao⁴ (dào)** - Pour (– tea).

132. 倜 **T'i⁴ (tì)** - Cautios, polite.

仓 133. 倉 **Ts'ang¹ (cang)** - Storehouse, warehouse.

134. 借 Chieh⁴ (jiè) - Lend, borrow.

倜 135. 俶 T'i⁴ (tì) - Same as 132.

136. 假⁹ Chia³ (jiâ) - False. Chia⁴ (jià) - Leave of absence, holiday.

137. 偕 Hsieh² (xíe) - Together with, jointly.

138. 健 Chien⁴ (jiàn) - Strong, healthy; stengthen, invigorate.

139. 偶 Ou³ (ôu) - Image; even (number), couple; unexpectedly.

逼 140. 偪 Pi¹ (bi) - Force, compel; press for (– payment), extort.

141. 偏 P'ien¹ (pian) - Slanting, leaning; partial, prejudiced.

142. 偷 T'ou¹ (tou) - Steal, pilfer; stealthily, secretly.

143. 停 T'ing² (tíng) - Stop, cease, discontinue.

144. 偈 Chieh² (jié) - Martial; diligent.

咱 145. 偺 Tsan² (zán) - I, we (incl. person or persons spoken to).

侧 146. 側 Ts'e⁴ (cè) - Side (right –); incline, turn toward.

147. 做 Tso⁴ (zuò) - Make, do, act; be, become (– a teacher).

侦 148. 偵 Chen¹ (zhen) - Detect, spy; investigate.

伟 149. 偉 Wei³ (wêi) - Great, mighty (wêidà).

150. 偃 Yen³ (yân) - Fall or lie on one's back; desist, cease.

151. 傅¹⁰ Fu⁴ (fù) - Teach(er); apply (– paint).

伧 152. 傖 **Ch'ang¹ (cang)** - Rude, rough.

效 153. 傚 **Hsiao⁴ (xiào)** - Imitate, follow example of; efect(ive).

154. 傢 **Chia¹ (jia)** - Tool or utensil (**jiahuo**); furniture (**jiaju**).

杰 155. 傑 **Chieh² (jíe)** - Hero, outstanding person; prominent.

156. 傀 **K'uei³ (kûi)** - Gigantic; puppet (**kuîlêi**) (– government).

157. 傍 **Pang⁴ (bàng)** - Near, close to.

备 158. 備 **Pei⁴ (bèi)** - Prepare, get ready; equipped with.

伞 159. 傘 **San³ (sân)** - Umbrella.

债 160. 債 ¹¹ **Chai⁴ (zhài)** - Debt.

传 161. 傳 **Ch'uan² (chuán)** - Pass on. **Chuan⁴(zhuàn)** - Biography; commentaries.

162. 傻 **Sha³ (shâ)** - Stupid; thoughtless; stunned.

仅 163. 僅 **Chin³ (jîn)** - Only; merely. **Chin⁴ (jìn)** - Almost; nearly.

倾 164. 傾 **Ch'ing¹ (qing)** - Incline, lean; collapse; pour (– tea).

偻 165. 僂 **Lü³ (lû)** - Hunchback(ed).

166. 傲 **Ao⁴ (ào)** - Proud, haughty; defy, brave (– the storm).

伤 167. 傷 **Shang¹ (shang)** - Wound, injury; hurt, injure.

仙 168. 僊 **Hsien¹ (xian)** - Celestial being (fairy, genie); immortal.

169. 催 **Ts'ui¹ (cui)** - Urge, press; hasten.

伛 170. 傴 **Yü³ (yǔ)** - Hunchbacked, with one's back bent (**yǔlǔ**).

佣 171. 傭 **Yung¹ (yong)** - Hire (– a laborer); servant.

侨 172. 僑 [12] **Ch'iao² (qiáo)** - Person living abroad (Chinese –).

173. 僭 **Chien⁴ (jiàn)** - Usurp, overstep one's authority or duty.

雇 174. 僱 **Ku⁴ (gù)** - Hire, rent (– a car); employ (– a worker).

175. 僚 **Liao² (liáo)** - Official; colleague.

仆 176. 僕 **P'u² (pú)** - Servant. *P'u¹ (pu)** - Fall forward.

177. 僧 **Seng¹ (seng)** - Buddhist monk, monk.

象 178. 像 **Hsiang⁴ (xiàng)** - Resemble; image, portrait.

179. 廝 **Szu¹ (si)** - Male servant; fellow (nice –); together (play –).

伪 180. 僞 **Wei³ (wěi)** - False; fake; counterfeit; puppet (– regime).

侥 181. 僥 **Chiao³ (jiǎo)** - By a stroke of luck (**jiǎoxìng**); lucky.

仪 182. 儀 [13] **Yi² (yí)** - Bearing; ceremony; gift; apparatus.

价 183. 價 **Chia⁴ (jià)** - Price, value.

184. 僵 **Chiang¹ (jiang)** - Stiffened, numb; deadlocked.

侥 185. 儌 **Chiao³ (jiǎo)** - Same as 181.

俭 186. 儉 **Chien³ (jiǎn)** - Thrifty, frugal.

亿 187. 億 **Yi⁴ (yì)** - A hundred million (100, 000, 000).

188. 儆 Ching[3] (jǐng) - Warn, admonish.

侩 189. 儈 K'uai[4] (kuài) - Broker, agent, middleman.

190. 儊 Ch'u[4] (chù) - Rough, rugged.

侬 191. 儂 Nung[2] (nóng) - You.

192. 僻 P'i[4] (pì) - Secluded; rare (– word).

傻 193. 儍 Sha[3] (shâ) - Same as 162.

侪 194. 儕 Ch'ai[2] (chái) - Associates, people of the same class.

俦 195. 儔 Ch'ou[2] (chóu) - Companion.

196. 儒[14] Ju[2] (rú) - Confucianism, Confucianist; scholar.

尽 197. 儘 Chin[3] (jǐn) - As .... as possible. Chin[4] (jìn) - Exhausted; to the utmost.

偿 198. 償[15] Ch'ang[2] (cháng) - Repay; compensate for; fulfill.

199. 儡 Lei[3] (lêi) - Destroy, run; (kuîleî) puppet (– government).

优 200. 優 Yu[1] (you) - Excellent, outstanding.

201. 儭[16] Ch'en[4] (chèn) - Line (fleece –d coat), lining; contrast.

储 202. 儲[17] Ch'u[3] (chû) - Store up (– grain).

203. 儳 Ch'an[3,4] (chân, chàn) - Irregular, uneven; obstinate.

俪 204. 儷[19] Li[4] (lì) - A pair, couple, married couple.

攒 205. 儹 Tsan[3] (zân) - Accumulate, hoard up, save.
Ts'uan[2] (cuán) - Assemble. Same as HAND (1) 146, 260.

伊 206. 儼 Yen³ (yân) - Solemn; dignified; just like (yânrán).

倘 207. 儻 T'ang³ (tâng) - If, supposing, in case (– sth. is wrong).

MELON 瓜

Picture of the melon plant and its fruit 瓜 .

1. 瓜 Kua¹ (gua) - Melon, gourd; wintermelon (donggua).

2. 瓞 Tieh² (dié) - Young melon or gourd, just coming out.

3. 瓠 Hu⁴ (hù) - Calabash (bottle gourd).

4. 瓢 P'iao² (píáo) - Ladle made of gourd; wooden dipper.

5. 瓤 Jang² (ráng) - Pulp, pith, kernel.

MILLET 黍

Representing the plant 禾 , the seeds of which are put ∩ in water 巛 , to produce spirits: 黍

1. 黍 Shu³ (shû) - Glutinous (sticky) millet.

2. 黎 Li² (lí) - Multitude, many; dawn (líming).

粘 3. 黏 Nien² (nián) - Sticky (– rice). Chan¹ (zhan) - Glue; stick (v).

MINISTER 臣

Picture of a minister making a deep bow 臣 before the Emperor. (The character was turned upright for compactnes 臣 .)

1. 臣 Ch'en² (chén) - Minister, statesman, courtier.

卧 2. 臥 Wo⁴ (wò) - Lie down (– to sleep).

临 3. 臨 Lin² (lín) - Approach; about to (– leave); copy (– painting).

MOON 月

Picture of a crescent moon 〽.

1. 月 Yüeh[4] (yuè) - Moon; month.
2. 有 [2] Yu[3] (yôu) - Have, possess; exist, there is.
3. 服 [4] Fu[2] (fú) - Clothes, dress; serve; obey; accustomed to.
4. 朋 P'eng[2] (péng) - Friend, companion.
5. 朕 [6] Chen[4] (zhèn) - I, we; sign, omen.
6. 朔 Shuo[4] (shuò) - First day of a lunar month; north (– wind).
7. 朗 [7] Lang[3] (lâng) - Bright; clear and distinct (read –ly).
望 8. 望 Wang[4] (wàng) - Look afar; visit; hope; reputation.
9. 朝 [8] Ch'ao[2] (cháo) - Court (imperial); dynasty; facing (– West).
10. 期 Ch'i[1] (qi) - Period (of time); expect; by appointment.
11. 朢 [10] Wang[4] (wàng) - Same as 8.
12. 朦 [14] Meng[2] (méng) - Dim, hazy, dim moonlight (**ménglóng**).
胧 13. 朧 [16] Lung[2] (lóng) - See 12 (in **ménglóng**)

MORTAR 臼

Representing a mortar ∪ *with crushed material* ⁖ *in it:* 臼 .

1. 臼 Chiu[4] (jiù) - Mortar, mortar-shaped object; joint (of bones).

2. 臾 [2] Yü² (yú) - Moment, instant (xuyú).

3. 舁 [3] Yü² (yú) - Lift, carry (on a pole).

4. 舀 [4] Yao³ (yâo) - Ladle out (– soup); bale out water; ladle.

5. 舂 [5] Ch'ung¹ (chong) - Pound (v) in a mortar; pestle.

6. 舅 [7] Chiu⁴ (jiù) - Uncle (mother's brother).

与 7. 與 [7] Yü³ (yû) - Give; help; and. Yü⁴ (yù) - Take part in.

兴 8. 興 [9] Hsing¹ (xing) - Prosper; start. Hsing⁴ (xìng) - Interest (with –).

举 9. 舉 [11] Chü³ (jû) - Raise; start; elect; whole, all (– those present).

旧 10. 舊 [12] Chiu⁴ (jiù) - Old, worn; secondhand; former (– capital).

MOUND 阜 . 阝

Representing a terraced embankment ⌒ with steps ☰ leading to a forest (ooo trees):

1. 阜 Fu⁴ (fù) - Mound; abundant.

2. 阡 [3] Ch'ien¹ (qian) - Footpath between fields.

3. 防 [4] Fang² (fáng) - Guard against, defend; dyke.

厄 4. 阨 [4] E⁴ (è) - Strategic point; narrow road; obstruction; distress.

5. 阱 Ching³ (jîng) - Trap, pitfall, pit.

6. 阻 [5] Tsu³ (zû) - Hinder, obstruct, stop.

7. 附 Fu⁴ (fù) - Attach; be near, get close to; agree with.

8. 阿 **A[1] (a)** - Prefix, as in: **Afūhàn (Afghanistan), A Bao (name)**.

9. 陂 **P'o[1] (po)** - Uneven. **Pei[1] (bei)** - Embankment; swamp.

10. 陀 **T'o[2] (tuó)** - Top (toy) **(tuóluó)**.

11. 限 [6] **Hsien[1] (xiàn)** - Limit, boundary; limit, restrict.

12. 降 **Chiang[4] (jiàng)** - Drop, fall. **Hsiang[2] (xiáng)** - Surrender.

13. 陋 **Lou[4] (lòu)** - Humble, mean; ugly; vulgar.

14. 陌 **Mo[4] (mò)** - Path between fields; road.

阵 15. 陣 [7] **Chen[4] (zhèn)** - Line of troops; period of time.

16. 陟 **Chih[4] (zhì)** - Ascend, promote.

17. 陛 **Pi[4] (bì)** - Steps to the throne.

18. 除 **Ch'u[2] (chú)** - Get rid of; divide; besides (– tea, also rice).

升 19. 陞 **Sheng[1] (sheng)** - Rise, ascend; raise, promote; litre.

20. 陡 **Tou[3] (dôu)** - Steep; suddenly, abruptly.

21. 院 **Yüan[4] (yuàn)** - Courtyard; public office.

陈 22. 陳 [8] **Ch'en[2] (chén)** - Display; old, stale.

23. 陷 **Hsien[4] (xiàn)** - Pitfall, trap; capture; sink into.

24. 陵 **Ling[2] (líng)** - Mound; tomb, mausoleum.

陆 25. 陸 **Lu[4] (lù)** - Land. **Liu[4] (liù)** - Six (elaborate form).

26. 陪　P'ei[2] (péi) - Accompany.

27. 陶　T'ao[2] (táo) - Pottery, earthenware; cultivate; happy.

陰 28. 陰　Yin[1] (yin) - Feminine; negative; moon. (See 34.)

队 29. 隊[9]　Tui[4] (duì) - Line (row of people); team, group; squad.

阶 30. 階　Chieh[1] (jie) - Steps, stairs; rank (military –).

31. 隆　Lung[2] (lóng) - Grand; prosperous; intense; swell, bulge.

32. 隋　Sui[2] (suí) - Sui dynasty (581-618 AD).

堤 33. 隄　Ti[1] (di) - Dyke, embankment.

阳 34. 陽　Yang[2] (yáng) - Masculine; positive; sun. (See 28.)

35. 隍　Huang[2] (huáng) - Dry moat outside the city wall.

36. 隅　Yü[2] (yú) - Corner.

37. 隘[10]　Ai[4] (ài) - Narrow; pass (mountain –).

38. 隙　Hsi[4] (xì) - Crack, crevice; opportunity.

39. 隔　Ke[2] (gé) - Separate; at an interval of, every (– hour).

陨 40. 隕　Yün[3] (yûn) - Fall from the sky or from out of space.

41. 障[11]　Chang[4] (zhàng) - Hinder, obstruct; barrier.

际 42. 際　Chi[4] (jì) - Boundary; inter- (–national); on the occasion of.

邻 43. 鄰[12]　Lin[2] (lín) - Neighbour(ing), near, adjacent (– seat).

险 44. 險 [13] Hsien² (xiân) - Danger, risk; nearly (– fall into the river).

随 45. 隨 Sui² (suí) - Follow, comply with; let (sb. do as he likes).

隐 46. 隱 [14] Yin³ (yîn) - Hidden, concealed, latent, dormant.

47. 隮 Chi¹ (ji) - Ascend, mount.

MOUNTAIN 山

Picture of a mountain range ⌂ .

1. 山 Shan¹ (shan) - Mountain, hill.

2. 岔 [4] Ch'a⁴ (chà) - Branch off; fork (where roads meet).

3. 岑 Ts'en² (cén) - High pointed hill.

4. 岐 Ch'i² (qí) - Double-peaked hill; ambiquity.

冈 5. 岡 [5] Kang¹ (gang) - Ridge (of a hill).

6. 岸 An⁴ (àn) - Bank, shore, coast; lofty.

7. 岩 Yen² (yán) - Rock, cliff.

8. 岳 Yüeh⁴ (yuè) - High mountain; wife's parents.

9. 峰 [7] Feng¹ (feng) - Peak, summit; hump (camel's –).

10. 峻 Chün⁴ (jùn) - High (of mountains); severe (– penalty).

11. 峪 Yü² (yù) - Valley, ravine.

岛 12. 島 Tao³ (dâo) - Island.

13. 崇 [8] Ch'ung² (chóng) - High, lofty; worship.

14. 崎 Ch'i² (qí) - Uneven; rugged (qíqu) (– mountain path).

15. 崩 Peng⁴ (beng) - Collapse, burst.

16. 崖 Ya² (yá) - Precipice, cliff.

17. 嵌 [9] Ch'ien⁴ (qiàn) - Inlay (– w. mother-of-pearl).

18. 崽 Tsai³ (zâi) - Son; young animal, whelp.

19. 嵩 [10] Sung¹ (song) - High (of mountains), lofty.

20. 嶂 [11] Chang⁴ (zhàng) - Range of peaks.

岖 21. 嶇 Ch'ü¹ (qu) - Rugged (qîqu) (– mountain path).

岭 22. 嶺 [14] Ling³ (lîng) - Mountain range; mountain ridge.

岳 23. 嶽 Yüeh⁴ (yuè) - Same as 8.

24. 巍 [18] Wei¹ (wei) - Towering, lofty.

巅 25. 巔 [19] Tien¹ (dian) - Mountain peak, summit.

岩 26. 巖 [20] Yen² (yán) - Same as 7.

MOUTH 口

Picture of the mouth 𠮩 .

1. 口 **K'ou³ (kôu)** - Mouth; opening; entrance.

2. 召 ² **Chao⁴ (zhào)** - Call together, convene, summon.

3. 只 **Chih³ (zhî)** - Only, merely.

4. 叱 **Ch'ih⁴ (chì)** - Scold, rebuke; shout out, hoot at.

5. 叩 **K'ou⁴ (kòu)** - Knock (– at the door); kowtow.

6. 叫 **Chiao⁴ (jiào)** - Shout, cry; call, name (– baby).

7. 可 **K'e³ (kê)** - Approve; can, may; fit (it –s him perfectly).

8. 古 **Ku³ (gû)** - Ancient, age-old; paleo-(–botany).

9. 句 **Chü⁴ (jù)** - Sentence, phrase.

10. 另 **Ling⁴ (líng)** - (An)other, extra; separate (– bank account).

11. 叭 **Pa¹ (ba)** - Sound imitation (*boom!* , etc.).

12. 叵 **P'o³ (pô)** - Impossible; cannot, unable.

13. 史 **Shih³ (shî)** - History.

14. 司 **Szu¹ (si)** - Manage; department (– of foreign affairs).

15. 台 **T'ai¹ (tái)** - Platform, stage, terrace; eminent; Taiwan.

16. 叨 **T'ao¹ (tao)** - Enjoy favors.

17. 叼 **Tiao¹ (diao)** - Hold in the mouth.

18. 叮　Ting[1] (ding) - Sting (mosquito –); reiterate (to make sure)

19. 右　Yu[4] (yòu) - Right, right side.

20. 后　Hou[4] (hòu) - Empress (huánghòu). * Behind; after.
　　　* As the simplified form of 後

21. 向　Hsiang[4] (xiàng) - Direction (wind –); face (–ing West).

22. 合　Ho[2] (hé) - Close, shut; combine, join (– efforts).

23. 吁　Hsü[1] (xu) - Sigh. Yü[4] (yù) - Appeal, plead.

24. 吉　Chi[2] (jí) - Lucky, auspicious.

25. 吃　Ch'ih[1] (chi) - Eat; wipe out; incur (– loss).

26. 各　Ko[4] (gè) - Each, every.

27. 吏　Li[4] (lì) - Government official (in ancient China), mandarin.

28. 名　Ming[2] (míng) - Name; reputation; famous, well-known.

29. 吊　Tiao[4] (diào) - Hang, suspend; condole; revoke (– license).

30. 吐　T'u[3] (tû) - Spit out, disclose. T'u[4] (tù) - Vomit.

31. 吆　Yao[1] (yao) - Cry out, call out (one's merchandise).

32. 同　T'ung[2] (tóng) - Same, similar; together; and, as well as.

33. 吵　Ch'ao[3] (châo) - Quarrel, make noise.

34. 吱　Chih[1] (zhi) - Squeak (of mice), chirp (of birds), etc.

35. 呈　Cheng[2] (chéng) - Assume (– color); submit; offer, present.

36. 吹　Ch'ui¹ (chui) - Blow; boast; break off (– engagement).

37. 吩　Fen¹ (fen) - Order, command, instruct (fenfu).

38. 吠　Fei⁴ (fèi) - Bark (of a dog).

39. 否　Fou³ (fŏu) - No, not; deny (fŏurèn).

40. 含　Han² (hán) - Hold in the mouth; contain; nurse (– hatred).

41. 吼　Hou³ (hŏu) - Roar, howl.

42. 吸　Hsi¹ (xi) - Inhale; absorb; attract (magnet –s iron).

43. 告　Kao⁴ (gào) - Tell, inform, announce; sue, indict.

44. 叫　Chiao⁴ (jiào) - Cry out, shout; call, name (– a baby).

45. 君　Chün¹ (jun) - Ruler, monarch; honorable.

46. 吝　Lin⁴ (lìn) - Miserly, stingy.

47. 呂　Lü³ (lû) - Musical pipe; vertebrae, backbone.

48. 呐　Na⁴ (nà) - Shout loudly (nàhân).

49. 吧　Pa¹ (ba) - Final particle (w. no meaning).

50. 吞　T'un¹ (tun) - Swallow, gulp down; annex (– country).

51. 吮　Shun³ (shûn) - Suck.

52. 吻　Wen³ (wên) - Lips; kiss.

53. 吾　Wu² (wú) - I, my; we, our (– country).

吴 54. 吳 **Wu²** (wú) - One of the Three Kingdoms (229-280 AD).

55. 呀 **Ya¹** (ya) - *Ah! Oh!*

56. 吟 **Yin²** (yín) - Recite, hum, chant.

57. 听 **T'ing¹** (ting) - Hear, listen; obey; allow, let.

58. 周⁵ **Chou¹** (zhou) - Circumference; week; cycle (kilo–).

59. 咋 **Cha⁴** (zhà) - Bite. **Cha³** (zâ) - How? Why?

60. 咒 **Chou⁴** (zhòu) - Incantation; curse.

61. 咐 **Fu** (fu) - Order, command; tell, instruct (**fenfu**).

啊 62. 呵 **Ho¹** (he) - Breathe out; scold; *Ah! Oh!* .

63. 呼 **Hu¹** (hu) - Exhale; shout, cry; whistle (the wind is –ing).

64. 和 **Ho²** (hé) - Peace(ful), harmony(-ious); mild, gentle.

65. 咕 **Ku¹** (gu) - Sounds made by pigeon, chicken, etc.

66. 咎 **Chiu⁴** (jiù) - Fault, blame.

67. 命 **Ming⁴** (mìng) - Life; fate; command; assign (name, etc.).

68. 呢 **Ne**(ne) - Final particle. **Ni²** (ní) - Woolen fabric.

69. 咆 **P'ao²** (páo) - Roar.

70. 呸 **P'ei¹** (pei) - *Pah! Bah! Pooh!*

71. 呻 **Shen¹** (shen) - Groan, moan (**shenyin**).

71A. 咖 **Ka¹** (ga) - In "galî" (curry). 71B. 喱 **Li²** (lí) - In "galî" (curry).

M 23

72. 咂 **Tsa¹ (za)** - Suck, sip (– of wine); taste carefully.

73. 呱 **Ku¹ (gu)** - Cry of infant. **Kua¹ (gua)** - Clip-clop (**guada**).

74. 味 **Wei⁴ (wèi)** - Taste, flavor, smell; interest, enjoyment.

75. 咏 **Yung³ (yông)** - Chant, intone.

76. 哎⁶ **Ai¹ (ai)** - Expression of discontent (*Aiya!*).

77. 咫 **Chih³ (zhî)** - Ancient measure of length (ca. 8 Chin. in.).

78. 响 **Hsiang³ (xiâng)** - Sound; loud; sound (v).

79. 咸 **Hsien² (xián)** - Salty, salted.

80. 哈 **Ha¹ (ha)** - Exhale, breathe out.

81. 哄 **Hung³ (hông)** - Deceive. **Hung⁴ (hòng)** - Uproar; noisy.

82. 咳 **K'o² (ké)** - Cough.

83. 咧 **Lieh³ (liê)** - Grin (– w. pain).

84. 咯 **Kê¹ (ge)** - Sound by hens. **K'a³ (kâ)** - Cough up (– bone).

85. 咩 **Mieh¹ (mie)** - Bleating of sheep (sound imitation).

86. 哀 **Ai¹ (ai)** - Sorrow, grief; pity.

87. 品 **P'in³ (pîn)** - Article, goods; grade; character (of person).

88. 哂 **Shen³ (shên)** - Smile.

笑 89. 咲 **Hsiao⁴ (xiào)** - Laugh, smile; ridicule.

陶 90. 咷 T'ao² (táo) - Cry loudly, wail (háotáo).

91. 咱 Tsan² (zán) - I, me;, we (speaker and addressed).

92. 哉 Tsai¹ (zai) - *Alas! Why!* (interjection, exclamation).

93. 咨 Tzu¹ (zi) - Consult, take counsel.

94. 哇 Wa¹ (wa) - *Wah!* (outburst of crying).

95. 咬 Yao³ (yâo) - Bite, gnaw; bark (of a dog).

96. 咽 Yen¹ (yan) - Pharynx, throat. Yan⁴ (yàn) - Swallow.

97. 哲 Che² (zhé) - Wise; sage (wise man); philosophy (zhélî).

98. 哮 Hsiao¹ (xiao) - Heavy breathing; roar, howl (of wind).

99. 哼 Heng¹ (heng) - Groan; hum (– a tune).

100. 哥 Ke¹ (ge) - Elder brother.

101. 哽 Keng³ (gêng) - Choke (w. grief, emotion).

102. 哭 K'u¹ (ku) - Cry, weep.

103. 哩 Li (li) - Adverb, final particle.

呹 104. 唚 Ch'in⁴ (qìn) - Belch out, vomit.

105. 哪 Na³ (nâ) - Which. Na (na) - Final particle.

106. 唉 Ai¹ (ai) - *Yes!* Ai⁴ (ài) - *Ai!* (exclamation of regret, etc.)

107. 哦 O² (é) - Chant (– a poem), hum (– a tune).

108. 哺 **Pu³ (bû)** - Feed (a baby).

109. 唇 **Ch'un² (chún)** - Lips.

110. 哨 **Shao⁴ (shào)** - Sentry, outpost; chirp, whistle.

111. 唆 **So¹ (suo)** - Instigate.

112. 唐 **T'ang² (táng)** - T'ang dynasty (618-907 AD).

员 113. 員 **Yüan² (yuán)** - Member (Party –); professional.

114. 唱 **Ch'ang⁴ (chàng)** - Sing, call loudly.

115. 啤 **P'i² (pí)** - Beer (píjiû).

116. 啄 **Cho² (zhuó)** - Peck (at) (of birds: – rice grains).

117. 啜 **Cho⁴ (chuò)** - Suck, sip, drink noisily; sob, wail.

118. 唬 **Hu³ (hû)** - Bluff; scare, frighten.

119. 啃 **K'en³ (kên)** - Gnaw, nibble, bite, chew.

启 120. 啓 **Ch'i³ (qî)** - Open, start; inform; note (– of thanks).

121. 唳 **Li⁴ (lì)** - Cry of wild geese or crane.

122. 唵 **An¹ (an)** - Gobble up.

123. 啊 **A¹ (a)** - *Ah!* (exclamation of surprise, admiration).

124. 商 **Shang¹ (shang)** - Shang dynasty (10-11th BC); trade.

125. 售 **Shou⁴ (shòu)** - Sell; carry out (– plan).

126. 啡 **Fei¹ (fei)** - For sound transliteration, e.g., **(kafei)** - coffee.

127. 啐 **Ts'ui⁴ (cuì)** - Spit (out).

128. 唾 **T'o⁴ (tuò)** - Spit; saliva.

哑 129. 啞 **Ya³ (yâ)** - Mute, dumb; hoarse.

问 130. 問 **Wen⁴ (wèn)** - Ask, inquire, interrogate.

131. 唯 **Wei² (wéi)** - Alone; only.

132. 喳⁹ **Cha¹ (zha)** - Chirp (of birds).

133. 唧 **Chi¹ (ji)** - Chirp (of crickets) **(jiji)**; spurt, squirt (- of water).

134. 喘 **Ch'uan³ (chuân)** - Pant, breathe heavily; asthma.

135. 喊 **Han³ (hân)** - Cry out, shout; call (– a person).

136. 喜 **Hsi³ (xî)** - Happy, joyful; be fond of, like.

衔 137. 啣 **Hsien² (xián)** - Hold in the mouth; harbor (– resentment).

138. 喝 **Ho¹ (he)** - Drink. **Ho⁴ (hè)** - Shout, cry out.

139. 喧 **Hsüan¹ (xuan)** - Noisy.

唤 140. 喚 **Huan⁴ (huàn)** - Call (out), shout.

乔 141. 喬 **Ch'iao² (qiáo)** - Tall, high, lofty; disguise.

吃 142. 喫 **Ch'ih¹ (chi)** - Eat, drink (– tea); swallow; suffer, bear.

143. 喉 **Hou² (hóu)** - Larynx, throat, gullet.

丧 144. 喵 **Miao¹ (miao)** - *Miaow !* (of cat).

145. 喇 **La¹ (la)** - Chatter, talk fast.

丧 146. 喪 **Sang¹ (sang)** - Funeral; mourning. **Sang⁴ (sàng)** - Lose.

147. 善 **Shan⁴ (shàn)** - Kind, friendly, good, virtuous.

148. 喃 **Nan² (nán)** - Chatter; murmur (**nannán**).

149. 啻 **Chih⁴ (zhì)** - Stop at; different from; only.

单 150. 單 **Tan¹ (dan)** - Single, odd (number); list (food - <menu>).

151. 啼 **T'i² (tí)** - Cry, weep aloud; animal's cry (e.g., cock's crow).

152. 喂 **Wei⁴ (wèi)** - *Hello!* (in phone conv.); feed (- chickens).

153. 喒 **Tsan² (zán)** - Same as 91.

154. 喻 **Yü² (yù)** - Explain; understand; analogy.

嗔 155. 嗔¹⁰ **Ch'en¹ (chen)** - Be angry at.

156. 嗤 **Ch'ih¹ (chi)** - Sneer, jeer, laugh at (**chixiào**).

157. 嗐 **Hai⁴ (hài)** - *Haiya!* (expression of disappointment).

158. 嗅 **Hsiu⁴ (xiù)** - Smell, sniff, scent (about).

吗 159. 嗎 **Ma⁰,³ (ma, mâ)** - Used as question mark (?).

160. 嗓 **Sang³ (sâng)** - Larynx, throat; voice.

161. 喿 **Tsao⁴ (zào)** - Chirp (of birds); clamor (confused noise).

嗇 162. 嗇 Se⁴ (sè) - Miserly, stingy.

163. 嗜 Shih⁴ (shì) - Have a liking for; be addicted to (– liquor).

164. 嗣 Szu⁴ (sì) - Succeed, inherit; posterity, descendant.

啼 165. 嗁 T'i² (tí) - Same as 151.

166. 嗉 Su⁴ (sù) - Crop of a bird (sùzi).

呛 167. 嗆 Ch'iang⁴ (qiàng) - Irritate. Ch'iang¹ (qiang) - Choke.

168. 嗟 Chieh¹ (jie) - Sigh, lament.

169. 嗡 Weng¹ (weng) - Hum (of bees), drone, buzz.

尝 170. 嘗¹¹ Ch'ang² (cháng) - Taste (food); ever.

171. 嘛 Ma (ma) - What, etc. (colloquial).

172. 嘉 Chia¹ (jia) - Praise; good, excellent.

173. 嘁 Ch'i¹ (qi) - Chatter away; jabber (qiqichacha).

呕 174. 嘔 Ou³ (ôu) - Vomit.

哔 175. 嗶 Pi⁴ (bì) - Serge (hard-wearing woollen cloth) (biji).

176. 嗽 Sou⁴ (sòu) - Cough.

叹 177. 嘆 T'an⁴ (tàn) - Sigh; praise.

178. 嘈 Ts'ao² (cáo) - Noise, noisy.

啧 179. 嘖 Tse² (zé) - Dispute, quarrel.

180. 嘲[12] **Ch'ao² (cháo)** - Ridicule, deride.

181. 嘱 **Chu³ (zhû)** - Enjoin; advise; urge; order (– rest).

182. 嘎 **Ka¹,² (ga, gá)** - *Ka* (sound transliteration).

183. 嘬 **Tso¹ (zuo)** - Suck.

184. 嘟 **Tu¹ (du)** - Honk (the car is –ing).

哗 185. 嘩 **Hua² (húa)** - Noise, clamor(ous).
Hua¹ (hua) - Sound imitation (*clang!* , etc.)

186. 噏 **Hsi¹ (xi)** - Inhale, suck up, absorb.

唠 187. 嘮 **Lao² (láo)** - **(láodao)** Chatter; garrulous.

188. 嘿 **Hei¹ (hei)** - *Hey!* (interjection).

叽 189. 嘰 **Chi¹ (ji)** - Chirp (of birds); whisper **(jigu)**.

190. 嘴 **Tsui³ (zûi)** - Mouth.

191. 噓 **Hsū¹ (xu)** - Breathe softly, utter a sigh; scald, burn.

幽 192. 嘯 **Szu¹ (si)** - Whistle.

193. 噎 **Yeh¹ (ye)** - Choke.

194. 噫[13] **Yi¹ (yi)** - Alas!

195. 噙 **Ch'in² (qín)** - Hold in the mouth (– pipe); hold tears in.

196. 器 **Ch'i⁴ (qì)** - Utensil, tool.

197. 噤 **Chin⁴ (jìn)** - Keep silent; shiver (– w. cold).

吨 198. 噸 **Tun¹ (dun)** - Ton, tonnage (**dunwèi**).

嗳 199. 嗳 **Ai⁴ (ai)** - *Oh!* (expression of regret).

恶 200. 噩 **O⁴ (è)** - Wicked, evil; fierce (– battle).

哝 201. 噥 **Nung² (nóng)** - Murmur (**nóngnong**).

喷 202. 噴 **P'en¹ (pen)** - Spurt, spray. **P'en⁴ (pèn)** - In season.

203. 噪 **Tsao⁴ (zào)** - Chirping (of birds); clamor.

哕 204. 噦 **Yüeh³ (yuê)** - Vomit.

205. 嚎¹⁴ **Hao² (háo)** - Howl, wail.

咛 206. 嚀 **Ning² (níng)** - Urge or instruct repeatedly (**dingníng**).

吓 207. 嚇 **Ho⁴ (hè)** - Threaten. **Hsia⁴ (xià)** - Frighten, intimidate.

208. 嚏 **T'i⁴ (tì)** - Sneeze.

噜 209. 嚕¹⁵ **Lü¹ (lu)** - Rumble, roll (**gulu**).

向 210. 嚮¹⁶ **Hsiang⁴ (xiàng)** - Direction; turn towards, face (–ing East).

咙 211. 嚨 **Lung² (lóng)** - Throat (**hóulóng**).

咽 212. 嚥 **Yen¹ (yan)** - Throat; pharynx. **Yen⁴ (yàn)** - Swallow; gulp down.

213. 嚷¹⁷ **Jang³ (rǎng)** - Shout, yell.

严 214. 嚴 **Yen² (yán)** - Strict, stern; tight (shut –).

215. 嚼¹⁸ **Chiao² (jiáo)** - Chew, masticate.

嚚 216. 嚻 **Hsiao¹ (xiao)** - Clamor, make loud noise.

217. 囊¹⁹ **Nang² (náng)** - Bag, sac.

罗 218. 囉 **Luo² (luó)** - Net; collect; gross (12 dozens). **Luo¹ (luo)** -
(luosuo) - Long-winded; wordy.

嘱 219. 囑²¹ **Chu³ (zhû)** - Enjoin, urge, instruct.

啮 220. 齧 **Nieh⁴ (niè)** - Gnaw, bite.

221. 囔²² **Nang¹ (nang)** - Murmur.

MOVE ON 辵

Representing the long strides made by a person: 辵

巡 1. 巡³ **Hsün² (xún)** - Patrol (night –); round (of drinks).

2. 廷⁴ **T'ing² (tíng)** - Court (feudal or imperial).

3. 延⁵ **Yen² (yán)** - Prolong, delay, postpone; send for (– doctor).

4. 廸 **Ti² (dí)** - Guide, lead forward, initiate.

5. 廹 **P'o⁴ (pò)** - Compel, force; urgent, pressing; approach.

回 6. 廻⁶ **Hui² (huí)** - Return; answer; chapter.

7. 建 **Chien⁴ (jiàn)** - Build, construct; establish, found.

N

NET 网 . 罒 . ⺳ . 罓

Picture of a net .

1. 网 **Wang³ (wâng)** - Net; catch with a net.
2. 罕 3 **Han³ (hân)** - Rarely, seldom (– seen), rare (– animal).
3. 罔 **Wang³ (wâng)** - Deceive; no, not.

挂 4. 罣 6 **Kua⁴ (guà)** - Hang; concerned; register (– at hospital).

5. 罩 8 **Chao⁴ (zhaò)** - Cover, shade (lamp–).

置 6. 置 **Chih⁴ (zhì)** - Place, put; establish; buy (– furniture).

7. 罪 **Tsui⁴ (zuì)** - Crime; guilt, fault; hardship.

罚 8. 罰 [9] **Fa[2] (fá)** - Punish.

9. 署 **Shu[3] (shû)** - Public office; arrange; sign (– agreement).

骂 10. 罵 [10] **Ma[4] (mà)** - Abuse, scold, curse.

罢 11. 罷 **Pa[4] (bà)** - Stop, cease; dismiss; finish.

罗 12. 羅 [14] **Lo[2] (luó)** - Net; catch w. a net; sieve; gross (12 dozens).

羁 13. 羈 [19] **Chi[1] (ji)** - Bridle, control, detain.

NOSE (1) 自

Picture of a nose 自 .

1. 自 **Tzu[4] (zì)** - Self, oneself; of course; from, since.

2. 臬 **Nieh[2] niè)** - Target; standard, criterion.

3. 臭 **Ch'ou[4] (chòu)** - Stinking, smelly; disgusting.

NOSE (2) 鼻

The nose 自 on the human body (represented by 畀): 鼻

1. 鼻 **Pi[2] (bí)** - Nose.

2. 鼾 **Han[1] (han)** - Snore.

3. 齁 **Hou[1] (hou)** - Much too sweet or salty; awfully (– hot).

懹 4. 齉 **Nang[4] (nàng)** - Snuffle, sniff repeatedly.

NOT 无．旡

A man (represented by his two feet 儿) unable to stand up, because of an obstacle 工 : 无.

无 1. **无** Wu² **(wú)** - Nothing, none; without; not, no.

2. **旡** Wu² **(wú)** - Same as 1.

3. **既** Chi⁴ **(jì)** - Already; since (– you are here); as well as.

O

OFFEND 辛

To offend (a pestle 辛 producing a grinding action) one's superior 二: 辛.

1. 辛 **Hsin¹ (xin)** - Hot (of taste); hard, toilsome, bitter.

2. 辜 **Ku¹ (gu)** - Guilt; crime; let down, fail to live up to **(gufu)**.

3. 辟 **Pi⁴ (bì)** - Monarch, sovereign; keep away, avoid.

4. 辣 **La⁴ (là)** - Peppery, hot (of taste); vicious, ruthless, cruel.

5. 辨 **Pien⁴ (biàn)** - Discriminate, distinguish.

办 6. 辦 **Pan⁴ (bàn)** - Do, manage; set up (– factory); bring to justice.

辞 7. 辭 **Tz'u² (cí)** - Phraseology; take leave; decline.

8. 瓣 **Pan⁴ (pàn)** - Petal (of flower); segment or section (of fruit, seed), clove (of garlic); fragment, piece.

辩 9. 辯 **Pien⁴ (biàn)** - Argue, dispute, debate.

OLD 老 . 耂

Hair ⊎ and beard ∩ that have changed in color (a person ⟩ who has changed his position ⋃ – is upside down): 耂 .

1. 老   **Lao³ (lâo)** - Old, aged; very (– far).

2. 考   **K'ao³ (kâo)** - Give or take examination, test, investigate.

3. 者   **Che³ (zhê)** - Pronoun for person or thing; this (– time).

4. 耆   **Ch'i² (qí)** - Over sixty years of age; very old.

5. 耄   **Mao⁴ (mào)** - Advanced in years (60-90 years old).

ONE 一

One stroke, to represent the number 'one' : 一 .

1. 一   **Yi¹ (yi)** - One, single; same (– height); whole (– winter).

2. 丁   **Ting¹ (ding)** - Fourth; male adult; diced (– vegetables).

3. 七   **Ch'i¹ (qi)** - Seven.

4. 丈   **Chang⁴ (zhàng)** - Unit of length (3.33 m); measure (land).

5. 下   **Hsia⁴ (xià)** - Below, under; inferior; next (– bus).

6. 三   **San¹ (san)** - Three; many (– times).

7. 上   **Shang⁴ (shàng)** - Up, above; superior; previous; ascend.

8. 丐   **Kai⁴ (gài)** - Beg; beggar.

9. 不   **Pu⁴ (bù)** - Not, no.

10. 丑 Ch'ou³ (chôu) - Ugly, disgraceful, shameful.

11. 丘 Ch'iu¹ (qiu) - Mound; grave. [4]

12. 丕 P'i¹ (pi) - Great (– performance). **P'ei¹ (pei)** - Unequaled.

13. 丙 Ping³ (bîng) - Third (– grade).

14. 世 Shih⁴ (shì) - Generation; age, era; world (shìjiè).

15. 且 Ch'ieh³ (qiê) - For the time being; in addition; both...and....

16. 丞 Ch'eng² (chéng) - Aid; assist(ant). [5]

17. 丢 Tiu¹ (diu) - Throw (away); lose (– face).

两 18. 兩 Liang³ (liâng) - Two, both (– sides); few; tael (weight). [7]

19. 並 Ping⁴ (bìng) - Combine, merge; equally.

OPPOSITION 舛

Two objects placed back to back 㐄屮 .

1. 舜 Shun⁴ (shùn) - Emperor Sun (2,255 BC).

2. 舞 Wu³ (wû) - Dance; brandish (– a sword).

OX 牛 . 牜

Representing an ox (seen from behind): only the two hind legs and tail are seen 十 *; the head is shown with the horns* 丫 : 半 .

1. 牛 Niu² (niú) - Ox, cattle.

2. 牟 [2] **Mou² (móu)** - Usurp, encroach; seek (– profit).

3. 牝 **P'in⁴ (pìn)** - Female of some birds and animals.

4. 牢 [3] **Lao² (láo)** - Firm, stable, durable; pen (pig–); prison.

5. 牡 **Mu³ (mû)** - Male of animals; peony (**mûdan**).

6. 牧 [4] **Mu⁴ (mù)** - Tend (watch over) cattle (sheep).

7. 物 **Wu⁴ (wù)** - Thing, matter; content, substance.

8. 牲 [5] **Sheng¹ (sheng)** - Domestic animal; animal sacrifice.

9. 牯 **Ku³ (gû)** - Bull.

10. 特 [6] **T'e⁴ (tè)** - Special (– permit); unusual; secret agent, spy.

11. 牸 [7] **Tsu⁴ (zì)** - Domesticated cow.

牽 12. 牽 **Ch'ien¹ (qian)** - Pull, haul, lead (– ox to water); involve.

13. 犁 **Li² (lí)** - Plough.

14. 犀 **Hsi¹ (xi)** - Rhinoceros.

15. 犄 [8] **Chi¹ (ji)** - Corner (**jijiâo**) (– of table).

16. 犍 [9] **Chien² (jian)** - Bullock (**jianniú**).

17. 犒 [10] **K'ao⁴ (kào)** - Reward w. food and drink.

犊 18. 犢 [15] **Tu² (dú)** - Calf.

牺 19. 犧 [16] **Hsi¹ (xi)** - Sacrificial animal; sacrifice.

P

PECK 斗

Ten 十 ladles 卩, which was a peck (measuring unit): 卩十.

1. 斗 **Tou³ (dôu)** - Peck (dry measure).**Tou⁴ (dòu)** - Contest

2. 料 **Liao⁴ (liào)** - Expect; material (raw –); grain (as feed).

3. 斜 **Hsieh² (xié)** - Oblique, slanting, tilted.

4. 斛 **Hu² (hú)** - Dry measure (ca. 5 pecks).

5. 斟 **Chen¹ (zhen)** - Pour (tea or wine).

PERIOD 辰

A woman who bends over 厂 (cp. 人 person) to conceal her menses (a sitting woman with apron 匜): 辰 .

1. 辰 **Ch'en² (chén)** - Time, epoch, period.

2. 辱　**Ju³ (rǔ)** - Disgrace; bring disgrace.

农　3. 農　**Nung² (nóng)** - Agriculture; peasant, farmer.

PERSEVERE 夊

A person 丿 who steps forward slowly despite shackles ㇏ : 夊 .

1. 復　**Fu⁴ (fù)** - Duplicate; turn around, toss (–in bed); answer.

2. 夏　**Hsia⁴ (xià)** - Summer; Xia dynasty (21st-16th century BC).

PESTLE 干

Picture of a pestle 午 .

1. 干　**Kan¹ (gan)** - Pestle; interfere; oppose; have to do with.

2. 平　**P'ing⁴ (píng)** - Level, even; smooth; peaceful; common.

3. 年　**Nien² (nián)** - Year, annual; age.

4. 开　**Ch'ien¹ (qian)** - Even, level.

并　5. 幷　**Ping⁴ (bìng)** - Combine, merge; equal(ly); and, moreover.

6. 幸　**Hsing⁴ (xìng)** - Good fortune, luck; fortunately; hope (v).

干　7. 幹　**Kan⁴ (gàn)** - Trunk (– line); do (– business); capable.

PIG 豕

Picture of a pig 豕.

1. 豕 Shih³ (shǐ) - Pig, hog, swine.

2. 豚 T'un² (tún) - Suckling pig, pig.

3. 象 Hsiang⁴ (xiàng) - Elephant; appearance, image; resemble.

4. 豦 Chü⁴ (jù) - Wild boar.

5. 豪 Hao² (háo) - Eminent person; forthright; heroic.

猪 6. 豬 Chu¹ (zhu) - Pig, swine, hog.

7. 豫 Yü⁴ (yù) - Beforehand (arrange –), in advance (pay –).

PIG'S SNOUT 彑 . 彑 . 彐

Representing a pig's snout 彑.

录 1. 彔 Lu⁴ (lù) - Record, write down; annals; employ, hire.

2. 彗 Hui⁴ (huì) - Broom.

汇 3. 彙 Hui⁴ (huì) - Gather, classify; collection; remit (money).

PIT 凵

Representing a hole in the earth 凵 .

1. 凵 K'an³ (kân) - Pit, hole in the earth

2. 凶 Hsiung¹ (xiong) - Ominous; ferocious; crop failure.

3. 凸 T'ieh⁴ (tiè). T'u¹ (tu) - Convex; projection; swelling.

4. 凹   Ao[1] (ao) - Concave; hollow; indentation; depression.

5. 出   Ch'u[1] (chu) - Go out; produce (– coal); happen, take place.

6. 函 [6]   Han[2] (hán) - Case, envelope; letter, document.

PLOW 耒

Representing a plow – the wooden (木 tree) handle and a piece of wood with dents in it 耂 : 耒 .

1. 耒   Lei[3] (lêi) - Plow handle, plow.

2. 耗 [4]   Hao[4] (hào) - Cosume, cost; waste; bad news.

3. 耕   Keng[1] (geng) - Plow, till, cultivate.

4. 耙   Pa[4] (bà). P'a[2] (pá) - Rake, harrow.

5. 耘   Yün[2] (yún) - Weed.

6. 耦 [9]   Ou[3] (ôu) - Even (number); pair, couple; mate, spouse.

7. 耨 [10]   Nou[4] (nòu) - Weed, hoe.

PROCEED 辵 . 辶 . 辶

To proceed step by step (the foot 止 and 彳 three footsteps): 辵 .

1. 迄 [3]   Ch'i[4] (qì) - Up to, until; so far, up to the present.

2. 迅   Hsün[2] (xùn) - Fast, swift, quick.

3. 迂   Yü[1] (yu) - Circuitous, winding; conservative; pedantic.

4. 返 [4]   Fan[3] (fân) - Return.

5. 近 **Chin⁴ (jìn)** - Near, close; approach (–ing ninety); intimate.

6. 迕 **Wu⁴ (wù)** - Resist, oppose; disobey (– decree).

7. 迓 **Ya⁴ (yà)** - Welcome, meet.

8. 迎 **Ying² (yíng)** - Welcome; receive.

9. 迦 **Chia¹ (jia)** - Used in transliteration (for its pronunciation).

10. 逈 **Chiung³ (jiông)** - Far away; widely different.

11. 迫 **P'o⁴ (pò)** - Compel, force; urgent, pressing; approach.

12. 述 **Shu⁴ (shù)** - State, tell; narrate.

13. 迨 **Tai⁴ (dài)** - Wait until; before (– it rains).

14. 迭 **Tieh² (dié)** - Alternate, change; repeatedly.

15. 迪 **Ti² (dí)** - Lead forward, guide, direct.

16. 追 **Chui¹ (zhui)** - Chase (after), pursue; trace (back), recall.

回 17. 迴 **Hui² (huí)** - Return, go back; chapter (in book).

18. 迻 **Yi ²(yí)** - Move, change residence; remove; shift.

19. 逆 **Ni⁴ (nì)** - Oppose; contrary to; disobey.

20. 迷 **Mi² (mí)** - Be confused; infatuated, mad after (– money).

21. 迸 **Peng⁴ (bèng)** - Burst forth, break out (applause –).

22. 送 **Sung⁴ (sòng)** - Deliver; give; accompany, see sb. off.

这 25. 這 Che⁴ (zhè). Chei⁴ (zhèi) - This. (with superscript 7 above 這)

23. 逃 T'ao² (táo) - Run away, escape, flee.

24. 退 T'ui⁴ (tùi) - Retreat, withdraw, recede.

25. 這 Che⁴ (zhè). Chei⁴ (zhèi) - This.

26. 逞 Ch'eng³ (chěng) - Boast; indulge, give free rein to.

27. 逐 Chu² (zhú) - Chase, expel; one by one.

28. 逢 Feng² (féng) - Meet, come across.

29. 逛 Kuang⁴ (guàng) - Stroll, roam.

连 30. 連 Lien² (lián) - Link, join, connect; including (– you).

31. 逋 Pu¹ (bu) - Abscond, flee.

32. 逝 Shih⁴ (shì) - Pass (– the time); pass away, die.

33. 逍 Hsiao¹ (xiao) - Free and unrestrained (xiaoyáo), at ease.

34. 速 Su⁴ (sù) - Fast, speedy; invite (un–ed guests).

35. 逗 Tou⁴ (dòu) - Stay, loiter; provoke (– laughter); play with.

36. 透 T'ou⁴ (tòu) - Penetrate, pass through; thoroughly (– done).

37. 途 T'u² (tú) - Road, way, route.

38. 通 T'ung¹ (tong) - Go through; open (– road); common.

39. 造 Tsao⁴ (zào) - Make, manufacture; train; go to; crop.

周 40. 週 Chou¹ (zhou) - Circumference; go round; cycle; week. (with superscript 8 above 週)

41. 逮 **Tai⁴ (dài)** - Reach, until (– now). **Tai³ (dâi)** - Catch, seize.

进 42. 進 **Chin⁴ (jìn)** - Advance, proceed; enter; receive (– income).

43. 逸 **Yi⁴ (yì)** - Ease, leisure; escape; be lost; excel (– others).

9

44. 遐 **Hsia² (xiá)** - Distant, far; long, lasting; advanced in age.

45. 遑 **Huang² (huáng)** - Leisure; pressed, urged.

过 46. 過 **Kuo¹ (guo)** - Excessive. **Kuo⁴ (guò)** - Cross; pass through.

47. 遏 **O⁴ (è)** - Check, hold back, stop.

48. 遍 **Pien⁴ (biàn)** - All over (– the world); time (two –s).

49. 逼 **Pi¹ (bi)** - Force, compel; press for, extort.

50. 遂 **Sui⁴ (suì)** - Succeed (be succesful); thereupon, then.

逿 51. 遢 **Tang⁴ (dàng)** - Fall (v); miss.

达 52. 達 **Ta² (dá)** - Extend; reach; distinguished.

53. 道 **Tao⁴ (dào)** - Road, path, way; method, principle.

54. 遁 **Tun⁴ (dùn)** - Escape, flee; evasive (– answer).

违 55. 違 **Wei² (wéi)** - Disobey, violate (– rules); be separated.

56. 逾 **Yü² (yú)** - Exceed, go beyond.

57. 遇 **Yü⁴ (yù)** - Meet; treat (– sb. nicely); opportunity.

运 58. 運 **Yün⁴ (yùn)** - Transport, carry; luck (good –).

10

59. 遣 Ch'ien³ (qiân) - Dispatch, send; dispel (– fear).

60. 遛 Liu⁴ (liù) - Saunter, stroll; fill (– gap).

逊 61. 遜 Hsün⁴ (xùn) - Abdicate, give up (power); modest, inferior.

递 62. 遞 Ti⁴ (dì) - Hand over, pass; successively (increase –).

遥 63. 遙 Yao² (yáo) - Distant, remote, far; long (– journey).

远 64. 遠 Yüan³ (yuân) - Remote, far, distant (– relative).

11

65. 遮 Che¹ (zhe) - Cover, protect; block (off), keep out (– rain).

迟 66. 遲 Ch'ih² (chí) - Slow (in action or thinking); late.

适 67. 適 Shih¹ (shì) - Suitable; just (– right); comfortable.

遁 68. 遯 Tun⁴ (dùn) - Escape, flee; hide away.

69. 遭 Tsao¹ (zao) - Meet with; suffer (– setbacks); time (two –s).

12

遗 70. 遺 Yi² (yí) - Lose; something lost; leave behind.

绕 71. 遶 Jao⁴ (rào) - Wind (v), circle (v); revolve; make detour.

辽 72. 遼 Liao² (liáo) - Far; faraway; distant.

73. 遴 Lin² (lín) - Choose, select sb. for a post (línxuân).

选 74. 選 Hsüan³ (xuân) - Select, choose.

迁 75. 遷 Ch'ien¹ (qian) - Move, shift, change.

76. 遵 Tsun¹ (zun) - Abide by, obey, follow; observe.

还 77. 還 **Huan² (huán)** - Return; repay. **Hai² (hái)** - Still (more). ¹³

78. 遽 **Chü⁴ (jù)** - Hastily (decide –); frightened.

迈 79. 邁 **Mai⁴ (mài)** - Walk w. great strides; step; stride; surpass; excel; old; aged.

80. 避 **Pi⁴ (bì)** - Avoid, shun (– evil), evade (– issue).

81. 邀 **Yao¹ (yao)** - Invite; seek (– approval).

迩 82. 邇 **Erh³ (êr)** - Near (far and –). ¹⁴

边 83. 邊 **Pien¹ (bian)** - Side (this –); edge (– of table), border, limit. ¹⁵

逻 84. 邏 **Lo² (luó)** - Patrol (make a round). ¹⁹

PURSUE 夂

A man 𠂉 who walks despite an obstacle 乀 : 夂.

1. 夆 **Feng¹ (feng)** - Butt (v), oppose.

R

RAIN 雨 . 雲

Drops of water ⸗ falling down \ from clouds ⋀ suspended from the sky ⁻ : 雨 .

1. 雨   **Yü³ (yû)** - Rain.

2. 雪   **Hsüeh³ (xuê)** - Snow.

云   3. 雲   **Yün² (yún)** - Cloud.

4. 雷   **Lei² (léi)** - Thunder; mine (– sweeper).

5. 零   **Ling² (líng)** - Zero; odd (– job); fractional, part (spare –).

6. 雹   **Pao² (báo)** - Hail.

电   7. 電   **Tien⁴ (diàn)** - Electricity; cable, telegram (**diànbào**).

8. 需   **Hsü¹ (xu)** - Need, want, requirement.

9. 震 **Chen⁴ (zhèn)** - Shake, quake; shock(ed).

10. 霉 **Mei² (méi)** - Mildew, mould.

11. 霈 **Pei⁴ (pèi)** - Soaking rain.

12. 霄 **Hsiao¹ (xiao)** - Clouds, sky, heaven (– and earth).

13. 霆 **T'ing² (tíng)** -Thunderbolt.

沾 14. 霑 **Chan¹ (zhan)** - Moisten. wet, soak; benefit by.

15. 霓 **Ni² (ní)** - Rainbow.

16. 霖 **Lin² (jîn)** - Continuous heavy rain.

17. 霎 **Sha⁴ (shà)** - Instant, moment.

18. 霞 **Hsia² (xía)** - Rosy clouds; morning glow; evening glow.

19. 霜 **Shuang¹ (shuang)** - Frost.

雾 20. 霧 **Wu⁴ (wù)** - Fog, mist, fine spray.

21. 霰 **Hsien⁴ (xiàn)** - Graupel (snow mixed w. hail).

22. 露 **Lu⁴ lù)** - Dew; show, expose; syrup (fruit –).

23. 霸 **Pa⁴ (bà)** - Feudal chief; tyrant, tyrannize.

24. 霹 **P'i¹ (pi)** - Thunderbolt (**piléi**).

霁 25. 霽 **Chi⁴ (jì)** - Clearing up of the sky.

霳 26. 靂 **Li⁴ (lì)** - Thunderbolt (**pilì**).

灵 27. 靈 Ling² (líng) - Clever; effective; soul, spirit (línghún).

RAT 鼠

Picture of a rat, showing its head with whiskers 🐀 *, legs and tail* 鼡 : 鼠.

1. 鼠 Shu³ (shû) - Rat, mouse.

2. 鼬 Yu⁴ (yòu) - Weasel.

3. 鼫 Shih⁴ (shì) - Long-tailed marmot.

RAWHIDE 革

A pair of hands 🖐 *stretching out a sheep's skin* 羊 : 革.

1. 革 Ke² (gé) - Leather, hide, reform; remove from office.

2. 靪 Ting¹ (ding) - Patch, piece of cloth.

3. 靴 Hsüeh¹ (xue) - Boots.

4. 靶 Pa³ (bâ) - Target.

5. 鞋 Hsieh² (xíe) - Shoes, slippers.

巩 6. 鞏 Kung³ (gông) - Consolidate, strengthen.

7. 鞍 An¹ (an) - Saddle.

8. 鞘 Ch'iao⁴ (qiào) - Scabbard, sheath (for sword).

9. 鞝 Chang³ (zhâng) - Leather sole.

10. 鞠 Chū¹ (ju) - Rear, bring up, nourish; bend (– the body).

11. 鞫 Chū¹ (ju) - Investigate judicially.

12. 鞭 Pien¹ (bian) - Whip, lash, flog.

缰 13. 韁 Chiang¹ (jiang) - Bridle, halter, reins.

鞑 14. 韃 Ta² (dá) - Tartar (Dádá).

REACH 至

A bird with wings backward 𝔾 coming down and reaching the earth
土 : 㞢.

1. 至 Chih⁴ (zhì) - Reach, arrive; until, to; most (– precious).

2. 致 Chih⁴ (zhì) - Extend, send; cause (– damage); fine, delicate.

台 3. 臺 T'ai² (tái) - Platform; stage; table; broadcasting station;
short for Taiwan.

4. 臻 Chen¹ (zhen) - Attain, reach (– one's goal)

RED 赤

Representing an angry man 大 – his face turning red (火 fire): 灻 .

1. 赤 Ch'ih⁴ (chì) - Red; naked, bare (–handed).

2. 赦 She⁴ (shè) - Pardon, forgive.

3. 赧 Nan³ (nân) - Blush.

4. 赫 Ho⁴ (hè) - Bright; glorious; hertz (kilo-).

5. 赭 Che³ (zhê) - Reddish brown; ochre (zhêshí).

REVELATION 示 . 礻

Emanations 川 from heaven 二, *revealing signs from heaven:* 示.

1. 示 **Shih⁴ (shì)** - Show, make known, instruct.

2. 社 **She⁴ (shè)** - Society, association.

3. 祀 **Szu⁴ (sì)** - Offer sacrifices to the gods.

4. 祉 **Chih³ (zhǐ)** - Blessedness, happiness.

只 5. 祇 **Ch'i² (qí)** - God of the Earth; great; repose, rest; merely; only.

6. 祈 **Ch'i² (qí)** - Pray (– for rain), implore, beg, request.

只 7. 祗 **Chih³ (zhǐ)** - Reverence, respect; merely, only. * **Chih¹ (zhi)** - Single; one only; (N).

8. 祝 **Chu⁴ (zhù)** - Wish, express good wishes.

9. 祜 **Hu⁴ (hù)** - Blessing, bliss.

10. 祕 **Mi⁴ (mì)** - Secret, keep sth. secret.

11. 神 **Shen² (shén)** - God, deity; spirit, mind; expression, look.

12. 祟 **Sui⁴ (suì)** - Evil spirit, ghost.

13. 祖 **Tsu³ (zǔ)** - Ancestors.

14. 祚 **Tso⁴ (zuò)** - Dignity, honor.

15. 祠 **Tz'u² (cí)** - Ancestral temple.

佑 16. 祐 **Yu⁴ (yòu)** - Protect, bless (may God – us).

17. 票 **P'iao⁴ (piào)** - Ticket; banknote, bill; psn. held for ransom.

18. 祥   Hsiang² (xiáng) - Auspicious (– omen); lucky, good luck.

19. 祧   T'iao¹ (tiao) - Ancestral shrine; become heir to.

20. 祭   Chi⁴ (jì) - Offer a sacrifice to; wield (– a magic wand).

21. 禁   Chin⁴ (jìn) - Prohibit, forbid; imprison; taboo.

禄 22. 祿   Lu⁴ (lù) - Official's salary; prosperity, happiness.

23. 裯   Tao³ (dâo) - Same as 32.

24. 稟   Ping³ (bîng) - Report to superior; petition; endowed with.

祯 25. 禎   Chen¹ (zhen) - Auspicious, propitious.

26. 福   Fu² (fú) - Good fortune, happiness, blessing.

祸 27. 禍   Huo⁴ (huò) - Misfortune, calamity, disaster.

御 28. 禦   Yü⁴ (yù) - Drive (carriage); imperial; keep out (– cold).

29. 禧   Hsi³ (xî) - Auspicious (– event); happy (– occasion).

禅 30. 禪   Ch'an² (chán). Deep meditation; Buddhist (adj). **Shan⁴ (shàn)** - Abdicate **(shànràng).**

礼 31. 禮   Li³ (lî) - Ceremony, rite; courtesy, etiquette; gift, present.

祷 32. 禱   Tao³ (dâo) - Pray, supplicate, beg.

33. 禳   Jang² (ráng) - Prayer or sacrifice offered for averting evil.

RICE 米

Four grains of rice, scattered ╳ due to thrashing ┼ : 米.

1. 米 **Mi³ (mǐ)** - Rice (uncooked); metre.

2. 籽 **Tzu³ (zǐ)** - Seed (cotton –).

3. 粉 **Fen³ (fěn)** - Powder, flour; white(wash); pink **(fěnhóng)**.

4. 粒 **Li⁴ (lì)** - Grain, granule, kernel, pellet.

5. 粘 **Chan¹ (zhan)** - Paste up. **Nien² (nián)** - Glutinous (– rice).

6. 粕 **P'o⁴ (pò)** - Dregs (undesirable part) of rice.

7. 粗 **Ts'u¹ (cu)** - Thick (– rope); rough, coarse; rude, vulgar.

8. 粥 **Chou¹ (zhou)** - Rice gruel, porridge, congée.

9. 粟 **Su⁴ (sù)** - Millet.

10. 粳 **Ching¹ (jing)** - Nonglutinous rice.

11. 粱 **Liang² (liáng)** - Fine strain of millet; choice food.

12. 粲 **Ts'an⁴ (càn)** - Bright, beautiful; smiling broadly **(cànrán)**.

13. 粹 **Ts'ui⁴ (cuì)** - Pure (– white), unadulterated, unmixed.

14. 精 **Ching¹ (jing)** - Refined; essence, spirit; smart; semen.

15. 粽 **Tsung⁴ (zòng)** - Glutinous rice dumpling wrapped in leaves.

16. 糊 **Hu¹ (hu)** - Plaster (– cracks). **Hu² (hú)** - Paste (v)(n).

17. 糕 **Kao¹ (gao)** - Cake, pastry and cakes **(gaodiân)**.

18. 糗 Ch'iu^3 (qiû) - Roughly crushed grain; dry food.

谷 19. 穀 Ku^3 (gû) - Grain, cereal.

20. 糖 T'ang^2 (táng) - Sugar; candy, sweets.

粪 21. 糞^{11} Fen^4 (fèn) - Dung, manure; apply manure.

22. 糠 K'ang^1 (kang) - Chaff, husk, bran.

23. 糙 Ts'ao^1 (zao) - Unpolished rice (caomî); coarse, rough.

縻 24. 糜 Mi^2 (mí). Mei^2 (méi) - Rice gruel, porridge; rotten.

25. 榑 T'uan^2 (tuán) - Same as 29.

26. 糟 Tsao^1 (zao) - Dreg; rotten, messed up; poor (– health).

粮 27. 糧^{12} Liang^2 (liáng) - Grain; food; provisions; grain tax.

28. 糯^{14} No^4 (nùo) - Glutinous, sticky (– rice).

团 29. 糰 T'uan^2 (tuán) - Rice dumpling. *Round; unite, group; (N).

RIVER 川 巛

A big stream formed by smaller streams 巛.

1. 川 Ch'uan^1 (chuan) - River, stream; plain (flat land).

2. 州 Chou^1 (zhou) - Administrative division; prefecture.

3. 巡 Hsün^2 (xún) - Patrol, make one's round; round (of drinks).

4. 巠 Ching^1 (jing) - Underground streams.

5. 巢 Ch'ao^2 (cháo) - Nest; liar, den (cháoxué).

ROD 丨

A vertical stroke representing a rod 丨.

1. 丫 **Ya¹ (ya)** - Bifurcation, fork.

2. 中 **Chung¹ (zhong)** - Center. **Chung⁴ (zhòng)** - Hit (- target).

3. 串 **Ch'uan⁴ (chuàn)** - String (together); bunch, cluster; (shish)kebab.

ROLL 疋 . 正

The foot 止 *in motion* ◡ : 疋.

1. 疋 **P'i³ (pi)** - Rolled up piece (- of cloth), bale.

2. 疏 **Shu¹ (shu). Su¹ (su)** - Distant (- relative); dredge **(shudâo).**

3. 疑 **Yi² (yí)** - Suspect, doubt(ful).

RUN 走

A man with his head bent downward 夭 *who runs (* 止 *foot) quickly:*
走.

1. 走 **Tsou³ (zôu)** - Walk, go, run; leave, depart.

2. 赴 **Fu⁴ (fù)** - Go to, attend (- meeting).

3. 起 **Ch'i³ (qì)** - Rise, get up; build; draft (- constitution); begin.

4. 趁 **Ch'en⁴ (chèn)** - Take advantage of; while (- you're here).

5. 超 **Ch'ao¹ (chao)** - Exceed, ultra-(-modern), super- (-power).

6. 趄 **Ch'ieh⁴ (qiè)** - Slanting, inclined.

7. 越 **Yüeh⁴ (yuè)** - Climb (jump) over; exceed (- the limit).

8. 趔 Lieh[4] (liè) - Stagger, reel, stumble (lièqie).

9. 趒 T'iao[4] (tiào) - Leap, jump; beat (his heart –s fast).

赵 10. 趙 Chao[4] (zhào) - Hasten to; visit.

赶 11. 趕 Kan[3] (gǎn) - Catch up with (gǎnshàng); rush through.

12. 趣 Ch'ü[4] (qù) - Interest(ing), amusing.

趋 13. 趨 Ch'ü[1] (qu) - Hasten, hurry; trend, tendency (qushì).

14. 趮 Tsao[4] (zào) - Quick-tempered, rash.

跃 15. 趯 Yüeh[4] (yuè) - Leap, jump.

趱 16. 趲 Tsan[3] (zǎn) - Urge, hasten, hurry (rush) through.

S

SALT 鹵

A vessel ⊗ containing grains of salt ∴ : ⊗.

鹵 1. 鹵   **Lu³ (lû)** - Rock salt; stew (in soy sauce); gravy for noodles, etc.

咸 2. 鹹   **Hsien² (xián)** - Salty, salted (– egg); all (– benefit from it).

盐 3. 鹽   **Yen² (yán)** - Salt, common (table) salt **(yánba)**.

碱 4. 鹼   **Chien³ (jiân)** - Alkali, soda (washing –).

SCHOLAR 士

One who has knowledge of all things (between the two units one –
and 十 : 士.

1. 士   **Shih⁴ (shì)** - Scholar.

2. 壬   **Jen² (rén)** - The 9th of the Ten Heavenly Stems.

壮 3. 壯 **Chuang⁴ (zhuàng)** - Strong, magnificent; strengthen.

壶 4. 壺 **Hu² (hú)** - Jug, pot (tea-), can (oil–), bottle, flask; kettle.

5. 壹 **Yi¹ (yī)** - Elaborate form of 'one' (used on checks, etc.).

寿 6. 壽 **Shou⁴ (shòu)** - Longevity; life (long –), age.

SEAL 卩.㔾

The right half of a broken seal 卩 given to a government official by the Emperor (who held the left half ㄥ).

1. 卯 **Mao³ (mâo)** - The period from 5 to 7 in the morning.

2. 印 **Yin⁴ (yìn)** - Seal, stamp; print (n)(v); tally with.

3. 危 **Wei¹ (wei)** - Danger(ous), endanger; dying; high, steep.

4. 却 **Ch'üeh⁴ (què)** - Step back, drive back; refuse; but, yet.

5. 卵 **Luan³ (luân)** - Ovum, egg, roe (of fish).

6. 卷 **Chüan³ (juân)** - Roll. **Chüan⁴ (juàn)** - Book, volume.

7. 巹 **Chin³ (jîn)** - Wedding cup.

8. 卸 **Hsieh⁴ (xiè)** - Unload; strip (– a machine); get rid of.

9. 卹 **Hsü⁴ (xù)** - Pity, sympathize with; give relief.

10. 谷卩 **Ch'üeh⁴ (què)** - Same as 4.

11. 即 **Chi² (jí)** - Reach (beyond –); at once; even, even if (**jíbiàn**).

12. 卿 **Ch'ing¹ (qing)** - Minister or high official in ancient times.

SEE 見

The eye 目 of a person (a being standing on two legs 儿): 見.

見 1. 見 **Chien⁴ (jiàn)** - See, *vide* (see); view, opinion; exposed to.

规 2. 規⁴ **Kuei¹ (guī)** - Compasses; regulation; advise; plan.

觅 3. 覓 **Mi⁴ (mì)** - Seek, look for, hunt for.

视 4. 視⁵ **Shih⁴ (shì)** - Look at, look upon; inspect.

腆 5. 覥 **T'ien³ (tiǎn)** - Blush; ashamed, brazen (– faced).

亲 6. 親⁹ **Ch'in¹ (qīn). Ch'ing⁴ (qìng)** - Relative; intimate; kiss.

觐 7. 覲¹¹ **Chin⁴ (jìn)** - Appear before the emperor; go on pilgrimage.

觑 8. 覷¹² **Ch'ü⁴ (qù)** - Look at, gaze, steal a glance.

觉 9. 覺¹³ **Chüeh² (júe)** - Perceive, feel, sense; awake, become aware.

览 10. 覽¹⁵ **Lan³ (lǎn)** - See, view; read.

觌 11. 覿 **Ti² (dí)** - Meet.

观 12. 觀¹⁸ **Kuan¹ (guān)** - Look at; view (n). **Kuan⁴ (guàn)** - Taoist temple

SEIZE 隶

A hand ⇉ that catches a running animal by its tail 木: 隶.

隶 1. 隸 **Li⁴ (lì)** - Subordinate, slave, servant.

SELF 己

Representing the threads of the weft: two transversal ⼆ and one longitudinal | ; at the bottom is the shuttle ⼃ : 㠯. (Etymology?)

1. 己　**Chi³ (jǐ)** - Self, oneself; I, myself; personal, private.

2. 已　**Yi³ (yǐ)** - Cease, stop; already; too (– much).

3. 巳　**Szu⁴ (sì)** - The sixth of the Twelve Earthly Branches.

4. 巴 [1]　**Pa¹ (ba)** - Hope; stick to; near; *ba* as in *Ba*námâ (Panama).

5. 巷 [6]　**Hsiang⁴ (xiàng)** - Lane, alley.

6. 巽 [9]　**Hsün⁴ (xùn)** - The fifth of the Eight Diagrams; mild.

SHEEP 羊 . 羊

Picture of a sheep seen from behind: the horns ⺷ , four feet and a tail 丰 : 羊 .

1. 羊　**Yang² (yáng)** - Sheep, goat.

2. 羌 [2]　**Ch'iang¹ (qiang)** - Ancient tribe in the west of China.

3. 美 [3]　**Mei³ (mêi)** - Beautiful, pretty; good.

4. 羔 [4]　**Kao¹ (gao)** - Lamb, kid, fawn.

羞 5. 羞 [5]　**Hsiu¹ (xiu)** - Shy, bashful; shame, feel ashamed.

6. 羚　**Ling² (líng)** - Antelope, gazelle.

7. 羡 [6]　**Hsien⁴ (xiàn)** - Envy, admire.

义 8. 義 [7]　**Yi⁴ (yì)** - Righteousness; just (– cause); false (– hair).

9. 群 **Ch'ün² (qún)** - Flock, herd; crowd, group, complex.

10. 羨 **Hsien⁴ (xiàn)** - Same as 7.

11. 羲 **Hsi¹ (xi)** - Legendary monarch Fu Hsi.

12. 羸 **Lei² (léi)** - Thin, lean, skinny.

13. 羹 **Keng¹ (geng)** - Soup, broth.

膻 14. 羶 **Shan¹ (shan)** - Rank odor of sheep or goat.

SHELL 貝

Picture of a 'cowrie' shell, used as money in ancient China 貝 .

贝 1. 貝 **Pei⁴ (bèi)** - Cowrie (small shell), shell(fish).

贞 2. 貞 **Chen¹ (zhen)** - Chaste, pure, virtuous, faithful.

负 3. 負 **Fu⁴ (fù)** - Carry on the back; rely on; lose; owe; minus.

贡 4. 貢 **Kung⁴ (gòng)** - Tribute (pay –).

财 5. 財 **Ts'ai² (cái)** - Wealth, property, money.

贩 6. 販 **Fan⁴ (fàn)** - Deal in (– grain); traffic (drug –); dealer.

货 7. 貨 **Huo⁴ (huò)** - Goods, commodity, merchandise.

贯 8. 貫 **Kuan⁴ (guàn)** - Pass through, linked together; birthplace.

贫 9. 貧 **Pin² (pín)** - Impoverished; garrulous, talkative.

贪 10. 貪 **T'an¹ (tan)** - Covet, greedy for (– money), corrupt.

责 11. **責** Tse² (zé) - Duty, responsibility; reproach, blame.

贮 12. **貯** Chu⁴ (zhù) - Store up, hoard.

费 13. **費** Fei⁴ (fèi) - Expense, fee; spend; waste(ful).

贺 14. **賀** Ho⁴ (hè) - Congratulate.

贶 15. **貺** K'uang⁴ (kuàng) - Bestow, confer upon, grant.

贻 16. **貽** Yi² (yí) - Bequeath, hand down, present.

贵 17. **貴** Kuei⁴ (gùi) - Expensive, costly; precious; noble, honorable.

买 18. **買** Mai³ (mǎi) - Purchase, buy.

贸 19. **貿** Mao⁴ (mào) - Trade.

贬 20. **貶** Pien³ (biǎn) - Demote, degrade; censure.

贲 21. **貴** Pen¹ (ben). Pi⁴ (bì) - Bright, beautifully adorned.

贰 22. **貳** Erh⁴ (èr) - Elaborate form for 'two' (used on checks, etc.).

贷 23. **貸** Tai⁴ (dài) - Loan; borrow, lend; pardon.

贴 24. **貼** T'ieh¹ (tie) - Paste up, stick, glue; subsidize.

赀 25. **貲** Tzu¹ (zi) - Estimate; money, expenses.

贿 26. **賄** Hui⁴ (hùi) - Bribe.

赅 27. **賅** Kai¹ (gai) - Complete, full; provided for, prepared.

贾 28. **賈** Ku³ (gǔ) - Merchant; conduct business.

赂 29. **赂** **Lu⁴ (lù)** - Bribe, bribery (**huìlù**).

赁 30. **賃** **Lin⁴ (lìn)** - Rent, hire.

贼 31. **賊** **Tsei² (zéi)** - Thief, enemy; injure.

资 32. **資** **Tsu¹ (zi)** - Money, wealth; expenses; qualification.

赈 33. **賑**[7] **Chen⁴ (zhèn)** - Relieve, relief (– funds); aid (**zhènjì**).

宾 34. **賓** **Pin¹ (bin)** - Guest, visitor (**binkè**).

赊 35. **賒** **She² (she)** - Trade on credit.

账 36. **賬**[8] **Chang⁴ (zhàng)** - Account (– book).

赒 37. **賙** **Chou¹ (zhou)** - Bestow.

质 38. **質** **Chih⁴ (zhì)** - Character; quality; substance; simple.

赋 39. **賦** **Fu⁴ (fù)** - Endow with, give; compose poem; land tax.

贤 40. **賢** **Hsien² (xián)** - Virtuous; able, talented.

赉 41. **賚** **Lai⁴ (lài)** - Bestow, confer, grant.

卖 42. **賣** **Mai⁴ (mài)** - Sell; betray; do the utmost; show off.

赔 43. **賠** **Pei² (péi)** - Compensate; suffer a loss.

赏 44. **賞** **Shang³ (shâng)** - Bestow, grant; reward; enjoy, appreciate.

赐 45. **賜** **Tz'u⁴ (cì)** - Bestow, confer, grant.

贱 46. **賤** **Chien⁴ (jiàn)** - Cheap; humble; contemptible.

赖 47. 賴 [9] **Lai⁴ (lài)** - Rely on, depend on; deny, put blame on sb.

赌 48. 賭 **Tu³ (dŭ)** - Gamble, bet.

赚 49. 賺 [10] **Chuan⁴ (zhuàn)** - Gain, earn. **Tsuan⁴ (zuàn)** - Deceive.

购 50. 購 **Kou⁴ (gòu)** - Purchase, buy.

赛 51. 賽 **Sai⁴ (sài)** - Race, match, competition; surpass.

剩 52. 賸 **Sheng⁴ (shèng)** - Surplus; remnant, left over, residue.

赘 53. 贅 [11] **Chui⁴ (zhuì)** - Redundant, superfluous, repetition.

赞 54. 贊 [12] **Tsan⁴ (zàn)** - Support, patronize; praise, commend.

赠 55. 贈 **Tseng⁴ (zèng)** - Offer as present.

赡 56. 贍 [13] **Shan⁴ (shàn)** - Support (one's parents); supply; abundant.

赢 57. 贏 **Ying² (yíng)** - Win, gain; profit; beat (– sb. at chess).

赃 58. 贓 [14] **Tsang¹ (zang)** - Stolen goods, booty; bribes.

赎 59. 贖 [15] **Shu² (shú)** - Redeem (sth. pawned); ransom (– money).

赝 60. 贋 **Yen⁴ (yàn)** - Counterfeit, false, spurious, fake.

赣 61. 贛 [17] **Kan⁴ (gàn)** - Other name for Kiangsi (Jiangxi) province.

SHELTER 广

A hut 𠆢 which is half-finished that serves as a shelter: 广 .

1. 庄 ³ **Chuang¹ (zhuang)** - Village; firm; manor; serious, grave.

2. 床 ⁴ **Ch'uang² (chuáng)** - Bed, couch; (N).

3. 庇 **Pi⁴ (bì)** - Protect, shield, shelter.

4. 序 **Hsü¹ (xù)** - Order, sequence; introduction, preface.

5. 府 ⁵ **Fu³ (fũ)** - Government office; mansion; prefecture.

6. 庚 **Keng¹ (geng)** - The seventh of Ten Heavenly Stems; age.

7. 庖 **P'ao² (páo)** - Kitchen, cook.

8. 底 **Ti³ (dĩ)** - Bottom; rough draft; end (– of the month); reach.

9. 店 **Tien⁴ (diàn)** - Shop, store; inn.

10. 度 ⁶ **Tu⁴ (dù)** - Measure; degree; limit; spend (– the day).

11. 庠 **Hsiang² (xiáng)** - Asylum, college, school.

库 12. 庫 ⁷ **K'u⁴ (kù)** - Warehouse, storehouse, granary.

13. 庭 **T'ing² (tíng)** - Courtyard; Court of Justice.

14. 座 **Tso⁴ (zuò)** - Seat, stand, pedestal.

15. 康 ⁸ **K'ang¹ (kang)** - Healthy; peaceful.

16. 庵 **An¹ (an)** - Hut, cottage; Buddhist convent.

17. 庶 **Shu⁴ (shù)** - Numerous; of or by the concubine; so that.

18. 庹 T'o³ (tuô) - Arm spread, span.

19. 庸 Yung¹ (yong) - Common(place); mediocre; inferior.

9

厢 20. 廂 Hsiang¹ (xiang) - Side-room; (train) compartment; (theatre) box.

厕 21. 廁 T'sê⁴ (cè) - Toilet, lavatory.

10

厦 22. 廈 Hsia⁴ (xià). Sha⁴ (shà) - Tall building; mansion.

23. 廊 Lang² (láng) - Porch, verandah; corridor, gallery.

24. 廋 Sou¹ (sou) - Conceal; search for.

25. 廉 Lien² (lián) - Honest, pure, incorrupt; cheap.

11

廒 26. 廒 Ao² (aó) - Granary.

荫 27. 廕 Yin¹ (yin) - Shade. Yin⁴ (yìn) - Shady; shelter.

12

厂 28. 廠 Ch'ang³ (châng) - Factory, plant, workshop.

厨 29. 廚 Ch'u² (chú) - Kitchen.

废 30. 廢 Fei⁴ (fèi) - Abandon, abolish, waste (– time); useless.

广 31. 廣 Kuang³ (guâng) - Wide, vast, extensive; numerous.

庙 32. 廟 Miao⁴ (miào) - Temple, shrine.

13

廪 33. 廩 Lin³ (lîn) - Public granary.

16

庐 34. 廬 Lu² (lú) - Hut, cottage.

22

厅 35. 廳 T'ing¹ (ting) - Hall (dining –); office (public –).

SILK 系 . 糸

Small threads from cocoons ষ twisted (木 spindle) into a thicker one 糸 .

1. 系 **Mi⁴ (mì)** - Silk.

2. 系 **Hsi⁴ (xì)** - System; connection; department; fasten; be.

3. 糾 **Chiu¹ (jiu)** - Entangle; gather together; correct.

4. 紂 **Chou⁴ (zhòu)** - Last emperor Shang Dynasty (ca. 1766 BC).

5. 紇 **Ke¹ (ge)** - Tribe of the Uigurs (**Huíhé**).

6. 紅 **Hung² (hóng)** - Red.

7. 紉 **Jen⁴ (rèn)** - Sew, stitch; thread a needle.

8. 紈 **Wan² (wán)** - Fine silk fabric.

9. 紀 **Chi⁴ (jì)** - Discipline; record; age, epoch, period.

10. 約 **Yüeh¹ (yue)** - Make appointment; restrain; frugal; about.

11. 紙 **Chih³ (zhǐ)** - Paper.

12. 紛 **Fen¹ (fen)** - Confused, disorderly; profuse, numerous.

13. 紡 **Fang³ (fǎng)** - Spin (– cloth); thin silk cloth.

14. 級 **Chi² (jí)** - Rank, grade; step (stone –s).

15. 納 **Na⁴ (nà)** - Admit, accept; pay (– taxes).

16. 紟 **Chin¹ (jin)** - Lapel (of coat).

纱 17. 紗 **Sha¹ (sha)** - Yarn (cotton –); gauze (wire –).

纾 18. 紓 **Shu¹ (shu)** - Slow, relax.

纯 19. 純 **Ch'un² (chún)** - Pure, unmixed; simple.

20. 索 **So³ (suô)** - Rope; search; demand.

21. 素 **Su⁴ (sù)** - White; plain, simple; vegetable (– diet); usually.

纹 22. 紋 **Wen² (wén)** - Lines (– on one's hand); grain (fine –ed).

23. 紊 **Wen³ (wên)** - Disordered, confused.

细 24. 紬 **Ch'ou² (chóu)** - Silk fabric; silk (– handkerchief).

终 25. 終 **Chung¹ (zhong)** - End; death; finally; whole, all.

26. 累 **Lei³ (lêi)** - Accumulate, continuous. **Lei⁴ (lèi)** - Tired.

绊 27. 絆 **Pan⁴ (bàn)** - Loop; trip over, stumble.

绅 28. 紳 **Shen¹ (shen)** - Gentry.

绍 29. 紹 **Shao⁴ (shào)** - Continue, carry on.

细 30. 細 **Hsi⁴ (xì)** - Thin, slender, delicate; soft (– voice); careful.

组 31. 組 **Tsu³ (zû)** - Organize, form (– cabinet); organization, group.

32. 紫 **Tsu³ (zî)** - Purple, violet.

绒 33. 絨 **Jung² (róng)** - Floss (silk –); cloth.

绛 34. 絳 **Chiang⁴ (jiàng)** - Crimson, deep purplish red.

绞 35. 絞 **Chiao³ (jiâo)** - Twist, strangle; hang (– by the neck).

结 36. 結 **Chieh² (jié)** - Knot; tie, unite, consolidate, settle.

给 37. 給 **Kei³ (gêi)** - Give, present, grant; for, for the benefit of.

络 38. 絡 **Lo⁴ (luò)** - Net-like object; complex; spin (– yard).

继 39. 絏 **Hsieh⁴ (xiè)** - Fetters, bonds, chains; tie up.

40. 絮 **Hsü⁴ (xù)** - Cotton; talkative

丝 41. 絲 **Szu¹ (si)** - Silk; shredded (– meat); threadlike thing (e.g. wire); trace (minute amount).

统 42. 統 **T'ung³ (tông)** - System; gather into one, unite; all.

绝 43. 絕 **Chüeh² (jué)** - Cut off; exhaust; superb; extremely.

经 44. 經⁷ **Ching¹ (jing)** - Longitude; menstruation; pass through.

绢 45. 絹 **Chüan⁴ (juàn)** - Thin silk; silk taffeta.

捆 46. 綑 **K'un³ (kûn)** - Tie up, bundle up, bind.

绑 47. 綁 **Pang³ (bâng)** - Tie, bind.

48. 绣 **Hsiu⁴ (xiù)** - Embroider(y).

绥 49. 綏 **Sui² (suí)** - Pacify; tranquilize; peaceful.

绽 50. 綻⁸ **Chan⁴ (zhàn)** - Split, burst.

绸 51. 綢 **Ch'ou² (chóu)** - Same as 24.

绰 52. 綽 **Ch'o⁴ (chuò)** - Spacious; ample.

绿 53. 綴 **Chui⁴ (zhuì)** - Sew together; compose (– essay); decorate.

绯 54. 緋 **Fei¹ (fei)** - Dark red.

纲 55. 綱 **Kang¹ (gang)** - Main rope of net; key link; outline; class.

紧 56. 緊 **Chin³ (jǐn)** - Tight(en); urgent; strict; short of money.

绫 57. 綾 **Ling² (líng)** - Damask silk.

绺 58. 絡 **Liu³ (liǔ)** - Skein (– of silk thread).

绿 59. 綠 **Lü⁴ (lǜ)** - Green.

纶 60. 綸 **Lun² (lún)** - Black silk ribbon; fishing line; sybthetic fibre.

绵 61. 綿 **Mien² (mián)** - Silk floss; continuous, unbroken; soft.

线 62. 線 **Hsien⁴ (xiàn)** - Thread, line; route; boundary; clue.

彩 63. 綵 **Ts'ai³ (cǎi)** - Color; variegated silk; applause; prize.

综 64. 綜 **Tsung¹ (zong)** - Put together, sum up, integrate.

网 65. 網 **Wang³ (wǎng)** - Net(work); catch w. net.

维 66. 維 **Wei² (wéi)** - Hold together; maintain; think(ing).

缓 67. 緩 **Huan³ (huǎn)** - Slow(ly); delay, postpone; recuperate.

缄 68. 緘 **Chien¹ (jian)** - Seal (up), close, keep shut (– one's mouth).

练 69. 練 **Lien⁴ (liàn)** - Silk; train (v), practise; experienced.

编 70. 編 **Pien¹ (bian)** - Weave; arrange; compose; volume (– I).

线 71. 線 Hsien⁴ (xiàn) - Same as 62.

绪 72. 緒 Hsü⁴ (xù) - Thread; task, undertaking; beginning.

缔 73. 締 Ti⁴ (dì) - Form (– friendship); conclude (– treaty).

缎 74. 緞 Tuan⁴ (duàn) - Satin.

缉 75. 緝 Ch'i¹ (qi) - Arrest; stitch.

纬 76. 緯 Wei³ (wêi) - Woof, weft; latitude (ten degrees north –).

缘 77. 緣 Yüan² (yuán) - Reason (for no –); fringe; relationship.

致 78. 緻 Chih⁴ (zhì) - Send; devote; cause (v); delicate.

缒 79. 縋 ¹⁰ Chui⁴ (zhuì) - Let down w. a rope.

缚 80. 縛 Fu⁴ (fù) - Fasten, tie up, bind.

县 81. 縣 Hsien⁴ (xiàn) - County, district, prefecture.

缢 82. 縊 Yi⁴ (yì) - Hang (– oneself).

绦 83. 縚 T'ao¹ (tao) - Silk ribbon.

绉 84. 縐 Chou⁴ (zhòu) - Crape, crepe.

缙 85. 縉 Chin⁴ (jìn) - Carnation silk, red silk.

萦 86. 縈 Ying² (yíng) - Entangle; encompass.
  ₁₁Jung² (róng) - Entwine, wind around.

87. 繁 Fan² (fán) - Numerous; propagate, multiply.

缝 88. 縫 Feng² (féng) - Sew, stitch.

纤 89. 縴 **Ch'ien⁴ (qiàn)** - Towline (rope for towing boat).

缧 90. 縲 **Lei² (léi)** - Fetters, rope for binding prisoners; bind w. rope.

缕 91. 縷 **Lü³ (lǔ)** - Thread; wisp (– of smoke); in detail.

缫 92. 繅 **Sao¹ (sao)** - Reel (v) silk from cocoons.

缩 93. 縮 **So¹ (suo)** - Shrink, draw back, withdraw.

绩 94. 績 **Chi¹ (ji)** - Twist (– hemp); merit.

纵 95. 縱 **Tsung⁴ (zòng)** - Vertical; release, let go; jump up; even if.

总 96. 總 **Tsung³ (zōng)** - Sum up; chief, general (– office); always.

缤 97. 繽 **Yen³ (yân)** - Lengthen; prolong; extend.
繇 98. 繇 **Yin⁴ (yìn)** - Sew, stitch.
Yu² (yóu) - Flourishing; cause.

织 99. 織¹² **Chih¹ (zhi)** - Weave, knit.

褙 100. 繈 **Ch'iang³ (qiâng)** - Swaddling clothes (**qiângbâo**).

翻 101. 繙 **Fan¹ (fan)** - Interpret, translate.

绕 102. 繞 **Jao⁴ (rào)** - Wind (v); circle (v); revolve; make detour.

缭 103. 繚 **Liao² (liáo)** - Sew; linger (**liáorâo**).

伞 104. 繖 **San³ (sân)** - Umbrella, umbrella-shaped object.

缮 105. 繕 **Shan⁴ (shàn)** - Repair; copy, write out.

绣 106. 繡 **Hsiu⁴ (xiù)** - Same as 48.

穗 107. 繐 Sui⁴ (suì) - Ear or spike of grain.

系 108. 繫 [13] Hsi⁴ (xì) - System; department; faculty; tie, fasten.
Chi⁴ (jì) - Tie, fasten, bind.

绘 109. 繪 Hui⁴ (huì) - Draw, paint.

缴 110. 繳 Chiao³ (jiǎo) - Pay (– tax); hand over; capture (– weapons).

茧 111. 繭 Chien³ (jiǎn) - Cocoon; callus.

缰 112. 繮 Chiang¹ (jiang) - Bridle, halter, reins.

绳 113. 繩 Sheng² (shéng) - String, cord, rope; restrain.

缘 114. 繸 Sui⁴ (suì) - Tassel, fringe.

绎 115. 繹 Yi⁴ (yì) - Unravel, unfold, sort out, explain.

继 116. 繼 [14] Chi⁴ (jì) - Continue, succeed, follow; then.

辫 117. 辮 Pien⁴ (biàn) - Plait, queue, pigtail, braid.

118. 纂 Tsuan³ (zuǎn) - Compile, edit; bun, hair worn in a knot. [15]

缠 119. 纏 Ch'an² (chán) - Wind, wrap; implicate; pester, annoy.

纩 120. 纊 K'uang⁴ (kuàng) - Cotton; fine floss silk.

累 121. 纍 Lei³ (lêi) - Accumulate; continuous.

续 122. 續 Hsü² (xù) - Continue; add.

纤 123. 纖 [17] Hsien¹ (xian) - Minute, fine.

才 124. 纔 Ts'ai² (cái) - Ability, talent, person of talent; then, just now.

纓 125. 纓 **Ying¹ (ying)** - Tassel, fringe, ribbon.

缆 126. 纜²¹ **Lan³ (lân)** - Hawser, towing or mooring rope; cable.

SKIN 皮

The skin ⌒ stripped off by a hand ⇒ holding a knife ⊃ : 㕘.

1. 皮 **P'i² (pí)** - Skin; leather, fur; sheet (iron –); rubber (– band).

疱 2. 皰 **P'ao⁴ (pào)** - Blister.

3. 皴 **Ts'un¹ (cun)** - Chapped (– hands); cracked.

皱 4. 皺 **Chou⁴ (zhòu)** -Wrinkle, crease.

SMALL 小

An object ハ split ∣ into two: 小.

1. 小 **Hsiao³ (xiâo)** - Small, little; a short time; young (– lady).

2. 少 **Shao³ (shâo)** - Few, little; a short while; be short of; lose.

3. 尖 **Chien¹ (jian)** - Point (– of needle), tip; sharp (– voice).

4. 尚 **Shang⁴ (shàng)** - Still (– too soon); yet (not –); esteem.

SOUND 音

Showing the mouth ▽, the tongue 舌, the sound – produced in the mouth and the sound waves coming out from the mouth ＝: 音.

1. 音 **Yin¹ (yin)** - Sound, tone; news.

2. 韶 **Shao² (sháo)** - Beautiful, splendid, excellent.

韵 3. 韻 **Yün⁴ (yùn)** - Musical sound, tone; rhyme; charm.

响 4. 響 **Hsiang³ (xiâng)** - Sound (n)(v), noise; loud; ring (v); echo.

SPEAK 曰

A word ∟ spoken out by the mouth ㄩ : 彐 .

1. 曰 **Yüeh¹ (yue)** - Speak, say, call, name (– a baby).

2. 曳² **Chuai⁴ (zhuài)** - Pull, drag, haul. (Same as **HAND 64**).

3. 曲 **Ch'ü¹ (qu)** - Crooked, curved; wrong, unjust(ifiable).

4. 更³ **Keng¹ (geng)** - Change; (night)watch.

5. 曷⁵ **He² (hé)** - Why? How? When? What?

书 6. 書⁶ **Shu¹ (shu)** - Book; write; letter.

7. 曼⁷ **Man⁴ (màn)** - Graceful; prolonged, extended.

8. 曹 **Tsao² (cáo)** - Company, class; people of the same class.

9. 替⁸ **T'i⁴ (tì)** - Substitute; decline, deteriorate; for, on behalf of.

10. 朁 **Ts'an³ (cân)** - Nevertheless, if, suppose.

11. 曾 **Tsêng¹ (zeng)** -Great grand (– child)**Tseng² (céng)**Already.

12. 最 **Tsui⁴ (zuì)** - To the highest degree; most (at –), best (the –).

会 13. 會⁹ **Hui⁴ (huì)** - Assemble, meet; association; be able to.

SPLITWOOD (LEFT) 爿

The left half of a tree 朿 : 爿 .

床 1. 牀 Ch'uang² (chuáng) - Bed; (N).

跄 2. 牄 Ch'iang⁴ (qiàng) - Walk fast; stagger (qiàngliàng).

墙 3. 牆 Ch'iang² (qiáng) - Wall.

SPLITWOOD (RIGHT) 片

The right half of a tree 朿 : 片 .

1. 片 P'ien¹ (pian) -Film; card (name –); disc (record –).
   4 P'ien⁴ (piàn) - Slice; flake (snow –); fillet (fish –).

2. 版 8 Pan³ (bân) - Printing block; edition; page (front –).

3. 牌 P'ai² (pái) - Plate, tablet; card; brand (well-known –).

笺 4. 牋 Chien¹ (jian) - Writing paper; letter; annotation.

5. 牒 Tieh² (dié) - Official document, records; certificate.

6. 牖 11 Yu³ (yôu) - Lattice window.

牍 7. 牘 15 Tu² (dú) - Ancient writing tablet; letter; documents.

SPOON 匕

Representing an ancient spoon: 六 .

1. 化 Hua⁴ (huà) - Change; melt, dissolve: chemistry; -ize.

2. 北 Pei³ (bêi) - North.

3. 匙 Ch'ih² (chí) - Spoon (tea –). Shih (shi) - Key (yàoshi).

SPROUT 屮

Picture of a new shoot of a plant , i.e. a sprout: Ψ .

1. 屯 **T'un² (tún)** - Store up (– grain); station (– troops); village.

SQUARE 方

Representing the square earth with the four regions at the corners: 卐 .

1. 方 **Fang¹ (fang)** - Square; side; method; prescription; just.

于 2. 於 ⁴ **Yü² (yú)** - To (loyal –); in (born – 1800); than (larger –).

3. 施 ⁵ **Shih¹ (shi)** - Carry out; exert; bestow; apply (– fertilizer).

4. 斾 **P'ei⁴ (pèi)** - Pennon, streamer, flag.

5. 旅 ⁶ **Lü³ (lǚ)** - Travel; brigade, troops.

6. 旁 **P'ang² (páng)** - Side (road–); other, else (anything –).

7. 旄 **Mao² (máo)** - Yak's tail; banner.

8. 旋 ⁷ **Hsüan² (xuán)** - Revolve, return; soon. **Hsüan⁴ (xuàn) -** Whirl (–wind).

9. 族 **Tsu² (zú)** - Clan, race, class.

10. 旌 **Ching¹ (jing)** - Banner (ancient type on mast).

11. 旗 ¹⁰ **Ch'i² (qí)** - Flag, banner.

幡 12. 旛 ¹⁴ **Fan¹ (fan)** - Banner (funeral –), streamer (before shrine).

STAND 立

A man 大 standing on the ground —: 立.

1. 立 $_5$ **Li⁴ (lì)** - Stand; set up (– rules); immediate (– reply).

2. 站 $_6$ **Chan⁴ (zhàn)** - Stand; stop, station; center (service –).

3. 章   **Chang¹ (zhang)** - Chapter; regulation; seal; badge, medal.

4. 竟 $_7$ **Ching⁴ (jìng)** - Finish; whole (– night); eventually.

5. 竦   **Sung³ (sông)** - Be afraid; encourage.

6. 童   **T'ung² (tóng)** - Boy; virgin; bare (– hills).

7. 竣 $_8$ **Chün⁴ (jùn)** - Complete, finish.

竖   8. 竪   **Shu⁴ (shù)** - Vertical, upright, perpendicular, erect.

9. 靖 $_9$ **Ching⁴ (jìng)** - Peace(ful), pacify.

10. 竭   **Chieh² (jié)** - Exhaust, use up.

11. 端 $_{15}$ **Tuan¹ (duan)** - End (both –s); beginning; reason; carry.

竞   12. 競   **Ching⁴ (jìng)** - Compete, contest **(jìngsài)**.

STONE 石

Showing a stone ○ in a cliff ⌐ : ⌐○.

1. 石 Shih² (shí) - Stone, rock.

2. 砍 K'an³ (kân) - Chop, hack, cut off; throw sth. at.

3. 砒 P'i¹ (pi) - Arsenic.

4. 砂 Sha¹ (sha) - Sand, gravel, grit.

5. 砌 Ch'i⁴ (qì) - Pave, lay bricks or stones; stone step.

6. 砦 Chai⁴ (zhài) - Stockade, stronghold; camp (military).

7. 砥 Chih³ (zhî) - Whetstone; smooth.

8. 砰 P'eng¹ (peng) - Sound of falling material.

9. 砲 P'ao⁴ (pào) - Cannon, piece of artillery.

10. 砣 T'o² (tuó) - Stone roller.

11. 砭 Pien¹ (bian) - Stone needle used in acupuncture; pierce.

12. 破 P'o⁴ (pò) - Damaged, worn-out; cleave; capture (– city).

13. 砸 Tsa² (zá) - Pound (v), break, smash; fail, bungle (– a job).

14. 朱 硃 Chu¹ (zhu) - Vermillion, scarlet, bright red; cinnaber.

15. 研 研 Yen² (yán) - Grind; study, investigate.

16. 硫 Liu² (liú) - Sulphur.

17. 硝 Hsiao¹ (xiao) - Nitre, saltpeter; tan (– leather).

18. 硬   Ying⁴ (yìng) - Hard, firm; stiff (– neck); good, able.

硯 19. 硯   Yen⁴ (yàn) - Ink slab, inkstone.

碌 20. 碌 ⁸   Lu⁴ (lù) - Commonplace; mediocre; laborious, busy.

21. 硼   P'eng² (péng) - Boron, natural borax.

22. 碓   Tui⁴ (duì) - Foot-operated pestle for hulling rice.

23. 碑   Pei¹ (bei) - Upright stone tablet; stele.

24. 碎   Sui⁴ (suì) - Break to pieces; broken (– glass); talkative.

25. 碗   Wan³ (wân) - Bowl.

26. 碣 ⁹   Chieh² (jié) - Stone plate, stone tablet.

27. 碰   P'eng⁴ (pèng) - Bump, run into (– psn.); take one's chance.

28. 碧   Pi⁴ (pì) - Green and blue jade; bluish green, blue.

29. 碟   Tieh² (dié) - Small dish; small plate, saucer.

30. 磕 ¹⁰   K'o¹, K'e¹ (ke) - Bump (– against door); knock out (– ash).

31. 磊   Lei³ (lêi) - Heap of stones; open and upright (lêiluò).

碼 32. 碼   Ma³ (mâ) - Sign for number; stack; wharf; yard (yd.).

33. 碾   Nien³ (niân) - Roller; grind, crush, flatten; husk (- rice).

34. 磐   P'an² (pán) - Huge rock (pánshí).

35. 磅   Pang⁴ (bàng) - Pound; scales; weigh.

确 36. 確　Ch'üeh⁴ (què) - True, reliable, authentic; firm (– belief).

37. 磋　Ts'o¹(cuo) - Rub, polish; (cuoshang) consult, negotiate.

38. 磁　Ts'u² (cí) - Magnetism; chinaware, porcelain.

碜 39. 磣　Ch'en³ (chên) - (yáchen): gritty (food), coarse (language).

砖 40. 磚　Chuan¹ (zhuan) - Brick, tile.

41. 磡　K'an⁴ (kàn) - Mountain cliff.

42. 磬　Ch'ing⁴ (qìng) - Stone chimes, inverted (percussion) bell.

43. 磨　Mo² (mó) - Rub, grind, polish; dawdle, waste time.

矶 44. 磯　Chi¹ (ji) - Rock projecting over the water.

磺 45. 磺　Huang² (huáng) - Sulphur.

46. 磴　Teng⁴ (dèng) - Ledge, cliff; stone steps.

47. 礁　Chiao¹ (jiao) - Reef, hidden or sunken rocks.

础 48. 礎　Ch'u³ (chû) - Plinth, subbase, pedestal.

碍 49. 礙　Ai⁴ (ài) - Obstruct, hinder.

矾 50. 礬　Fan² (fán) - Vitriol, sulphate.

矿 51. 礦　K'uang⁴ (kuàng) - Ore, mineral deposit; mine (coal –).

砺 52. 礪　Li⁴ (lì) - Whetstone; whet, sharpen.

STOOL 几

Picture of a stool 几.

1. 几 **Chi[1] (jǐ)** - Stool, low table.

2. 凡 **Fan[2] (fǎn)** - Common(place), ordinary; earth; every, all.

3. 凰 **Huang[2] (huáng)** - Phoenix (fènghuáng).

凯 4. 凱 **K'ai[3] (kǎi)** - Victory (-ious), triumph(ant).

5. 凳 **Teng[4] (dèng)** - Stool, bench.

6. 凭 **P'ing[2] (píng)** - Lean against; rely on; evidence.

STOP 止

Representing the foot-at-rest, showing the heel L , the toe ⌐ and the ankle ⴔ of a foot: 止 .

1. 止 **Chih[3] (zhǐ)** - Stop (– pain); to (– date), till (– now); only.

2. 正 [1] **Cheng[4] (zhèng)** - Straight; correct; main (– hall); chief.

3. 此 [2] **Tz'u[3] (cǐ)** - This (– moment).

4. 步 [3] **Pu[4] (bù)** - Step, pace; walk; situation.

5. 歧 [4] **Ch'i[2] (qí)** - Forked (– road), divergent, different (– views).

6. 武 **Wu[3] (wǔ)** - Military, martial; valiant, fierce.

7. 歪 [5] **Wai[1] (wai)** - Askew, slanting; crooked; devious, evil.

岁 8. 歲 [9] **Sui[4] (suì)** - Year (end of the –; one – old).

历 9. 歷 [12] **Li⁴ (lì)** - Undergo; previous; successive; calendar.

归 10. 歸 [14] **Kuei¹ (gui)** - Return (– home); give back; converge, come together.

STOPPER 西 . 西 . 西

Picture of a stopper ⊽ on a bottle ⌐⌐ : ⌐ᵀ⌐.

1. 西 **Hsi¹ (xi)** - West(ern); foreign (– countries).

2. 要 **Yao⁴ (yào)** - Important; want to; must; suppose (– it rains).

3. 覃 **T'an² (tán)** - Extend (– favors); deep (– in thought).

4. 覆 **Fu⁴ (fù)** - Cover (n)(v); overturn, capsize (–d boat).

STRENGTH 力

Picture of a muscle in its sheath: ⟅⟆ .

1. 力 **Li⁴ (lì)** - Strength, power, force.

2. 加 [3] **Chia¹ (jia)** - Add, increase; plus (one – one is two).

3. 功 **Kung¹ (gong)** - Merit; achievement; skill.

4. 劣 [4] **Lieh⁴ (liè)** - Bad, inferior (– quality).

5. 助 [5] [5] **Chu⁴ (zhù)** - Assistance, aid, help.

6. 劫 **Chieh² (jié)** - Rob, plunder; coerce; calamity, disaster.

7. 劬 **Ch'ü² (qú)** - Fatigued; diligent; hardworking; toil (v).

8. 努 **Nu³ (nû)** - Put forth (– strength); bulge.

9. 劾 [6] **Ho² (hé)** - Expose sb's misdeeds; impeach, indict.

劲 10. 勁 [7] **Ching⁴ (jìng)** - Strong, sturdy. **Chin⁴ (jìn)** - Strength, spirit.

11. 勉 **Mien³ (miân)** - Encourage, strive, urge.

12. 勃 **Po² (bó)** - Suddenly.

13. 勇 **Yung³ (yông)** - Brave, valiant, courageous.

务 14. 務 [8] **Wu⁴ (wù)** - Business, affair; engaged in; must **(wùbi)**.

15. 勒 [9] **Le⁴ (lè)** - Rein in (– horse). **Lei (lei)** - Tie or strap sth. tight.

16. 勘 **K'an¹ (kan)** - Collate; investigate; proofread.

动 17. 動 **Tung⁴ (dòng)** - Move, get moving; change; arouse.

劳 18. 勞 [10] **Lao² (láo)** - Work, labor; fatigue; merit, worthy action.

胜 19. 勝 **Sheng⁴ (shèng)** - Win (– lawsuit); surpass; wonderful.

20. 勤 [11] **Ch'in² (qín)** - Diligent; frequently; duty; attendance.

剿 21. 勦 **Chiao³ (jiâo)** - Suppress, put down (– bandits).

22. 募 **Mu⁴ (mù)** - Raise (– money); enlist (– soldiers).

势 23. 勢 **Shih⁴ (shì)** - Power; influence; circumstance; male genitals.

勋 24. 勳 [14] **Hsün¹ (xun)** - Merit; achievement.

励 25. 勵 [15] **Li⁴ (lì)** - Encourage, urge, stimulate.

劝 26. 勸 [18] **Ch'üan⁴ (quàn)** - Advise, persuade; encourage.

STRIKE 殳

The hand ⇒ making a violent motion ⌃ in order to strike:

1. 殳 **Shu¹ (shu)** - Ancient bamboo spear.

2. 段 ⁵ **Tuan⁴ (duàn)** - Section, segment; paragraph (**duànluò**).

3. 殷 ⁶ **Yin¹ (yin)** - Abundant, rich; eager; hospitable.

杀 4. 殺 ⁶ **Sha¹ (sha)** - Kill, slaughter; fight; weaken; reduce.

壳 5. 殼 ⁸ **Ch'üeh⁴ (què)** - Husk, shell (egg –).

6. 毀 ⁹ **Huî³ (huî)** - Destroy, ruin; defame, slander.

7. 殿 **Tien⁴ (diàn)** - Hall, palace, temple; rear (– of army).

8. 毅 ¹¹ **Yi⁴ (yì)** - Firmly, resolutely.

殴 9. 毆 **Ou¹ (ou)** - Beat, hit, strike.

STYLUS 聿

A hand ⇒ holding a stylus | writing a line — on a tablet ⬡:

1. 聿 **Yü⁴ (yù)** - Pen(cil); thereupon; narrate.

2. 肄 **Yi⁴ (yì)** - Study, learn.

肃 3. 肅 **Su⁴ (sù)** - Respectful; solemn; majestic.

4. 肆 **Szu⁴ (sì)** - Four (elaborate form); wanton (– massacre).

5. 肇 **Chao⁴ (zhào)** - Start, initiate, cause (– accident).

SUN 日

Picture of the sun ⊙ .

1. 日　　**Jih⁴ (rì)** - Sun; day, daily; time (spring –).

2. 旦　　**Tan⁴ (dàn)** - Dawn, daybreak.

3. 旨　　**Chih³ (zhǐ)** - Purpose, decree; tasty, excellent (– wine).

4. 旬　　**Hsün⁴ (xún)** - Ten days; ten years (8 – <80 yrs> old man).

5. 旭　　**Hsü⁴ (xù)** - Rising of the sun; dawn.

6. 早　　**Tsao³ (zǎo)** - Morning (early –); long ago (know him –).

7. 旱　　**Han⁴ (hàn)** - Drought, dry (–land rice); overland (– travel).

8. 昂　　**Ang² (áng)** - Soaring, high (– in price); hold high (– head).

9. 昌　　**Ch'ang¹ (chang)** - Prosperous, flourishing.

10. 昊　　**Hao⁴ (hào)** - Luminous; grand; vast.

11. 昏　　**Hun¹ (hun)** - Dusk; dark, dim; confused; faint.

12. 易　　**Yi⁴ (yì)** - Easy; amiable; (ex)change.

13. 昆　　**K'un¹ (kun)** - Elder brother; descendants.

14. 明　　**Ming² (míng)** - Bright, clear; open; next; Ming dynasty.

15. 昔　　**Hsi¹ (xi)** - The past, formerly.

升 16. 昇　　**Sheng¹ (sheng)** - Ascend, rise; promote; litre (l.).

17. 旺 **Wang⁴ (wàng)** - Prosperous; vigorous.

18. 昭 ⁵ **Chao¹ (zhao)** - Clear (– explanation), obvious **(zhaozhù)**.

19. 春 **Ch'un¹ (chun)** - Spring (season); lust, obscene; vitality.

20. 昧 **Mei⁴ (mèi)** - Be ignorant of; stupid; hide, conceal.

21. 昵 **Ni⁴ (nì)** - Close, intimate.

22. 是 **Shih⁴ (shì)** - To be; correct; yes; this, that.

23. 星 **Hsing¹ (xing)** - Star, heavenly body; bit (tiny –).

24. 昨 **Tso² (zuó)** - Yesterday.

25. 映 **Ying⁴ (yìng)** - Shine; reflect.

26. 晃 ⁶ **Huang³ (huâng)** - Dazzling. **Huang⁴ (huàng)** - Sway.

27. 晌 **Shang³ (shâng)** - Noon, midday (– meal).

时 28. 時 **Shih² (shí)** - Time, season; hour; present (at –); sometimes.

晋 29. 晉 **Chin⁴ (jìn)** - Advance, promote; Jin dynasty (265-420 AD).

30. 晏 **Yen⁴ (yàn)** - Late (get up –).

31. 晨 ⁷ **Ch'en² (chén)** - Morning.

昼 32. 晝 **Chou⁴ (zhòu)** - Daytime.

33. 晦 **Hui⁴ (huì)** - Dark, obscure.

34. 晚 **Wan³ (wân)** - Night; late; younger (– generation).

35. 晤 **Wu⁴ (wù)** - Meet, see face to face.

36. 智 ⁸ **Chih⁴ (zhì)** - Wisdom, wit.

37. 景 **Ching³ (jǐng)** - View, scene(ry); situation; admire.

38. 晷 **Kuei² (guǐ)** - Shadow (cast by sun); sundial; time (spare –).

39. 晾 **Liang⁴ (liàng)** - Dry in the sun or air; air (v).

40. 普 **P'u³ (pǔ)** - General; **(pǔbiàn)** - universal, widespread.

41. 晶 **Ching¹ (jīng)** - Bright, brilliant; crystal; quartz.

42. 晴 **Ch'ing² (qíng)** - Fine (– weather); clear (– sky).

43. 晰 **Hsi⁴ (xi)** - Clear, distinct.

44. 暇 ⁹ **Hsia² (xiá)** - Leisure (– time).

45. 暗 **An⁴ (àn)** - Dark (– room); secret, hidden; vague (– idea).

46. 暖 **Nuan³ (nuán)** - Warm, genial.

47. 暑 **Shu³ (shǔ)** - Heat (summer –), hot weather.

48. 暌 **K'uei² (kuí)** - Separate, apart.

晕 49. 暈 **Yün¹ (yun)** - Dizzy; faint. **Yün⁴ (yùn)** - Halo (of moon).

畅 50. 暢 ¹⁰ **Ch'ang⁴ (chàng)** - Smooth; uninhibited; joyful.

51. 暮 ¹¹ **Mu⁴ (mù)** - Sunset, dusk, evening; late (– autumn).

昵 52. 暱 **Ni⁴ (nì)** - Same as 21.

53. 暴 **Pao⁴ (bào)** - Violent; cruel; hot-tempered; stand out.

暂 54. 暫 **Tsan⁴ (zàn)** - Temporarily; of short duration.

晓 55. 曉 **Hsiao³ (xiâo)** - Dawn, daybreak; know.

56. 暨 **Chi⁴ (jì)** - And, also, together with; up to (– now); till.

历 57. 曆 **Li⁴ (lì)** - Experience (v), go through (– hardship); calendar.

昙 58. 曇 **T'an² (tán)** - Cloudy; covered with clouds.

59. 曙 **Shu³ (shû)** - Dawn.

60. 曜 **Yao⁴ (yào)** - Sunlight; shine.

旷 61. 曠 **K'uang⁴ (kuàng)** - Spacious; carefree; neglect.

62. 曝 **Pao⁴ (bào)** - Dry in the sun.

63. 曩 **Nang³ (nâng)** - Former, past, in olden days **(nângshí)**.

晒 64. 曬 **Shai⁴ (shài)** - Dry in the sun; shine upon (of the sun); bask.

SWEET 甘

Something sweet – being held in the mouth 甘 : 甘 .

1. 甘 **Kan¹ (gan)** - Sweet, pleasant; willingly, voluntarily.

什 2. 甚 **Shen² (shén)** - What? **(shénme). Shen⁴ (shèn)** - Very; extremely; more than. *** Shih² (shí)** - Miscellaneous.

3. 甜 **T'ien² (tián)** - Sweet, pleasant; sound (– asleep).

T

TAP 攴 . 攵

A hand holding a stick : 彐.

考 1. 攷 K'ao³ (kâo) - Test; investigate.

2. 改 Kai³ (gâi) - Alter, change, correct.

3. 收 Shou¹ (shou) - Receive, accept; collect (– taxes); harvest.

4. 攻 Kung¹ (gong) - Attack; study, specialize in.

5. 政 Cheng⁴ (zhèng) - Government; administration.

6. 放 Fang⁴ (fàng) - Release; make larger, add; place, put aside.

7. 故 Ku⁴ (gù) - Incident; reason; intentionally; old (– friends).

8. 效 Hsiao⁴ (xiào) - Effect(ive); imitate; devote one's life to.

9. 敕⁷ **Ch'ih⁴ (chì)** - Edict, imperial decree.

教 10. 教 **Chiao⁴ (jiào)** - Teach, instruct; religion.

11. 救 **Chiu⁴ (jiù)** - Rescue, save; relieve.

12. 敏 **Min³ (mĭn)** - Nimble, quick.

败 13. 敗 **Pai⁴ (bài)** - Defeat(ed), spoil (–ed meat); wither.

14. 敘 **Hsü⁴ (xù)** - Chat, talk, narrate.

15. 敞⁸ **Ch'ang³ (chăng)** - Spacious; open (leave door –).

敢 16. 敢 **Kan³ (găn)** - Bold; dare, venture.

17. 敝 **Pi⁴ (bì)** - Worn-out (– clothes); my, our.

18. 散 **San⁴ (sàn)** - Fall apart, scatter; medicinal powder.

19. 敦 **Tun¹ (dun)** - Sincere, honest.

20. 敬⁹ **Ching⁴ (jìng)** - Respectful(ly); offer respectfully.

21. 敲¹⁰ **Ch'iao¹ (qiao)** - Strike, knock (– at door), beat (– drum).

22. 敷¹¹ **Fu¹ (fu)** - Apply (– ointment); lay (– pipes); sufficient.

数 23. 數 **Shu³ (shŭ)** - Count. **Shu⁴ (shù)** - Number; several; fate.
Sho⁴ (shuò) - Often.

敌 24. 敵 **Ti² (dí)** - Enemy; oppose, fight against.

25. 整¹² **Cheng³ (zhēng)** - Whole (– day); in good order; repair.

敛 26. 斂¹³ **Lien³ (liăn)** - Hold back; restrain; collect (– taxes).

毙 27. 斃 **Pi⁴ (bì)** - Die; get killed; kill or execute (by shooting).

TEETH 齒

Representing teeth in the mouth :🦷*. (𠂤 Serves as phonetic only.)*

齿 1. 齒 **Ch'ih³ (chî)** - Teeth, tooth; age; mention.

齣 2. 齣 **Ch'u¹ (chu)** - Stanza, couplet, play, act. *Come out, etc.
(See **PIT** 5.)

龃 3. 齟 **Chü³ (jû)** - Discordant (teeth), irregular.

啃 4. 齦 **K'en³ (kên)** - Gnaw, nibble, chew. ** **Yin² (yín)** - Gum.
** Refers to the traditional form only.

龊 5. 齪 **Ch'uo⁴ (chuò)** - Grind teeth; auger; **(wòchuò)**: dirty, filthy.

龌 6. 齷 **Wo⁴ (wò)** - **(wòchuò)**: Dirty, filthy. (See 5).

TEN 十

Symbol for a unit: 十.

1. 十 **Shih² (shí)** - Ten.

2. 千 **Ch'ien¹ (qian)** - Thousand; very many.

3. 廿 **Nien⁴ (niàn)** - Twenty.

4. 升 **Sheng¹ (sheng)** - Rise, promote; litre (l.).

5. 午 **Wu³ (wû)** - Noon, midday (– meal); seventh.

6. 卉 **Hui⁴ (huì)** - Plants, herbs, various kinds of grass.

7. 半 **Pan⁴ (bàn)** - Half, semi-; halfway, partly.

8. 卓 ^{6} **Cho^1 (zhuo)** - Upright (stand -); outstanding, prominent.

协 9. 協 **Hsieh^2 (xié)** - Joint(ly), together (work -); assist.

10. 卑 **Pei^1 (bei)** - Low, inferior; humble.

11. 卒 **Tsu^2 (zú)** - Soldier; servant; end, die.

12. 南 ^{7} **Nan^2 (nán)** - South.

13. 博 ^{10} **Po^2 (bó)** - Rich (- resources), extensive; win (- praise).

THREAD 幺

Two cocoons ○ twisted into a thread: 𢆼 .

1. 幺 **Yao^1 (yao)** - Small, tiny; one (in games, etc.); youngest.

2. 幻 **Huan^4 (huàn)** - Imaginary; magic (- lantern); changeable.

3. 幼 **Yu^4 (yòu)** - Young; child(ren), the young (- people).

4. 幽 **Yu^1 (you)** - Secluded; hidden, secret; tranquil.

几 5. 幾 **Chi^3 (jǐ)** - How many; few. **Chi^1 (ji)** - Nearly. *Small table.

TIGER 虎

Representing the stripes of the tiger: 虍 .

1. 虎 ^{2} **Hu^3 (hǔ)** - Tiger; brave, fierce (-looking).

2. 虐 ^{3} **Nüeh^4 (nüè)** - Cruel, tyrannical.

3. 虔 [4] Ch'ien² (qián) - Pious, sincere.

处 4. 處 [5] Ch'u³ (chû) - Get along with; dwell, live. Ch'u⁴ (chù) - Place; department.

虚 5. 虛 [6] Hsü¹ (xu) - Empty, false; humble, weak.

虏 6. 虜 [7] Lu³ (lû) - Capture, take prisoner; prisoner (- of war).

号 7. 號 Hao⁴ (hào) - Name; number (no.); mark. Hao² (háo) - Howl, wail.

虞 8. 虞 Yü² (yú) - Supposition; deceive, cheat.

亏 9. 虧 [11] K'uei¹ (kui) - Lose, wane (of moon); thanks to, fortunately.

TILE 瓦

Representing a Chinese rooftile 瓦 , turned upright in order to take up minimum writing space: 瓦 .

1. 瓦 Wa³ (wâ) - Earthenware; watt (elec. power unit).

2. 瓶 P'ing² (píng) - Bottle, jug, vase, jar.

3. 瓷 Tz'u² (cí) - Porcelain, china (-ware).

瓯 4. 甌 Ou¹ (ou) - Bowl, cup.

5. 甑 Tseng⁴ (zèng) - Ancient rice steamer.

罂 6. 甖 [5] Ying¹ (ying) - Jar w. small mouth.

TONGUE 舌

The tongue 干 *shown outside the mouth* 曰: 丫.

1. 舌 **She² (shé)** - Tongue (ox –).

2. 舍 **She⁴ (shè)** - House, shed; my (humble) (– home).

3. 舐 **Shih⁴ (shì)** - Lick (the cow –s its calf).

4. 舒 **Shu¹ (shu)** - Stretch; unfold **(shuzhan)**.

5. 舔 **T'ien³ (tiân)** - Lick (the cat –s its tail).

铺 6. 鋪 **P'u⁴ (pù)** - Shop, store, stall.

TOOTH 牙

Representing a tooth: 与.

1. 牙 **Ya² (yá)** - Tooth; ivory (– chopsticks).

TORTOISE 龜

Representing a tortoise, showing its body 于, *its shell* 囱, *and its claws* 彡: 龜.

龟 1. 龜 **Kuei¹ (gui)** - Tortoise, turtle.

TRACK 内

Representing the hind legs 八 *and the tail* 丿 *of an animal – one that just left its track:* 欣.

1. 禹 **Yü³ (Yû)** - Emperor Yü, founder Hsia dynasty (2,205 BC).

2. 禽 **Ch'in² (qín)** - Birds (song –); poultry **(jiaqín)**.

TREE 木

Picture of a tree, showing the trunk |, *with the branches* ∨ *and the roots* ∧ : 朮.

1. 木   Mu[4] (mù) - Tree, wood(en); numb (– w. cold).

2. 札[1]   Cha[2] (zhá) - Ancient wooden writing tablet; letter.

3. 末   Mo[4] (mò) - Tip (– of hair); end (week–); powder, dust.

4. 本   Pen[3] (bên) - Root, origin(al); native (– soil); this; copy (N).

朮 5. 朮   Shu[2] (shú) - Medicinal plant.

6. 未   Wei[4] (wèi) - Not; the Eighth (of the Earthly Branches).

7. 朱[2]   Chu[1] (zhu) - Red, vermillion (zhuhóng); cinnabar.

8. 朽   Hsiu[3] (xiû) - Rotten, decayed; senile.

朵 9. 朵   To[3] (duô) - (N) for flowers, etc.

10. 束   Tz'u[4] (cì) - Thorn.

11. 杖[3]   Chang[4] (zhàng) - Cane, stick; flog (– a criminal).

勺 12. 杓   Shao[2] (sháo) - Ladle, spoon.

13. 杏   Hsing[4] (xìng) - Apricot.

14. 杆   Kan[1] (gan) - Pole, staff, rod.

15. 杠   Kang[4] (gàng) - Thick stick; carrying pole; (cross)bar; underlining; cross out.

16. 李   Li[3] (lî) - Plum, prune.

17. 呆 Ai² (ái) - Idiotic. Tai¹ (dai) - Dull; stay (– at home).

18. 杉 Shan¹ (shan) - Fir tree.

19. 束 Shu⁴ (shù) - Bind; bundle (– of flowers); restrain.

20. 杜 Tu⁴ (dù) - Shut out, stop, prevent.

21. 材 Ts'ai² (cái) - Material(s); talent, ability; timber.

22. 村 Ts'un¹ (cun) - Village, hamlet; rustic.

23. 杌 Wu⁴ (wù) - Stump of tree; square stool.

24. 枕⁴ Chen³ (zhên) - Pillow; rest head on (– pillow); block.

25. 枝 Chih¹ (zhi) - Branch, twig.

26. 杼 Chu⁴ (zhù) - Shuttle.

27. 杵 Ch'u³ (chû) - Pestle, pounder; pound (– washing clothes).

28. 果 Kuo³ (guô) - Fruit, result; resolute; really, indeed.

29. 林 Lin² (lín) - Wood, forest(ry), grove; circle(s) (literary –).

锨 30. 枚 Hsien¹(xian) - Shovel.

31. 枚 Mei² (méi) - (N), a numerator.

32. 杪 Miao³ (miâo) - Tip of, end of (– year).

33. 杷 Pa² (pá) - Loquat (pípa). (See pí 35.)

34. 板 Pan³ (bân) - Board, block (chopping –); hard, stiff.

35. 枇 P'i² (pí) - Loquat (pípa). (See pá 33).

36. 杯 Pei¹ (bei) - Cup, trophy.

37. 柿 Shih⁴ (shì) - Persimmon.

38. 析 Hsi¹ (xi) - Divide (– property); analyze.

39. 松 Sung¹ (song) - Pine tree; loose(n); dried minced meat.

东 40. 東 Tung¹ (dong) - East(ern); master, owner, host.

41. 枉 Wang³ (wâng) - Crooked; do wrong (– to psn.); in vain.

42. 杳 Yao³ (yâo) - Dark, obscure; far away and out of sight.

43. 查⁵ Ch'a² (chá) - Examine, investigate; consult (– dictionary).

44. 柴 Ch'ai² (chái) - Firewood.

45. 柘 Che⁴ (zhè) - Silkworm oak.

46. 栅 Cha⁴ (zhà) - Palisade, railings (zhàlan).

47. 枳 Chih³ (zhî) - Chinese orange; shrub thorns.

48. 柱 Chu⁴ (zhù) - Post, pillar, column (mercury –).

49. 枵 Hsiao¹ (xiao) - Hollow tree stump; hollow, empty.

50. 染 Jan³ (rân) - Dye (v); catch (– disease), acquire (– habit).

51. 柑 Kan¹ (gan) - Mandarin orange.

52. 柔 Jou² (róu) - Soft(en); flexible, yielding; mild, gentle.

53. 枷 Chia¹ (jia) - Pillory; shackles (jiasuô).

54. 架 Chia⁴ (jià) - Frame; shelf; put up (– bridge); fight, quarrel.

55. 柬 Chien³ (jiân) - Card (invitation –); note, letter.

56. 柩 Chiu⁴ (jiù) - Coffin w. corpse in it.

57. 柯 K'o¹ (ke) - Stalk, branch; axe-handle.

58. 枯 K'u¹ (ku) - Withered (– plants); dried up, dry (– well).

59. 柳 Liu³ (liû) - Willow.

60. 某 Mou³ (môu) - Certain (– person, etc.); some (to – extent).

61. 柄 Ping³ (bîng) - Handle (knife –), stem; power, authority.

62. 柏 Pai³ (bâi) - Cedar, cypress.

63. 柁 T'o² (tuó) - Girder (steel –).

64. 柒 Ch'i¹ (qi) - Seven (elaborate form on checks, etc.).

65. 柞 Tso⁴ (zuò) - Oak.

66. 柚 Yu⁴ (yòu) - Shaddock, pomelo fruit.

67. 桌⁶ Cho¹ (zhuo) - Table (dining –); desk.

68. 株 Chu¹ (zhu) - Tree trunk; plant; (N) for plant, trees.

69. 核 Ho² (hé). Hu² (hú) - Stone (peach –); walnut (hétao); nucleus; examine.

70. 桓 Huan² (huán) - Stone tablet before grave.

71. 根 **Ken[1] (gen)** - Root, base, foundation; piece (– of string).

72. 校 **Hsiao[4] (xiào)** - School; field officer.

杰 73. 桀 **Chieh[2] (jié)** - Tyrannical; Emperor Chieh (Hsia dynasty).

74. 格 **Ke[2] (gé)** - Squares formed by crossed lines; pattern.

75. 框 **K'uang[1,4] (kuang, kuàng)** - Frame (n)(v).

76. 桂 **Kuei[4] (guì)** - Cassia, cinnamon, laurel, bay leaf trees.

77. 栗 **Li[4] (lì)** - Chestnut; shudder, tremble.

78. 案 **An[4] (àn)** - Table; case (murder –); record, file; proposal.

79. 桑 **Sang[1] (sang)** - Mulberry tree.

80. 桃 **T'ao[2] (táo)** - Peach.

81. 桐 **T'ung[2] (tóng)** - Tung, paulownia, phoenix trees.

82. 栽 **Tsai[1] (zai)** - Plant (– trees); impose; tumble, fall.

83. 桅 **Wei[2] (wéi)** - Ship's mast.

84. 梵[7] **Fan[4] (fàn)** - Brahma; Buddhist (– temple).

85. 械 **Hsieh[4] (xiè)** - Tool, instrument; weapon; shackles.

栀 86. 栀 **Chih[1] (zhi)** - Cape jasmine (zhizi).

枭 87. 枭 **Hsiao[1] (xiao)** - Owl; fierce, brave, formidable.

杆 88. 桿 **Kan[3] (gân)** - Handle (pen –). *Kan[1] (gan)** - Pole (flag–).

89. 梗 **Keng³ (gêng)** - Stem (flower –); straight(en); obstruct.

90. 梨 **Li² (lí)** - Pear.

91. 梁 **Liang² (liáng)** - Beam; bridge; ridge.

92. 梅 **Mei² (méi)** - Plum, prune.

93. 梆 **Pang³ (bang)** - Watchman's rattle.

94. 梢 **Shao¹ (shao)** - Tip (– of branch).

95. 梳 **Shu¹ (shu)** - Comb (v)(n).

96. 梭 **So¹ (suo)** - Shuttle.

97. 梯 **T'i¹ (ti)** - Ladder, stairs.

条 98. 條 **T'iao² (tiáo)** - Twig; strip; item; (N).

99. 桶 **T'ung³ (tông)** - Bucket, barrel, tub.

100. 梃 **T'ing³ (tîng)** - Stalk, stick, club.

101. 梧 **Wu² (wú)** - Chinese parasol tree **(wútóng)**.

栈 102. 棧 **Chan⁴ (zhàn)** - Warehouse, shed; inn.

103. 棹 **Cho¹ (zhuo)** - Same as 67.

植 104. 植 **Chih² (zhí)** - Plant (v), grow, cultivate.

105. 椅 **Yi³ (yî)** - Chair.

106. 棋 **Ch'i² (qí)** - Chess (Chinese –).

弃 107. 棄 Ch'i⁴ (qì) - Discard, throw away; abandon.

108. 棘 Chi² (jí) - Jujube tree; thorny bushes.

极 109. 極 Chi² (jí) - Extreme(ly); pole (South, North –).

110. 棐 Fei³ (fěi) - Chinese *torreya*, or its nuts.

111. 棺 Kuan¹ (guan) - Coffin.

112. 棍 Kun⁴ (gùn) - Stick, club; rascal.

113. 棉 Mien² (mián) - Cotton; cotton-padded.

114. 棒 Pang⁴ (bàng) - Stick, club; excellent.

115. 棱 Leng² (léng) - Edge; corrugation, ridge (– of washboard).

116. 棚 P'eng⁴ (péng) - Awning; booth, shed.

117. 森 Sen¹ (sen) - Overgrown w. trees; in large numbers; gloomy.

栖 118. 棲 Ch'i¹ (qi) - Perch (of birds); stay (qishen) (no place to –).

119. 棠 T'ang² (táng) - Birchleaf pear (tánglí).

120. 棵 K'o¹ (ke) - (N) for trees, plants, vegetables.

栋 121. 棟 Tung⁴ (dòng) - Ridge pole; beam, pillar.

枣 122. 棗 Tsao³ (zǎo) - Jujube, Chinese date.

123. 椒 Chiao¹ (jiao) - Pepper(y), hot (– food).

124. 棕 Tsung¹ (zong) - Palm tree, palm fibre; brown (zongsè).

125. 椊 Tsu³ (zû) - Plug, cork.

126. 楂 Cha¹ (zha) - Chinese hawthorn (shanzha).

127. 椹 Shen⁴ (shèn). Jen⁴(rèn) - Mulberry (shangshèn, -rèn).

128. 楮 Ch'u³ (chû) - Paper mulberry; paper.

129. 楚 Ch'u³ (chû) - Clear, distinct; pain, suffering.

130. 椿 Ch'un¹ (chun) - Chinese mahagony tree.

131. 椽 Ch'uan² (chuán) - Rafter.

檀 132. 楥 Hsüan⁴ (xuàn) - Shoe last; hat block; shape w. last, block.

133. 楦 Hsüan⁴ (xuàn) - Same as 132.

134. 楷 K'ai³ (kâi) - Model, pattern.

135. 楞 Leng² (léng) - Same as 115.

136. 楣 Mei² (méi) - Intel of a door.

137. 楠 Nan² (nán) - Cedar (wood).

138. 楫 Chi² (jí) - Paddle, oar.

139. 楸 Ch'iu¹ (qiu) - Chinese catalpa tree.

杨 140. 楊 Yang² (yáng) - Willow, willow and poplar (yángliû).

业 141. 業 Yeh⁴ (yè) - Business, profession; estate; already.

142. 椰 Yeh¹ (ye) - Coconut tree; coconut.

143. 榆 Yü[2] (yú) - Elm.

144. 榨[10] Cha[4] (zhà) - Press; extract oil, juice (from sugarcane), etc.

145. 榛 Chen[1] (zhen) - Hazel tree, hazel nut (zhenzi).

146. 槌 Ch'ui[2] (chuí) - Mallet, wooden hammer.

147. 槁 Kao[3] (gâo) - Dry, withered; rotten.

构 148. 構 Kou[4] (gòu) - Construct, build; compose (literary work).

149. 榔 Lang[2] (láng) - Hammer (lángtou); bulky (lángkang).

150. 榧 Fei[3] (fêi) - Same as 110.

151. 榴 Liu[2] (liú) - Pomegranate.

杠 152. 槓 Kang[4] (gàng) - Same as 15.

153. 榜 Pang[3] (bâng) - List of succesful candidates; notice.

154. 槊 Shuo[4] (shuò) - Ancient long spear.

155. 榭 Hsieh[4] (xiè) - Raised pavilion.

156. 槐 Huai[2] (huái) - Locust tree.

157. 榫 Sun[3] (sûn) - Tenon, dovetail (sûntòu).

158. 榻 T'a[4] (tà) - Long, narrow and low bed; couch.

枪 159. 槍 Ch'iang[1] (qiang) - Rifle, gun; spear, lance.

荣 160. 榮 Jung[2] (róng) - Flourish; glory, honor.

161. 榕 Jung² (róng) - Banyan tree.

162. 樟 ¹¹ Chang¹ (zhang) - Camphor tree.

枢 163. 樞 Shu¹ (shu) - Pivot, hub, centre.

桩 164. 樁 Chuang¹ (zhuang) - Pile, stake, post.

165. 樊 Fan² (fán) - Fence, hedge; cage.

166. 概 Kai⁴ (gài) - General (– view); outline; bearing, deportment.

楼 167. 樓 Lou² (lóu) - Multi-story house; floor (second –), story.

乐 168. 樂 Yüeh⁴ (yuè) - Music. Le⁴ (lè) - Happy, joyful; enjoy.

模 169. 模 Mo² (mó) - Pattern, model, standard.

标 170. 標 Piao¹ (biao) - Signal, mark (n)(v), label (n)(v).

171. 槽 Ts'ao² (cáo) - Trough; groove, slot.

桨 172. 槳 Chiang³ (jiâng) - Oar, paddle.

样 173. 樣 Yang⁴ (yàng) - Shape, appearance; kind (many –s); style.

174. 橙 ¹² Ch'eng² (chéng) - Orange; orange color.

横 175. 橫 Heng² (héng) - Horizontal. **Heng⁴ (hèng)** - Perverse.

桦 176. 樺 Hua⁴ (huà) - Birch.

177. 橄 Kan³ (gân) - Olive (**gânlân**).

机 178. 機 Chi¹ (ji) - Machine, abbrev. for aeroplane; opportunity.

179. 橇 Ch'iao¹ (qiao) - Mud shoe, sledge, sleigh.

180. 橡 Hsiang⁴ (xiàng) - Oak; rubber tree.

桥 181. 橋 Ch'iao² (qiáo) - Bridge.

182. 橛 Chüeh² (jué) - Short wooden stake; peg.

183. 橘 Chü² (jú) - Tangerine, mandarin orange.

朴 184. 樸 P'u³ (pû) - Plain, simple.

树 185. 樹 Shu⁴ (shù) - Tree, plant; set up, establish.

186. 樵 Ch'iao² (qiáo) - Collect firewood; firewood.

187. 樽 Tsun¹ (zun) - Ancient wine vessel.

丛 188. 欉 Ts'ung² (cóng) - Crowd together; grove; collection.

189. 檄 Hsi² (xí) - Call to arms.

190. 檢 Chien³ (jiân) - Check (up), examine; restrain oneself.

桧 191. 檜 Kuei⁴ (guì) - Chinese juniper.

檩 192. 檁 Lin³ (lîn) - Purlin of a roof.

193. 檀 T'an² (tán) - Sandalwood (tánxiang).

档 194. 檔 Tang⁴ (dàng) - Shelves, files; cross-piece; grade (high –).

墙 195. 檣 Ch'iang² (qiáng) - Mast.

196. 檐 Yen² (yán) - Eaves (of house), ledge, brim (– of hat), visor.

196A. 檬 Meng² (méng) - In (níngméng) - Lemon (See 197A).

棹 197. 櫂 Chao⁴ (zhào) - Oar; row a boat.

柠 197A. 檸 Ning² (níng) - In (níngméng) : Lemon. (See 196A).

槛 198. 檻 Chien⁴ (jiàn) - Railing, cage. K'an³ (kân) - Threshold.

柜 199. 櫃 Kuei⁴ (guì) - Cupboard, cabinet (kitchen -).

槟 200. 檳 Pin¹ (bin). Ping¹ (bing) - Betel palm (binglang).

橹 201. 櫓 Lu³ (lû) - Scull (oar used at stern), sweep (long oar).

椟 202. 櫝 Tu² (dú) - Casket, case, box.

橼 203. 櫞 Yüan² (yuán) - Citron (jûyuán) (xiangyuán).

苹 204. 櫇 P'ing² (píng). P'in² (pín) - Apple tree.* Apple (píngguô).
(See GRASS 160A.)

栏 205. 欄 Lan² (lán) - Railing; pen (animal -); column (news -).

樱 206. 櫻 Ying¹ (ying) - Cherry (yingtáo).

权 207. 權 Ch'üan² (quán) - Right (- to vote); authority; weight.

栾 208. 欒 Luan² (luán) - Goldenrain tree.

档 209. 檔 Tang⁴ (dàng) - Same as 194.

榄 210. 欖 Lan³ (lân) - Olive (gânlân).

TRIPOD 鼎

Picture of an ancient caldron with three legs, of which two only can be seen: 鼎 .

1. 鼎 Ting³ (dîng) - Ancient caldron with three legs.

TURTLE 黽

Representing the turtle, showing its body 𓆏 and its gills ○: 𓆐 .

黾 1. 黽   **Min³ (mĭn)** -Turtle, toad, frog; put forth effort, strive for.

鼋 2. 鼋   **Yüan² (yuán)** - Large sea turtle.

TWO 二

Two strokes, representing the number "two" : ⁼ .

1. 二   **Erh⁴ (èr)** - Two, second, No.2.

2. 于   **Yü² (yú)** - In, at, to, out of (– ignorance).

3. 云²   **Yün² (yún)** - Say. * Cloud.
     * If the character appears as the simplified form of 雲 .

4. 互   **Hu⁴ (hù)** - Mutual(ly), reciprocal, each other.

5. 井   **Ching³ (jĭng)** - Well; orderly, in good order (jĭngráu).

6. 五   **Wu³ (wŭ)** - Five.

亙 7. 亙⁴   **Ken⁴ (gèn). Keng⁴ (gèng)** - Extend; stretch.

8. 些⁵   **Hsieh¹ (xie)** - A few, some (do – work), a little (– smaller).

9. 況⁶   **K'uang⁴ (kuàng)** - Condition, situation; moreover.

亚 10. 亞   **Ya⁴ (yà)** - Ugly, inferior, second; short for "Asia".

U

USE 用

Representing an ancient bronze vessel, to be used when making offers to the ancestors: 貝 *. (Etymology unknown.)*

1. 用   **Yung⁴ (yòng)** - Use(ful), employ; hence, therefore.

2. 甩   **Shuai³ (shuâi)** - Swing (– back and forth); throw, cast.

3. 甫   **Fu³ (fù)** - Just, just now.

4. 甬   **Yung³ (yông)** - Path leading to the front of building.

宁 5. 甯   **Ning² (níng)** - Peaceful. **Ning⁴ (nìng)** - Would rather.

V

VALLEY 谷

A narrow opening (日 mouth) which is situated between two high mountain walls 彳彡 : 俗 .

1. 谷 **Ku³ (gŭ)** - Valley. * Cereals, grain.
   * Refers to the simplified form when it stands for 穀 .
2. 谿 **Huo¹ (huo)** - Break, give up. **Huo⁴ (huò)** - Open(-minded).

VAPOR 气

Representing vapors rising from the soil 气 .

气 1. 氣 **Ch'i⁴ (qì)** - Gas, air; breath; smell; weather; spirit.

VILLAGE 里

The fields of eight families $\frac{1|4|6}{3|5|8}$ *surrounding a common well* • *, and the soil to be cultivated (± earth, a Radical, see p. 34):* 甡 .

1. 里   Li³ (lǐ) - Village, neighborhood. * Lining, inside.

2. 厘   Li² (lí) - Unit of length, weight, etc.; fraction, the least.

3. 重   Chung⁴ (zhòng) - Heavy. Ch'ung² (chóng) - Repeat.

4. 野   Yeh³ (yě) - Countryside; wild (– cat), rude.

5. 量   Liang² (liáng) - Measure. Liang⁴ (liàng) - Quantity.

厘   6. 釐   Li² (lí) - Same as 2.

* Only if the character appears as the simplified form of 裏 .

W

Rapid Access *available* **WATER** 水 . 氵 . 氺

A stream ⎨ *with whirls of water* ⸙ : ⫶.

1. 水 **Shui³ (shuǐ)** - Water, liquid; general term for river, etc.

2. 永 ¹ **Yung³ (yǒng)** - Perpetually, eternally, forever, always.

3. 汁 ² **Chih¹ (zhī)** - Juice (orange –); extract (beef –).

泛 4. 氾 **Fan⁴ (fàn)** - Same as 8 and 38.

5. 求 **Ch'iu² (qíu)** - Request, beg; strive for, seek; demand.

6. 汀 **T'ing¹ (tīng)** - Spit of land; low level beach along river.

7. 池 ³ **Ch'ih² (chí)** - Pool (swimming –), pond; floor (dance –).

泛 8. 汛 **Fan⁴ (fàn)** - Same as 4 and 38.

9. 汛 **Hsün⁴ (xùn)** - Flood (spring –), high water.

10. 汗 **Han⁴ (hàn)** - Perspiration, sweat.

11. 汝 **Ju³ (rû)** - You (– people).

12. 江 **Chiang¹ (jiang)** - River.

13. 汐 **Hsi¹ (xi)** - Nighttide.

14. 污 **Wu¹ (wu)** - Dirty, filthy; defile.

15. 汙 **Wu¹ (wu)** - Same as 14 and 69.

16. 沉 **Ch'en² (chén)** - Sink, settle down; profound; heavy.

17. 冲 沖 **Ch'ung¹ (chong)** - Infuse (– tea); rinse; rush; develop (– film). **Ch'ung⁴ (chòng)** - Vigorously; strong (– smell).

18. 汲 **Chi² (jí)** - Draw (– water from well).

19. 决 決 **Chüeh² (jué)** - Determine, decide; certainly; execute.

20. 没 沒 **Mo⁴ (mò)** - Sink, submerge; overflow.

21. 沒 **Mei² (méi)** - No, not. **Mo⁴ (mò)** - Sink, submerge, overflow.

22. 沐 **Mu⁴ (mù)** - Wash (– one's hair), bathe **(mùyù)**.

23. 沙 **Sha¹ (sha)** - Sand; granulated; hoarse (– voice).

24. 汽 **Ch'i⁴ (qì)** - Steam, vapor, gas.

25. 汰 **T'ai⁴ (tài)** - Discard, eliminate; rinse, wash out.

26. 沌 **Tun⁴ (dùn)** - Chaos; innocent as a child **(hùndùn)**.

27. 沏 **Ch'i¹ (qi)** - Steep, infuse (– tea).

28. 沁 **Ch'in⁴ (qìn)** - Fathom (the depth of water); penetrate.

29. 汪 **Wang¹ (wang)** - Deep and vast (- ocean); bark.

30. 沃 **Wo⁴ (wò)** - Fertile; irrigate.

31. 汩 **Ku³ (gû)** - Gurgle (**gûgû**).

32. 沛 **P'ei⁴ (pèi)** - Copious, abundant, full of (- energy).

33. 沼⁵ **Chao³ (zhâo)** - Pond, pool.

34. 泅 **Ch'iu² (qiú)** - Swim.

35. 沾 **Chan¹ (zhan)** - Moisten, wet; stain(ed); benefit from.

36. 注 **Chu⁴ (zhù)** - Pour; concentrate; register(ed) (- trademark).

37. 法 **Fa³ (fã)** - Law; method.

38. 泛 **Fan⁴ (fàn)** - Float; flood (v); general (- term).

39. 治 **Chïh⁴ (zhì)** - Govern; cure; harness; punish; study (v).

40. 沸 **Fei⁴ (fèi)** - Boil, boiling (- point).

41. 河 **Ho² (hé)** - River.

42. 泄 **Hsieh⁴ (xiè)** - Leak (- secret), let out, vent (- anger).

43. 泔 **Kan¹ (gan)** - Swill, hogwash (**ganshuî**).

44. 泣 **Chi⁴ (jì). Yï⁴ (yì)** - Weep in silence.

45. 沽 **Ku¹ (gu)** - Buy; sell.

46. 泯 **Min³ (mǐn)** - Vanish, destroy; die out **(mǐnmiè).**

47. 沫 **Mo⁴ (mò)** - Foam, broth (– on beer).

48. 泥 **Ni² (ní)** - Mud; sauce (apple –). **Ni⁴ (nì)** - Plaster (v).

49. 泡 **P'ao⁴ (pào)** - Bubble; steep, soak.

50. 波 **Po¹ (bo)** - Waves.

51. 泊 **Po² (bó)** - Be at anchor, moor (– a ship).

52. 泗 **Szu⁴ (sì)** - Mucus.

53. 泰 **T'ai⁴ (tài)** - Safe, peaceful; extreme, most.

54. 泉 **Ch'üan³ (quán)** - Spring (hot –)

55. 沿 **Yen² (yán)** - Follow, along. **Yen⁴ (yàn)** - Edge (– of water).

56. 油 **Yu² (yóu)** - Oil; fat; sauce; paint **(yóuqi).**

57. 泳 **Yung³ (yông)** - Swim.

58. 洲 ^6 **Chou¹ (zhou)** - Continent; islet (in river).

59. 泭 **Fu⁴ (fú)** - Swim.

60. 洽 **Ch'ia⁴ (qià)** - Be in harmony; consult, discuss.

61. 洪 **Hung² (hóng)** - Big, great, vast; flood **(hóngshuǐ).**

62. 活 **Huo² (huó)** - Live, alive; save (– psn's life).

63. 派 **P'ai⁴ (pài)** - Faction, school (– of thought); appoint.

64. 洒 Sa³ (sâ) - Sprinkle, spill (– soup).

65. 洗 Hsi³ (xǐ) - Wash, bathe; develop (– film); cleanse (xǐdí).

泄 66. 洩 Hsieh⁴ (xiè) - Same as 42 and 116.

67. 洞 Tung⁴ (dòng) - Hole, cavity; clearly (dòngchá).

68. 津 Chin¹ (jin) - Ferry; ford; saliva, sweat; moist(en).

污 69. 洿 Wu¹ (wu) - Same as 14 and 15.

70. 洋⁷ Yang² (yáng) - Ocean; foreign, Western-style; modern.

71. 浮 Fou² (fú) - Float, swim; superficial; temporary; excessive.

72. 海 Hai³ hâi) - Sea; great number of people.

73. 浩 Hao⁴ (hào) - Great; vast, vast and numerous (hàofán).

74. 浣 Huan⁴ (huàn) - Wash, bathe.

75. 浪 Lang⁴ (làng) - Wave, billow; unrestrained.

76. 流 Liu² (liú) - Flow (v)(n); drifting; circulate.

77. 浦 P'u³ (pǔ) - River mouth.

78. 涉 She⁴ (shè) - Wade (through); experience; involve.

79. 消 Hsiao¹ (xiao) - Disappear, eliminate, while away (– time).

80. 涕 T'i⁴ (tì) - Tears, mucus from nose.

81. 涎 Hsien² (xián) - Saliva.

82. 浸 **Chin⁴ (jìn)** - Immerse, soak.

83. 浴 **Yü⁴ (yù)** - Bathe, bath (sun –).

84. 涌 **Yung³ (yông)** - Gush (oil –ed out), surge, emerge.
Same as 130.

85. 淌⁸ **T'ang³ (tâng)** - Drip (– sweat), shed (– tears).

86. 涵 **Han² (hán)** - Contain, bear; submerge; culvert (hándòng).

87. 涸 **Ho² (hé)** - Dry up, dried; exhausted.

88. 混 **Hun⁴ (hùn)** - Mix; confused; pass off as (– genuine).

泪 89. 淚 **Lei⁴ (lèi)** - Tears, teardrops.

涼 90. 涼 **Liang² (liáng)** - Cool; disappointed.

91. 淋 **Lin² (lín)** - Pour, drench.

沦 92. 淪 **Lun² (lún)** - Sink, fall into; reduced to; ruined; submerged.

93. 深 **Shen¹ (shen)** - Deep, dark (– red); late (– summer).

94. 淑 **Shu¹ (shu)** - Virtuous (– woman), fine, kind and gentle.

95. 淳 **Ch'un² (chún)** - Pure, honest.

96. 涮 **Shuan⁴ (shuàn)** - Rinse; instant-boil.

97. 淡 **Tan⁴ (dàn)** - Light (– yellow), weak (– tea); tasteless, dull.

98. 淘 **T'ao² (táo)** - Wash (– rice), clean out; naughty (táoqì).

99. 添 **T'ien¹ (tian)** - Add, increase.

100. 淀 Tien⁴ (diàn) - Precipitate, form sediment; shallow lake.

101. 淒 Ch'i¹ (qi) - Chilly, cold; sad, miserable.

浅 102. 淺 Ch'ien³ (qiân) - Shallow; easy; light (color); short (time).

净 103. 淨 Ching⁴ (jìng) - Pure, clean; complete(ly), net (- weight).

104. 清 Ch'ing¹ (qing) - Clear; quiet; completely; Ch'ing dynasty.

105. 涯 Ya² (yá) - Limit, margin; shore.

106. 淹 Yen¹ (yan) - Immerse, submerge.

107. 液 Yeh⁴ (yè) - Liquid, fluid, juice.

108. 淫 Yin² (yín) - Excessive (- rains); wanton, lewd, obscene.

109. 淤 Yü¹ (yu) - Silt, filled w. silt; stasis (of blood).

渊 110. 淵 Yüan¹ (yuan) - Deep pool; deep, profound (yuanshen).

111. 渣 Cha¹ (zha) - Dregs, residue; crumbs (bread -).

112. 湛 Chan⁴ (zhàn) - Deep, clear (crystal -).

113. 湖 Hu² (hú) - Lake.

浑 114. 渾 Hun² (hún) - Turbid, muddy (- water); foolish.

115. 港 Kang³ (gâng) - Port, harbor; short for Hongkong.

泄 116. 渫 Hsieh⁴ (xiè) - Same as 42 and 66.

减 117. 減 Chien³ (jiân) - Subtract, reduce, decrease.

118. 渴 K'e³ (kê) - Thirsty; yearn for, long for (**kêwàng**).

119. 渠 Ch'ü² (qú) - Ditch, channel, gutter.

120. 渺 Miao³ (miâo) - Vast (– ocean); vague; tiny, negligible.

汤 121. 湯 T'ang¹ (tang) - Hot water; soup, broth; decoction.

122. 溲 Sou¹ (sou) - Soak; urinate.

123. 渡 Tu⁴ (dù) - Cross (– river); ferry.

测 124. 測 Ts'e⁴ (cè) - Survey, measure (**cèdù**).

凑 125. 湊 Ts'ou⁴ (còu) - Put together; happen by chance.

126. 溫 Wen¹ (wen) - Warm (up), lukewarm; gentle; kind, cordial; revise, review.

涡 127. 渦 Wo¹ (wo) - Whirlpool, eddy.

洇 128. 湮 Yin¹ (yin) - Soak, spread and sink (of ink on paper).

129. 游 Yu² (yóu) - Swim; travel, wander, roam.

涌 130. 湧 Yung³ (yông) - Same as 84.

10

准 131. 準 Chun³ (zhûn) - Allow; in accordance with; standard, norm; accurate; certainly; quasi-, para– (–military).

滑 132. 滑 Hua² (huá) - Slippery, smooth; slip, slide.

汇 133. 匯 Hui⁴ (huì) - Gather, collect(ion); remit (– money).

溷 134. 溷 Hun⁴ (hùn) - Dirty; turbid.

沟 135. 溝 Kou¹ (gou) - Ditch, trench, groove; ravine.

136. 溪 Hsi[1] (xi) - Creek, brook, rivulet.

137. 溜 Liu[1] (liu) - Glide; smooth. Liu[4] (liù) - Flow of water.

灭 138. 滅 Mieh[4] (miè) - Extinguish, exterminate, destroy; drown.

139. 溟 Ming[2] (míng) - Sea.

140. 溺 Ni[4] (nì) - Drown (- female infants); addicted to.

141. 溥 P'u[3] (pû) - Vast, broad; common, universal.

湿 142. 溼 Shih[1] (shi) - Wet, damp.

143. 溯 Su[4] (sù) - Go against stream; trace back, recall.

144. 滔 T'ao[1] (tao) - Inundate, flood; torrential (taotao).

145. 滋 Tzu[1] (zi) - Grow, multiply; spurt, burst.

146. 滓 Tsu[3] (zî) - Dregs, residue.

147. 溢 Yi[4] (yì) - Overflow, spill; excessive (- praise).

148. 源 Yüan[2] (yuán) - Source; income; cause (- of disease).

涨 149. 漲[11] Chang[3] (zhâng) - Rise. Chang[4] (zhàng) - Swell, expand.

滞 150. 滯 Chih[4] (zhì) - Stagnant, stoppage; unsaleable (- goods).

汉 151. 漢 Han[4] (hàn) - Chinese (adj); Han dynasty; male adult.

152. 溉 Kai[4] (gài) - Irrigate, water (- flowers), wash.

滚 153. 滾 Kun[3] (gûn) - Roll; get away; boil(ing).

154. 漏 Lou⁴ (lòu) - Divulge, leak out; missing (line is –).

155. 漓 Li² (lí) - (línlí) - Dripping wet; free from inhibition.

涟 156. 漣 Lien² (lián) - Ripples; unceasing flow (– of tears).

满 157. 滿 Man³ (mân) - Full, fill; expire; complete(ly); complacent.

158. 漫 Man⁴ (màn) - Overflow, flood (v); everywhere.

漠 159. 漠 Mo⁴ (mò) - Desert; indifferent.

沤 160. 漚 Ou⁴ (òu) - Soak, steep (v).

161. 漂 P'iao¹ (piao) - Float. P'iao³ (piâo) - Bleach; rinse.

渗 162. 滲 Shen⁴ (shèn) - Ooze (v), seep (v).

163. 漱 Shu⁴ (shù) - Gargle, rinse (– mouth).

164. 漩 Hsüan² (xuán) - Eddy, whirlpool.

165. 滴 Ti¹ (di) - Drip(ping), drops.

卤 166. 滷 Lu³ (lû) - Stew (in soy sauce), thick gravy.

167. 漕 Ts'ao² (cáo) - Water transport (esp. of grain).

浆 168. 漿 Chiang¹ (jiang) -Thick liquid; starch (v).Chiàng (jiàng) - Thick (– porridge).

渐 169. 漸 Chien⁴ (jiàn) - Gradually, step by step.

沪 170. 滬 Hu⁴ (Hù) - Short for Shanghai.

171. 漆 Ch'i¹ (qi) - Paint, lacquer, varnish.

172. 演 Yen³ (yân) - Perform, act, play (- role).

渔 173. 漁 Yü² (yú) - Fish (v), fishing (- village).

渍 174. 漬 Tzu⁴ (zì) - Steep, soak; stain (tea -s).

175. 潮 Ch'ao² (cháo) - Tide, upsurge; moist, damp.

176. 澈 Ch'e⁴ (chè) - Clear (as water), limpid.

177. 澄 Ch'eng² (chéng) - Clear. Teng⁴ (dèng) - Settle (of liquid).

溃 178. 潰 K'uei⁴ (kuì) - Burst (of dyke), break through; fester (kuìlàn).

浇 179. 澆 Chiao¹ (jiao) - Sprinkle water on, irrigate (jiaoguàn).

洁 180. 潔 Chieh² (jié) - Clean, neat.

涧 181. 澗 Chien⁴ (jiàn) - Ravine, gully.

182. 潦 Lao³ (lǎo) - Same as 184.

潜 183. 潛 Ch'ien³ (qián) - Latent, hidden; stealthily, secretly.

涝 184. 澇 Lao⁴ (lào) - Waterlogged (- areas), flooded.

泼 185. 潑 P'o¹ (po) - Sprinkle, spill (- soup); rude and unreasonable.

涩 186. 澀 Se⁴ (sè) - Astringent; hard-going, difficult (- reading).

187. 潲 Shao⁴ (shào) - Slant in (of rain); sprinkle; hogwash.

滩 188. 潬 T'an¹ (tan) - Beach, sandbank, shoal.

189. 潭 T'an² (tán) - Deep pool, big pond.

润 190. 潤 Jun⁴ (rùn) - Moist(en), lubricate; profit, benefit.

浊 191. 濁 Cho² (zhuó) - Muddy; deep and raucous (– voice); chaotic.

浣 192. 澣 Huan⁴ (huàn) - Same as 74.

193. 激 Chi¹ (ji) - Arouse, excite; violent; chill (– watermelon).

194. 澳 Ao⁴ (aò) - Bay, cove. (Aò) - Aomen (Macao).

浓 195. 濃 Nung² (nóng) - Dense, thick; strong (– liking).

涩 196. 澀 Se⁴ (sè) - Same as 186.

197. 澹 Tan⁴ (dàn) - Tranquil, placid.

198. 澡 Tsao³ (zǎo) - Bath, bathe.

泽 199. 澤 Tse² (zé) - Marsh, pool; lustre (of metals).

200. 濯 Cho² (zhuó) - Wash (– one's feet).

201. 濠 Hao² (háo) - Moat, ditch, trench.

202. 濡 Ju² (rú) - Immerse, moisten; linger.

滥 203. 濫 Lan⁴ (làn) - Overflow; excessive; indiscriminate.

204. 濛 Meng² (méng) - Drizzly, misty.

泞 205. 濘 Ning⁴ (nìng) - Muddy (nínìng).

滨 206. 濱 Pin¹ (bin) - Shore (sea–), bank (river–); be close to.
Same as 215.

湿 207. 濕 Shih¹ (shi) - Wet, damp.

涛 208. 濤 T'ao¹ (tao) - Great waves, billows.

济 209. 濟 Chi⁴ (jì) - Cross river; help. Chi³ (jǐ) - Many (jǐjǐ).

滤 210. 濾¹⁵ Lü⁴ (lü) - Strain, filter.

211. 瀑 P'u⁴ (pù) - Waterfall.

泻 212. 瀉 Hsieh⁴ (xiè) - Flow rapidly; have diarrhea.

渎 213. 瀆 Tu² (dú) - Show disrespect; ditch, drain.

溅 214. 濺 Chien⁴ (jiàn) - Splash, spatter.

濒 215. 瀕¹⁶ Pin¹ (bin) - Same as 206.

沥 216. 瀝¹⁷ Li⁴ (lì) - Drip; trickle; drop (n).

澜 217. 瀾 Lan² (lán) - Great waves, billows.

218. 灌¹⁸ Kuan⁴ (guàn) - Irrigate; pour, fill.

洒 219. 灑¹⁹ Sa³ (sâ) - Sprinkle, spill (– soup).

滩 220. 灘 T'an¹ (tan) - Same as 188.

221. 灒 Tsan⁴ (zàn) - Spatter, splash, scatter.

湾 222. 灣²² Wan¹ (wan) - Bend (river–); gulf, bay; moor (– ship).

WHEAT 麥

A plant (米 tree) with ears of grain ⹁⹁, and 夂 (a man 刀) who advances in spite of an obstacle ╲ , indicating the relentless development of the grain): 麥 .

麦 1. 麥 **Mai⁴ (mài)** - Wheat; common name for wheat, barley, etc.

麸 2. 麸 **Fu¹ (fu)** - Wheat bran.

曲 3. 麯 **Ch'ü¹ (qu)** - Leaven, yeast. *Crooked; wrong. **Chü³ (qū)** - Song.

4. 麴 **Ch'ü¹ (qu)** - Same as 3.

面 5. 麵 **Mien⁴ (miàn)** - Wheat flour, flour; noodles.

WHITE 白

The sun ☉ just rising above the horizon, causing the sky to become "white": 白 .

1. 白 **Pai² (bái)** - White; blank; pure; in vain, useless.

2. 百 **Pai³ (bâi)** - Hundred; numerous.

3. 皃 **Mao⁴ (mào)** - Looks (good –), appearance.

4. 皂 **Tsao¹ (zào)** - Black; soap.

5. 的 **Ti⁴ (dì)** - Bull's eye, target.

6. 皇 **Huang² (huáng)** - Sovereign, ruler, emperor, king.

7. 皆 **Chieh¹ (jie)** - All, each and every.

8. 皈 **Kuei¹ (gui)** - Religious ceremony to proclaim sb. member.

9. 皎 Chiao³ (jiâo) - Clear, bright (– moon).

10. 皓 Hao⁴ (hào) - White, bright (– moon).

11. 皖 Huan³ (huân) - Bright, luminous, glorious.

12. 皦 Chiao³ (jiâo) - Same as 9.

WIND 風

Motion of air 冂 and an insect 虫. (It was believed that insects were born when the wind blew.): 風.

风 1. 風 Feng¹ (feng) - Wind; style, custom; scene(ry); news.

刮 2. 颳 Kua¹ (gua) - Scrape; smear with; extort; blow (wind –s).

扬 3. 颺 Yang² (yáng) - Raise; toss, throw up; make known.

飀 4. 飀 Liu² (liú) - Sighing of wind.

飘 5. 飄 P'iao¹ (piao) - Float; flutter (of flags).

WINE JUG 酉

Picture of a wine jar 酉.

1. 酉 Yu³ (yôu) - Tenth (10th); 5.00 to 7.00 pm (yôushí).

2. 酋 Chiu² (qiú) - Chieftain, tribal chief.

3. 酊 Ting¹ (ding) -Tincture. Ting³ (dîng) - Drunk (mîngdîng).

4. 酌 Cho² (zhuó) - Pour out wine; drink; consider.

5. 配 P'ei⁴ (pèi) - Mate (of animals), match, mix; qualified.

6. 酒 Chiu³ (jiû) - Wine, liquor, spirits.

7. 酖 Chen⁴ (zhèn) - Given to drink, fond of wine.

8. 酣 Han¹ (han) - Drink to heart's content; merry from wine.

9. 酥 Su¹ (su) - Crispy, crunchy; weak (- limbs); shortbread.

10. 酡 T'o² (tuó) - Flushed with wine (of face).

11. 酬 Ch'ou² (chóu) - Toast w. wine; reward; entertain (- friends).

12. 酩 Ming³ (mîng) - Drunk (mîngdîng).

13. 酵 Chiao³ (jiào) - Ferment, yeast, leaven.

14. 酷 K'u⁴ (kù) - Cruel (- punishment), oppressive; extreme(ly).

15. 酸 Suan¹ (suan) - Acid (acetic -); sour; grieved; ache.

16. 醅 P'ei¹ (pei) - Unstrained liquor.

17. 醇 Ch'un² (chún) - Pure and rich wine; pure, unmixed.

18. 醋 Ts'u⁴ (cù) - Vinegar.

19. 醉 Tsui⁴ (zuì) - Drunk, tipsy; liquor-saturated (- crab).

20. 醃 Yen¹ (yan) - Preserve in salt, salted (- fish, meat).

21. 醒 Hsing³ (xîng) - Sober up, wake up; come to realize (xîngwù).

22. 醡 Cha⁴ (zhà) - Press to extract oil, juice (from sugar), etc.

23. 醜 Ch'ou³ (chôu) - Ugly, shameful, disgraceful.

丑

医 24. 醫 **Yi¹ (yī)** - Physician, doctor; cure, medicine (Chinese –).

25. 醪 **Lao² (láo)** - Undecanted wine (w. dregs unremoved).

酱 26. 醬 **Chiang⁴ (jiàng)** - Thick soy sauce, sauce (tomato –); jam (apple –).

27. 醭 **Pu² (bú)** - Mould on soy sauce, vinegar, etc.

28. 醮 **Chiao⁴ (jiào)** - Libation at wedding; remarry (of woman).

29. 醺 **Hsün¹ (xun)** - Intoxicated, drunk.

酿 30. 釀 **Niang⁴ (niàng)** - Ferment, brew; wine; lead to (– disaster).

衅 31. 釁 **Hsin⁴ (xìn)** - Smear w. blood (ceremonial); feud, quarrel.

酽 32. 釅 **Yen⁴ (yàn)** - Strong (– tea, etc.).

WINE VESSEL 㔭

A vessel filled with grain ※ and a ladle 〈 to remove the wine: 㔭.

郁 1. 鬱 **Yü⁴ (yù)** - Strongly fragrant; luxuriant; depressed.

WINGS 羽

Picture of a pair of wings: 羽羽.

1. 羽 **Yü³ (yû)** - Wings, feathers, plumes.

2. 翅 **Ch'ih⁴ (chì)** - Wing, fin (shark's –s).

3. 翁 **Weng¹ (weng)** - Old man; father; father-in-law.

4. 翎 **Ling² (líng)** - Plume, feather, quill.

习 5. 習 Hsi² (xí) - Practice; accustomed to, habit.

6. 翌 Yi⁴ (yì) - Next (- year).

7. 翕 Hsi¹ (xi) - Amiable and compliant; roll up, shut.

8. 翔 Hsiang² (xiáng) - Soar, hover over.

9. 翡 Fei³ (fēi) - Kingfisher; jadeite (fēicuì).

10. 翠 Ts'ui⁴ (cuì) - Kingfisher; emarald green; jadeite (fēicuì).

11. 翩 P'ien¹ (pian) - Flutter (butterflies -); elegant.

12. 翰 Han⁴ (hàn) - Writing brush; writing, letter.

13. 翳 Yi⁴ (yì) - Screen made of feathers; nebula, cataract.

14. 翼 Yi⁴ (yì) - Wings (of birds, aeroplane, etc.); assist (- ruler).

15. 翻 Fan¹ (fan) - Capsize; cross (- mountain); translate; reverse.

翘 16. 翹 Ch'iao² (qiáo) - Raise (- head); warped; eminent.
Ch'iao⁴ (qiào) - Turn upwards.

17. 耀 Yao⁴ (yào) - Shine, dazzle; boast.

WOMAN 女

Picture of a woman �.

1. 女 Nü³ (nǚ) - Woman, female; girl, daughter.

2. 奶 Nai³ (nâi) - Breasts (woman's); milk; breast-feed.

3. 奴 Nu² (nú) - Slave, enslave; bond servant.

4. 妁 Cho⁴ (zhuò) - Go-between, match-maker.

5. 妃 Fei¹ (fei) - Emperor's concubine, prince's wife; light pink.

6. 好 Hao³ (hâo) - Good, fine; friendly. Hao⁴ (hào) - Fond of.

7. 如 Ju² (rú) - According to, like (– lion); as good as; if.

8. 奸 Chien¹ (jian) - Wicked, treacherous; traitor.

9. 妄 Wang⁴ (wàng) - Absurd, proposterous, presumptious.

10. 妝 Chuang¹ (zhuang) - Make up (apply –); trousseau. 妆

11. 妨 Fang¹ (fang) - Harm. Fang² (fáng) - Hinder, obstruct.

12. 妓 Chi⁴ (jì) - Prostitute.

13. 妗 Chin⁴ (jìn) - Aunt (wife of mother's brother).

14. 妙 Miao⁴ (miào) - Wonderful, excellent; ingenious; subtle.

15. 妞 Niu¹ (niu) - Girl. 妞

16. 妣 Pi³ (bî) - Deceased mother (my –).

17. 妥 T'o³ (tuô) - Appropriate, proper; ready, settled.

18. 妒 Tu⁴ (dù) - Jealous, envious.

19. 妖 Yao¹ (yao) - Goblin, evil spirit; evil, bewitching.

20. 妍 Yen² (yán) - Beautiful.

21. 妯 Chou² (zhóu) - Sister-in-law (zhóulǐ).

22. 姑 Ku¹ (gu) - Aunt (father's sister).

23. 妹 Mei⁴ (mèi) - Younger sister.

24. 姆 Mu³ (mû) - Nanny, children's nurse (bâomû).

25. 妮 Ni¹ (ni) - Girl, lass (nizi).

26. 始 Shih³ (shî) - Start, beginning; only then.

27. 妻 Ch'i¹ (qi) - Wife (qizi).

28. 姐 Chieh³ (jiê) - Elder sister; sister; young woman.

29. 妾 Ch'ieh⁴ (qiè) - Concubine.

30. 姊 Tzu³ (zî) - Elder sister; sister.

31. 委 Wei³ (wêi) - Entrust; shift; true. Wei¹(wei) - Halfheartedly.

32. 姓 Hsing⁴ (xìng) - Family (clan) name, surname.

33. 姪 Chih² (zhi) - Niece; nephew.

34. 姨 Yi² (yí) - Aunt (mother's sister).

35. 姜 Chiang¹ (jiang) - Ginger.

奸 36. 姦 **Chien¹ (jian)** - Wicked; traitor; illicit sexual relation, adultery **(jianyín)**.

37. 姥 **Lao³ (lâo)** - Grandma (maternal grandmother) **(lâolao)**.

38. 姿 **Tzu¹ (zi)** - Looks (good –), appearance; gesture, posture.

39. 娃 **Wa² (wá)** - Baby **(wáwa)**.

40. 威 **Wei¹ (wei)** - Power; threaten by force **(weibi)**.

41. 姻 **Yin¹ (yin)** - Marriage; relation by marriage.

42. 娌 **Li³ (lî)** - Sisters-in-law (wives of brothers) **(zhóuli)**. ⁷

43. 娘 **Niang² (niáng)** - Mother, ma; young woman.

44. 娓 **Wei³ (wêi)** - Tirelessly (talk –).

45. 娣 **Ti⁴ (dì)** - Younger sister; bridesmaid.

46. 娠 **Shen¹ (shen)** - Pregnancy **(rènshen)**.

47. 娩 **Mien³ (miân)** - Childbirth.

娱 48. 娱 **Yü² (yú)** - Amuse, joy.

49. 娼 **Ch'ang¹ (chang)** - Prostitute. ⁸

妇 50. 婦 **Fu⁴ (fù)** - Woman, married woman; wife.

51. 婚 **Hun¹ (hun)** - Wed, marry; wedding, marriage **(hunyin)**.

52. 婪 **Lan² (lán)** - Greedy **(tanlán)**.

53. 婢 **Pei⁴ (bi)** - Slave girl, maid servant.

54. 婊 Piao³ (biâo) - Prostitute, whore (biâozi).

55. 婆 P'o² (pó) - Old woman, mother-in-law (husband's mother).

56. 娶 Ch'ü³ (qû) - Marry (take wife).

57. 婉 Wan³ (wân) - Obliging, gentle (– words) (wânzhuân).

58. 媛 Yüan² (yuán) [9] - Charming, bewitching, beautiful; beauty.

59. 媒 Mei² (méi) - Matchmaker, intermediary, medium (méijiè).

60. 媚 Mei⁴ (mèi) - Fawn on, flatter; charming, fascinating.

61. 嫂 Sao³ (sâo) - Sister-in-law (elder brother's wife) (sâozi).

62. 婷 T'ing² (tíng) - Graceful, elegant.

63. 婿 Hsü⁴ (xù) - Son-in-law; husband.

64. 嫌 Hsien² (xián) [10] - Suspicion; grudge; dislike.

65. 嫁 Chia⁴ (jià) - Marry (take husband); shift (– blame).

愧 66. 媿 K'uei⁴ (kuì) - Conscience-stricken, ashamed.

妈 67. 媽 Ma¹ (ma) - Mother, ma, mummy; addres to elder woman.

68. 媳 Hsi² (xí) - Daughter-in-law.

69. 嫉 Chi² (jí) - Be jealous, be envious; hate.

媪 70. 媼 Ao³ (âo) - Old woman.

71. 嫠 Li² (lí) [11] - Widow.

72. 嫩 **Nen⁴ (nèn)** - Delicate; light (– yellow); inexperienced.

73. 嫖 **P'iao² (piáo)** - Lewd, wanton; visit prostitutes.

74. 嫦 **Ch'ang² (cháng)** - Woman in the moon (legend) **(Cháng'é)**.

75. 嫡 **Tî² (dí)** - One's proper wife (not concubine); blood relative.

76. 嬉 **Hsi¹ (xi)** - Play, have fun. [12]

娴 77. 嫻 **Hsien² (xián)** - Refined; skilled (– in archery).

娇 78. 嬌 **Chiao¹ (jiao)** - Lovely, delicate; pamper, spoil.

奶 79. 嬭 **Nai³ (nâi)** - Same as 2. [14]

嫔 80. 嬪 **P'in² (pín)** - Emperor's concubine; woman court attendant.

婴 81. 嬰 **Ying¹ (ying)** - Baby, infant.

婶 82. 嬸 **Shen³ (shên)** - Aunt (father's younger brother's wife). [15]

娘 83. 孃 **Niang² (niáng)** - Mother, ma, mum. [17]

84. 孀 **Shuang¹ (shuang)** - Widow.

娈 85. 孌 **Lüan² (luán)** - Beautiful, fine. [19]

WORDS 言

The tongue 舌 and words (=sound waves) being produced by it: 言.

1. 言 Yen² (yán) - Word(s), speech: speak, say, talk.

讣 2. 訃 Fu⁴ (fù) - Obituary, death notice.

计 3. 計 Chi⁴ (jì) - Calculate, count; plan, scheme; gauge (rain –).

4. 訇 Hung¹ (hong) - Loud stunning noise (– of drums).

订 5. 訂 Ting⁴ (dìng) - Conclude; subscribe to; revise; put together.

训 6. 訓 Hsün⁴ (xùn) - Teach, train; example, model.

讯 7. 訊 Hsün⁴ (xùn) - Interrogate; dispatch, report, news.

记 8. 記 Chi⁴ (jì) - Remember, keep in mind; record (v)(n).

讦 9. 訐 Chieh² (jié) - Expose sb's past misdeeds.

讫 10. 訖 Ch'i⁴ (qì) - Settled (– in full); end (the –).

讪 11. 訕 Shan⁴ (shàn) - Mock, ridicule; embarrassed.

讨 12. 討 T'ao³ (tǎo) - Send punitive action; ask for; marry a woman.

托 13. 託 T'o¹ (tuo) - Lean on (to); entrust.

访 14. 訪 Fang³ (fǎng) - Visit (– friend); inquire about, search for.

许 15. 許 Hsü³ (xǔ) - Praise; permit; maybe; about, circa; a little.

诀 16. 訣 Chüeh² (jué) - Bid farewell; key to success.

讹 17. 訛 O² (é) - Erroneous; extort, blackmail.

讠内 18. 訥 Ne⁴ (nè) - Speak cautiously; stammer.

设 19. 設 She⁴ (shè) - Set up, establish, suppose, if.

讼 20. 訟 Sung⁴ (sòng) - Litigate; dispute, argue.

讶 21. 訝 Ya⁴ (yà) - Be surprised, wonder.

诈 22. 詐 Cha⁴ (zhà)⁵ - Cheat, swindle; pretend, feign.

诊 23. 診 Chen³ (zhên) - Examine (patient); diagnose (zhénbìng).

诏 24. 詔 Chao⁴ (zhào) - Proclaim; imperial edict (zhàoshu).

证 25. 証 Cheng⁴ (zhèng) - Prove, demonstrate; proof; certificate.

诅 26. 詛 Tsu³ (zû) - Curse (zûzhòu).

注 27. 註 Chu⁴ (zhù) - Pour; concentrate; stakes (gambling –).

讵 28. 詎 Chü⁴ (jù) - But, however.

29. 詈 Li⁴ (lì) - Revile, scold.

评 30. 評 P'ing² (píng) - Comment, criticize; judge (v).

诉 31. 訴 Su⁴ (sù) - Tell; complain, accuse; appeal (– to higher court).

诋 32. 詆 Ti³ (dî) - Slander, defame.

词 33. 詞 Tzu² (cí) - Words, phrases; classical poetical composition.

咏 34. 詠 Yung³ (yòng) - Sing, chant; hum.

诧 35. 詫 Ch'a⁴ (chà)⁶ - Be surprised.

36. 詹 Chan¹(zhan) - Rave, be delirious.

诛 37. 誅 Chu¹ (zhu) - Execute criminal; punish.

话 38. 話 Hua⁴ (huà) - Words, talk, speak about.

诩 39. 詡 Hsü³ (xû) - Boast, brag.

诣 40. 詣 Yi⁴ (yì) - Pay visit; scholarly achievement.

该 41. 該 Kai¹ (gai) - Ought to, should; that, the said (– psn.).

诘 42. 詰 Chieh² (jié) - Interrogate.

夸 43. 誇 K'ua¹ (kua) - Exaggerate; boast; praise.

诓 44. 誆 K'uang¹ (kuang) - Deceive, cheat.

诡 45. 詭 Kuei³ (guî) - Cunning, weird.

诙 46. 諛 Hui¹ (hui) - Humorous (huixié).

诔 47. 誄 Lei³ (lêi) - Eulogize, praise very highly.

诗 48. 詩 Shih¹ (shi) - Poetry, poem, verse.

试 49. 試 Shih⁴ (shi) - Try, test; examination (oral –).

详 50. 詳 Hsiang² (xiáng) - Detailed, in detail (speak –); details.

询 51. 詢 Hsün² (xún) - Inquire.

诠 52. 詮 Ch'üan² (quán) - Explanatory notes (quánshì).

志 53. 誌⁷ Chih⁴ (zhì) - Annals; keep in mind *Will, aspiration, ideal (high –s).

* Refers only to the simplified form, i.e. when it is a traditional form.

诚 54. 誠 **Cheng²** (chéng) - Sincere, honest; really, actually.

诲 55. 誨 **Hui⁴** (huì) - Teach, instruct.

认 56. 認 **Jen⁴** (rèn) - Know; recognize; admit.

诰 57. 誥 **Kao⁴** (gào) - Order, command; imperial mandate.

诫 58. 誡 **Chieh⁴** (jiè) - Warn, admonish; commandment (Ten C-s).

诳 59. 誆 **K'uang²** (kuáng) - Lies, falsehood (**kuángyû**).

60. 誓 **Shih⁴** (shì) - Swear; oath, pledge, vow.

说 61. 說 **Shuo¹** (shuo) - Speak; explain. **Shui⁴** (shuì) - Persuade.

诵 62. 誦 **Sung⁴** (sòng) - Recite, read aloud, chant.

诞 63. 誕 **Tan⁴** (dàn) - Birth(day); absurd; brag.

诮 64. 誚 **Ch'iao⁴** (qiào) - Censure, blame; satirize, ridicule.

诬 65. 誣 **Wu¹** (wu) - Accuse falsely (**wugào**).

误 66. 誤 **Wu⁴** (wù) - Mistake; miss (- train); by accident.

诱 67. 誘 **Yu⁴** (yòu) - Guide, induce; lure, seduce.

语 68. 語 **Yü³** (yû) - Language, words; speak.

诤 69. 諍⁸ **Cheng⁴** (zhèng) - Admonish, criticize sb's fault.

谄 70. 諂 **Ch'an³** (chân) - Flatter, fawn on (**chânmèi**).

谆 71. 諄 **Chun¹** (zhun) - Earnestly and tirelessly.

谊 72. 誼 Yi⁴ (yì) - Friendship.

诿 73. 諉 Wei³ (wêi) - Shirk, evade; put blame on other psn.

课 74. 課 K'e⁴ (kè) - Course, lesson (- one); class; levy (-taxes).

谅 75. 諒 Liang⁴ (liàng) - Forgive; suppose (I - you agree).

论 76. 論 Lun⁴ (lùn) - Discuss, talk about; essay; regard as.

谁 77. 誰 Shui² (shuí) - Who; someone, anyone.

谈 78. 談 T'an² (tán) - Talk, chat, converse; conversation, chit chat.

调 79. 調 Tiao⁴ (diào) - Transfer. T'iao² (tiáo) - Mix (well); mediate.

诹 80. 諏 Tsou¹ (zou) - Choose, select; consult (with).

请 81. 請 Ch'ing³ (qǐng) - Request, invite; please (- sit down).

谀 82. 諛 Yü² (yú) - Flatter(ing) (- words).

诸 83. 諸⁹ Chu¹ (zhu) - All, various; put into practice.

讽 84. 諷 Feng³ (fêng) - Satirize; chant, intone.

喧 85. 誼 Hsüan¹ (xuan) - Brawl, quarrel noisily; noisy.

谐 86. 諧 Hsieh² (xíe) - Harmonize; come to agreement.

谖 87. 諼 Hsüan¹ (xuan) - Cheat, swindle, deceive; forget.

讳 88. 諱 Hui⁴ (huì) - Avoid as taboo; taboo.

谏 89. 諫 Chien⁴ (jiàn) - Remonstrate, admonish.

谋 90. **謀** Mo² (móu) - Plan; work for; consultation (without -).

诶 91. **諳** An¹ (an) - Skilled in.

诺 92. **諾** No⁴ (nuò) - Promise; consent; yes.

谝 93. **諞** P'ien³ (piân) - Show off (- one's skill).

谥 94. **諡** Shih⁴ (shì) - Posthumous title.

谛 95. **諦** Ti⁴ (dì) - Carefully (listen -); examine closely; truth.

咨 96. **諮** Tzu¹ (zi) - Consult, seek advice from (zixún).

谓 97. **謂** Wei⁴ (wèi) - Say, call; meaning.

谒 98. **謁** Yeh⁴ (yè) - Visit a superior.

谚 99. **諺** Yen⁴ (yàn) - Proverb, common saying.

谕 100. **諭** Yü⁴ (yù) - Instruct, tell.

谎 101. **謊**[10] Huang³ (huâng) - Lie, falsehood.

讲 102. **講** Chiang³ (jiâng) - Speak (- English); discuss, explain.

谦 103. **謙** Ch'ien¹ (qian) - Humble, modest.

谜 104. **謎** Mi² (mí) - Riddle, puzzle: mystery.

谤 105. **謗** Pang⁴ (bàng) - Slander, speak ill of, defame.

谥 106. **諡** Shih⁴ (shì) - Same as 94.

谢 107. **謝** Hsieh⁴ (xiè) - Thank; decline; wither.

誉 108. 謄 T'eng² (téng) - Copy, transcribe.

诌 109. 謅 Chou¹ (zhou) - Fabricate, make up story.

谣 110. 謠 Yao² (yáo) - Rhymes, ballad; rumor.

谨 111. 謹 Chin³ (jǐn) - Careful, cautious; sincere (- thanks). [11]

谩 112. 謾 Man² (mán) - Deceive. Man⁴ (màn) - Disrespectful, rude.

谬 113. 謬 Miu⁴ (miù) - Erroneous, wrong (- view), false (- report).

谟 114. 謨 Mo² (móu) - Plan (well-organized -).

讴 115. 謳 Ou¹ (ou) - Sing; ballads.

谪 116. 謫 Chai¹ (zhai) - Reproach, blame; fault, error.

证 117. 證 Cheng⁴ (zhèng) - Same as 25. [12]

哗 118. 譁 Hua² (huá) - Noise, clamor.

讥 119. 譏 Chi¹ (ji) - Ridicule, mock; satirize.

谲 120. 譎 Chüeh² (jué) - Cheat, swindle; crafty (juézhà).

谮 121. 譖 Ts'an² (cán) - Slander, libel.

识 122. 識 Shih² (shí) - Know(ledge). Chih⁴ (zhì) - Remember; mark.

谭 123. 譚 T'an² (tán) - Talk, gossip; boast.

谯 124. 譙 Ch'iao² (qiáo) - Watchtower (qiáolóu).

毁 125. 譭 Hui³ (huǐ) - Slander. * Destroy completely. [13]

* Refers only to the simplified form, i.e when it is a traditional form.

议 126. 議 Yi⁴ (yì) - Opinion; discuss, deliberate; proposal (yǐ'àn).

127. 警 Ching³ (jǐng) - Warn; alarm (fire -); police (- box).

128. 譬 P'i⁴ (pì) - Compare, comparison; illustrate; parable.

谱 129. 譜 P'u³ (pǔ) - Table, chart; manual; write music for.

译 130. 譯 Yi⁴ (yì) - Translate, interpret.

护 131. 護 Hu⁴ (hù) - Guard, protect.
    14

誉 132. 譽 Yü⁴ (yù) - Reputation; praise.

读 133. 讀 Tu² (dú) - Read aloud; study (dúshu).
    15

雠 134. 讎 Ch'ou² (chóu) - Revise (- documents); enemy.
    16

变 135. 變 Pien⁴ (biàn) - Change, transform.

宴 136. 讌 Yen⁴ (yàn) - Feast, banquet; entertain (- at banquet).

谗 137. 讒 Ch'an² (chán) - Slander, defame.
    17

让 138. 讓 Jang⁴ (ràng) - Yield; offer (- tea); allow, let (- him in).

谶 139. 讖 Ch'an⁴ (chàn) - Prophesy; prognostic; omen.

赞 140. 讚 Tsan⁴ (zàn) - Praise; support (zànzhù); approve (zànchéng).
    19

谠 141. 讜 Tang³ (dǎng) - Honest, unbiased (- comment).
    20

谳 142. 讞 Yen⁴ (yàn) - Pronounce judgement; sentence (v.).

讟 143. 讟 Tu² (dú) - Slander, defame; complain, grumble.
    22

WORK 工

The ancient carpenter's square to symbolize 'work' : 工.

1. 工 **Kung¹ (gong)** - Work; workman; industry (chemical –).

2. 左 **Tso³ (zuô)** - Left, left-hand side; unorthodox, queer.

3. 巧 **Ch'iao³ (qiâo)** - Ingenious; cunning, artful; timely.

4. 巨 **Chü⁴ (jù)** - Gigantic, huge.

5. 巫 **Wu¹ (wu)** - Witch, wizard.

6. 差 **Ch'a¹,⁴ (cha, chà)** - Difference. **Ch'ai¹ (chai)** - Dispatch.

WRAP 勹

A man 人 (a being standing on his legs 人) who bends his legs to envelop a large object: 勹.

1. 勺   ¹ **Shao² (sháo)** - Spoon, ladle.

2. 勾   ² **Kou¹ (gou)** - Cancel; thicken (– soup); evoke; gang up with.

3. 勿 **Wu⁴ (wù)** - Do not (– smoke), not.

勾 4. 匀 **Yün² (yún)** - Even; divide evenly.

5. 包   ³ **Pao¹ (bao)** - Wrap (up); bag; swelling; charter (– plane).

6. 匆 **Ts'ung¹ (cong)** - Hastily, hurriedly.

7. 匈   ⁴ **Hsiung¹ (xiong)** - Thorax, chest; mind, heart.

8. 匉   ⁵ **P'eng¹ (peng)** - Noise of waves.

9. 匊 Chū[6]² (jú) - Handful; grasp.

10. 匋 T'ao² (táo) - Pottery, earthenware; happy (táorán).

11. 匍 P'u[7]² (pú) - (púfú¹²) - Crawl, creep; lie prostrate.

12. 匐 Fu[9]² (fú) - (pú¹¹fú) - Same as 11.

Y

YELLOW 黃

The fiery glow 炗 (a man 人 carrying a torch 币) from the fields
田 :黃.

1. 黃 **Huang² (huáng)** -Yellow.

黌 2. 黌 **Hung² (hóng)** - Ancient name for schoolhouse.

NOTES